# UNDERMINING RACIAL JUSTICE

**Histories of American Education**

*A series edited by Jonathan Zimmerman*

A list of titles is available at cornellpress.cornell.edu

# UNDERMINING RACIAL JUSTICE

## HOW ONE UNIVERSITY EMBRACED INCLUSION AND INEQUALITY

## MATTHEW JOHNSON

CORNELL UNIVERSITY PRESS

*Ithaca and London*

First published 2020 by Cornell University Press

Library of Congress Cataloging-in-Publication Data

Names: Johnson, Matthew (Matthew James), 1983–author.
Title: Undermining racial justice : how one university
    embraced inclusion and inequality / Matthew Johnson.
Description: Ithaca [New York] : Cornell University
    Press, 2020. | Series: Histories of American education |
    Includes index.
Identifiers: LCCN 2019024696 (print) |
    LCCN 2019024697 (ebook) | ISBN 9781501748585
    (hardcover) | ISBN 9781501748592 (pdf) |
    ISBN 9781501748608 (epub)
Subjects: LCSH: University of Michigan—Admission. |
    Discrimination in higher education—Michigan—
    Ann Arbor. | Affirmative action programs in
    education—Michigan—Ann Arbor. | Racism in higher
    education—Michigan—Ann Arbor. | Universities and
    colleges—Michigan—Ann Arbor—Admission. |
    African American college students—Civil rights—
    Michigan—Ann Arbor.
Classification: LCC LC212.422.M5 J64 2020 (print) |
    LCC LC212.422.M5 (ebook) | DDC 378.774/35—dc23
LC record available at https://lccn.loc.gov/2019024696
LC ebook record available at https://lccn.loc.gov
    /2019024697

Portions of Chapter 2 are adapted, with permission, from "Managing Racial Inclusion: The Origins and Early Implementation of Affirmative Action Admissions at the University of Michigan," *Journal of Policy History* 29, no. 3 (July 2017): 462–489.

# CONTENTS

# UNDERMINING RACIAL JUSTICE

# Introduction

## Preserving Inequality

There has never been a racial justice revolution in higher education. Beginning in the 1960s, black campus activists and their allies occupied buildings, but they never captured or seized control of universities and colleges; administrators never let that happen. Over the last sixty years, campus leaders embraced racial inclusion only so far as it could coexist with long-standing values and priorities created in an era when few black students had access to elite universities. Racial inclusion initiatives, then, helped bring unprecedented access to a new generation of black students, but they also reinforced and normalized practices and values that preserved racial disparities. In other words, administrators responded to black campus activists by making racial inclusion and inequality compatible.

I tell this story as it played out at the University of Michigan. Since the 1960s, UM has gained national recognition for its racial inclusion programs. University and college leaders from around the country began visiting Ann Arbor because they saw UM as a model of inclusion. For the same reason, opponents of affirmative action and racial sensitivity training targeted UM in op-eds, books, and lawsuits. Given UM's reputation, it was no surprise when the university found itself at the center of two of the most famous affirmative action lawsuits of the twenty-first century: *Gratz v. Bollinger* and *Grutter v. Bollinger* (2003). In the eyes of black students, though, UM has never represented a model of racial inclusion. Black students' share of the student body has never matched blacks' share of the state or national population, and the majority of black students have never reported satisfaction with the university's racial climate. Nevertheless, black students' critiques never stopped UM leaders from claiming that racial inclusion was one of the university's core values. This book explains why.

I argue that institutional leaders incorporated black student dissent selectively into the University of Michigan's policies, practices, and values, while preventing activism from disrupting the institutional priorities that campus leaders deemed more important than racial justice. This book, then, pays special attention to what administrators were trying to preserve in the face of activism. First and foremost, administrators wanted to sustain the university's elite status and preserve a system that measured institutional quality by the "merit" and "qualifications" of its student body. Second, university leaders wanted to preserve their goal of creating a model multiracial community on campus. That might not sound like a problematic priority, but the way administrators tried to engineer this multiracial community led to social alienation and high attrition rates for black students.[1]

I use the term "co-optation" to describe the process of selectively incorporating activism, while preserving long-standing values and priorities. One of the goals of this book is to uncover the repertoires of co-optation. Scholars of social movements recognize that activists rely on repertoires—basically, a toolbox of tactics that activists recognize as useful and often draw on. It's one reason that protests usually look similar. This book reveals how university officials developed their own repertoires to co-opt activism. These repertoires changed over time, but a select group of tools reappear throughout much of this book.[2]

First, university officials used a discourse of racial innocence to justify racial disparities and a poor racial climate. Black activists tried to get administrators to see these problems as symptomatic of institutional racism, but university leaders never adopted this activist framework. Instead, administrators preferred to see the university as a victim. In their eyes, UM was caught in a racist society that made it almost impossible to meet many of black activists' demands. They claimed that racism unfolding outside the campus walls created racial disparities on campus and produced the white students who hurled racist remarks at black students. Administrators had the best interests of black students at heart. Activists couldn't expect officials to overcome all these obstacles, administrators argued. This perspective helped rationalized the university's policies, which contributed to the inequality on campus and helped officials resist black activists' most powerful demands.

Second, executive administrators built an inclusion bureaucracy to channel activism into institutional offices and control the outcomes of dissent. Beginning in the late 1960s, administrators created an unprecedented number of positions, most of them filled by black officials, meant to respond to activists' demands. Administrators hoped that black students would abandon protest and work for change within bureaucratic channels alongside black officials. Campus leaders, though, rarely gave these new black officials the power and resources to implement new programs independently. White administrators had to approve and fund any proposal; this allowed campus leaders to exercise influence over the character of inclusion, moving dissent into a bureaucracy they could control.

Third, university administrators selectively used institutional knowledge about black students when crafting racial inclusion policies. Beginning in the 1960s, various groups fought over who could interpret black students' experience on campus. Social scientists, admissions officials, black staff members, and black students all tried to offer their own analysis of everything from black students' academic performance to their social environment. An important tool in maintaining control over inclusion, campus leaders found, was controlling who could offer legitimate forms of knowledge about black students. The groups they chose changed over time, as campus leaders sought out knowledge that could support their priorities and policy goals.

Finally, discipline became a key part of co-optation. Since the 1960s, the most confrontational protests have been the most effective in producing change at UM. These protests have also invited the harshest disciplinary methods. While administrators created institutional reforms in response to activism, they also took steps to deter confrontational protests by threatening to expel or criminally prosecute activists. For co-optation to work, administrators needed to exercise as much control as possible over the character of reform. The less administrators had to worry about dissent, the more control they had over racial inclusion.

Emphasizing the coercive process of co-optation raises important questions about intent. Did UM officials co-opt black student activism with the specific intent to perpetuate racial inequality? The simple answer is no. None of the university officials covered in this book since the 1960s fit well into the conventional backlash narrative, which focuses on the people who resisted the black freedom movement because of racial animus and a desire to protect white privilege. The most powerful UM administrators expressed sympathy for racial equity. In an ideal world, they wanted black students' representation on campus to match blacks' representation in the state population. They wanted black students to perform well in the classroom and thrive socially on campus. At times, this sympathy made it easier for activists to win concessions. After reading thousands of pages of correspondence among UM leaders, it's clear that administrators would have celebrated a student body that reflected the racial demographics of the state of Michigan and a racial climate that made black students feel welcome—but only if that happened on administrators' terms.

By highlighting administrators' sympathy for racial equity, I'm not privileging their motivations over the outcomes of their policies. While preserving racial inequality didn't motivate policies at UM, campus officials usually knew that their inclusion policies would likely maintain racial disparities. If administrators were surprised about the outcomes, they were often surprised by the degree of those disparities, not by the mere existence of inequality. Consequently, racial disparities at UM can hardly be called unintended outcomes. This isn't a book, then, about good intentions gone bad; this is a book about how people who created and maintained racial disparities still believed they had good intentions.

I wrote this book because I felt that the scholarship on the history of race and higher education lacked in-depth analyses of the implementation of racial inclusion initiatives over the last fifty years. Many historians have contributed to a flourishing literature on the black campus movement (BCM). Ibram X. Kendi, Joy Ann Williamson-Lott, Stefan Bradley, and Martha Biondi, just to name a few, have given us a fuller understanding of black campus activists' tactics, demands, and intellectual foundations. These excellent works pay attention to the people who ran universities, but scholars have yet to fully uncover the techniques administrators used to resist and co-opt activists' demands. Aside from administrators' use of the police and disciplinary campus codes, we still have an incomplete understanding of what black activists were up against in reforming higher education institutions.[3]

Part of the problem is that much of the scholarship on the black campus movement doesn't extend beyond the mid-1970s, when most scholars agree that the BCM fell apart. It's an inconvenient end date for anyone who wants to understand the legacies of the movement. At the University of Michigan, as at many universities across the country, the late 1970s and early 1980s represented an era of racial retrenchment. Black enrollment plummeted, and complaints about the campus racial climate increased. To understand the outcomes of activism, scholars need to extend their studies beyond the moment the movement lost its organizing power.[4]

Ending studies in 1975 also encourages celebratory scholarship that highlights the victories of activists and downplays their failures. This plays into the hands of conservative critics who believe colleges and universities have too easily succumbed to black protesters, bending to their every demand. That couldn't be further from the truth. Clearly, black campus activism led to important reforms, but scholarship on the movement too often overstates the impact of black activism and fails to explain how campus leaders retained control over the priorities and values of higher education. Without attention to this process, it's impossible to understand the persistent racial disparities on campuses across the country.

Scholars of critical race theory offer a model of institutional change that more closely resembles reality at elite universities. This book's focus on cooptation follows the insights of interest convergence and interest divergence, two fundamental ideas in critical race theory. In the context of higher education, these ideas posit that minorities can win institutional change only when the interests of whites and minorities align. Conversely, when minorities' proposals for institutional change don't align with whites' interests, those proposals will fail. Not all whites, just as not all minorities, think alike, of course. But whites with power over the University of Michigan have thought enough alike to create and preserve a set of core institutional interests that perpetuate inequality. As critical race theorists would expect, only black activist proposals that aligned with those interests had a chance for implementation at UM.[5]

One of the lessons of this book is that it's important not to confuse reform with disruptive institutional change. Reform introduces practices that can make the university more inclusive while preserving the core institutional priorities that have long sustained racial inequality, ensuring that disparities persist. Disruptive institutional change for racial equity is different; it sees the university's core values as the root of the problem. The goal of disruptive change, then, is to rethink the entire purpose and structure of elite institutions to create a truly equitable university. Black student activists offered disruptive ideas. They got reform instead.

Most universities don't make it easy to study the history of racial inclusion policies. I'll be the first to admit that I was naive about the difficulties I would face in writing this book. Once I started traveling the country in search of institutional records, I quickly learned why we know so little about racial inclusion programs, especially those created after the 1970s. While some archives are filled with internal documents concerning initiatives produced in the 1960s and 1970s, more recent records are difficult to find. Many universities have likely destroyed these records or kept them hidden. Some acknowledge their existence but refuse to let researchers access them.

There are reasons that universities haven't offered the type of historical documentation that scholars covet. In a world where anti–affirmative action lawsuits have become commonplace, there isn't much incentive for universities to provide lawyers with ammunition. Contributing to the problem, some universities have poor preservation practices regardless of the subject matter or legal threat. Whatever the reason, the lack of transparency has left racial inclusion policies shrouded in mystery. This book tries to take that mystery out of some of the nation's most contested practices.

Because of the lack of transparency, some scholars studying racial inclusion policies have looked outside university archives for answers. Usually they rely on published institutional sources meant for the public's eyes. Others depend on interviews with higher education officials. Scholars have to work with what is available, but these sources hide as much as they reveal. As I found once I dove into the institutional archives, published sources meant for the public often conceal the institution's most controversial policies and practices. They also rarely accurately explain the motivations behind the inclusion policies. I also found that interviews with former officials were important supplementary sources, but these officials frequently confided that their memories were hazy. Some were unwilling to talk about controversial issues, many never responded to interview requests, and at least one person lied to me.[6]

That's why getting into an institutional archive was so important to me. Archival sources aren't perfect, but I wanted to read the internal reports, memos, and personal correspondence that weren't produced for someone like me to see. I wanted to see how officials justified inclusion policies in the moment and if they anticipated the consequences of their decisions. I wanted to see how their inclusion policies shifted with the ebb and flow of activism, a changing political economy, and a growing backlash to affirmative action. I wouldn't be able to do this with small pieces of evidence that offered insight into a few years of policy making at one university and a few years of decisions at another.

Early in my research, I worried that I wouldn't be able to write this book. Eventually, though, I arrived at the University of Michigan. When I first set foot on campus, UM had just stepped out of the national spotlight. A few years earlier, the university had defended its affirmative action practices in two of the most highly publicized Supreme Court cases of the twenty-first century: *Gratz v. Bollinger* and *Grutter v. Bollinger* (2003). When I walked into the university's archives, I stood in front of the most significant collection of documents on racial inclusion practices that I had ever seen. I sat down and went to work. I returned summer after summer—and some winters—until I felt I could offer a book unprecedented in its historical coverage of the long-term implementation of racial inclusion initiatives.[7]

While the University of Michigan is the most transparent institution that I've encountered, its archives still hide stories that limit the scope of this book.

For example, I focus on undergraduate students for a reason. Undergraduate admission was more centralized, taking place within the Undergraduate Admissions Office. The office worked with the various schools and colleges to create selection criteria, but the admissions office carried out the duties of selection. This centralized office produced an incredible amount of paper. Memos, reports, and meeting minutes survived the long decades and ended up in the university's archives. Graduate and professional school admissions worked differently. Individual departments—and professional schools in some cases—control who enters their graduate programs; they haven't handed over the selection process to a centralized graduate admissions office. If these schools and departments have been good record keepers, they haven't been as transparent as the Undergraduate Admissions Office. Trying to tell the long history of affirmative action admissions for graduate students in the history department, for example, would be almost impossible through archival records. The university's law school has kept better records, but much of its affirmative action documentation won't be available to the public until 2020.[8]

In focusing on undergraduates, UM's largest college—the College of Literature, Science, and the Arts (LSA)—gets special attention in this book. LSA enrolled the vast majority of undergraduate students and the majority of black students. As such, executive administrators focused much of their resources and attention on LSA when crafting inclusion policies. It's not surprising, then, that conservative lawyers brought a lawsuit against LSA when they wanted to contest the university's undergraduate affirmative action admissions practices. *Gratz v. Bollinger* didn't challenge all of UM's undergraduate admissions practices; rather, it specifically targeted LSA's admissions policies.[9]

Because undergraduate students tied affirmative action admissions and efforts to improve the racial climate to affirmative action hiring, I also offer insight into the university's efforts to hire black faculty, staff, and administrators. Much of this hiring, like graduate admissions, unfolded within academic units, making this story difficult to tell. But because the university created a centralized office to oversee affirmative action hiring, I was able to uncover some of this story. As a result, this book reveals the importance of affirmative action hiring policies to black students' experience at UM. This is an issue that's often lacking in the scholarship on the history of affirmative action admissions, as affirmative action hiring and admissions are often studied separately. Black student activists, though, never saw these as isolated issues.

My hope is that in reading this book, you will understand what black activists have been up against in trying to transform higher education. External forces, of course, placed obstacles in the way of racial justice at UM. But this book is a reminder that some of the fiercest roadblocks to racial justice in selective colleges and universities have come from the people working within institutions who claimed to be champions of black students. Explaining how these administrators could see themselves as advocates of racial inclusion while overseeing an institution that perpetuated racial inequality is one of the central goals of this book.

# CHAPTER 1

# Bones and Sinews

When black student activists led a campus strike at the University of Michigan (UM) in 1970, they challenged entrenched ideas and practices that seemed so natural and embedded in the institution that administrators had never questioned them. Black students called these ideas and practices part of the "bones and sinews of the place."[1] Some of these bones and sinews had developed more than a century before black activists took over campus buildings at UM; others had developed not long before activists stepped foot on campus.

The institutional values and practices that justified an admissions system that created racial disparities began in the mid-nineteenth century. Two core values emerged at the first board of regents meetings in Ann Arbor. Campus leaders wanted to create a university on par with any in the United States, and they wanted the university to offer broad access to the people of Michigan. But over the course of the nineteenth and twentieth centuries, campus leaders chose to subordinate the ideal of access to the goal of attaining and sustaining UM's elite status. UM leaders saw exclusion as a necessary price to pay for creating an elite institution.

Other values developed in the aftermath of World War II. In the 1940s and 1950s, administrators slowly purged official practices that mandated or accommodated segregation in campus buildings and social clubs. In their place, campus leaders developed a vision of a model multiracial community on campus. They slowly incorporated the prevailing ideas of racial liberalism: an ideal that suggested that interracial contact and universalism would end individual prejudice in America. Administrators never anticipated—in fact, they never seriously considered—how the implementation of racial liberalism would impact black students. The ways that UM leaders crafted the model multiracial community led to a toxic racial climate at UM.

All institutions have a hierarchy of values. At the University of Michigan, crafting and then maintaining its identity as an elite public postsecondary institution has been its main priority since the mid-nineteenth century. Throughout UM's history, university officials have tried to marry their ambitions to create an elite university with their concerns about access and inclusion. But at every turn, UM leaders made policy decisions that privileged UM's status as an elite institution over the principle of access. Since the first regents' meetings in Ann Arbor, access has remained a secondary value—important but always subordinate to quality. Subordinating inclusion in the university's hierarchy of values would have long-lasting consequences for racial justice advocates at the University of Michigan.

In the university's first years, though, its foundational values were up for grabs. The university dates its founding to 1817, when Michigan was a small territory. Augustus Woodward, a territorial judge and alumnus of Columbia College, drafted the piece of legislation that created the university. He envisioned a university funded by tax revenues in order to provide an education at a low cost to students. For two decades, the Detroit university existed in name only. The turning point came in 1837, the same year that Michigan achieved statehood, when the university found a home on forty acres of land in Ann Arbor. Two years later, the University of Michigan finally began offering courses at the collegiate level, with six first-year students and one sophomore enrolled.[2]

Two competing values emerged when the regents began meeting in Ann Arbor. On the one hand, the regents believed that access should be an important principle at a public institution funded with public money. When the regents thought about the principle of inclusion in the early nineteenth century, they were thinking about access for men—UM restricted women's admission until 1870—regardless of social class. The regents wanted to ensure that the University of Michigan would not become an institution reserved for the children of wealth. After all, the common critique of public higher education, the regents reported in 1839, was that public funds were used to maintain the status of the economically advantaged "when the impoverished genius and talent had to struggle on without this Public facility." Providing a low-cost education, then, was central to the University of Michigan's mission in offering what the regents called an institution "of the People." While access for black men was probably not on their minds at that moment, the regents never created racial restrictions. Thus, prospective black students would not have to fight the same battles as women against official policies of exclusion. It would take a few decades, but UM admitted its first black student in 1853 and graduated its first black student, Gabriel Franklin Hargo, in 1870.[3]

Several models were available to an institution wishing to build a university "of the people" in the first half of the nineteenth century. This period marked great growth in higher education. The number of degree-granting postsecondary institutions rose from 25 in 1800 to 52 in 1820 and then to 241 in 1860. These new institutions ranged from professional schools to "multipurpose" colleges that tried to offer something for everyone, mixing "practical" courses with traditional college courses. Most often, these colleges incorporated preparatory instruction in order to admit students who lacked advance training at the high school level. Essentially, most of these institutions provided access to anyone who could pay tuition. This was as much out of necessity as out of a grand vision of accessibility and mass education. The biggest struggle that higher education institutions faced in the nineteenth century was finding enough students to pay for operating costs. Open admissions represented a way to survive.[4]

Regents at the University of Michigan did not copy these models. For all their allusions to a university "of the people," the regents also had aspirations of building an elite university on par with any in the United States and were willing to exclude most of the state's students in the process. UM modeled its curriculum and admissions standards on the most respected higher education institutions in the Northeast. An important characteristic of "elite" institutions at this time was their steadfast commitment to a liberal education built around a classics course, which was taught in Latin and Greek.[5] To gain admission to UM, first-year students took examinations in arithmetic, algebra, geography, Cicero's *Orations*, Sallust, Friedrich Jacobs's *Greek Reader*, and Latin and Greek prosody.[6] The board of regents made its intentions clear in 1841, stating that UM's admission requirements would place the university "on an equality with the best colleges in the United States." From the start UM leaders saw admission standards as a marker of elite status.[7]

These admission requirements weren't built to provide broad access to Michigan's residents. Before 1909, when the state legislature finally required counties to either build a high school or pay for its students to attend a high school elsewhere, many students in Michigan didn't have access to an education beyond the eighth grade. And access to just any high school didn't guarantee an education that prepared students to take an exam on Cicero. Michigan wasn't the only state that offered little training to prepare the public for admission to a school like UM. As late as 1940, more than 50 percent of Americans hadn't completed an education past the eighth grade. It was no secret that UM's admission requirements excluded the vast majority of young people in the United States. While this might have represented a political risk for the state institution, it presented an even greater financial risk, as UM officials would have to find enough students who were prepared for this type of study in order to pay for operating costs. Leaders at UM decided to take that risk.[8]

The board's choices in subsequent decades helped reinforce UM's hierarchy of values. For the first two decades in Ann Arbor, the university operated without a president. By 1852, the regents decided that the university needed a full-time leader. The board hired Henry Tappan, someone who would help build one of America's first modern research universities and, in doing so, ensure that inclusion remained a secondary institutional value. The regents knew they were getting someone with a grand vision. The year before, Tappan had gained widespread attention for his biting critique of American higher education in his book *University Education*, in which he suggested that not a single American postsecondary institution could truly call itself a "university" when compared to the German universities he saw in his travels. This wasn't someone who wanted UM to aspire to become the midwestern Harvard or Yale, like the regents had originally envisioned. Tappan wanted to create an entirely new American university that could aspire to compete with German universities.[9]

Tappan wasted no time initiating the first steps toward making UM a modern American research university. The new president quickly recruited distinguished faculty members. He put resources toward building a library equal to any in the United States that could support advanced research. He raised $15,000 for an observatory and brought an astronomer from Europe to use it. He oversaw a new laboratory of analytical chemistry and the erection of a new campus museum, which Tappan hoped would become one of the great museums of natural history in the United States. As historian Richard Geiger has concluded, "The University of Michigan was the only institution of higher education in the West that made academic quality its foremost value."[10]

Pursuing Tappan's vision continued to make access a secondary principle at UM. Creating a research university was expensive and required money and resources that the University of Michigan didn't have. Until 1869, when the university began receiving money from a state property tax, the main source of public funds came from public land sales. Michigan's territorial governors had invested in UM by providing the university almost twenty-five thousand acres of land to sell. About nineteen hundred of those acres came from Native American lands handed over to Michigan's territorial governor, Lewis Cass, at the Treaty of Fort Meigs. The rest of the land came from a federal grant. Michigan was one of seventeen states to receive federal land grants to create institutions of higher education before the more famous Morrill Land Grant Act of 1862. The university sold this land slowly through the nineteenth century. By 1881, when the regents had finally sold all the land, they had raised $547,000.[11]

Half a million dollars was no small sum in the nineteenth century, but it still couldn't support the type of growth that Tappan envisioned. The university needed more students to cover costs. At this moment, keeping so many people out of the university became a problem, as UM wasn't receiving enough money from tuition revenues to fund Tappan's vision. If the university's leaders were going to achieve their goals of building a university that resembled the German model, they needed a stable student population. Still, they weren't willing to rethink the connection between admission criteria and elite status.

Part of the solution to maintain selective admissions and create a stable student population came from out-of-state applicants. As the University of Michigan began building a modern research university in the second half of the nineteenth century, it gained respect throughout the country. Its newfound reputation sparked interest from students outside the state who qualified for admission at UM, which broadened its pool of potential students. But as a public university supported by state funds—although not as adequately as UM leaders would have liked—admitting too many out-of-state students posed a political problem. To avoid this, university officials needed to find a way to create a larger pool of in-state applicants who could meet selective admission requirements.[12]

In 1854, future University of Michigan president Henry Frieze offered a plan to increase in-state student enrollment. Like Tappan, Frieze was enamored with the German education system. He was especially impressed with a system that provided a pool of talented students for each successive level of education. If UM officials wanted a more reliable pool of students, they needed to get high school leaders to see college preparation as one of their core responsibilities. To do this, UM would tell high school administrators what type of curriculum was necessary for their students to attend the university, and any high school that wanted to provide that curriculum could do so voluntarily. University faculty would travel to participating high schools and certify those schools whose curriculum met UM's standards. Any student from a certified high school who completed the required coursework prescribed by UM and gained a letter of recommendation from the principal gained automatic admission to the University of Michigan. Students who didn't graduate from a certified high school could take an entrance exam to prove they were capable of completing UM's coursework. Adopted unanimously by the faculty in 1870, this system became known as the certification system. UM was the first to develop it in the United States, and it left its mark on universities across the country in the subsequent decades, becoming the most popular method of admissions in the country.[13]

These changes, though, came at a great cost to inclusion. Aside from the fact that many in-state students still lacked access to a high school education and the automatic admission it offered, rising tuition costs that fueled the skyrocketing operating cost of a rising research university priced UM out of the reach of many low-income students. Between 1869 and 1909, the cost of tuition tripled. Not surprisingly, the number of low-income students declined as tuition and fees rose. Before an era of federal and state financial aid, students had to find a way to pay for these rising costs. Into the twentieth century, loans represented the only need-based funds the university provided to low-income students. While low-income enrollment declined, the university's revenue from tuition receipts skyrocketed. In 1849, the University of Michigan brought in $1,006 from tuition revenues. By 1909, tuition receipts totaled $327,169. What began as a university that would provide low-cost tuition transformed into an institution that imposed costs that excluded many people in the state.[14]

While UM's efforts to become a modern research university limited access, they fulfilled UM leaders' aspirations to become an elite American university. By the turn of the century, observers recognized that a sea change in higher education was unfolding. There was now a group of universities that looked recognizably different from the rest of the postsecondary institutions. Their large size, commitment to graduate education and scholarly productivity, impressive libraries, and significant annual revenues set them apart. One of these observers, Edwin Slosson, called them the "Great American Universities." The University of Michigan was on Slosson's list, along with twelve others, including Johns Hopkins University, Columbia University, Harvard University, and the University of California.[15]

To get on this list, UM officials proved that they were willing to accept the declining number of low-income students as long as the university maintained its status as an elite institution. For all the allusions to an institution "of the people," University of Michigan leaders never saw inclusion as the institution's leading principle; they were always willing to sacrifice inclusion for status. By the early twentieth century, it was clear that university officials had a high tolerance for inequality.

Once the University of Michigan secured its position among a select group of elite American universities, maintaining its status became administrators' primary goal. This was no easy task. Although its position as a modern research university helped signal its elite status, faculty members and administrators still saw the academic preparation of the university's student body as an important signifier of UM's quality. In the first decades of the twentieth century—another period of growth in higher education—UM faculty members began to question whether UM's certification system provided the type of student body that could ensure its elite status. The problem was that the certification system was now making UM too accessible. More high schools were popping up around the state and gaining certification. As a result, UM's enrollment nearly doubled between 1910 and 1923, increasing from 5,339 to 10,500.[16]

UM officials and faculty weren't alone in worrying about the impact of the growing demand for higher education. Anxieties about growth surfaced at UM during a heated national debate about who should go to college. During the interwar years, the college-going population in the United States increased from 597,857 to just under 1.5 million.[17] Some vocal critics of rising college enrollment, such as George Vincent, professor of sociology at the University of Chicago, argued that only a small number of Americans were capable of postsecondary learning. According to Vincent, the population could be divided into three categories: 95 percent of the population constituted a "mediocre group," and the final 5 percent encompassed a group of "superior, exceptionally able people" and a group composed of the "inefficient, the criminal, the undesirable." Only the "superior, exceptionally able people," according to Vincent, should have a place in higher education. This meant Vincent believed that about 97 percent of the American population wasn't suitable for postsecondary study. On the other side of the argument, some higher education leaders saw colleges and universities as tools of social mobility in a changing economy that demanded more professionals and managers with a postsecondary degree. They were also rethinking both who was capable of college-level work and who postsecondary institutions should serve. Representatives of Washburn Municipal University, for example, suggested that "all students with adequate motivation for doing work on the collegiate level should go" to college. Responding to those claiming that only a small percentage of Americans were capable of higher learning, representatives of Washburn noted that the "group incapable of doing college work if adequately motivated is much smaller than is usually assumed." Representatives of Fresno State College agreed: "Students with honest purpose, ambition, and character—even if having only average intellectual ability"—should go to college.[18]

UM officials might have agreed that someone of "average intellectual ability" had a place in higher education—just not at the University of Michigan. UM officials felt that the status of the university depended on keeping "average" students out of UM. They believed that they needed to protect UM's status when inclusion and access went too far.

Concerns about the future of UM's elite status produced new questions about the effectiveness of the certification system. Efficiency remained one of the virtues of admission by certificate. Large admissions staffs proved unnecessary because the system left much of the hard work of selecting students up to the high school principals of certified schools. The deans of each college were able to handle and review all applications without the help of an admissions office. Its key virtue was also a problem, though. Without much control over principals' decisions, administrators enjoyed little recourse when the faculty was unhappy about the quality of the students. The only tools the faculty had to control the academic preparation of incoming students were revoking the certification of particular high schools or changing course requirements for high school students. Evidence suggests that UM's colleges generally pursued the latter. If faculty members in the College of Literature, Science, and the Arts (LSA) were concerned about the preparation of students in mathematics, the dean added trigonometry to the course requirements. Not enough language preparation? LSA added more Latin or Greek courses to the requirements. But simply adding courses to the required curriculum didn't necessarily equate to a better high school education. Students were still coming to UM unprepared in the eyes of the faculty.[19]

Amid these fears about student quality, the regents hired Clarence Little, one of the nation's leading eugenicists, to lead the university in 1925. Eugenicists believed that Anglo-Saxons were biologically superior and feared that their purity was at risk. They also shared a common faith that people could be easily placed in categories through simple tests, such as intelligence tests, which became popular after World War I. These pseudoscientists used intelligence tests to promote the sterilization of the "feebleminded" and justify immigration restriction. Eugenics became so popular in the early twentieth century that 376 universities taught courses on the subject.[20]

While Little never called for admission restrictions based on race or ethnicity, he incorporated his faith in eugenics at UM by centralizing undergraduate admissions and introducing new testing tools to identify students who couldn't meet the intellectual demands of the university's curriculum. In 1925, the board of regents approved the first step of this plan: creating a registrar's office. In 1927, the regents also approved the Bureau of University Research, which soon turned into the Office of Educational Testing (OET). Little gave these offices opportunities to evaluate students in new ways. When Little first arrived at UM, he brought with him from the University of Maine a program called Freshman Week. This program, instituted at Michigan in the fall of 1927, required all admitted first-year students to take a battery of standardized tests. One of these tests, the SAT, had roots in eugenics. Its creator, Carl Brigham, was a eugenicist who wrote *A Study of American Intelligence*, in which he claimed "American intelligence is declining, and will proceed with an accelerating rate as the racial admixture becomes more and more extensive."[21]

Little didn't eliminate the certification system. Nevertheless, he created offices that would eventually lead to a new admissions system based on standardized tests and high school grades. The introduction of the registrar's office proved to be one of Little's long-lasting contributions to admissions reform. Ira Smith became the office's first leader. Smith came to UM with fifteen years of experience in the registrar's and admissions offices at the University of Illinois and the University of Chicago, respectively. To call Smith's new fiefdom at UM an office might be too generous. His staff included an editorial assistant and a secretary. Together, they handled all first-year admission applications; transfer applications continued to go to the deans of each respective college. At this point, there still wasn't much for a registrar to do with in-state applicants who went to a certified school. Smith would simply check for a principal's recommendation and make sure that the student took the required high school courses. Only out-of-state applicants and in-state students who didn't attend a certified school needed serious evaluation.[22]

Smith's limited power in the admissions process didn't stop him from thinking about how to identify those students the faculty desired. Smith started collecting whatever information he could about students, then added additional questions to admissions applications in order to collect more data. Initially, Smith didn't expect that his data collection would undermine the certification system. He thought he could improve student advising if he could forecast which students would struggle academically at UM. Still, in collecting data and trying to predict how students would perform at UM, he was slowly trying to gain more power over the admissions process within the constraints posed by the certification system. Smith was gaining confidence that he could forecast students' success better than high school principals could. So when Smith saw a student who he thought would struggle at UM—despite the fact that the student had a principal's recommendation, had graduated from a certified high school, and had taken the required coursework—he called the principal and questioned the official's decision. Sometimes he would convince the principal that the student would be better served by going to another college.[23]

The Principal-Freshman Conference represented another tool Smith used to gain more influence over the certification system. At these annual conferences, Smith met with the principals of high schools that sent students to UM, sharing all his data about which students succeeded in college. Basically, Smith was trying to train principals the same way he might train an admissions counselor. He made the point that principals were sending students to UM who were unprepared and emphasized that new techniques in sorting students were necessary for principals to make more informed decisions about which students to recommend for an elite institution.[24]

Still, there were limits to Smith's power in incorporating these tools in the admissions process. While Smith believed he could forecast students' performance at UM better than the certification system, his prediction tools were flawed. In reality, although he might be able to predict with some degree of accuracy how the top and bottom high school students would perform at UM, he found that students in the middle were "completely unpredictable." Since over 50 percent of UM students fell into that category, Smith had no idea how most UM students would perform. But that didn't stop Smith from continuing to put students into categories and making these labels a part of university practice.[25]

Those at UM who were actually trained to analyze data were more transparent about the problems of forecasting. Researchers in the OET—the other office Little created—began examining all the prediction tools the university had at its disposal to forecast which students would leave UM before graduating. OET researchers weren't as optimistic about these tools as Smith was, likening admissions to a life insurance company trying to predict the life span of an applicant. With such mixed results in forecasting students' performance, the certification system held strong through WWII, despite grumbles from faculty.[26]

Ironically, the research office Little created slowed the incorporation of standardized tests at UM. Nevertheless, Little's efforts would have long-term consequences. Little left the university in 1929, but the research he sparked on prediction tools continued long after he left. That research evolved after World War II, eventually providing the data necessary to justify making the SAT an admissions requirement at UM.

On the surface, at least, the University of Michigan's obsession with student quality set UM apart from elite institutions in the Northeast, which worried that focusing too closely on academic credentials would bring too many socially undesirable students to campus. Ivy League institutions such as Harvard, Yale, and Princeton were especially concerned that Jewish students with high test scores were overtaking their campuses. Even with a eugenicist leading the

University of Michigan from 1925 to 1929, the issue of religion didn't infuse public discussions about admissions practices like it did at some Ivy League institutions. There was no organized effort at the University of Michigan in the 1920s and 1930s to introduce admissions practices, such as quotas, specifically designed to exclude Jewish students from undergraduate admissions.[27]

Furthermore, UM officials didn't create quotas or other policies specifically designed to limit black enrollment when the number of black students on campus climbed in the early twentieth century. UM hosted one of the largest black student populations among historically white colleges and universities (HWCUs) during this period. In 1912, UM hosted thirty-nine black students, which meant that only two HWCUs in the United States enrolled more. An estimate from the 1920s put about sixty black students on campus out of ten thousand—or 0.6 percent of the student population. UM's record as a top enroller of black students among HWCUs speaks more to the poor record of other institutions than UM's commitment to racial inclusion. Considering that the black population of the state rose from 1.6 percent to 3.5 percent between 1920 and 1930, significant racial disparities still existed in UM's student body.[28]

The priorities behind UM's admissions system created these disparities. Preserving the university's elite status was always the driving purpose behind UM's admissions practices. UM officials didn't craft admissions policies to challenge racial inequality. Only an admissions system that thought little about inequality could measure students' merit by their academic capabilities at the moment of admission. In other words, UM's admissions system didn't think about how students' academic capabilities might change after four years—or even two years—of study at UM. They measured merit by how students would perform at UM the moment they stepped onto campus. That type of definition simply reproduced the advantages and disadvantages of race and wealth outside UM's walls. There were, of course, other definitions of merit available. For example, officials could have defined merit by the predicted academic capabilities of students after four years of study at UM, when students had a chance to overcome educational disadvantages. Furthermore, if university officials made equity an important part of its mission, officials could have defined merit by which students would best use their education to disrupt structures of inequality after they left UM. But university officials never considered these alternatives.[29]

UM's definition of merit meant that its admissions system worked in harmony with the discriminatory educational policies in Detroit. African Americans began moving to Michigan in larger numbers beginning in World War I. Most of these black migrants settled in Detroit, where they were met with discrimination and repression. This behavior extended into the school system. Beginning in the 1920s, the Detroit school district created a curriculum tracking system that divided students into different coursework plans based on tests that claimed to measure students' abilities. Black students were overwhelmingly placed in coursework that prepared them for industrial labor, not postsecondary study. Black students in the Motor City were half as likely to be on the college preparatory track than white students. For the few black students on the college preparatory track, white principals remained the gatekeepers to their admission at the University of Michigan. As late as 1955, there were two black principals in the entire Detroit school system, including all primary and secondary schools.[30]

The certificate system created a perfect recipe for racial discrimination. Evidence from UM's records suggests that the university distributed certifications to high schools liberally, especially in southeastern Michigan, where most black residents lived. But lack of certification wasn't the problem. The problem was that black students didn't just have to graduate from a certified high school to gain admission to UM; they also had to complete a specific set of college preparatory courses. The tracking system made that extremely difficult. And for the few black students who did have access to such courses, they had to get a letter of recommendation from their principal. Thus, the same white high school administrators who were complicit in a discriminatory system decided whether a black student would get into UM. The University of Michigan's undergraduate admissions system was "color-blind" only in the sense that UM officials didn't look at an applicant's race when deciding who to admit. Instead, they outsourced the process of selection to secondary-school officials engaged in racial discrimination. If black students could run the gauntlet of discrimination in Detroit's school system and qualify for admission, UM officials would permit their entry.[31]

Black students' access to the University of Michigan didn't improve when UM officials eliminated the certification system. The final nail in the certification system's coffin came during yet another explosion in college enrollment. The rising demand for college education after World War II revealed another problem with the certification system: it was a poor tool for controlling enrollment growth. Again, the certification system was making UM too accessible, which potentially threatened the university's status.

If the 1920s enrollment growth concerned officials and faculty, the post–World War II growth created a crisis. The demand for higher education was unparalleled in American history. During the 1939–40 academic year, American postsecondary institutions enrolled about 1.5 million students. Ten years later, enrollment had almost doubled, reaching close to 2.7 million. By 1960, the number reached 3.6 million. UM wasn't immune to the growing demand for higher education. In 1940, 1,730 students made up the entire first-year class. Immediately after the war, Ira Smith received almost 1,500 undergraduate applications in a single day. The post–World War II baby boom and growing high school enrollments around the country made it clear to UM administrators that the demand for higher education wouldn't return to pre–World War II levels anytime soon—if ever.[32]

UM officials had only a few tools they could use to control undergraduate student growth. First, because nonresidents didn't have access to the certification system and the automatic admission that it provided to qualified students—with the exception of a few high schools in neighboring states—Smith could curtail nonresident enrollment. And that's exactly what he did, but he did so strategically, picking which out-of-state students to privilege and which to deny. He ensured that out-of-state applicants from the children of alumni would still have access to the university. To limit enrollment, he discriminated against out-of-state women, restricting their access unless they were veterans or legacy applicants. Elisabeth Lawrie, the assistant registrar, justified discrimination against these women, arguing that it would not "be any great hardship on women. There is not now a pressing need for women to rush through their college work."[33]

These tools put only a small dent in the surging demand for access to UM, and for those committed to maintaining UM's status as an elite institution, these particular tools posed a threat to the university's quality. Postwar growth was putting stress on the university's infrastructure and faculty. UM had only so many faculty members, so many seats in classrooms, and so many beds in dormitories. UM faculty and administrators worried that the university would have to compromise its academic standards to accommodate the demand for higher education after World War II.[34]

Structural changes within higher education exacerbated concerns about student quality. UM's status as a modern research university made it unique in the early twentieth century. By the post–World War II period, more postsecondary institutions were claiming research status. As President Harlan Hatcher recalled, "The pre-eminence of Michigan as we had known it, in the previous 100 years, practically, was no longer unique." As officials searched for ways to set UM apart from these emerging research universities, the academic preparation of UM's student body became even more important as a marker of the university's elite status.[35]

In response to concerns over student quality and rapid growth spread across the country, elite universities began raising their admission standards. UM officials watched this process with trepidation. Charles Odegaard, the LSA dean at the time, warned that the "pressure from mediocre students to gain admittance [to UM] will increase" as they get shut out of other elite schools. If UM didn't shut them out too, he suggested, its elite status would diminish. In effect, more flexible admissions systems allowed competing institutions to have more control over sorting the "high ability" students from the "mediocre" students as application numbers skyrocketed. In this context, the "mediocre" student became a dangerous threat to UM's status.[36]

What happened next reveals a recurring pattern that would eventually have an impact on the evolution of affirmative action at UM. When a particular group was deemed a threat to the university's elite status, it faced an intellectual assault that justified its exclusion. In the 1950s, "mediocre students"—some of the same students who were deemed qualified in previous decades—were portrayed as a waste of university resources and a drain on the faculty's time. These students, the argument went, stymied the intellectual growth of "superior" students in the classroom and unfavorably influenced the social and extracurricular environment of these same students outside the classroom. Even worse, the presence of too many "mediocre" students made it difficult to recruit "superior" students who wanted to be challenged by their peers. For a university that prized faculty research, low-performing students were also problematic because, according to one UM researcher, they produced "unnecessary problems for a busy and scholarly faculty." In other words, helping "mediocre" students produce satisfactory work diverted too much of the faculty's time away from research.[37]

UM officials also introduced diversity language to justify the exclusion of previously qualified in-state students in order to enroll a large number of nonresidents. In the immediate post–World War II period, out-of-state students' share of the student body dropped significantly to accommodate the surge of in-state applicants. Faculty members and administrators loathed the practice of limiting nonresident enrollment to control growth. Out-of-state students were valuable to UM because they paid more money, but just as important, they were considered better students. Out-of-state students faced more stringent admission standards, and their presence, UM officials believed, was necessary to maintain the university's elite status. Of course, this is how administrators and faculty discussed out-of-state students internally. Recognizing that it wasn't the best tactic to tell Michigan taxpayers and state legislators that their children were intellectually inferior to the students UM could recruit from outside the state, UM administrators and faculty publicly stressed how in-state students benefited from the diversity that out-of-state students brought to UM. Words like "national character," "cosmopolitan," and "heterogeneity" filled the public statements that justified the large numbers of nonresidents at

UM. Some people called this diversity rationale into question. Weren't there areas in the state that were almost totally unrepresented at UM? Wouldn't students from Michigan's Upper Peninsula bring different perspectives to UM, just like students from Ohio? These were marginal voices, however, that never gained much traction at UM. After all, diversity in this context was always about justifying UM's quest to get large numbers of the nation's "best" students.[38]

UM officials pursued two paths to preserve UM's status in this new era of mass higher education. First, they pushed for the expansion of already existing postsecondary state institutions and the creation of new ones to accommodate the students they considered mediocre. The idea here was that the University of Michigan would receive pressure from the state legislature to admit "mediocre" students if other outlets were not available. To relieve this pressure, UM president Harlan Hatcher proved instrumental in expanding the number of junior colleges in the state and encouraging the growth of Michigan State University.[39]

Second, faculty and administrators became more willing to entertain a new admissions system. In the postwar period, the university moved away from the automatic admission guaranteed by the certification system and replaced it with a new system that gave admissions officers the power to select both in-state and out-of-state students. A new admissions office, inaugurated in 1949, led this transformation. Clyde Vroman became the university's first admissions director. Vroman was an unusual choice to lead an admissions office. A high school dropout, he eventually graduated from high school in 1933 at the age of twenty-nine. Nine years later, he had a PhD in secondary education and a master's degree in music, all from the University of Michigan. He began teaching music and education courses at UM until he received an offer to lead the admissions office. Without any prior experience, he helped transform admissions into a professional practice at the University of Michigan.[40]

Despite his lack of experience, Vroman was able to do what Smith couldn't. He convinced faculty and administrators that he could predict how students would perform at UM better than high school principals could. He offered an admissions system that would focus on high school grades, standardized test scores, and a college preparatory curriculum. Vroman made the SAT a requirement on an experimental basis for out-of-state applicants in 1955 and for in-state applicants in 1961. After claiming its validity in selecting students, Vroman made the exam a permanent part of the application process for out-of-state students in 1957 and for in-state students in 1963.[41]

Vroman wouldn't have been able to do this without the support of social scientists. Ira Smith's innovations fell victim to skeptical researchers; Vroman's admissions innovations received the full intellectual support of the university's research arm. In particular, Vroman received the support of Benno Fricke. Fricke served as the assistant chief of the university's Evaluation and Examination Division, a research office created in 1945. Fricke's job involved analyzing the predictive value of the common admissions tools used in the United States. He concluded that UM could no longer rely on principals to predict which students could graduate from UM. The most accurate predictors of students' performance, according to Fricke, were their high school grade point averages and SAT scores. He sold these practices to the faculty as "objective" and "considerably accurate."[42]

Fricke offered a sense of order and fairness to a system that was going to exclude even more in-state applicants than had the certification system. But a look at Fricke's internal reports suggests that these prediction tools were a lot messier than Fricke had let on to the faculty. In one internal report he admitted, "It is reasonably safe to say that the accuracy with which freshman grades are predicted has not changed over the past thirty years." Much like Smith, Fricke could only predict with a high degree of certainty the performance of students with high school grades and standardized test scores in the top and bottom fifth of UM's current students. In other words, Fricke couldn't successfully predict the performance of 60 percent of students in their first year at UM.[43]

Nevertheless, this wasn't a problem for Fricke. He suggested that UM should simply increase the number of students whose SAT scores and high school performance put them in the top fifth of applicants. In other words, he wanted the admissions office to focus on students whose performance was easily predictable. These were the valuable students. As a goal, Fricke wanted to reduce the number of students whose performance was difficult to predict to 15 to 25 percent of the university's student body. The unpredictable students, a full sixty percent of UM's undergraduate population, suddenly became potential threats to the university's quality.[44]

The consequences of Fricke's research and the university's move to modify admissions standards based on standardized test scores proved monumental in determining how university officials would define merit and talent. Sixty percent of UM's student body now threatened UM's quality, not because UM researchers could predict their poor academic performance but because researchers *couldn't* predict how they would perform. There were many brilliant students in this group, but there were also many students deemed "mediocre" and low performing. Because researchers like Fricke couldn't sort the brilliant from the rest, everyone in this group was deemed a risk to the university's quality. Fricke, in other words, transformed predictability into merit.[45]

These new admissions tools were likely popular because they gave UM an aura of selectivity that allowed it to claim elite status in an emerging period of mass education. As I mentioned previously, mass higher education disrupted the stratification of higher education. Elite universities began to rely even more on their selectivity and the quality of their student bodies to claim their elite status.[46]

All of this speaks to how the SAT gained legitimacy and authority as a measurement tool at the University of Michigan when so much of the internal research suggested that it was unreliable in identifying talented students. When research was translated into public statements, the messiness became orderly. The environment of fear about the future quality of UM also likely helped the UM community overlook—or at least ask fewer questions about—much of this messiness. The benefits of the new admissions system offered a new sense of confidence that UM could maintain its elite status.[47]

In sum, the primary purpose of these new admissions tools was never to accurately predict the "best" students; rather, the primary purpose was to preserve the university's elite status. Preserving status has always been put above fairness and inclusion at the University of Michigan. In fact, regardless of the SAT's poor utility in predicting the ability of students, once SAT scores became a reliable tool for sustaining UM's reputation, doing away with the test proved almost impossible.

Much like the certification system, the new admissions system continued to ignore the social world of applicants. When Benno Fricke studied the correlation between SAT scores and academic performance at UM, he gave no attention to race. Because UM students took these exams once they arrived on campus, it's likely that only a few black students were part of Fricke's studies. As late as 1963, a generous estimate put two hundred black first-year students on campus. The numbers wouldn't have mattered because Fricke didn't ask test takers for their racial identity. This lack of attention to race helped UM present the SAT as a legitimate tool for measuring the merit of all students effectively, regardless of their background.[48]

The fact that UM leaders implemented the SAT with no discussion of race shows just how easily the exam shed its eugenics legacy. Faculty members and administrators started to disconnect testing from eugenics in the 1920s, when Clarence Little introduced standardized tests during Freshman Week. Administrators and faculty members never challenged the SAT because it was rooted in racial pseudoscience. Early researchers questioned its effectiveness, not its racist origins or consequence for black applicants. It's unclear how many people within the university community shared Little's faith in eugenics. Faculty members didn't directly reference eugenics when discussing admissions reform in public meetings and reports. Perhaps most faculty members were attracted to Little's faith in standardized tests only because they hoped it would preserve the university's status. Whatever the reason, they were still willing to overlook (or accept) the reforms' connection to racial pseudoscience. This speaks to how UM officials and faculty normalized racism. The UM community embraced the tools of eugenics while ignoring the racist ideology behind standardized testing. This process of de-racializing the test made it easier for UM officials to incorporate it as a tool in the 1950s and ignore the racial disparities it produced.[49]

Racial disparities, of course, plagued the SAT and brought criticism from civil rights groups. The SAT, though, wasn't the only admissions mechanism that ignored the social world of students and produced disparities. By continuing to place emphasis on a college preparatory curriculum in admissions decisions, officials kept the fate of black students' admission in the hands of Detroit officials. The problem was that black students' access to college preparatory courses didn't greatly improve during the postwar period. Black parents protested against the poor quality of their children's education, especially the lack of college preparatory courses. But reform was slow, and efforts to integrate the city's schools through busing initiatives in the early 1960s were met with harsh resistance from white parents.[50]

Before the 1960s, only one school within the University of Michigan considered the social world of black applicants when crafting admissions practices. By the late 1940s, UM's medical school recognized the structural factors that gave white students advantages in the admissions system. With these structural problems in mind and believing that there was a pressing need for black doctors, the medical school set up UM's first affirmative action admissions program. There is so little documentation of this program that it's unclear when it started. But since the earliest affirmative action admissions program recorded thus far began in the early 1960s, UM's medical school was years ahead of what scholars consider the pioneers of affirmative action in higher education.[51]

The program fell victim to protest. Surprisingly, these challenges to the medical school's affirmative action program came from the Committee to End Discrimination (CED), a coalition of many different student groups on campus. When students began to pressure the medical school to reform its admissions practices in spring 1949, none of the students in CED understood that the school's practices benefited black applicants. Students only knew that the medical school asked for students' race and religion on applications in addition to requesting a photograph. To them, this was prima facie evidence of discrimination against black applicants.[52]

CED members didn't come up with this assumption about the dangers of racial identification and discrimination on their own. These students found inspiration in the growing popularity of racial liberalism that followed World War II. Racial liberals saw racism as one of the great social problems in the United States that threatened American democracy. Within universities, they imagined a world without formal barriers designed to limit or exclude African Americans. In their eyes, eliminating race as an important institutional category was fundamental to this process. *To Secure These Rights*, the famous report President Harry Truman commissioned from his Committee on Civil Rights, gave the students a road map, listing the types of policies universities used to discriminate against black students. Questions about race were an obvious red flag, but so too were requests for photographs, as the medical school had implemented. The students cited the committee's report when they attacked the medical school.[53]

Students' pressure on the medical school heated up in the fall of 1949. CED representatives participated in a series of meetings with Wayne Whitaker, chair of the medical school's admissions committee. Whitaker took a cautious approach by trying to reassure the students that the medical school did not discriminate. The committee, according to Whitaker, "regard[s] the problems of race and religion as insignificant" in determining who to admit. But Whitaker's attempts to reassure CED did not end the organization's campaign. And it was clear that CED was making inroads with the university's administration. In February 1950, administrators organized a committee to study CED's claims about discrimination. Only then did Whitaker reveal the true purpose of the medical school's questions about race.[54]

The fact that the medical school used racial identification to improve access for black students made little difference to CED. Students continued to pressure UM officials to remove requests for photographs and questions about race from applications. By the end of 1950, a committee led by Professor Harold M. Dorr made the recommendation to every college and school at UM that "pre-admission photographs and questions regarding race, religion, national origin, and ancestry be eliminated from admission forms." Soon thereafter, a representative of UM's president's office announced that Dorr's recommendation was now university policy. The medical school officially changed its forms in fall 1951.[55]

The pressure from the CED and the administration's new policy had an immediate impact on black students' access to the medical school. A national survey of medical schools in the late 1940s revealed that UM's medical school enrolled more black students than any other HWCU. In the midst of the backlash to affirmative action, however, black enrollment fell by half. Later, by the 1970s, declining numbers of black students would signal that there was a potential problem with racial inclusion policies. But for racial liberals, a decline in black students did not necessarily signal a problem, as they didn't measure success by the number of black students on campus. Ensuring that race played no role in choosing people for jobs or admission was more important to racial liberals than implementing a policy that raised black enrollment. In fact, counting the number of black students or employees—a key part of measuring success for future affirmative action proponents—violated the principles of racial liberalism. After all, counting by race made race an important category, something racial liberals wanted to avoid. That's why the students who protested against the medical school's affirmative action program didn't rethink their position when black enrollment fell after the school modified its admissions policies. The outcomes of admissions policies were less important than a color-blind process of selecting students.[56]

The color-blind admissions process produced poor outcomes for black students across the university. By 1963, the first time UM officially reported black enrollment, approximately two hundred black students were on UM's campus—or 0.5 percent of the student body. That means that if the estimate of black students from the 1920s is correct, which placed sixty black students on campus (0.6 percent of a smaller student body), black students' share of the UM student population actually declined slightly between the 1920s and early 1960s. This is especially significant considering that the black population in the state rose dramatically during this period. In Detroit, for example, African Americans' share of the city's population rose from 4.1 percent to 28.9 percent between 1920 and 1960.[57]

Retaining control over what constituted fairness and racism represented a key tool that allowed UM administrators to claim racial innocence, even as few black students gained access to the university. Racial liberalism helped rationalize admissions policies that created disparities while prohibiting admissions criteria designed specifically to increase black enrollment. Despite UM leaders' focus on the process of selecting students, they were noticeably silent on how the university's admissions process was unfair to black students. Demanding pictures as part of the admissions process signaled unfairness. Standardized tests that greatly disadvantaged black students were fair. Questions about race suggested prima facie evidence of discrimination. Admissions criteria that focused on a college preparatory curriculum, largely inaccessible to black students, represented fairness. Racial liberalism never kept race out of university policies; it simply helped UM officials claim that they cared about racial inclusion while muting discussions about how the university's admissions policies reinforced discrimination in primary and secondary schools. Even when university leaders later rejected some of the principles of racial liberalism and adopted affirmative action, they never rejected racial innocence. Racial innocence continued to be an effective weapon for avoiding any institutional culpability for racial disparities.

As UM leaders were undermining the university's first affirmative action admissions program, they were crafting special admissions programs for other groups. These programs gave administrators the confidence that they could incorporate the principle of inclusion without disrupting the entire admissions system. Minor modifications could be made to implement inclusion and preserve the university's elite status.

UM's special admissions practices for international students were emblematic of efforts to reconcile access with the more important value of institutional quality after World War II. UM's increasingly exclusive admissions policies called international students' access into question. The University of Michigan had a long history of admitting international students. As early as 1858, international students constituted 4.5 percent of the student body. The university carried that tradition through the twentieth century. By the mid-1950s, 960 international students were on campus, accounting for 5.5 percent of UM's students. Few universities in the United States matched that number, and UM consistently ranked among the top three enrollers of international students in the country. China represented UM's most fruitful recruiting ground. Between 1854 and 1954, no U.S. university came close to educating the number of Chinese students that UM enrolled.[58] But as UM initiated new tools of applicant selection, UM's registrar, and later the admissions office, had a difficult time evaluating applications from international students. Many of the international students who were admitted had little knowledge of English and struggled in their coursework, which sparked complaints from faculty.[59]

International students' struggles, however, didn't stop UM from admitting them. University officials created special admissions criteria for international applicants. Still, UM officials created rules to ensure that special admissions programs would preserve the university's hierarchy of values. First, any special admissions program had to serve a social need that the university had an interest in addressing. In international students' case, in times of war university officials felt they had a responsibility to educate students in war-ravaged countries without access to postsecondary training. In peacetime, assumptions about American universities' responsibility to modernize "backward" places drove administrators' commitment to admitting international students. UM officials pitched international student enrollment by recounting the work of UM alumni who had returned to their home countries and "built railways and river locks in China, . . . promoted Turkey's strategic network of highways," and "attacked the scourge of the Nile, the liver fluke, which is carried in its contaminated waters." Their work would also have obvious benefits for the United States, administrators argued. These graduates would go back to their home countries and develop business relationships with American corporations. For example, a Chilean engineer educated at UM would become "familiar with American models and specifications and is bound to import American machinery rather than British or German." UM officials also saw the presence of international students as a tool to challenge the growing importance of nationalism. Leaders at UM saw nationalism as a modern problem that led to the world wars of the twentieth century. Admitting international students, in administrators' eyes, facilitated a cultural exchange that would get UM students to "think in terms of humanity at large, not as self-centered and isolated national groups." In the special admissions process for international students, then, UM officials saw the opportunity to contribute to a new world where American businesses would have greater access to global markets, UM alumni would solve the social problems of "backward" places, and world wars would be relics of the past.[60]

These arguments alone still weren't enough to justify international students' admission. The second rule ensured that proponents of special admissions had to show that the program wouldn't undermine the university's elite status. In this case, proponents had to show how admitting large numbers of international students who often struggled in their coursework would not hurt the university's quality. Advocates used the diversity rationale, arguing that international students broadened the educational experience of U.S. citizens at the University of Michigan. Through contact with "diverse personalities," American students would widen their "understanding of life and people." It was an education that students could not get simply by learning about different cultures through classroom lectures. The university set up a place on campus that was supposed to facilitate this engagement between American and international students. The International House provided campus housing for many of the international students, developed programing that promoted the positive traits of different cultures, and sought to bring American students into contact with international students. International students, according to the diversity rationale, improved the educational experience of American students, which justified their special admissions criteria.[61]

Officials also crafted special admissions practices for men. In the eyes of most administrators and faculty members, the problem with moving to an admissions system that admitted students based on high school grade point averages, high school standing, and standardized test scores was that women often outperformed men on these measurements. Officials in LSA decided that they needed to limit women's enrollment. As a model, they could have used the Ivy League's practices of discriminating against Jewish applicants by introducing subjective personality factors that were supposedly lacking in women. Instead, LSA officials crafted a new policy of proportionalism, which required that a man be admitted for every woman admitted. The fact that LSA officials were so open about the proportional system suggests that they weren't concerned about backlash to policies that formally limited women's enrollment. Administrators and faculty members who were concerned about women's rising representation at UM never explained why they thought this was a problem, perhaps because the people involved thought the problem was obvious.[62]

If administrators didn't need to articulate the reasons behind these practices, they still needed to address concerns about quality by showing how the special admissions practices for men wouldn't hurt the academic capabilities of the student body. Their rationale required some intellectual jujitsu. By almost all measurements, the data on women's high school and UM performance suggested that they outperformed men. The chair of LSA's oversight committee on undergraduate admissions even reported that women were responsible for improving the quality of the first-year class. Women, on average, also achieved higher grade point averages at UM. But that didn't stop advocates of women's restriction from mobilizing evidence to support their case. Despite the fact that women performed better in their coursework at UM, they left LSA before graduating in higher numbers than did men. UM officials never considered the social factors that pressured women to leave higher education in the post–World War II period. Instead, the data led advocates of women's restriction to argue that women matured much earlier than men, which explained their superior performance in high school, on standardized tests, and even in their first years at UM. Admissions tools, they argued, were flawed because they privileged a group with high attrition rates and didn't consider the late development of male students. Using this logic, letting in more male students actually improved the quality of the university because more men successfully completed the university's upper-level courses.[63]

The justifications for men's special admissions practices show that UM officials were capable of considering alternatives to an important feature of the admissions system that had long preserved racial disparities. UM measured merit based on a candidate's qualifications at the time of application. An alternative, which they used here for men, was to measure merit by predicting the academic capabilities of a student after four years of study at UM. UM officials, of course, never considered this method for black students.

It's worth pausing for a moment to point out the difference between the evidence necessary to challenge the validity of traditional admissions tools for a particular group and the evidence necessary to support the diversity rationale. The diversity rationale, used for international students, wasn't as easy to measure and test. In the mid-twentieth century, there were no tools set up to determine whether American citizens benefited from their contact with international students. People on campus took international students' positive contributions for granted. That didn't mean that nobody worried about the academic preparation of international students, but the diversity rationale made no guarantees about their academic performance. International students added value through their presence on campus; they didn't face the same burden of proving they were just as capable of completing the coursework as any other student. But when the rationale for a special admissions program hinged on challenging the validity of admissions tools, advocates faced a different standard. University researchers had already set up a sophisticated, if flawed, system that measured whether admissions tools effectively predicted students' performance. Any claim that these admissions tools didn't measure a particular group effectively, then, seemed easy to assess and required empirical evidence. That's why advocates of special admissions practices for men relied heavily on data to support their cause.

So far, I've highlighted the obstacles UM officials faced in showing how special admissions programs wouldn't hurt the quality of the university. There were, however, exceptions to this rule. UM's post–World War II program for veterans, for example, found a place at UM without reconciling the perceived tension between quality and inclusion. Veterans' admissions policies didn't just deviate from the normal high school curriculum required for admission; rather, the university was willing to admit veterans who hadn't graduated from high school. As long as the veteran applicant showed a chance of doing satisfactory work and had completed three years of high school, the applicant was granted admission. UM officials argued that veterans deserved special treatment because of their service. The success of this program speaks to the special place military service held during the period and the temporary nature of this program. It was understood that the special admissions practices for veterans would last only a couple of years and, consequently, would not have any long-term consequences for the university's quality.[64]

Two other groups—legacies and athletes—enjoyed access to special admissions criteria without the need to regularly articulate how their presence didn't hurt the university's quality. In evaluating out-of-state applicants, the university privileged the children of alumni. The university also evaluated applications from potential athletes differently. In internal reports and faculty meeting minutes, special admissions practices for legacies and athletes were usually discussed without any rationale. Only in the case of the sons and daughters of international students did an official suggest that special admissions practices were necessary in order to create a "Michigan tradition" in other countries. The fact that university officials rarely had to articulate these rationales suggests that alumni and athletes enjoyed a special privilege where few people ever questioned their presence and access to special admissions practices.[65]

Still, these programs wouldn't have existed if administrators and faculty members didn't see value in these two groups. The university community connected both alumni and athletes to the university's prestige. Running an elite university was expensive, and donations from alumni were essential to maintaining the university's status. In 1921, President Martin Burton called the university's alumni a "moderate-sized army," standing at fifty-two thousand. He recognized that alumni donations were responsible for much of the university's equipment and recently constructed buildings. Two-fifths of all the university's property and operating funds came from alumni. When officials added up all the university's money, property, and equipment that hadn't come from the state government, they revealed that alumni donations amounted to $22,721,634.17. Special admissions practices for legacies, then, became one way to keep this important donor pool happy. Special admissions practices for athletes also had value because they helped the university administration satisfy alumni. Beginning in the early twentieth century, few things were more important to alumni than a winning football team. Getting the best football talent, regardless of whether these athletes qualified for admission, represented a tool to keep alumni money flowing.[66]

These special admissions programs created problems for black students. In the short term, the programs meant that white and non-U.S. citizens would largely benefit from special admissions, while black students faced a system that produced harsh racial disparities. In the long term, the principles of special admissions created obstacles for future activists who wanted to make the university more accessible to black students. The idea that inclusion required only minor modifications through a special admissions program weakened black activists' calls to ditch the university's admissions practices and build a new system from scratch based on the principle of racial justice. The programs' obsession with quality also meant that black students had to prove their merit constantly, always under suspicion that their presence undermined the university's status.

UM's admissions system clearly excluded many black students, but the university's admissions policies were not the only factors that kept black students' representation below 1 percent of the student body for the better half of the twentieth century. For the small group of black students who could afford to attend UM and overcame the obstacles put in their way by local school districts, UM's toxic racial climate created an additional roadblock. Black students needed to be willing to come to and stay on a campus with a reputation as an uninviting place for minorities. Thus, the social environment, not just the selection and funding procedures, excluded black students.

While UM admitted and graduated black students long before many other universities in the United States, the history of UM's racial climate mirrors that of most HWCUs. Before the post–World War II period, the University of Michigan did little to end discriminatory practices on or off campus. At least into the 1920s, black students were prohibited from attending college dances and using the university swimming pool. University housing was also segregated into World War II. In fact, until 1930, black women could not live on campus. In the classroom, black students might find themselves in the classes of U. B. Phillips, a historian who characterized slavery as a benevolent institution, or A. Franklin Shull, a zoologist who believed that whites were genetically superior to African Americans. Moreover, between 1925 and 1929, black students traversed a campus led by a prominent eugenicist. Off campus, black students found segregated restaurants and discriminatory housing practices. Black students' efforts to challenge this environment were met with retribution from UM administrators.[67]

After World War II, university administrators ended official policies of racial segregation, yet they maintained practices that allowed white students to act on their prejudices. As late as 1959, the housing office allowed students to request to live with a member of the same racial group, asking the question on applications: "Are you interested in a roommate of a nationality, or race other than your own?" These policies enjoyed strong support from UM students. One 1949 survey recorded that 59 percent of UM students supported the housing office's practice of obtaining students' racial information before making housing assignments. Only 9 percent of students stated that they would like to live with a black student. The irony here is that in the same year that a student movement used the ideal of color blindness to end affirmative action in the medical school, the majority of UM students supported the collection of racial information in the housing office that protected white students from rooming with black students.[68]

Executive administrators also undermined some efforts to eliminate discriminatory practices. An investigation revealed that the constitutions of thirty-three fraternities and three sororities on campus included racially discriminatory clauses. In November 1950, in a close vote of twenty to eighteen, the student legislature approved a proposal to mandate that all campus fraternities and sororities remove discriminatory clauses within six years. UM president, Alexander Ruthven vetoed the plan. Ruthven and his successor, Harlan Hatcher, also refused to call on the Ann Arbor City Council to pass fair practices laws, despite evidence that black students faced discrimination off campus. Segregated restaurants and barber shops dotted Ann Arbor's map. Other businesses might serve black patrons but stated preferences for white employees. In the case of a local ambulance service provided by Staffan Funeral Home, the owner didn't hire black students because he feared objections from white employees. Finding housing off campus also frustrated black students. In some cases, the discriminatory practices of rental companies were well known. The largest rental complex in Ann Arbor, Pittsfield Village, openly discriminated on the basis of race. In some cases, landlords were explicit, telling black applicants that they would not rent to people of color. In 1961, the Office of Student Affairs received reports of sixty-eight landlords that discriminated on the basis of "race, creed or national origin." But in cases where individual landlords didn't state their racial preferences in advertisements, black students looking for housing could only hope that meant that the owner was willing to rent to a person of color.[69]

The university had a close relationship with some of the discriminatory rental companies in Ann Arbor. The university provided mortgages to developers, expanding Ann Arbor's apartment stock. It's unclear just how many mortgages the university held, but it's clear that it profited from at least one company that practiced racial discrimination. In the late 1950s, Cutler Hubble Company of Detroit obtained a mortgage from the university to build two Ann Arbor apartment buildings, Arbordale Manor and Parkhurst. The Michigan Civil Rights Commission and the Ann Arbor Human Relations Commission later found that the company discriminated against prospective black tenants.[70]

Still, the late 1940s represented a clear moment of transition, as racial liberalism began to take hold slowly and unevenly among administrators. The university became an intellectual hub for research on interracial relations when the Research Center for Group Dynamics moved from the Massachusetts Institute of Technology to UM in 1948. Suddenly the university was sponsoring race relation workshops in Detroit and supporting new research that supported the premises of racial liberalism. In August 1952, for example, the center led the intergroup relations workshop "Human Relations in School and Community." The workshop brought sixty-two educators and eight active community members from around the country to learn "how to meet the problems of intergroup tension and conflict as these arise in school and community." One of the workshop's field trips took participants to Detroit to review the work of the Mayor's Interracial Committee in "Negro-White" relations.[71]

By the 1950s, the university had implemented some of the proposals offered by the Student Government Council's Human Relations Board. In the case of off-campus housing, one of the board's first steps was to make sure the university did not serve as a vehicle for discriminatory landlords. New policies followed that prohibited landlords who discriminated on the basis of race from advertising in any of the university's venues or publications. Some landlords removed their advertisements; others remained insistent that the university should help landlords discriminate. Even after learning about the policy, Marcia Minnis, a local landlord, asked if a university official could just send white women to her house. Nevertheless, the policy gave black students access to the housing advertisements of landlords who had at least signed a document agreeing not to use race as a factor in choosing tenants. It also gave black students an opportunity to make complaints to an organization with some power, as the board could prohibit a landlord's access to a valuable advertising outlet.[72]

By the end of the 1950s, UM leaders took the university's most significant step in implementing racial liberalism. In 1959, the board of regents passed a bylaw stating that the university "shall not discriminate against any person because of race, color, religion, creed, national origin, or ancestry." The housing office subsequently eliminated questions on applications that allowed students to request a roommate of the same racial group. At the turn of the decade, the ideal of color blindness was embedded in university policy.[73]

As racial liberalism took hold, university officials began to embrace the idea of creating a model multiracial community, seeing an opportunity to use the university to address white prejudice. George Palmer, a professor at UM's law school and a member of the governing body of student housing, explained these ideals when he argued for an end to housing policies that allowed students to choose to live only with people of their own racial background. Palmer claimed that if a student who holds racial prejudices "associates with a member of such a group long enough to learn something about his qualities as a human being, it is possible that he will change his attitude toward this group." Only by ending racial separation and encouraging interracial contact could UM help "purge . . . something that lies heavy on the conscience of the American people; the treatment of the Negro."[74]

Racial liberals like Palmer made two assumptions, both rooted in post–World War II racial liberalism, about how to address racism and create a model multiracial community. First, interracial contact was vital to improving race relations. Second, expressions of racial identity harmed race relations. Racial liberals put their faith in universalism, which highlighted the similarities and deemphasized the differences between whites and blacks. A shared

American identity, the assumption went, was essential for members of different racial groups to see their common human identity.

These assumptions created a toxic racial climate for black students. Officials' emphasis on interracial contact helped them see black students as tools in changing white students. Black students' interactions with white students was essential in getting white students to overcome their prejudice. Universalism also helped officials see black culture as something to be overcome, not celebrated. Black culture threatened the shared American identity, which administrators believed was vital to improving race relations.

Notice the subtle differences between the ways in which university officials tried to improve relationships between American citizens and international students, and the ways in which they tried to improve relationships between white and black students. The end goal was the same. In both cases, university officials wanted students to see each other as human beings, not as citizens of different countries or members of a different racial group. But the path to see each other as humans was different. Sure, contact between the two groups was important, but for international students, university officials emphasized the positive cultural traits of different nationalities. It would be out of respect for those positive cultural differences that American citizens would learn to overcome stereotypes, see value in cultural differences, and ultimately see international students as equal human beings. But improving relations between white and black students followed a different model. Downplaying cultural differences and emphasizing a shared American identity was fundamental to getting different racial groups to see each other simply as human beings.

This speaks to how racial liberals viewed black culture. Chinese students, according to UM officials, brought with them a culture that UM students should appreciate and could learn from. Racial liberals didn't see the same positive value in black culture. Emphasizing the importance of a shared American—white middle class—identity was as much a critique of African American culture as a grand vision of racial progressivism. It's no surprise, then, that words like "culturally deprived" filled racial liberals' descriptions of African Americans. In UM officials' eyes, black students brought a cultural identity that was threatening. It added no value to the university, and it offered nothing to white students and faculty.[75]

It's no surprise that these ideas created a toxic racial climate. Nobody at the University of Michigan thought to ask black students what they thought of these "color-blind" policies. In fact, no UM official commissioned a study on black students' social experience until the late 1960s. The lack of black voices in administrative and staff positions helped UM officials believe they were acting in the best interest of black students. There were no black administrators;

there were no black regents. As late as 1963, the university employed only eight black faculty members at or above the rank of instructor. As a result, whites controlled the institutional knowledge about black students without any input from African Americans.[76]

William Boone, a master's student at UM, was the only researcher who thought to ask black students about the university's racial climate before the late 1960s. In 1940, he asked black students at UM, "Do you feel that your social life within the University community is adequate?" Eighty-five percent of students responded negatively. He found that black students "rarely participated in any of the social activities" and that "their contacts [with white students] were mostly entirely academic in nature." The students' conclusions were filed away with other UM theses. No social scientist at UM asked these questions again for almost thirty years.[77]

Scholars who listened to black students at other HWCUs during the post–World War II period found that black students expressed similar frustration with the racial climate. A late 1950s study of two groups of black students— one group that attended a historically white midwestern university and one group that attended a historically black southern university—tested the perceptions black students held about higher education. The survey found that black students thought HWCUs and HBCUs offered different advantages. Black students who attended the HBCU concluded that they were trading the academic prestige of an HWCU for a social life. These black students reported feeling "more at ease in an all Negro group" and had an easier time adjusting to college life. They also noted that they valued the opportunity to learn about black history and study contemporary problems that African Americans faced—topics that were lacking at many HWCUs. Nevertheless, they thought that the education they received at their historically black institution was inferior to that offered at a predominantly white institution. Black students at the HWCU, in contrast, cited the lack of a social life as the most notable disadvantage of attending such an institution, but they chose to make that sacrifice because of the perceived academic advantages of historically white universities.[78]

When social scientists finally began examining UM's racial climate in the late 1960s, they found that black students reported similar feelings about UM. In response to these studies and campus protests, UM leaders began questioning some of the assumptions behind UM's model multiracial community. Administrators eventually reconsidered their commitment to universalism and accepted the idea that celebrating black culture was compatible with improving race relations. Nevertheless, despite criticism from black students, UM leaders held steadfast to their commitment to interracial contact as the key tool for changing white students.

In 1964, the University of Michigan created an undergraduate affirmative action program that signaled its most dramatic step toward policies of racial inclusion. But the long-standing developments over the course of the nineteenth and twentieth centuries would loom large over these new racial inclusion initiatives. The university's hierarchy of values, which privileged UM's elite status over inclusion, would hang over affirmative action like a black cloud. Racial liberalism never sought to disrupt this hierarchy; rather, it sought to preserve it in the wake of pressure for racial justice. Affirmative action proponents would have to prove that they, too, weren't trying to disrupt the institution's hierarchy of values.

Just as university officials had a high tolerance for racial disparities in its admissions decisions, they also had a high tolerance for a poor racial climate. The model multiracial community failed to address black students' social alienation on campus. Nevertheless, UM leaders would cling to the goal of creating a model multiracial community on campus that privileged combating prejudice over addressing black students' alienation. Black students' experience on campus remained a secondary concern.

# CHAPTER 2

# The Origins of Affirmative Action

Affirmative action was never forced on the University of Michigan. The pressure that led to the university's first undergraduate affirmative action admissions program came from a federal bureaucrat and the president of the United States, who were both responding to black activism for workplace justice. Yet this pressure never threatened UM with the loss of lucrative federal contracts or potential court cases. University officials risked little if they chose to reject affirmative action admissions policies. UM adopted affirmative action in 1964 because people at the top of the institution wanted the university to change.

This environment of weak federal coercion created a perfect recipe for co-optation. After the initial dose of federal pressure, UM officials took control of the purpose and character of affirmative action, creating a program that preserved the university's long-established priorities and values. It's no surprise, then, that between 1964 and 1967, black enrollment rose from only 0.5 to 1.65 percent of the student body. Still, tripling black students' representation on campus was nothing to scoff at. But given that African Americans constituted more than 10 percent of the state population, affirmative action made a small dent in the racial disparities at the University of Michigan.[1]

It's unlikely that the black activists fighting for workplace justice in the early 1960s ever thought their protests would impact the admissions office at the

University of Michigan. These activists were tired of ineffectual federal, state, and local fair employment laws. Take Philadelphia as an example. The city hosted a fair practices employment law, and the State of Pennsylvania had a similar law on the books. African Americans initially saw potential in these antidiscrimination laws. They brought complaints of discrimination to the proper government agencies, but little came of most investigations. African Americans continued to suffer from high unemployment rates, and employers faced few repercussions for discriminating.[2]

Federal executive orders were supposed to add another layer of protection for black workers. Executive orders banning discrimination among federal contractors had become standard since President Franklin Roosevelt signed Executive Order 8802 during World War II, which stated that there "shall be no discrimination in the employment of workers in defense industries or government because of race, creed, color, or national origins." Roosevelt signed the order reluctantly, only after A. Philip Randolph threatened to bring 100,000 demonstrators to Washington, D.C., to march for fair employment practices. When Congress refused to make the Fair Employment Practices Committee—the agency that enforced Roosevelt's executive order—permanent after the war, President Harry Truman and then President Dwight Eisenhower signed executive orders prohibiting discrimination among federal contractors and created their own agencies to enforce the orders.[3]

The problem with these executive orders was that they gave enforcement agencies little power to force businesses to change their hiring practices. The agencies had small budgets and staff for investigations, and no authority to cancel contracts. But that didn't stop bureaucrats from experimenting with new investigative methods and concepts of racial justice. Early enforcement agencies relied on an individual-complaint model. In other words, they waited for a worker to file a discrimination complaint and then looked for evidence of discrimination. The initial goal was to make sure that race played no role in hiring practices. By the end of Eisenhower's term, though, officials in his President's Committee on Government Contracts (PCGC) were already moving beyond the individual-complaint model, judging employers' compliance based on whether the racial composition of their workforces matched the racial composition of the surrounding community. PCGC officials also began using their limited power to pressure some businesses to practice racially attentive hiring policies. Still, with little authority to force companies to comply, the agency didn't produce the wide-scale transformation required to change African Americans' confidence in federal antidiscrimination measures. Civil rights groups were vocal critics of the program and demanded stronger enforcement.[4]

These lackluster antidiscrimination laws led to a grassroots campaign for affirmative action in 1960. Activists like Leon Sullivan in Philadelphia believed that change would come only from pressuring businesses directly. Sullivan and his organization, the 400 Ministers, leaned on a popular tactic of the 1930s known as "Don't buy where you can't work." The slogan said it all. Sullivan called for boycotts of businesses that discriminated against black workers. He started with Tastykake, a Philadelphia company whose products were popular within the black community. Sullivan didn't want the company to reaffirm its antidiscrimination policies; he wanted the company to hire black workers immediately. When Tastykake refused, the group led a six-month boycott of the company's products. At the end of the campaign, Tastykake hired two black truck drivers, two black clerical workers, and four black female production workers. The group went on to successfully boycott twenty-nine other companies operating in Philadelphia, including Pepsi-Cola and Sunoco. When asked why he supported using race as a positive factor in hiring black employees, Sullivan argued that it was a means of redress for past discrimination: "Black men have been waiting for a hundred years, white men can wait for a few months." Similar campaigns in Detroit, Milwaukee, St. Louis, Chicago, New York, Boston, and Seattle signaled a new period of black activism.[5]

The fact that a new wave of activism was unfolding in an election year was significant. The more aggressive and confrontational civil rights movement that emerged in 1960, which included workplace activism and the famous sit-ins, pushed the Democratic Party in an uncomfortable direction. Party officials faced the difficult challenge of courting black voters, who expected more from the federal government, while hanging on to the party's control of the South. John F. Kennedy moved cautiously through his campaign, often trying to court the support of civil rights leaders through closed door meetings rather than through strong public statements. But Kennedy's party took a stronger stand. The Democratic Party Platform of 1960 reflected the new surge of civil rights activism, especially activism for jobs. The document reassured black voters that a "Democratic Administration will use its full executive powers to assure equal employment opportunities." Throughout the platform's civil rights section, jobs claimed equal footing with other civil rights issues, such as education, fair housing, voting, and access to public facilities.[6]

When Kennedy won the nomination and then the general election, he faced the difficult task of responding to calls for stronger equal opportunity employment policies. Those policies eventually landed at the University of Michigan.

A black University of Michigan alumnus brought the grassroots movement for workplace justice to campus. In the early 1960s, Hobart Taylor Jr. wasn't a nationally known civil rights figure poised to push UM to adopt affirmative action admissions. Taylor joined the National Association for the Advancement of Colored People (NAACP) in the 1940s but wasn't an active member. Taylor preferred to advance civil rights outside the spotlight. In his hometown of Detroit, he was the president of a mortgage company set up specifically to help African Americans who struggled to get loans for homes outside predominantly black neighborhoods. As a lawyer, he was also involved in court cases that tackled racial segregation in housing and restaurants. These were all important initiatives, but they didn't put Taylor on the national map of prominent civil rights activists.[7]

If Taylor wasn't the son of a wealthy donor, he would never have been an important figure in the rise of affirmative action. Taylor found a role in federal affirmative action policies because he was one of the well-connected people that Lyndon Johnson leaned on during his campaign for the presidency and then vice presidency in 1960. Taylor grew up in Houston, born into a family with strong political connections. His father was a multimillionaire businessman who provided key financial backing for Lyndon Johnson's Senate run in 1948 and found himself as a delegate at the 1956 Democratic National Convention. By the early 1960s, Hobart Taylor Jr. had graduated from the University of Michigan Law School and, having grown out of his father's shadow, was practicing as an attorney in Detroit. While the young attorney didn't follow in his father's entrepreneur footsteps, he continued the family tradition of supporting Johnson. So when Johnson was campaigning and wanted to meet with Michigan's liberal leaders, he asked Taylor to organize the meetings. And when Johnson needed advice on civil rights issues, Taylor was one of the people he called on.[8]

The road that led Taylor to UM's doorstep began in 1961. After Kennedy's presidential victory, Johnson, as vice president, oversaw Kennedy's first attempt to address employment discrimination among federal government contractors—what would become Executive Order 10925. Johnson called on Taylor for help. When the young lawyer arrived in D.C., Johnson handed him an early draft of the executive order, secured him a room at the Willard hotel, and told Taylor to start revising.[9]

Taylor's most famous contribution to the executive order came in the form of a single concept. The order included a provision that stated, "Each employer shall take action" to ensure it doesn't discriminate. But what did that mean? Taylor thought that the executive order needed a concept that people could give meaning to, courts could interpret, and could evolve over time. Something like the "equal protection" clause of the Fourteenth Amendment, he thought. Sitting there, typing up a draft of the executive order, Taylor inserted a term that would soon gain resonance across the country and endure for many decades. He first considered "positive action," then finally settled on a term he considered more alliterative: "affirmative action." In explaining a federal contractor's responsibilities, the final version read, "The contractor will take affirmative action to ensure that applicants are employed, and that employees are treated during employment, without regard to their race, creed, color, or national origin."[10]

After Kennedy signed the order in March, Taylor continued to consult on new policies and regulations for the President's Committee on Equal Employment Opportunity (PCEEO)—the agency set up to enforce the executive order. Taylor's role might have ended there if black workers were satisfied with the order's implementation. Instead, the PCEEO quickly came under attack from civil rights advocates. Especially distasteful to black activists was the Plans for Progress (PfP) program. PfP was the brainchild of Robert Troutman, a Georgia lawyer and friend of the Kennedy administration. Participation in PfP gave companies an opportunity to create their own voluntary inclusion plans and sidestep some of the PCEEO's oversight powers. The NAACP, just one of the many critics of the program, called PfP "virtually useless." Johnson called on his longtime political ally for help, hoping a change in management would temper criticism. In August 1962, Hobart Taylor became executive vice chair of the PCEEO.[11]

This is where the story of hiring and university admissions began to come together. Taylor was well aware of the calls from civil rights groups to exert more pressure on companies to reform hiring practices, but he was also worried that focusing too narrowly on hiring practices might limit the outcomes of the executive order. In light of deindustrialization, he was especially concerned about the prospects of employment for the large pool of unemployed and underemployed young African Americans in urban America. If there was a place to learn about the consequences of deindustrialization, it was Taylor's hometown of Detroit. Between 1948 and 1967, the city lost 130,000 manufacturing jobs. Just forty-five miles from the University of Michigan, African Americans suffered the brunt of deindustrialization in the Motor City, experiencing unemployment rates almost three times as high as whites during the early 1960s.[12]

Taylor thought he knew what needed to happen. If manufacturing jobs were dwindling, black workers needed better access to jobs in the growing white-collar sector. The problem was that Taylor believed the PCEEO could do only so much to advance blacks' access to this sector. Unless more African Americans gained college degrees—increasingly a qualification for these jobs—the PCEEO's intervention would have little impact. Taylor spent the early

1960s giving speeches highlighting the constricting market for manufacturing jobs and the growing need for black students to be trained for professional positions. Taylor, of course, wasn't the first to point to the importance of blacks' access to the white-collar sector; civil rights groups had long promoted the importance of access to higher education and white-collar positions. But Taylor was now acting on this idea from a position of power within the federal government.[13]

Taylor's emphasis on training also reflected a strategy of the Kennedy administration. Kennedy's early policies followed a school of economists that promoted "manpower development," which stressed that providing African Americans the skills to compete in the workplace was the key to lifting them out of poverty. As much as Taylor's ideas complemented manpower development thinking, he was quietly critiquing one aspect of Kennedy's program by focusing on the need for postsecondary training. When Kennedy thought about manpower development, he usually had in mind training for blue-collar jobs. By focusing on deindustrialization and the need for higher education, Taylor pointed out one of the flaws in Kennedy's assumption that providing training and access to manufacturing jobs would offer the solution to black unemployment rates.[14]

When Taylor finally decided to use his power to advance African Americans' access to postsecondary institutions, black enrollment in historically white institutions was bleak. About 70 percent of black college students were enrolled in HBCUs. Even though African Americans made up about 6 percent of American college students, few enrolled in universities that white-led businesses would consider elite. In fact, black enrollment at the University of Michigan looked remarkably similar to that of some of the public flagship universities in the South that had only recently opened their doors to black students. In the early 1960s, black students accounted for about 0.5 percent of the University of Michigan's enrollment, which matched black students' share of the student body at Louisiana State University–Baton Rouge. At the University of Texas, black students actually represented a larger share (0.7 percent) of the student population.[15]

Still, using Executive Order 10925 to reform admissions practices was a complicated process, since the order said nothing about admissions. Taylor started by focusing on universities he knew well. As an alumnus of the University of Michigan's law school, UM was on his radar. The University of Michigan was also a convenient target for an agency set up to oversee federal contractors, as UM was one of the largest recipients of federal defense contracts among postsecondary institutions (only the Massachusetts Institute of Technology and Columbia University received more money). To intervene at UM,

Taylor began by using the executive order's compliance reporting system, which gave the PCEEO the authority to demand information from federal contractors on the racial identity of their employees. In March 1962, Taylor came calling for a demographic breakdown of the University of Michigan's workforce.[16]

UM's board of regents initially refused to fully cooperate with the PCEEO. The very collection of racial data, they thought, violated the color-blind principles they had implemented since World War II. The major assumption behind these policies was that by removing race as a relevant institutional category, a university could take away opportunities for racial prejudice to influence institutional practices. In light of these changes, regent Donald M. D. Thurber of Detroit lamented that "it would be regrettable if we were forced to take this type of census," since it "would only focus attention on something on which we've lost consciousness." The university's vice president for business and finance, Wilbur Pierpont, proposed a response to the PCEEO. He suggested that UM document the number of university employees (approximately 10,253) but explain that racial statistics were not available. Pierpont recommended that UM attach a copy of its nondiscrimination policy and an explanation that the "maintenance of such records is inconsistent with the bylaw and the long-standing philosophy which indicates that these [racial] distinctions have no place at the University." All the regents approved Pierpont's proposal. The university's response read like a lecture to the PCEEO. Regent Allan Sorenson stated that "philosophically this answer is ahead of federal action"—meaning that the federal government had not yet entered the progressive world of color blindness.[17]

Taylor responded quickly to the University of Michigan's initial attempt to avoid providing racial statistics. He didn't care that the university chose not to keep records of its employees' racial identity. Taylor suggested that UM "turn in a count based on a visual check" and told administrators that they could keep this information separate from the university's regular personnel data. In December 1962, only after continued pressure from Taylor, the university agreed to provide the PCEEO with a racial census.[18]

The University of Michigan completed the study in February 1963. To the public, the university reported that black employees made up 10.4 percent of UM's workforce. The reality, however, was more complex. At the time, the bulk of UM's black employees worked in service and manual labor positions. The university employed only eight black faculty members at or above the rank of instructor. Employment data like this, which showed racial disparities in workforces, gave the PCEEO a tool to justify intervention at work sites. Rather than relying on individual complaints of discrimination, the PCEEO used workforce data as prima facie evidence of discrimination. To the PCEEO, the data suggested that there was something clearly wrong with the university's hiring practices.[19]

Following the release of workforce data, Taylor organized conferences with UM and Wayne State University (WSU) of Detroit—which had recently gone through a similar struggle with the PCEEO over racial data—to clarify the universities' responsibilities in complying with Kennedy's executive order. It's doubtful that UM or WSU officials ever expected to discuss admissions practices at these conferences. After all, they agreed to a meeting to talk about employment data with the head of an agency that oversaw hiring practices. The first of their Detroit meetings with Taylor did just that, focusing on the universities' compliance reports submitted to the PCEEO. The second conference, however, must have surprised university officials. There, Taylor focused on both hiring practices concerning black faculty members and educational opportunities for black students.[20]

Of course, the process of using the executive order to reform admissions practices required more than a discussion about educational opportunities for African Americans at a compliance meeting. Taylor didn't have the coercive tools to force universities to change their admissions practices. The PCEEO *did* have the authority to revoke contracts, but it was unlikely that Taylor could cancel a contract because a university chose not to modify admissions practices—something well outside the language of the executive order. But even if admissions practices had been part of the executive order, Taylor preferred not to revoke contracts. Taylor believed that the success of affirmative action programs hinged on making institutional officials feel like "participants and innovators" in government policymaking. Despite the fact that Johnson brought him onto the PCEEO because of black activists' criticism of Plans for Progress, Taylor still liked PfP's voluntary formula of institutional change. In Taylor's mind, institutional change worked best when managers were able to carry out affirmative action "as part of their program rather than because they were compelled to do it by law." Force from above wasn't as effective, Taylor surmised, because to get a real institutional commitment to implement affirmative action, "you have to change a man's mind from being negative and doing what he's doing under force to do something he's doing."[21]

Taylor's emphasis on voluntary compliance highlights the fact that affirmative action admissions was never forced on University of Michigan officials. The poor record of PfP in effecting widespread change is a testament to just how easily institutional leaders could meet compliance standards without making any significant reforms. For weak government coercion to give black students unprecedented access to UM, the interests of Taylor and at least one well-placed executive administrator at UM needed to align. Luckily for Taylor, he found a powerful ally sympathetic to his goals in Roger Heyns, UM's vice president for academic affairs—the person who oversaw the university's Office of Undergraduate Admissions.[22]

Unlike board of regent members, Heyns was more comfortable with affirmative action. By the time the PCEEO entered into the fray at UM, Heyns had already taken steps to modify admissions policies. In 1962, he met separately with Francis Kornegay of the National Urban League and representatives from the local NAACP chapter about implementing new methods to increase black enrollment. Neither of these groups threatened to protest if Heyns didn't implement affirmative action, but the meetings marked an important turning point. Not much is known about Heyns's views on affirmative action before 1963. Perhaps Heyns was already sympathetic to racially attentive solutions to inequality or perhaps the arguments of activists convinced him that affirmative action was necessary. Whatever he thought about racial equity before these meetings, though, Heyns would spend the rest of his administrative career supporting efforts to expand opportunities for black students in higher education, beginning at UM and then as chancellor at the University of California–Berkeley. By February 1963, Heyns began discussions with UM's admissions and public relations offices about the possibilities of increasing access for black students. In proposing that the university take proactive steps to make itself more inclusive, he was suggesting that color-blind policies were not enough.[23]

But if a powerful administrator already supported affirmative action, why was Taylor's intervention necessary to spark reform? Answering this is important in understanding the relationship between coercion—even weak coercion—and institutional change. Before Taylor's intervention, Heyns's meetings had not led to any firm plans for new admissions policies or any committees to study the feasibility of an affirmative action program. It's not clear why Heyns didn't pursue affirmative action admissions more aggressively after his early meetings with civil rights groups. Perhaps he worried that he wouldn't be able to cultivate enough institutional support at that time. What *is* clear is that Heyns used PCEEO pressure to advance a program that he already supported. In UM's case, federal pressure didn't force a recalcitrant administrator to implement a program he disagreed with; instead, federal intervention created an opportunity for a well-placed administrator to advance his own goals. As historian Timothy Minchin found in his work on the southern textile industry, blaming institutional reform on outside coercive pressure represented an important tactic in institutional officials' toolbox that could temper internal resistance. In other words, internal opponents were less likely to challenge institutional reforms if they thought those reforms were being forced on an institution rather than simply recommended as an administrative innovation. In UM's case, the ability to frame admissions reform as a federal compliance measure likely gave Heyns a moment of opportunity to create an affirmative action admissions program.[24]

As Heyns began to figure out how to advance affirmative action admissions at UM during the summer, he gained an important ally in University of Michigan president Harlan Hatcher. Hatcher came to support Heyns's efforts after receiving his own dose of federal pressure, this time from President Kennedy. Like the pressure from Taylor, Kennedy never threatened to cut off federal contracts or grants. In June 1963, Kennedy invited 175 education leaders, including Hatcher, to hear his desperate plea for assistance. The president wanted education leaders to help solve the high dropout rates of urban school districts and create educational opportunities for black high school graduates left with few job prospects. Without their aid, Kennedy feared that the nation would face urban rebellions.[25]

The White House meeting occurred during an especially difficult time in Kennedy's tenure as president. The previous month, Americans watched the violent resistance to civil rights demonstrations in Birmingham, Alabama, on their televisions—demonstrations that included demands for equal opportunity hiring in downtown businesses. At the same time, African Americans' protests against workplace discrimination outside the South didn't end after Kennedy issued Executive Order 10925. By 1963, construction sites funded with government money became places of protest around the country. In Philadelphia, for example, protesters occupied the mayor's office for twenty-one hours, demanding that the mayor guarantee black workers access to jobs on city-funded construction sites. These jobs were typically controlled by trade unions that excluded black workers or relegated them to the lowest-paying positions. Similar protests rocked Harlem, Brooklyn, and Newark. In the midst of these uprisings, Kennedy received reports from Secretary of Labor Willard Wirtz and other advisers expressing their concerns about "danger spots" around the country, or places of potential violence in America's cities. One memo came from G. Mennen Williams, the former governor of Michigan, who advised Kennedy that "large segments of the Negro population are losing confidence in interracial approaches to the problems of gaining full civil rights."[26]

Thus in June 1963, Kennedy was trying to prevent urban uprisings and gain black activists' confidence in the federal government as an ally. One of Kennedy's solutions has been well documented. Just three days after his meeting with Hatcher, Kennedy signed Executive Order 11114, which amended

Executive Order 10925 to include racial discrimination on federally contracted construction projects. Less well known are Kennedy's efforts to convince higher education officials to reform admissions policies. By summer 1963, Kennedy had come to the same conclusion that Taylor had come to years earlier: skills-based training for blue-collar jobs coupled with antidiscrimination enforcement, even if successful, was still going to leave a lot of African Americans without employment opportunities. Given warnings about potential unrest in urban areas, Kennedy was particularly concerned about the consequences of large populations of young African Americans, despite vocational training, not finding jobs after leaving high school. This was why Harlan Hatcher was at the White House in June 1963.[27]

The White House meeting gave Heyns a powerful ally within the institution. Historical records don't show whether Hatcher was already sympathetic to affirmative action or if his meeting with Kennedy pushed him to reform his views. What *is* clear is that when students and faculty returned from the summer recess in September 1963, Hatcher delivered his State of the University speech, in which he outlined the university's new commitment to tackle the problems Kennedy discussed at the White House. Hatcher unveiled an initiative to "re-examine [UM's] responsibilities to high schools in which there are a substantial number of Negro pupils" and where the "urgent problems" are "high dropout rate or lack of motivation." Months before the university ever outlined the details of an affirmative action admissions program, he suggested that the university might have to create different admissions criteria for "students from deprived backgrounds." Hatcher threw his support behind Heyns to address these issues.[28]

The University of Michigan was about to change because two of UM's most powerful leaders were willing to make those changes. Activists for racial justice who forced the federal government into action had yet to threaten UM directly, and the federal bureaucrats and politicians who responded to protest never forced an affirmative action admissions program on UM. The weak coercive power of the federal government also meant that federal officials had handed over the implementation of affirmative action to UM's leaders. Administrators went to work crafting affirmative action in their own vision.

What happened next shows the limitations of weak government pressure. Voluntary compliance created the perfect environment for co-optation. Administrators took control of the purpose, scope, and character of affirmative action admissions. From the start, UM officials never imagined affirmative action as a disruptive tool; rather, they envisioned affirmative action as a tool to align UM's more expansive racial inclusion commitment with the university's existing priorities and values. Not surprisingly, black enrollment rose slowly in the 1960s.

UM already had an established set of rules for special admissions programs to ensure that inclusion initiatives didn't disrupt the university's core values. Recall from chapter 1 that these rules created a two-part rationale that most special admissions programs followed. First, proponents needed to explain the social need that the university had an obligation to address. Second, proponents had to prove that the program wouldn't undermine the university's elite status.

President Hatcher offered the first piece of the rationale when he introduced plans for a new affirmative action initiative to the university community in September 1963. Hatcher reminded his audience of UM's long history of addressing social problems, stating that racial inequality was just the next social problem that the university would help solve. Still, he preserved the university's racial innocence in justifying affirmative action: the problem wasn't that the university discriminated against black students; rather, the problem of racial discrimination and inequality operated outside the university's walls.[29]

Rationales that directly challenged the university's racial innocence never gained traction among UM leaders. In October 1963, Leonard Sain, a black assistant principal in Detroit, filled a new position at UM to develop the university's new affirmative action program. Sain offered a critical view of the university, claiming that UM's policies were at least partly responsible for the racial disparities on campus. While he did not accuse the university of overt discrimination, he suggested that the university was guilty of "sins of omission." That meant that the university didn't use race as a factor to consciously exclude black students but rather constructed color-blind policies that, when put into practice, effectively identified and supported only talented middle-class white students. Sain pointed out that the university's admissions criteria, for example, relied on standardized test scores and put a lot of weight on whether students took a college preparatory curriculum. These policies gave no thought to identifying talented black students who were being educated in discriminatory educational environments. And even if black students did meet UM's admissions criteria, many could not afford to attend due to the fact that the university provided little financial support for low-income students. In Sain's rationale, then, the University of Michigan needed affirmative action to address its own harmful policies, not just the societal discrimination unfolding off campus. Arguments like this, which challenged the university's racial innocence, never became popular among UM leaders.[30]

Leonard Sain enjoyed more success offering an argument that showed how affirmative action wouldn't harm the university's elite status. He emphasized that alternative admissions tools would bring only talented and "qualified" black students. Affirmative action, in other words, would simply create an admissions system that identified black students who were as talented as any white student who walked onto campus. Implicit in this argument, of course, was a critique of the university's admissions system and, in turn, the university's racial innocence. Administrators, though, were willing to accept the implicit critiques that came with reconciling inclusion and quality. They refused to accept any explicit critiques that blamed the university for racial disparities.[31]

This type of rationale proved important in protecting affirmative action from resistance. It helped temper concerns that affirmative action would undermine the university's elite status. It's one of the reasons why administrators who crafted these types of rationales believed they had good intentions. But subordinating racial inclusion to the university's elite status also placed great limitations on the types of possible reform. Any inclusion initiative that threatened UM officials' stringent definition of quality would never find a place at the university.

UM leaders' aversion to political and legal risk also shaped the character of affirmative action. In 1963, exchange programs between HWCUs and HBCUs represented the approach that carried the least political and legal risk. Howard University and Williams College, Tougaloo Southern Christian College and Oberlin College, and Spelman College and Barnard College, to name just a few, set up student exchange programs in the early 1960s. By the time Sain came to campus, Harlan Hatcher had already initiated an exchange program at UM. The same day Hatcher listened to President Kennedy's speech at the White House, Hatcher sat down with Luther Foster of the Tuskegee Institute. The two discussed a student and faculty exchange program between the universities. What made the program especially attractive was that it represented a low-risk commitment for university administrators. Because students attended UM for only a semester, administrators did not have to worry about opponents arguing that the students' presence lowered the quality of the institution. Furthermore, the program offered an opportunity to bring black faculty members to the university without the long-term commitments of tenure.[32]

By fall 1963, though, it was clear that UM leaders wanted to go further than the faculty and student exchange programs, which had been popular in the early 1960s. It was Sain's job to figure out how much further UM would go. Sain quickly learned that using race in identifying students was a contentious issue that had to be handled carefully. Racial liberalism had institutionalized color blindness in leaders' thinking, making racially attentive policies immediately suspect. In Sain's first initiative, he wanted to create a racial census of the student body. Nobody at the university knew how many black students were on campus in 1963. Admissions applications didn't include questions about race, and the registrar's office didn't record such information. So the census involved the painstaking process of counting black students—that is, faculty members and residence hall directors looked for black students in their classes and housing complexes, recorded their names, and sent them to Sain. Some faculty members were uncomfortable with the race-conscious aspects of the survey. One English professor wrote to Sain, "I have explained to the staff the purposes of the survey and have endeavored to answer questions in such a way to quiet anxieties. These anxieties do exist" and "are likely to spread through the student body." The faculty in the School of Education also shared their concerns. They invited Sain to meet with them because they felt uneasy about identifying students by race and were worried about how students would react to this practice. When Sain met with these faculty members, his notes show that he was prepared to talk about the legal merits of the census.[33]

Despite concerns raised by members of the university community, enough faculty and staff members participated in the survey for Sain to release the results in February 1964. The census recorded 148 black undergraduate and 25 black graduate students at UM. There were only 32 black first-year students on campus, and about 25 percent of them were athletes. Perhaps trying to account for probable errors resulting from the census's methods, Sain estimated that two hundred black students attended the university full time. This meant that black students made up 0.8 percent of the first-year class and 0.5 percent of the university's total enrollment. A "pathetically small number," Sain lamented.[34]

Sain knew the university's policies had to change in order to improve black students' access, but he was constantly reminded of the environment he had to work within. For example, when Sain arrived on campus, the regents were involved in a battle with the university's Human Relations Board, which had uncovered a long-standing endowed scholarship designated exclusively for whites by its benefactor. While the regents refused to begin the potentially lengthy legal process of changing the criteria of an endowed scholarship, they promised to put pressure on all future donors to remove any discriminatory clauses. Ironically, this policy worked to preserve the scholarship for whites while prohibiting attempts to fund scholarships reserved for African Americans. When an anonymous donor offered to fund an annual scholarship for black students who lacked the money to attend the university, the board of regents accepted the donation only after pressuring the donor to remove any reference to race that would "have discriminated in favor of a Negro student." It represented another example of racial liberalism sustaining white privileges and offering roadblocks to racial inclusion. Internal battles like this must have further revealed to Sain the land mines involved in creating an affirmative action program that used race as a factor in selecting and funding students.[35]

Any official talented at reading the political winds off campus could also find plenty of evidence that using race as a factor in admissions and financial aid was risky. Opponents to what would become the Civil Rights Act of 1964 were condemning the proposed legislation as a quota bill that would give special preferences to minorities over whites. Moreover, no affirmative action admissions program had been tested in court. Eleven years before the Supreme Court heard oral arguments in America's first anti–affirmative action admissions case, *DeFunis v. Odegaard* (1974), and fifteen years before Justice Lewis Powell provided his famous opinion in *Regents of the University of California v. Bakke* (1978), the constitutional merits for affirmative action admissions programs were up for grabs.[36]

When UM began crafting its affirmative action program, racially attentive practices weren't widely accepted in higher education. In 1963, perhaps only four universities practiced affirmative action admissions, all of which were in the Ivy League. Harvard University created an affirmative action program in 1961, Dartmouth University joined in 1962, and Columbia University and the University of Pennsylvania implemented programs in 1963. All these programs were modest and weren't widely publicized.[37]

It's unclear if UM officials knew about these early Ivy League programs, but they learned the limits of acceptable inclusion initiatives from peer institutions crafting inclusion policies in 1963. During the summer and fall, UM officials participated in conferences with other universities and colleges on how to advance racial inclusion. UM also hosted a conference of its own—with the help of Hobart Taylor and the PCEEO—in October. Although it was clear that many conference participants endorsed racially attentive efforts to advance equity, the initiatives proposed suggested that not all racially attentive practices were acceptable. The most popular programs discussed at these meetings included scholarship and recruiting programs for black students or for disadvantaged students of all races. None of the reports from these conferences recorded a proposal to create special admissions criteria exclusively for black students.[38]

For a risk-averse institution, an affirmative action program that focused exclusively on black students was out of the question. Ultimately, Sain made compromises in order to reduce the likelihood of resistance. While Sain had black students in mind when he wrote the new admissions policies, he emphasized that the program would be open to all students, regardless of race, "whose economic and social backgrounds has [*sic*] been of deprivation and disadvantaged." Still, Sain crafted admissions practices for the program that he hoped would broaden access for black students. He put more weight on high school counselor evaluations than on grade point averages and standardized test scores. Sain also allowed students the option to interview with an admissions counselor. Moreover, all the students admitted through the program would receive generous grant packages that covered most of their expenses. The program did not yet have a name, but it would soon be called the Opportunity Scholarship Program and, by June, the Opportunity Awards Program (OAP).[39]

Not forgetting Hobart Taylor's role in the origins of OAP, Roger Heyns wrote to Taylor that he hoped the program would double the number of black first-year students from the previous year. Taylor would later send the names of promising black students for the program to consider.[40]

Sain returned to his position in the Detroit public school system in spring 1964, months before the first class of OAP students set foot on campus. Despite the "colorblind" criteria of OAP, successors understood the main purpose of the program: recruit and admit more black students. Just like Sain, though, these black officials worked within the political constraints of the university. Their efforts to implement an affirmative action program safe from any resistance limited the number of black students who benefited from the program.

In the sixties, two officials were responsible for the day-to-day operations of OAP. Once Sain left, the university hired one counselor and one admissions officer to run the program. These new OAP officials were African Americans who saw their jobs at UM as an opportunity to improve access for black students. Consider John Chavis, who took the counseling position. Chavis had grown up in Toledo, Ohio, and felt that discrimination in his hometown had stymied his early social mobility opportunities. He worked as a porter for a year and a half after graduating from high school. Only after he was drafted and spent five years in the army did he finally attend the University of Toledo at the age of twenty-six, likely on the GI Bill. When his alma mater finally began an affirmative action recruitment program in the late 1960s, he wrote, "Perhaps the effort, as late as it seems to me, will save others of my race from a lifetime of catching-up." This was what drove Chavis. He wanted to provide the type of opportunities for young black students that were missing for him in his younger years.[41]

As committed as these officials were to increasing black enrollment, potential opposition to affirmative action made implementing a safe affirmative action program difficult. Outlining potential opposition to OAP after 1964 is tough because the historical record has left little evidence of the views of most of the university community on affirmative action. Officials never polled faculty and students on their views, and contentious debates over OAP don't appear in faculty meeting minutes of the 1960s. The broadest survey of faculty opinions on affirmative action came from a questionnaire sent to individual department chairs in 1966, which requested information on whether each department actively recruited black graduate students and faculty. In response to the question "Do you make any special efforts to recruit Negro students?" sixteen respondents replied affirmatively and eighteen replied negatively. Only two of the respondents suggested that their departments might apply different admissions criteria for black graduate students. Still, the survey suggested that there was at least some support for affirmative action initiatives, while also bringing to light adamant opposition. The responses of opponents were filled with statements such as "I trust that discriminating practices will not be directed against Caucasians and Eurasians?" and "The University should consider . . . individuals without regard to race." The survey irked three department chairs so much that they attached letters protesting any suggestion that departments should take race into account. John M. Allen, chair of the zoology department, wrote that special recruiting practices for black students and faculty were "contrary to my own ideas as well as those of my colleagues." Responses like these probably further reinforced OAP officials' belief that they needed to downplay the significance of race in their program for undergraduate students.[42]

This speaks to how institutional change unfolded in the early 1960s, when officials implementing OAP tried to protect the program from resistance. OAP benefited from the fact that universities began to take on the bureaucratic structures of large organizations. Over the course of the twentieth century, faculty increasingly ceded control of management duties to professional offices that worked underneath executive administrators. In the process, much of the day-to-day management duties of undergraduate admissions, financial aid, and counseling operated outside the view of most of the university community. This allowed OAP officials some autonomy to craft and implement policies without the close oversight of people who would have likely brought more resistance if they knew about the program's practices.[43]

Still, OAP officials couldn't create any policy they saw fit. Fear of opposition limited their choices. Even though the university's bureaucratic structure could hide some of their policies, they were careful in crafting their admissions practices. OAP officials created admissions and recruiting practices that could increase black students' access while also allowing administrators to promote the program's benefits for white students. Initially, resisting the impulse to put questions about race on admissions applications was important to that process. The university banned racial classifications on applications in the early

1950s, and pushing to amend this practice might have signaled that OAP was only interested in admitting black applicants. Instead, officials added a box on applications that allowed students to apply as an OAP candidate. Without the ability to identify race on applications, recruiters cultivated a predominantly black pool of applicants to OAP in order to admit mostly black students. Importantly, those black applicants needed to understand that they had to check the Opportunity Awards Program box on their admissions application; otherwise, students would be evaluated like any other applicant. To do this, the OAP counselor traveled to high schools with large black enrollments, developed contacts with high school counselors of predominantly black schools, and built relationships with community institutions in black communities to spread information about OAP.[44]

Officials' efforts to avoid resistance, though, limited recruiting efforts. For example, the OAP recruiter consciously avoided majority-white high schools—even those schools with black students. Aware of potential legal and political challenges to the program, officials wanted to escape challenges from white students if they realized OAP targeted African Americans. They also, of course, needed to limit the number of white students who applied, because the success of OAP depended on ensuring that black students dominated the applicant pool. Yet this practice also ensured that black students in majority-white schools did not receive information about the program through school visits.[45]

Whatever the limitations of OAP's policies, its recruiting practices provided an overwhelmingly black applicant pool that ensured black students would dominate OAP admissions. In the fall of 1964, sixty-seven of the seventy Opportunity Awards Program students were black. In subsequent years, black students would continue to represent about 90 percent of the program's enrollment.[46]

These disparities suggest that OAP doesn't fit well into the categories that scholars have created to make sense of different affirmative action programs. Scholars have divided practices into soft and hard affirmative action. "Soft" refers to programs that use race as a factor in recruiting and financial aid practices but not as part of the admissions process. In contrast, "hard" refers to programs that use race as a factor in selecting which students to admit. On the surface, OAP might look like a soft program, since applications did not ask for students' race. But closer inspection reveals how OAP blurs the lines between soft and hard. Despite the fact that admissions officers didn't officially know the racial background of applicants—unless the student took advantage of the interview option or a recommendation letter referenced the student's background—race-conscious recruiting practices created a predominantly black pool of applicants for a special admissions program that used different

criteria to evaluate applications. So the line between an admissions officer seeing an applicant's race on an application and the "color-blind" admissions process of OAP, in which admissions officers evaluated applicants with a high
degree of certainty about their race, is blurry indeed.[47]

Once admissions officials began admitting students to the program, the racial disparities within OAP made promoting its benefits for white students a
difficult task. To avoid backlash, they needed to downplay the racial attentiveness of the program. Early descriptions of OAP suggest that officials weren't
prepared for the public relations game. Administrators' descriptions of the program fluctuated from a program open to all students but focused on bringing
African Americans to campus, to a program exclusively for black students. One
early article went so far as to explain that OAP meant to "counteract some of
the obstacles faced by Negro students interested in coming" to UM, without
mentioning that white students were also able to apply. A 1968 OAP leaflet
noted that applicants must be "member[s] of a disadvantaged minority group."
Nevertheless, after OAP's first year, administrators were generally more careful in downplaying the significance of race in recruiting and selecting students
for the program. For example, in 1967, John Chavis claimed that race actually
played no role in selecting students for OAP. He explained that the program
focused on "poverty and cultural criteria," not race. Black students made up a
disproportionate number of OAP students, he argued, because they constituted a disproportionate share of the "disadvantaged" population in the United
States.[48]

UM leaders' discomfort with racial attentiveness also allowed them to resist new frameworks of measuring discrimination and racial progress. Beginning with Hobart Taylor, federal compliance agencies were trying to get UM
officials to see numbers as the primary way to view compliance and racial progress. The PCEEO used racial disparities as prima facie evidence for discrimination. But even when university officials responded to Taylor's pressure and
created an affirmative action program, they didn't adopt his framework for
measuring progress. Administrators wanted to focus on the process of selecting students, not the outcomes. According to UM officials, the important questions for measuring whether the process of selection was fair were these: Did
admissions officers admit every black student who had a chance to graduate
from UM? Was the OAP recruiter visiting every predominantly black high
school? If the answer to these questions was yes, affirmative action was working well. In fact, in 1965, administrators still hadn't developed any tools to
keep track of black enrollment. OAP administrators knew how many black
students were in that program, but nobody knew how many black students
were enrolled outside OAP.[49]

So while affirmative action changed the admissions selection process at UM, it didn't radically alter the framework UM officials used to measure progress. This is another reason UM administrators could convince themselves that they were committed to racial inclusion, even while black students composed a tiny percentage of the university's student body. In their eyes, the number of black students didn't represent an accurate measure of the university's commitment to inclusion. Effort, not numbers, represented the best measurement of the university's commitment.

Even the support services available to OAP became tied up with public relations efforts to downplay the role that race played in the program. Aside from Chavis's counseling position, the university didn't provide any special academic services for the program's students once they were on campus. Publicly, Chavis used this to safeguard OAP from potential opposition. For anyone concerned that the program gave special treatment to the overwhelmingly black pool of OAP students once they were on campus, Chavis reassured them that "there is no attempt to obtain any kind of . . . preferential treatment for them. In fact, we go to a great deal of trouble to make certain this does not happen." Resisting special academic services for black students might have helped shield the program from resistance, but it also helped limit the support available to these students. This point wasn't lost on John Chavis. Behind the scenes, he complained about the lack of resources devoted to helping black students succeed.[50]

Chavis's criticism sheds light on a major problem that more University of Michigan officials began to recognize: trying to improve African Americans' access to UM while downplaying racial attentiveness greatly limited racial justice efforts. But in the first years of OAP, officials thought that downplaying the role of race in OAP was necessary to protect the program from backlash. As two black officials concluded in 1968 when surveying the political environment, "For P.R. and other appropriate reasons . . . it is not proper at this point to restrict our programs to Blacks only."[51]

By fall 1966, OAP faced its first crisis. Of the seventy original OAP students, only thirty-six remained in the program. The numbers got even worse, as only nineteen of these students had graduated by summer 1968. Eleven enrolled for a fifth year. An unsympathetic evaluation called the first class of OAP students "hastily recruited."[52]

These numbers produced a crisis because affirmative action imported past concepts about performance that rationalized exclusion. Affirmative action never disrupted the prevailing institutional knowledge that students left the university before graduating because they were academically underprepared.

Attrition rates, then, represented the most popular measuring stick to determine whether a group of students was academically capable. The high attrition rates of OAP students called into question claims that affirmative action would bring only "qualified" students to UM. The future of OAP was at stake.

The crisis raised important questions: Who were the legitimate producers of knowledge about black students? Who would administrators trust to explain the academic capabilities of black students? Who would administrators trust in determining whether OAP officials' admissions tools let in "unqualified" students? The answers to those questions shows how administrators incorporated affirmative action carefully. White social scientists became the legitimate producers of knowledge about black students. The black officials who admitted and supported black students had little voice in interpreting black students' performance. Black students, too, had no voice in interpreting attrition in OAP's early years. Black students became the objects of research, not active participants. The marginalization of black voices in institutional research limited the conclusions social scientists offered to explain attrition, which further constrained the scope of affirmative action.

White social scientists took for granted the prevailing assumption that students left UM before graduating because they were academically unprepared and thus "unqualified." According to white social scientists, the solution to black OAP student attrition rates was to figure out better ways to predict which OAP students could graduate from the University of Michigan. One of the most important of these social scientists was Ruth Eckstein, a researcher in the Counseling Division of the Bureau of Psychological Services at UM. She began by using the university's traditional admissions tools to predict which black OAP students performed well at UM. In 1965, though, she found that high school performance was a poor prediction instrument. The statistical correlation between OAP students' high school class standing and their first-year student grade point average at UM was 0.02. In contrast, in a random sample of 255 Michigan first-year students, the correlation between high school class standing and college grade point average was 0.43. In sum, high school class standing had almost no value in predicting OAP students' first-year student grade point average at the university.[53]

Initially, the SAT looked like a better predictor of OAP students' performance. In 1965, Benno Fricke, a longtime UM researcher and proponent of standardized testing, concluded that the predictive value of the SAT for OAP and non-OAP students was almost identical. This was a potentially devastating conclusion for proponents of affirmative action, who argued that the SAT poorly predicted black students' academic performance. The next year, though, another researcher challenged Fricke's findings. When Fricke examined SAT scores, he grouped men and women together and examined only OAP students' first-semester performance. Doris Miller, a researcher in UM's Center for Research on Learning and Teaching, reexamined the data by looking at men and women separately and examining GPAs for the entire first year. She found surprising results. Miller discovered that while the SAT held strong predictive value for OAP women, it was a poor tool in predicting how OAP men would perform at UM. Among the first group of OAP men, their SAT scores ranged from 659 to 1330, with a median of 997. Almost half of the students who scored below 997 achieved a GPA of 2.0 or above at UM, and 60 percent of the men who scored above the median achieved a GPA below 2.0. Perhaps even more surprising, more OAP men who scored above the median on the SAT left UM after their first year. When Miller extended the study to include OAP students admitted in 1965, she found that the SAT continued to be a poor predictive tool for men in the program.[54]

The major problem with all this research was that social scientists interpreted attrition through a narrow lens. In a glaring omission, social scientists never looked at the grades of black students who left the university before graduating. They simply assumed that black students who left were failing their courses. Nobody considered that factors other than academic preparation could explain attrition. By the late 1960s and early 1970s, black students and a new cast of black administrators helped give new meaning to black students' attrition rates. They emphasized the impact of the university's racial climate on black student attrition. Once social scientists began listening to black students and officials, they soon found that most of the black students who left the university before graduating were in good academic standing. The selection procedures, then, weren't UM's biggest obstacle in improving black retention rates.[55]

While social scientists offered important research that supported claims that traditional admissions tools poorly predicted black students' performance, the research left the admissions office with two problems. First, the office still didn't have a reliable admissions tool to predict black students' academic performance at UM. Second, admissions officers still didn't know that the majority of black students who were leaving UM before graduation were in good academic standing. These problems led to conservative admissions practices in the mid-1960s. As a result, OAP grew slowly in its first years. By 1967, black students' share of the undergraduate student body tripled. Nevertheless, black students still only constituted 1.6 percent of the undergraduate student body.[56]

The slow growth of black enrollment highlighted UM's co-optation of federal pressure. Hobart Taylor left the university alone to develop its own program, with no federal oversight, and black campus activism had yet to push administrators beyond campus leaders' desired "safe" affirmative action practices. OAP offered a glimpse of a program designed with administrators' priorities and ideals in mind. It was an example of a program designed without external forces pushing university leaders to adopt policies that administrators believed were unviable or challenged UM's priorities. When UM finally received a stronger dose of federal pressure in 1966, administrators fought to preserve the affirmative action policies that they had already created. Co-optation was a long-term process. It required constant vigilance.

In 1966, Walter Greene, acting regional director of the Department of Defense's Contract Compliance Office in Detroit, arrived at the University of Michigan to lead a compliance investigation. Much had changed since Hobart Taylor intervened at UM. The Civil Rights Act of 1964, passed and signed just four months after UM officials announced OAP, brought UM under a new microscope. Title VI of the act was broader than Kennedy's executive order that originally sparked UM's affirmative action program. It simply read, "No person in the United States shall, on the ground of race, color, or national origins, be excluded from participation in, be denied the benefits of, or be subjected to discrimination under any program or activity receiving Federal financial assistance." The language was so broad that it covered everything from hiring practices to admissions procedures to dormitory room assignments. The University of Michigan, of course, fell under Title VI because it was a major federal contractor. But by 1966, it wouldn't have mattered if UM was receiving money from federal contracts. The Higher Education Act of 1965, which provided federal loans and grants to students, had created another stream of federal money to the University of Michigan every year. In fact, once the federal government began to play a vital role in funding students' education, it became difficult for universities to lie outside the scope of Title VI.[57]

One of the problems involved in implementing the Civil Rights Act of 1964, though, was that the federal bureaucracy was unprepared to enforce the legislation. The Department of Housing, Education, and Welfare (HEW), which oversaw student loan and grant distribution through the Higher Education Act of 1965, was overwhelmed by the new responsibilities of investigating compliance, especially since it also bore the brunt of investigating primary and secondary school segregation. So HEW officials looked for help. They asked the Department of Defense (DoD) to lead a Title VI compliance investigation of the University of Michigan on HEW's behalf. This was why Greene was at the University of Michigan in 1966.[58]

When Greene began his compliance review at UM, he sought out black students, faculty, and staff to interview. Here was an opportunity for the black community at UM to offer their own views of the university. They didn't hold back their criticism. Greene relied heavily on these interviews when he wrote his report, in which he concluded that the university had an image problem, as black communities in the state saw UM as an institution for "rich white kids." Greene also found many problems in the university's Opportunity Awards Program, which contributed to the poor representation of black students on campus. Greene concluded that OAP's recruitment efforts were insufficient and needed to be expanded. Regular reviews of admissions practices were also necessary. In other words, high-level administrators needed to take on a more significant oversight role. He also recommended that UM devote more resources to recruiting black students outside the state. Finally, Greene wanted UM to take steps to hire more black employees. Ironically, after Hobart Taylor intervened at UM to enforce Kennedy's executive order concerning hiring practices, UM had created an affirmative action admissions program but no centrally managed affirmative action hiring program. Departments were free to create (or choose not to create) hiring programs with no support or oversight. Greene suggested that the university needed an equal opportunity office, whose director would hold a position at the vice president level, directly responsible to UM's president. The office would investigate the policies of all departments, educate people involved in hiring on proper equal employment practices, and receive and investigate complaints concerning discrimination. Perhaps seeing that UM officials were more inclined to support affirmative action admissions than hiring polices, Greene tied the outcomes of affirmative action admissions to hiring initiatives. He suggested that new affirmative action hiring policies were necessary to fix the university's public image, which would in turn bring more black students to UM.[59]

Just a few months later, Greene returned to UM to carry out another investigation, this time under the authority of President Lyndon Johnson's Executive Order 11246. The order, which Johnson signed in 1965, replaced Kennedy's previous affirmative action hiring orders and restructured the bureaucracy of equal opportunity compliance. Still, the language concerning government contractors looked similar to Kennedy's Executive Order 10925. The order stated that contractors "will take affirmative action to ensure that applicants are employed, and that employees are treated during employment without regard to race, creed, color, or national origin." When Greene arrived, he found that UM had done little to implement any of the recommendations he had made at the conclusion of his Title VI investigation, not least of which was the creation of an office of equal opportunity, which he still wanted. Greene requested written affirmative action plans from each department, explaining efforts to improve equal opportunity employment practices.[60]

Greene had run into a problem, which he shared with Hobart Taylor. University of Michigan officials didn't see Greene as a threat to their lucrative federal contracts. The problem wasn't that the DoD didn't have the power to cancel contracts—that was well within its authority. The problem was that the DoD was generally unwilling to cancel contracts—and if University of Michigan officials didn't already know this, Greene's supervisor had indirectly reminded them of it. Greene's investigations of the University of Michigan had invited national attention, and when a writer for *Science* interviewed Greene's supervisor, Jack Moskowitz, about UM's compliance investigation, the DoD official emphasized that the agency offered only recommendations, not orders. Moskowitz then said that only flagrant failure to comply would lead the DoD to cancel a contract. So far, he said, no university had been judged so out of step that the DoD revoked a contract.[61]

So Greene, like Hobart Taylor, needed sympathetic allies within the university's executive administration to carry out these reforms. But unlike Taylor, Greene didn't find them. The problem wasn't that executive administrators now refused to support affirmative action. Though there had been personnel changes—Roger Heyns had left to become chancellor at UC Berkeley—UM administrators continued to support affirmative action. The problem was that in 1965, executive administrators believed that the university was already doing enough to advance racial inclusion. In this environment, Greene experienced a different response than Taylor had. UM officials attacked Greene's authority, painting him as a know-nothing bureaucrat. In fact, A. Geoffrey Norman, UM's vice president for research, suggested that "if there are to be more reviews of this type, the Department of Defense should get a group which understands universities."[62]

University officials used the narrative of racial innocence to show that Greene didn't appreciate all the factors outside UM's control that led to racial disparities. According to administrators, Greene didn't understand the political obstacles UM officials faced. Greene mentioned that the black students he interviewed suggested that the university needed to expand its affirmative action program to include black students outside the state. Extending OAP to out-of-state black students would be easy if officials put questions about racial identity on applications. Admissions officials could then take race into account for any black applicant, regardless of residential status. But administrators had created OAP's admissions practices in order to avoid claims that the program took race into account at the point of selection. It took a lot of effort and money to increase black enrollment without the ability to see a prospective student's race when evaluating an application. An OAP official had to travel to predominantly black high schools, recruiting students and teaching them how to apply for the OAP program. It was hard enough to do this when the recruiter focused on predominantly black schools within the state; using OAP to increase out-of-state black enrollment would take resources that administrators never imagined devoting to affirmative action. OAP would need enough money and people to travel the country, identifying and visiting predominantly black high schools. Even if the university were willing to devote enough money to do this, administrators thought that using taxpayers' money to fund out-of-state students would invite backlash. In fact, administrators thought that even using university funds to pay for recruiting trips outside the state would spark consequences from the state legislature. In response to Greene, the university wrote that "as a public institution whose instructional activity is funded primarily from state tax sources," UM "cannot recruit students from outside Michigan." Greene just didn't understand the political environment, UM officials concluded.[63]

Administrators also claimed that Greene didn't appreciate the obstacles involved in identifying "qualified" black students and faculty members. "Given population characteristics, limited scholarship endowment, and high admissions standards, the U-M student population is primarily white," UM's response read. Attrition rates of OAP were already high, and social scientists struggled to find viable tools to predict black students' performance at UM. In light of the problems UM officials faced in finding useful alternative admissions tests for OAP students, UM argued that "restructuring admissions criteria to eliminate unintended bias . . . is not easy to accomplish." In other words, identifying racial disparities in UM's enrollment was easy, but UM officials claimed that Greene didn't appreciate how difficult it was to build a new system that could predict which OAP students would graduate from UM. Similarly, UM officials claimed that Greene didn't appreciate the small pool of black faculty members in the United States, which limited the university's affirmative action hiring efforts.[64]

There was a sense of helplessness in these writings, as administrators tried to portray themselves as victims of a larger system of inequality. In other words, administrators became the victims of a public school system that poorly prepared black students for postsecondary study. They were victims of housing and employment discrimination that made it difficult for black students to pay the university's tuition. And they were victims of standardized tests—tests UM officials chose to adopt—that failed to predict black students' performance.

By portraying themselves as victims, UM officials were trying to preserve their preferred frameworks for measuring discrimination and racial progress. They were asking Greene to evaluate their effort in pursuing affirmative action in light of all the obstacles, not the outcomes of UM's policies. The number of black students and faculty on campus, administrators claimed, were poor ways to measure compliance with the Civil Rights Act of 1964 and Executive Order 11246. UM officials wanted Greene to take into account all the impediments the university faced in pursuing affirmative action and asked him to give UM officials some credit for all their efforts.

Without sympathetic allies in powerful positions inside UM and without the authority to force administrators to implement changes, Greene failed to spark the institutional reforms he sought. It would take black campus activism to force more substantive change.

The Opportunity Awards Program changed the course of history at the University of Michigan. The black freedom movement's struggle for affirmative action hiring practices affected UM in unexpected ways. When Hobart Taylor initiated meetings with UM, it's unlikely that any university official thought the university would receive pressure to create an affirmative action admissions program. But that's exactly what happened. The year 1963 proved a historic turning point at the University of Michigan, as UM officials responded positively to federal pressure and created the university's first undergraduate affirmative action admissions program.

Nevertheless, from the moment UM officials introduced OAP, they co-opted the purpose and character of affirmative action, ensuring that inclusion would be a secondary priority. UM leaders reminded the university community that OAP was only viable because it didn't harm the university's most important priority: institutional excellence. UM officials also ensured that black students couldn't identify their race on applications, protecting the university from legal and political threats but also making recruiting and selection especially difficult. Moreover, UM leaders made white social scientists the legitimate producers of knowledge about black students. In the early years of OAP, these social scientists never considered the nonacademic factors behind black student attrition, which helped justify the low enrollments in OAP. Finally, UM leaders resisted pressure to measure the success of OAP by the outcomes of the program. It would take black student protest to challenge these mechanisms of co-optation.

# CHAPTER 3

# Rise of the Black Campus Movement

University of Michigan leaders weren't ready for black campus activism. In the first half of the 1960s, administrators felt the victories of the black freedom movement largely through the actions of the federal government. They took comfort in the fact that black activism was still something unfolding off campus. That all changed in the late 1960s.

Weak federal coercion proved easier to co-opt than protest. Black activism that took over buildings and shut down classes threatened university operations. The activists also offered more radical visions of inclusion than federal bureaucrats had. Black campus activists didn't want new policies that fit easily into the existing values and priorities of the university; they wanted to create an institution that saw racial justice as the driving force of its mission.

A new president led the University of Michigan through these protests. Arriving at the university in January 1968, Robben Fleming introduced a new managerial strategy to co-opt activism. He introduced new measures to get black student activists to work with officials to create institutional change rather than resort to campus disruptions. His efforts worked briefly to stem the tide of black student protests in the late 1960s, but they ultimately failed when Fleming didn't provide the types of policies and initiatives that would satisfy activists. By 1970, black student activists organized the most successful student strike in the university's history, calling into question whether UM leaders could retain control of the meaning and character of racial inclusion.

There wasn't much that campus leaders feared more in the late 1960s than campus unrest—not federal intervention, nor a few vocal black faculty members calling for change on committees. By 1967, campus rebellion—and the potential violence that came with it—was a real possibility on college campuses.

Initially, UM leaders most feared the New Left. These were students who, in historian Robert Cohen's words, were "'committed to redressing social and political inequalities of power,' challenging cold war nationalism, and renewing 'the atrophied institutions of American democracy' by creating 'new institutions of popular participation to replace existing bureaucratic structures.'" The free speech movement signaled a shift in campus activism at HWCUs and introduced higher education leaders to the threat of the New Left. In fall 1964, students, led by Mario Salvo, applied the civil disobedience techniques of the civil rights movement to challenge a ban on political advocacy in a formerly designated free speech area on campus. On October 1, students formed a blockade around a police car as police officers arrested a prominent violator of the political advocacy ban. In the months that followed, students used tactics that would become commonplace on college campuses in the 1960s, such as staging sit-ins.[1]

By 1966, the New Left's antiwar protests began to dominate campus activism. The close connection between higher education and the Vietnam War made campuses a natural site for protest. Draft boards depended on postsecondary institutions to provide information about the eligibility of their students. Some universities provided research for the military; many more provided space for the military and companies that manufactured weapons of war to recruit new soldiers and employees. While 1966 saw a growing number of protests, 1967 proved to be a turning point. Antiwar activism enveloped campuses across the country as students marched and occupied campus buildings, sparking direct confrontations between student activists and police.[2]

Although administrators at UM avoided the violent conflicts between students and law enforcement in 1966 and 1967, UM leaders knew the campus wasn't filled with apathetic students. In fact, it was becoming one of the epicenters of the New Left. UM students, like Tom Hayden and Bill Ayers, were important figures in one of the New Left's most prominent organizations, Students for a Democratic Society (SDS). It's no coincidence that UM was also home to the first teach-ins on the Vietnam War. Especially frightening to campus leaders, students started turning to some of the confrontational actions they had seen at other universities.[3]

The black campus movement didn't raise the same concerns among UM leaders in the mid-1960s. UM's black students had yet to organize a formidable protest organization. In fact, black students at UM received criticism from their white peers for being too moderate, too slow to put up a significant fight for racial justice on campus. Nevertheless, a black campus movement was building across the country. Black campus activists took, in historian Joy Ann Williamson-Lott's words, "Black Power principles and molded them to fit their specific context." The movement took Black Power's emphasis on racial pride and called for an intellectual and cultural revolution on college campuses that saw the value of black culture and history. The movement also adopted Black Power's international perspective, especially the intellectual framework of colonialism. The black campus movement called on universities to use their resources to empower black communities and make them more autonomous. Finally, black student activists used Black Power's principle of self-determination. For some, this meant creating autonomous universities. For most, though, it meant gaining more autonomy within their own institutions, as they demanded that black students control programs and spaces on campus and influence admissions and hiring decisions.[4]

In 1966 and early 1967, the black campus movement didn't garner the same media attention that the antiwar movement received. Still, the movement was gaining strength. Black student unions, which would become key organizations in the movement, formed at HWCUs across the country. At Merritt College, future Black Panthers Bobby Seale and Huey Newton successfully fought for the nation's first black history course at a historically white institution. Activists at Merritt built on this success to fight for a full-fledged black studies program. Especially in the early years, though, student activists at HBCUs drove the movement. Howard University students fought for a "militant Black university" and organized a strike in May 1967. Students at Texas Southern University rose in rebellion in the spring of 1967 and faced violent repression, as police fired 3,000 bullets into a dormitory and arrested 488 students.[5]

If the black campus movement seemed like a distant threat to UM administrators, one event reminded them that black activism wasn't far from UM's doorstep. The Detroit Rebellion of 1967 began in the early morning hours of June 23. The city's entrenched racial inequality and police abuse in black communities sparked the uprising. By the time the rebellion ended, 43 people were dead, and 657 were injured; about 2,500 buildings were damaged; and 132 city blocks had seen fires. No urban rebellion of the 1960s matched these numbers. It's difficult to underestimate the role of the Detroit Rebellion at UM. Once black students at UM organized and began protesting, the Detroit Rebellion hung over their demands. Unfolding just 45 miles from UM's campus, it provided a reference point for administrators as they thought about the potential consequences of dissent.[6]

In the midst of campus and urban uprisings, the University of Michigan searched for a new president. In March 1966, Harlan Hatcher announced that he would retire as president of the university at the end of 1967. The regents saw Hatcher's retirement as an opportunity to hire someone who could guide the university through what they expected would become a new period of campus demonstrations. It was clear that the regents needed a president who had experience managing dissent. At that time, there were different models available to administrators for dealing with campus unrest. Repression represented one popular response. Some university and college leaders saw the police and National Guard as frontline deterrents for campus activism and were quick to turn to guns and batons. University of Michigan regents decided to pursue a different model to control activism. They were looking for a president who could prevent violent confrontations between students and the police, while still limiting dissent.[7]

Robben Fleming emerged as the regents' top candidate. Fleming was especially attractive because, as chancellor at the University of Wisconsin (UW), he had experience managing student dissent. The Madison campus was quickly becoming a hotbed of antiwar activism. Just a few months before his interview, Fleming had defused a seventy-two-hour sit-in at UW's Administration Building without a violent conflict between students and law enforcement. Fleming sympathized with some of the students' antiwar and civil rights positions and believed that activism, within certain constraints, had a place on campus. He also hesitated to use the police, fearing the bloody scenes that unfolded on other campuses. Student activists certainly didn't see Fleming as a great ally, but he also didn't win any friends among hard-line Wisconsin politicians, UW faculty members, and regents. On one of the rare occasions in which the police intervened and arrested students, Fleming bailed them out with a personal check.[8]

Fleming's long career mediating and studying labor disputes was also attractive. Before taking on executive administrative duties, he served as a professor and director of the Industrial Relations Center at the University of Wisconsin and then as the director of the University of Illinois's Institute of Labor and Industrial Relations. He also served as an arbitrator for labor disputes, ranging from the medical claims of a particular worker to a longshoremen strike in New York. In Fleming, the regents weren't hiring the typical campus administrator; they were getting someone who had dealt with labor strikes and student protests, had been yelled at in negotiations, and was confident that a resolution could be reached in even the most difficult circumstances.[9]

When Fleming arrived in Ann Arbor to interview for the job in 1967, he spent almost the entire evening with the regents discussing how he would handle student protests. Unlike some presidents, who preferred to shut down dissent with guns and billy clubs, Fleming told the regents that he saw the police and the National Guard as last resorts. This was the type of answer most of the regents were looking for. The regents hired Fleming because they thought he was best qualified to quiet student unrest without the use of force.[10]

Just a few months after Fleming left the University of Wisconsin, his successor took a harder line against student activists. Fleming left behind a growing antiwar movement that was becoming more confrontational. When students occupied another building on campus, police in riot gear stormed the building, some swinging night sticks at students' heads. As the tear gas evaporated, the bloody scene became clear.[11]

Fleming didn't think that he was going to escape these types of confrontational protests at UM. When Fleming took the job at Michigan, university presidents, in his words, "were falling like flies." He thought he had a 50 percent chance to survive as UM's president without getting fired. Despite his experience as a negotiator, there were too many things that were out of his control. Before he accepted the job at UM, he asked himself if he really wanted to be president anywhere. The answer was yes, but he took the job with much trepidation about the future.[12]

When Fleming took over the position at UM on January 1, 1968, the black campus movement that was making its mark on other college campuses was still small and fledgling in Ann Arbor. Fleming thought organizations like SDS would take up much of his time. He didn't know that his predecessors' resistance to reforms proposed by black students and professors had created an environment of discontent.[13]

Before Fleming arrived at UM, black students had yet to lead a protest, but they were proposing reform. In 1966, Richard Ross, a black student at UM, submitted a proposal for a black history course taught by a black faculty member. The chair of the history department, W. B. Wilcox, responded to Ross with a simple message: nobody in the history department was prepared to teach a course on black history, and there were no "qualified" black scholars that UM could hire. Ross returned with a virtual who's who list of established and up-and-coming black historians, including Vincent Harding and John Blassingame. Wilcox then offered another rationale for his resistance. Focusing too much on racial identity, Wilcox surmised, would undermine race relations. In Wilcox's eyes, the course would "emphasize . . . separateness at just the time when their assimilation is the crucial problem before the country." Ross wasn't ready to organize a formal protest movement just yet. He created a petition drive to show widespread support across the campus for a black history course. In March 1968, Ross submitted the petition to Wilcox with 498 signatures. Wilcox again changed his position. Now he claimed to be sympathetic to black students' cause. He believed the history department needed a black history course but reminded students that finding a qualified person to teach it would be difficult. He asked the students to be patient.[14]

By 1968, it was difficult for black students to be patient because the black history course wasn't the only inclusion initiative that the Hatcher administration had failed to implement. The struggle for a black history course unfolded as UM continued to resist Walter Greene's proposed reforms. Black students watched as black faculty members fought, and largely failed, to implement Greene's policy suggestions.

In the mid-1960s, black students didn't have any strong allies in executive positions to fight for change. The two black officials involved in OAP represented the only full-time positions devoted to implementing racial inclusion. There wasn't a single African American who held a post as an executive administrator. Every dean was white. The president and all the vice presidents were white. And until 1967, all the regents were white. Despite UM's affirmative action admissions program, UM administrators marginalized black voices.[15]

Only one official committee on campus incorporated black voices to make recommendations concerning racial inclusion. Allan Smith, the vice president for academic affairs, created the University Steering Committee on the Development of Academic Opportunities in 1965. The committee chair, engineering professor Norman Scott, called the committee the university's "conscience." Even this committee was overwhelmingly white, but it included two of the earliest black professors in UM's tenure system, Ralph Gibson and Albert Wheeler. Gibson graduated with a Bachelor of Science degree from UM in 1945. He decided to stay at Michigan for graduate school, earning a master's degree in 1947 and a PhD in 1959. After serving as an instructor in the Department of Pediatrics, he was hired as an assistant professor in 1963. Albert Wheeler also had a long history at UM. He earned his PhD in public health from UM in 1943, became a research assistant at the university the next year, and was hired as the university's first black tenure-track faculty member in 1953.[16]

In the years before Fleming arrived, Wheeler, in particular, used his position on the committee to pressure executive administrators to implement Greene's recommendations. He was especially interested in placing African Americans in administrative positions. In his mind, UM's policy decisions suffered from an absence of black perspectives. He pointed out that administrators' confidence that they were doing everything they could to implement racial inclusion was only possible because they didn't consult blacks within the university community. As a starting point, Wheeler wanted the president to follow Greene's recommendations and create a civil rights office, with a director and staff directly responsible to the president. This person would develop and implement an affirmative action hiring program at the university. A black official should lead this office, Wheeler suggested, but not just any black official. "A warm, brown body" shouldn't be the only qualification, he explained. Wheeler was well aware that institutions practiced what he called "Administrative Nullification"—the practice of hiring and rewarding black officials who were easily intimidated and unwilling to critique the policies of their white supervisors. In an environment like Michigan's, where critical black voices faced retribution, Wheeler wanted black administrators with activist experience who wouldn't be intimidated.[17]

In the end, the steering committee didn't go as far as Wheeler would have liked. Still, the predominantly white committee developed a set of policy recommendations that pushed executive administrators in unprecedented directions. The committee's recommendations, which they sent to Vice President Smith, didn't include a civil rights office with a black leader, but the committee suggested that the university create a budget reserve designed to hire black faculty members and offer postdoctoral fellowships or instructor positions to help minority candidates gain the experience necessary to be competitive for tenure-track positions. The committee also offered affirmative action hiring recommendations, suggesting that departments should offer jobs to minority candidates over whites if their qualifications were equal. Finally, the committee developed an affirmative action plan that required departments to report the steps they would take to improve black representation. As part of this plan, departments needed to include numerical goals to increase black graduate enrollment, nonacademic staff, and faculty.[18]

Smith accepted some of the recommendations, but he was never willing to use the full power of the executive administration to influence hiring decisions within UM's schools, colleges, and departments. There were no consequences for any department that chose not to set up a reserve fund or create postdoctoral fellowship positions for black candidates. Smith also didn't provide incentives to encourage departments to pursue affirmative action policies. For example, he didn't offer to fund or partially fund any budget reserve or fellowship. By the summer of 1968, only the Medical School had set up reserve funds to hire black candidates. Not surprisingly, the university's student newspaper reported that affirmative action hiring initiatives were "sporadic and decentralized."[19]

Smith proved more open to centralized planning to advance racial equity in staff positions. In summer 1967, the personnel office hired a new black official, Clyde Briggs, to increase minority representation in nonacademic staff positions. In less than a year, Briggs had set up an administrative internship program, a fellowship program that provided experience in UM's health science laboratories, and a program that provided work experience as dental assistants. All these programs recruited students from HBCUs. Briggs was also responsible for the university's public relations efforts, educating minority communities about UM's affirmative action hiring plans. Finally, he set up training programs to make UM minority employees competitive for promotions. All these efforts led to greater minority representation in nonacademic staff positions. By April 1968, forty-three HBCU students had taken advantage of the internship and fellowship programs. Furthermore, Briggs's programs had brought hundreds of new minority employees to campus in nonacademic positions. Still, Briggs's position speaks to the areas where white administrators were willing to give black officials the power to make significant institutional changes. Most of these placements were in service positions. Only seven minority candidates were hired in professional and managerial categories. White officials were comfortable giving Briggs the power to transform hiring practices for low-level nonacademic staff positions, yet white leaders on campus were unwilling to give black officials the authority to transform administrative and faculty hiring.[20]

This was the environment that Fleming walked into in 1968. Black students were frustrated. Trying to work with administrators through petition drives and meetings just led to excuses and requests to wait a little longer. At the same time, they watched university administrators ignore most of Walter Greene's recommendations. They saw few new black faces in faculty and administrative positions. By April 1968, administrators' resistance to the inclusion initiatives proposed by black students and faculty members produced the kindling for protest that just awaited a spark. That spark came from a bullet in Memphis, Tennessee.

On April 4, 1968, just three months after Fleming took the helm at the university, a white supremacist killed Martin Luther King Jr. Within hours, cities across the country exploded in rebellion. In Washington, D.C., alone, twenty-one thousand people were arrested. UM administrators realized that King's assassination could spark campus protest. Even before UM's black student activists could organize a demonstration, administrators offered reforms to try to avoid disruptions. On April 8, William Haber, dean of LSA, wrote to Ross that the history department would conduct a "vigorous and affirmative search for a Negro scholar" and create a new lecture series on black culture. Haber's efforts didn't have the intended effect.[21]

At 9 a.m. on April 11, the phone rang at the president's campus home. Fleming learned that more than one hundred black students were occupying the Administration Building. The students, who had arrived two hours earlier, carried all the necessary tools for a building occupation: blankets, food, and pillows. Within thirty minutes, the students had chained the doors of the building shut and posted a list of demands. They then prepared to watch King's funeral on television.[22]

The students' demands were short but ambitious. They demanded that the university create a Martin Luther King scholarship program and a faculty chair in King's name. The students called for "University activity in the community" and the implementation of Walter Greene's recommendations. Finally, the students wanted the athletic office to appoint blacks to the athletic staff and replace a black admissions official who had recently resigned.[23]

Outside the building, staff and students tried to figure out what was going on. It was their first encounter with black campus protest in the 1960s. White employees gathered in the parking lot and waited for instructions. White students who were sympathetic to the protest quickly gathered on the Administration Building's steps. Some made signs—"Support Our Black Brothers" and "Ann Arbor—All American City for All." Others collected money to buy lunch for the protesters. Some simply sat on the steps to show their support.[24]

Around noon, after the television coverage of King's funeral had ended, Fleming arrived in front of the chained doors. The discussion was quick, and the students agreed to leave in exchange for a meeting with the president the following Monday. Just like that, the occupation was over. Five hours. No arrests. It lacked the drama of the well-covered black campus protests of 1968, and yet the brief occupation led to important reforms. In the months that followed, the university created the Martin Luther King Memorial Scholarship Fund, hired more black instructors, appointed a new assistant director of admissions, hired two black assistant coaches, and started plans to form a closer relationship with Ann Arbor's black community. UM also created a black studies major, something that hadn't been included in the demands. The concessions represented the first major victory of the black campus movement at UM.[25]

Fleming didn't want to be known as the president who could settle building takeovers quickly; he wanted to set up an environment that would prevent disruptions altogether. He wanted activists to work with bureaucrats for a change, rather than protest. This was the goal of his co-optation strategy: limit campus disruptions and move dissent into the institutional bureaucracy, where campus leaders could exercise as much control over the implementation of racial inclusion as possible.[26]

Black students' lack of faith in campus administrators represented an early obstacle for Fleming. The Hatcher administration had marginalized black voices, leaving students to believe that they had to protest in order to make their voices heard. Thus, making students feel like their voices mattered to administrators represented the first step in co-opting dissent. In the aftermath of the lock-in, campus leaders began criticizing past methods of dealing with black students' proposals. Leaders painted Wilcox, the chair of the history department, as the villain of the building lock-in and a symbol of bad management. Administrators believed that Wilcox's resistance to a black history course had caused the frustration that led black students to take over the Administration Building. As one regent told Fleming, Ross's moderate approach, which he called the "polite and courteous 'please'" of meetings and petitions, was the type of dissent that the administration needed to encourage. The way to inspire black student activists to work within administrative channels was to reward activists who politely asked for reforms by complying with any request that administrators felt was reasonable. Wilcox's resistance to Ross's moderate tactics was "absurd," the regent told Fleming.[27]

Fleming tried to signal to black student activists that the administration valued their voices by defending the students involved in the lock-in, calling their demands "perfectly legitimate." He also decided not to punish the students involved in the protest. "We've had this terrible, terrible tragedy," Fleming said of King's assassination. "You can't expect the normal rules to apply." He also testified in front of the U.S. House of Representatives Special Subcommittee on Education, justifying black students' protests as a response to the "dreadful inequities which continue to exist." In his testimony, he criticized politicians who wanted to take federal financial aid away from individual students who participated in campus demonstrations. In defending black activists in public, he legitimized the claims and grievances of black students.[28]

Fleming's endorsement of black student activists infuriated some alumni and put Fleming on the FBI's radar. Alumni filled Fleming's mailbox with angry letters that criticized his defense of black student protesters and his refusal to use law enforcement or disciplinary codes to punish them. The FBI also noticed Fleming's response to activism. COINTELPRO, an FBI domestic counterintelligence program that J. Edgar Hoover started in 1956 to challenge the Communist Party USA, found its way onto the University of Michigan's campus in the 1960s as the program expanded to target the New Left and Black Power groups. Just two months after the Administration Building lock-in, a

COINTELPRO report raised concerns that a "new, weak President" who was "adverse to having any 'show-down' with agitators" now ran the University of Michigan. Some of the critical letters that Fleming received likely came from the FBI. The bureau believed that UM was susceptible to public outcry because the university depended on alumni donations. Part of the FBI's counterintelligence strategy included sending letters to UM administrators and board members, complaining that university leaders weren't doing enough to suppress campus protests.[29]

Fleming also tried to signal to students that inclusion was a priority by devoting his own time and effort to securing scholarship money. Inclusion was rarely on the radar of President Hatcher after he endorsed OAP in 1963. The day-to-functions, long-term planning, and publicity all fell to the black officials running the program. Fleming, in contrast, made more of an effort to act on behalf of inclusion. He proved especially important in winning donations from wealthy donors to support the Martin Luther King Memorial Fund. The fund represented one of black students' most important demands. Activists wanted to increase the number of black students on campus, but they knew that any recruiting effort would require more money. The months following the lock-in brought additional urgency to the King fund. Black student applications to OAP rose, but OAP's financial aid funding didn't immediately increase in the spring and summer of 1968. OAP could have accepted an additional one hundred students for fall 1968 if it had had the money.[30]

Fleming understood the importance of the MLK fund—especially since he didn't want to redistribute significant resources from the university's general fund to OAP—and knew that the program couldn't rely solely on small individual donations. The state's largest corporations would have to support the scholarship program, he concluded. So Fleming started courting the state's automakers. The ways in which Fleming solicited these funds helped reinforce the relationship between affirmative action admissions and federal affirmative action hiring policies that put pressure on companies to expand their minority workforce. Writing to the vice president of public relations at General Motors, Fleming suggested that the University of Michigan and the automaker "share a common dilemma—access to an adequate pool of trained leadership among non-white and disadvantaged." Fleming emphasized the benefits General Motors would receive if UM graduated more black students. General Motors and other manufacturers had made great strides in expanding opportunities for the "lesser skilled," according to Fleming, but "trained and talented black people for managerial and supervisory positions are scarce." UM could expand that pool of prospective black managers and supervisors for GM if the corporation helped fund more scholarships at the university.

The argument worked. GM and Ford made donations to expand funding for black students.[31]

Fleming's actions were part of a larger strategy to wrestle control of inclusion from protesters. He made visible efforts to win the faith of black student activists by showing that his administration was committed to institutional change. He hoped that faith would push black students to abandon confrontational protests and work within the university's bureaucracy to create reforms. The bureaucracy was a place where Fleming and other campus leaders felt they could exercise significant power and influence over the future of inclusion. More protest, on the other hand, could lead to concessions that administrators felt were unviable and violated the university's priorities.

If the goal was to get students to work within the university's bureaucracy for change, Fleming needed to give them bureaucrats to work with. Fleming and his fellow administrators created an unprecedented number of full-time positions devoted exclusively to developing and implementing new racial inclusion practices. All these new positions marked the rise of an inclusion bureaucracy—a new set of positions devoted to working with black student activists, listening to their concerns, and proposing institutional reforms. The bureaucracy was set up to move dissent into institutional channels that administrators felt they could control. It was also set up to anticipate dissent and create initiatives that could stymie activism before it started.

Fleming created an assistant to the president position, filled by a new black administrator, to oversee this inclusion bureaucracy and help manage black student dissent. He hired William Cash, a black UM alumnus, who joined the University of Michigan as a professor of education in 1968. Fleming's plan was to bring all the staff involved in inclusion initiatives together in a single committee called the Human Relations Committee (HRC). Cash, as the chair, would provide oversight and coordination of all initiatives.[32]

The HRC brought together inclusion officials around the university hired before and after the 1968 lock-in. LSA dean William Haber hired two black officials after the Administration Building lock-in. Like Fleming, Haber believed that if the university didn't address black students' concerns quickly, administrators could expect more protests. J. Frank Yates became assistant to the dean to develop new programs that would prevent further unrest. Yates was still a graduate student in the psychology department when he took the position. Now, while working on his doctorate, he was tasked with developing new inclusion initiatives in UM's largest college. Haber didn't stop there. He also appointed Nellie Varner, a black political science professor, as special assistant to the dean, to develop new courses on "Negro affairs" across LSA.

Haber saw the calls for black history as just the first step in a larger movement for curricular reform. He wanted Varner to create new courses before black students began demanding change.[33]

George Goodman rounded out the new black officials hired to fulfill inclusion initiatives. Goodman's position represented one of black student activists' demands during the 1968 lock-in. The only black admissions official had left, and the students wanted the position filled immediately. What students didn't know was that they almost prevented Goodman's interview. Goodman arrived for his interview on the day of the lock-in. When he walked up to the Administration Building, he found a group of black students guarding chained doors. "I'm here for an interview," Goodman told the students. "I understand there is a position open and I'm trying to get hired." The students removed the chains, let him enter, and immediately locked the door again. In doing so, the students fulfilled one of their demands without knowing it.[34]

A few officials already working at the university also joined the Human Relations Committee. John Chavis and Clyde Briggs, two black officials hired in previous years to lead affirmative action initiatives, also served. Joining them were white officials, such as John Feldkamp, director of housing, and William Haber, who had stepped down from his position as dean not long after the lock-in to lead the university's efforts to hire more black faculty members.[35]

Showing what happens when black officials are allowed to weigh in on policy decisions, the committee immediately challenged long-held assumptions. Chief among them was that improving race relations hinged on downplaying racial difference. The committee went to work crafting innovations that used the university's resources to embrace and promote black cultural identity. White executive leaders accommodated these ideas within limits as campus leaders tried to keep tight control of the inclusion bureaucracy.

HRC officials were most successful in reforming UM's curriculum. Since 1966, black student activists had been pushing for a curriculum that addressed black students' needs. It's not a surprise, then, that curricular reform was high on the committee's priorities. The earliest initiative, though, came from a professor outside the committee. Otto Graff, a professor in the German department and director of the Honors College, hired Harold Cruse to teach a new course: The American Cross Cultural Phenomenon in Black and White: Interpretations and Reevaluations. Cruse was one of America's most famous black intellectuals, as he had just published the highly touted *The Crisis of the Negro Intellectual*. Wilcox, the chair of the history department, saw an opportunity. He still hadn't hired a scholar to teach a black history course. Cruse was only supposed to be at UM for one semester in the Honors College, but Wilcox convinced Cruse to stay for another semester to teach a black history course. Cruse ended up staying at the University of Michigan for almost twenty years.[36]

The HRC worked to build on Cruse's position by creating new classes on the black experience. Nellie Varner led this effort. Varner's actions could have led to a disconnected web of courses in the college's various departments, but Varner helped turn the dean's vision for new courses on "Negro affairs" into the University of Michigan's first black studies degree program. The process took a year, but in spring 1969 the program began to take shape. It included three introductory courses, a senior seminar, and five interdisciplinary courses that would all be requirements for the program. The foundational introductory course was the class on black history that Ross and his supporters had been calling for since 1966. In April, the faculty of LSA voted without any recorded dissent to approve the University of Michigan's first black studies major.[37]

By that time, black students had become better organized and began to shape the future of black studies. In 1969, undergraduate students formed the Black Student Union (BSU). From the start, Ron Harris led the organization. The BSU wanted to institutionalize the university's commitment to research on issues relevant to black people by creating a center to oversee black studies. The center, according to the BSU, would help black students develop racial pride and better understanding of black history and culture. Students' proposal for the center also offered a new vision of the university's responsibilities to black communities outside the university. UM didn't simply have an obligation to admit "disadvantaged" black students and move them into the professional class. The university needed to train people who could return with the technical skills to help black communities. Still, the students argued, the "problems of the community are too critical for" the University of Michigan "to rest solely on the development of formally educated black citizens" who would use their skills to help black communities. The center was supposed to directly aid black communities through "technical assistance and the short-term transmission of relevant and useful information."[38]

Members of the new inclusion bureaucracy worked to make black students' proposal a reality. J. Frank Yates, a member of the Human Relations Committee, developed the formal proposal for the center. Yates proved to be a strong supporter of black student activists during his career and sympathetic to the ways black students framed their grievances and demands. His efforts to rewrite the proposal, though, show that uneven power relationships put black officials in difficult positions. To pitch the center to white faculty and administrators, Yates removed the psychological language and need for racial pride that filled the original proposal. He found black students' goal to push the university to use its resources to serve black communities in the state easier to pitch to white administrators. Yates included strong statements about the university's duty to "re-orient itself toward the black community and racial issues . . . through various auxiliary functions." To do this, Yates played on administrators' fears of another Detroit Rebellion, promoting the center as an intellectual hub that would help prevent future urban uprisings. As mentioned before, the 1967 rebellion made black protest more threatening and helped motivate administrators to make preemptive reforms. At the same time, the rebellion made studying the problems that black communities faced all the more pressing to UM administrators and faculty members. Yates's proposal gained Fleming's support. The president approved a committee of faculty, administrators, students, and community leaders to create plans for the new center.[39]

Yates's influence reveals how co-optation could work subtly, seemingly outside the hands of white administrators. Black officials rarely enjoyed the autonomy and independent funding necessary to create programs on their own; instead, they had to appeal to white supervisors for financial support and policy approvals. It's one of the reasons campus leaders felt they could control the inclusion bureaucracy. It's also the reason black officials often felt that they had to make difficult choices between policy victories and the framing that activists preferred. To win important reforms, black officials reframed some of black students' language in ways that would appeal to white administrators and faculty. The consequence, of course, was that reframing language often meant muting the problems black students wanted to emphasize. Before proposals reached the hands of white administrators, then, the process of co-optation had often already begun.

During the 1968–69 academic year, the inclusion bureaucracy was working as Fleming had envisioned it. Black students were working within institutional channels, and proposals for institutional change had replaced building takeovers. Accommodating demands, however, became more problematic when black students and inclusion bureaucrats began challenging executive administrators' vision of a model multiracial community.

"My own feeling is," Fleming wrote in November 1968, "that we were doing something good, we deliberately desegregated dormitories. Perhaps this was in error, and doubtless we were too insensitive to the wishes of the black students." Fleming wrote this just after meeting with a group of black campus activists calling themselves "Pro-Black Students," led by Ron Thompson. The students complained about UM's color-blind housing policies. According to the group, the tension between black and white students assigned to live together resulted in students finding ways to change rooms in order to live with members of their own racial group by the end of the semester—even though university policy prohibited this practice. Allowing black students to room to-gether from the beginning of the academic year, Thompson told Fleming, would help them avoid the uncomfortable feelings that accompanied room-ing with a white student.[40]

Demands like these tested Fleming's managerial strategy. Listening to black voices and confirming that their critiques were legitimate represented vital tools in preventing black activism, he thought. But allowing black students to choose to live separately challenged all his assumptions about race relations. Fleming, like campus leaders in previous decades, wanted to set up a model multiracial community at UM. He wanted to use the campus to address white prejudice and improve the interactions between white and black students. One of the basic tenets of post–World War II racial liberalism still carried great weight among white administrators when they thought about how to create this model community. Recall that racial liberalism suggested that universal-ism and interracial contact were key to creating a new world without racism. In the late 1960s, administrators began to question universalism, slowly em-bracing the idea that celebrating cultural difference was compatible with the model community. They were unwilling, though, to reconsider the idea that interracial contact offered the key to improve race relations. Any effort to cre-ate spaces for black students to socialize or live together was met with skepti-cism or, more often, outright resistance.

The Detroit Rebellion of 1967 only made the model community more pressing to UM administrators. It also heightened their concern about the con-sequences of segregation. The Kerner Report, the government study com-missioned to diagnose the causes of urban uprisings in the 1960s, reinforced Fleming's commitment to interracial contact. The report's most famous line resonated with Fleming. The report's authors claimed that America was be-coming "two societies, one black, one white—separate and unequal." To Flem-ing, this meant that racial separatism was at the heart of America's race problems. He later used the quote when he testified on student unrest in front of the U.S. House of Representatives Special Subcommittee on Education, add-ing, "We are losing our last real chance for a society in which we can be one people." As the future of race relations seemed to be at stake, administrators saw demands for racially exclusive spaces as counterproductive to the model community.[41]

Still, Fleming worried about simply rejecting Ron Thompson's proposal. When Fleming responded to Thompson by writing that "doubtless we were too insensitive to the wishes of the Black students," he employed a common tactic in his arsenal by suggesting that black students' concerns were legitimate. Then he delegated the job of creating an alternative housing reform measure to the vice president of student affairs, Barbara Newell, who then delegated the job to John Feldkamp, the university's twenty-nine-year-old white director of university housing and HRC member.[42]

The problem with accommodating black students' demands was that Feldkamp shared Fleming's commitment to improving race relations and believed that interracial contact was vital to the model community. Feldkamp had been on the front lines of the fight to implement racial integration policies at UM. Until 1959, housing applications gave students the option of living with members of their own racial group. When the housing office took questions of racial preference off applications, Feldkamp and other housing officials had to defend the policies of integration against white parents' objections. He worried that returning to old policies, which allowed students to choose roommates based on race, would "accommodate Black identity desire but would also cater to elements of the White community who are highly prejudiced to other races."[43]

Still, by the end of 1968, Feldkamp understood that the practice of assigning students to dorm rooms without regard to race was not playing out the way he had hoped. Racial tension continued, and black students were clearly suffering. As he evaluated black activists' housing proposal, alternatives to color-blind housing assignments were already available at a few other universities. Cornell University, for example, created separate residence halls for black men and women who chose to live there voluntarily. Feldkamp, though, was uncomfortable with solutions that gave black students their own living spaces. He went to work trying to craft a living space that preserved interracial contact while also emphasizing the value of racial identity. Feldkamp suggested that the housing division could designate a specific building with a "pro-Black, Black, or Afro-American identity." Black students could choose to live there on a voluntary basis, but to continue facilitating interracial interaction, white students who were "sincerely interested in Blacks" could also live in the building.[44]

Even after Feldkamp reframed the proposal to fit with white administrators' interest in improving race relations, the plan never came to fruition. Feldkamp told black activists that the plan wasn't feasible for the next school year, as the planning process for housing was already underway. He also warned them of the contentious political process that came with trying to implement such a plan. It's unclear who ultimately squashed Feldkamp's proposal, but it disappeared from the housing office's discussions in 1968. The housing office wouldn't face another proposal for black living units until 1972.[45]

While the proposal never came to fruition, Fleming began to emphasize the university's commitment to celebrating black identity. Fleming had already embraced proposals, like black studies, which suggested the university was slowly rejecting the ideal of assimilation. But he had yet to articulate publicly how black culture was now part of his vision of a model multiracial community. On the one-year anniversary of Martin Luther King's assassination, Fleming laid out his new vision of racial inclusion in a public speech. "If I understand what my white eyes tell me," he explained to the audience, "there is no necessary conflict between Black pride, Black consciousness, Black dignity, Black power, and an integrated society." Then, in what could have come out of the mouth of any of UM's black student activists, he said, "The Black man, like the white man, needs pride, dignity, and confidence. Having been nurtured for so long and under so many circumstances in a culture which deprives him of these qualities, is it to be expected that he can participate in an integrated society on an equal basis?"[46]

Fleming's message resembled how administrators had seen the value of international students for decades. Seeing nationalism as a major problem that led to world wars, UM officials had argued that promoting and appreciating other countries' cultures would improve international relations. Now Fleming saw cultural appreciation as a tool to solve racial tension on campus. Changes unfolding at the national and local levels likely helped him apply this approach to relations between white and black students. In the late 1960s, black cultural expression found a new place in mainstream popular culture, and these changes were visible in Ann Arbor. Blues festivals, black poetry readings, and black art festivals became popular in the city. African Americans weren't the only ones attending these events. Black culture was suddenly becoming cool among white students—something to be consumed. It would have been unlikely for Fleming to see the expression of black identity as a pathway to better race relations if he didn't see white students' growing interest in and respect for black culture.[47]

The end goal for Fleming, though, was always for students to see their common humanity. Fleming hoped that even when the university celebrated cultural differences, race would become "accidental differences," and people of all races would see each other as "members of a human brotherhood." This was Fleming's effort to reconcile universalism and the celebration of racial identity. To see their common humanness, students needed to meet each other on equal cultural footing, the argument went. Respect for another's culture was the pathway to seeing a common human bond.[48]

Fleming's speech and the rejection of the housing policy showed how administrators kept control over the priorities of inclusion. Although administrators modified racial liberalism, they never reconsidered the purpose of the model multiracial community. Black activists argued that the merits of inclusion initiatives shouldn't be judged on whether they improved how white and black students interacted; they should be judged on whether they improved African Americans' experience on campus. In the hierarchy of institutional priorities, though, improving race relations always trumped addressing black students' social alienation on campus. These goals were not always mutually exclusive, but they weren't always mutually reinforcing, either. The problem for black students who called for racially exclusive space on campus was that the poor racial climate for black students had never been enough to justify an inclusion program. Any program that black students proposed would have to also explain how white students would benefit. Conversely, programs designed to improve race relations never faced the burden of showing how they would address black students' social alienation.

Perhaps most frustrating to black activists, UM administrators still made little progress in implementing Walter Greene's recommendations—one of the demands of the 1968 lock-in. Greene had focused on initiatives that increased black student and faculty representation on campus. The HRC tried to develop policies that advanced Greene's policy suggestions, but the committee once again ran into obstacles, as executive administrators exercised control over the outcomes of the committee's work.

Increasing the number of black students at UM was at the top of the committee's agenda. The MLK fund would help support more students whom the admissions office deemed "qualified," but that wouldn't be enough to make significant gains, committee members thought. Part of the problem was that George Goodman worked within a difficult set of circumstances. UM provided only enough resources for one OAP recruiter. Goodman, alone, had to travel the state, recruit students, and teach them how to identify themselves on the admissions application.[49] William Cash and his fellow committee members also believed that OAP admissions requirements were too strict. There were many black applicants, they thought, who could graduate from UM but weren't given a chance because of OAP's admissions criteria.[50]

Cash wanted a new admissions program—what he called a "high-risk" program—to expand OAP. To do that, the committee needed to tackle the problem of attrition. OAP students left UM before graduating at twice the rate of non-OAP students. The program's attrition rates made it difficult, at least in the eyes of white administrators, to justify significantly expanding OAP. When Cash's committee addressed the issue, the popular assumption on campus was still that students left UM before graduating because they were academically underprepared. Consequently, all the early research conducted at UM tried to find better ways to predict which black students could handle the academic demands of the university. Researchers examined students' SAT scores, high school GPAs, high school class standing, and curricular choices once on UM's campus, but they were stumped. The tools officials had available to predict black OAP students' academic performance at Michigan offered little value in predicting whether they would graduate. In some cases, the lower students scored on traditional admissions tools, the better they performed. None of this evidence, though, suggested to administrators and researchers that factors other than academic preparation could explain attrition.[51]

The HRC disrupted white social scientists' control over knowledge about black students and gave black officials a voice in interpreting black student attrition rates. J. Frank Yates led the way. White officials who embraced the narrative of racial innocence rarely looked for deficiencies in UM's practices. Black officials, in contrast, often assumed that the institution bore some responsibility for the problems black students faced. Yates believed that relying on the admissions office to find the "right" students in order to reduce attrition rates ignored the things that the university could do on campus to improve retention. Rather than viewing attrition rates as an admissions problem, Yates blamed OAP attrition on the university's poor supportive services programs. According to Yates, university administrators failed in their duties to create an environment that helped black students succeed. For example, throughout the first six years of OAP, only one counselor was assigned to provide services for all the black students in the program. If the university was committed to increasing black enrollment and graduation rates, Yates suggested, it would need to shift its attention from better prediction tools to better academic support services.[52]

Yates also called attention to the role of the racial climate in attrition. Until Yates took his management position in 1969, no UM official had recognized that black students' social experience on campus could help explain their higher attrition rates. Affirmative action admissions, academic support services, and programs that affected black students' social lives were all intimately connected in Yates's eyes. Evaluations of black students' performance, he argued, overlooked the "psychological problems" black students faced in adjusting "to the University atmosphere." The experience of living as a black student in an overwhelmingly white space was inherently problematic and created intense feeling of alienation, he argued. The social alienation that black students faced at a predominantly white institution, then, needed to be addressed if the university wanted to lower OAP attrition rates. This represented the first time an official at UM had claimed that the university's racial climate could help explain black student attrition rates.[53]

In 1969, Yates proposed the Freshman Year of Studies program, which would seek to address these issues through counseling and study sections. An important part of the program identified courses that OAP students struggled with the most during their first year on campus. These included introductory courses in English, chemistry, botany, physics, zoology, and mathematics. The program would require OAP students to sign up for an additional section attached to these courses, which would offer help in preparing for exams and assignments. The second piece of the program required more black counselors to help black students deal with issues of social alienation they experienced at the University of Michigan.[54]

The "high-risk" admissions program attracted the support of the new LSA dean, William Hays. "I think it's important that we now begin to recruit a larger number of Black students, and that . . . almost certainly means that we should begin to explore some relative relaxation in admissions standards," Hays wrote. The dean liked the program because it addressed his own concerns that a more aggressive affirmative action program would lead to higher attrition rates. The admissions program could only work, he surmised, if the university implemented an equally aggressive support program.[55]

Once Yates proposed the program, he learned a lesson that many black administrators would learn throughout the late 1960s and early 1970s: grand programmatic visions were difficult to pursue with little power and money. Assistant to the dean might sound like an important position, but it was a position created to provide recommendations for new programs. Yates had no power over personnel or money to pursue programs on his own. Hays supported the project but didn't fund it. Instead, Hays wrote to President Fleming to ask for $15,000 to $20,000 to implement the program. Fleming wrote back that he had "committed my own free funds rather heavily in the direction of disadvantaged students, and I'm not sure I can justify using more of them for this one purpose." In 1969, it seemed that Yates's initiative was dead.[56]

The results from the University of Michigan's affirmative action hiring policies for faculty represented another disappointing inclusion initiative for black students. During the 1968–69 academic year, 40 of 2,356 (1.7 percent) UM faculty members were black, and 74 of 4,168 (1.7 percent) full-time professional staff were black. In contrast, African Americans made up 40 percent of UM's service workforce. Black students who protested in 1968 called on administrators to implement Greene's recommendations to increase black faculty and administrators. The initiatives UM leaders introduced in the late 1960s didn't suggest that those numbers would improve anytime soon.[57]

In the aftermath of the 1968 lock-in, Allan Smith, vice president for academic affairs, developed the university's first official affirmative action plan. Smith informed units that "preference will be given to minority group applicants for employment, with special cognizance being given for potential growth" as long as "minimum qualifications are met." Smith also forced units to create affirmative action hiring goals and explain the "positive compensatory action" that the university was taking to increase black representation. Smith's plan, though, didn't introduce a system of accountability. It was especially difficult to hold units accountable when the university kept no official records of the racial background of individual employees.[58]

Again, William Cash proved important in offering policy solutions. For years, UM leaders were uncomfortable with recording an individual's racial background. But by the late 1960s, HEW began demanding more accurate data on race and ethnicity from universities and colleges. During the 1969–70 academic year, HEW postponed its compliance reporting requirements to allow universities to improve their racial collection techniques. Cash took advantage of this environment to convince campus leaders to change the way the university recorded racial identity. He introduced a new system of counting employees that no longer hinged on the visual counts of departments. Employees were now asked to provide their racial identity for record-keeping purposes. The process was voluntary, as employees had the option not to identify themselves. Nevertheless, Cash believed this system was much more reliable than asking supervisors to look at each employee and report their racial identity.[59]

If Cash hoped that better reporting would lead to better accountability, he would be sorely disappointed. The university's 1969 Equal Employment Opportunity Affirmative Action Plan was essentially an education program. Cash was tasked with making sure the people who did the hiring knew how to recruit and interview minority candidates. The plan also included a program to analyze data "for effectiveness and for areas of improvement." Yet there was no plan to build on Greene's intervention and continually update affirmative action hiring goals. More importantly, there was no plan to hold anyone accountable for not meeting goals. According to the plan, Cash would conduct periodic audits of a unit's affirmative action program in order to offer "counsel and assistance regarding equal employment opportunity matters." There were no consequences for refusing to take affirmative action seriously.[60]

Cash found himself in a common position for a black official. Essentially, he served as an educator to white people on campus. He documented problems and recommended new policies, but this black official assigned to oversee affirmative action hiring had no power to hold anyone accountable.

When HEW officials arrived for a compliance review in 1969, government officials found that the university's affirmative action hiring program was inadequate. The university clearly wasn't measuring progress against any goals. As part of the review, UM agreed to start setting firm hiring goals, regularly reporting its hiring decisions, and measuring equal opportunity progress against its affirmative action goals. Still, it would take more black student activism for university leaders to translate this agreement into policy.[61]

By the beginning of the fall 1969 semester, it seemed like Fleming's co-optation techniques were working the way he had envisioned. Even though many of black activists' demands remained unresolved, Fleming could still show activists concrete changes. The MLK fund and Goodman's recruiting efforts raised black enrollment to 1,000 students—709 undergraduates and 291 graduate students—for the first time in UM's history. A black studies program was already underway, even though the black studies center was moving slowly through administrative channels.[62] New offices and positions, filled mostly with black officials, were there to listen to black students' concerns and create policy proposals—even if those proposals didn't always lead to concrete initiatives. Importantly, all the initiatives in place didn't reroute significant resources away from programs that Fleming considered vital to the university's quality. The true measure of the effectiveness of co-optation, though, was the lack of black campus protest.[63]

During the 1968–69 academic year, Fleming watched black students at UM work within the inclusion bureaucracy for change while hundreds of protests for racial justice enveloped college campuses. Historian Ibram X. Kendi has called the 1968–69 academic year the "apex year the movement" for a reason. It was a year when demands for inclusion eclipsed antiwar demonstrations on college campuses. One of the most significant began in November 1968. Black students at San Francisco State University (SFSU) led the longest demonstration in the black campus movement's history, lasting five months. S. I. Hayakawa, SFSU's president, turned the campus into a police state. Hundreds of protesters were jailed, including 450 on a single day. Others were beaten, carried off with their clothes covered in blood. At Cornell University, black student protesters took over a campus building, demanding, among other things, a campus investigation into recent racist incidents on campus. After the negotiations ended, cameras flashed as the students walked out of Straight Hall armed with guns. At Columbia University, Students for a Democratic Society (SDS) and Student Afro-American Society (SAS) protesters took over five buildings on campus, protesting a gymnasium that would take away important public space for the black community. Over 720 students were arrested, many of them beaten and dragged out of buildings.[64]

Some of the most violent police reactions to protests unfolded at HBCUs. At North Carolina A&T University, campus activists joined with local high school activists protesting a school board decision. As police arrived on campus,

Willie Grimes, a North Carolina A&T student who wasn't involved in the protest, was killed on campus while walking to a restaurant. The campus exploded. Students exchanged gun fire with law enforcement officials. The National Guard arrived with a tank and air support, which dropped tear gas from the sky onto students in a dormitory.[65]

While black student activists at UM were working for change within the university's bureaucracy during the 1968–69 academic year, other groups on campus showed Fleming what could happen when his co-optation techniques failed. SDS frightened Fleming. In response, he tried to use some of the same co-optation techniques to tame the organization. He accommodated as much protest as possible to avoid police confrontations and spoke out against the Vietnam War, but SDS continued to protest.[66]

In May 1969, Fleming contacted a local attorney for advice. He was interested in potentially suing the campus chapter of SDS, placing a financial burden on the organization that might lead to its demise. He even considered suing the parents of SDS students involved in property damage.[67] He was so frightened about contact between the police and SDS that he also wanted advice on the measures he could take to avoid violence. In case he did have to call the police, would officers be willing to accompany Fleming into an occupied building unarmed, Fleming asked? No, the lawyer answered. Could he ask police officers to retreat if they experienced forceful resistance from students, Fleming inquired? Probably not, the lawyer answered. "Retreat is much more difficult once open defiance occurs." The attorney advised that Fleming stood the best chance of avoiding confrontation if campus leaders worked with the police and carefully selected which officers entered the building.[68]

A month after Fleming asked the lawyer for advice, he watched as his nightmare became a reality. The confrontation between law enforcement and students, along with members of the Ann Arbor community, began on June 16, 1969, when a police officer pulled over a motorcyclist performing stunts on South University Avenue, which runs through the main campus. A large crowd gathered, threatening the officer. When the officer retreated, the crowd took over the street and threw a party. The next day, local activists and students tried to barricade South University Avenue and create a "people's party." When a police officer tried to remove the barricade, a brick or a bottle flew at the police car. The crowd grew, and police with riot gear arrived on South University Avenue. When law enforcement officials asked the crowd to disperse, more bottles flew at police.[69]

On the second day, Sheriff Doug Harvey arrived. Harvey was well known among campus administrators. "He was just like the sheriffs that were depicted in parts of the South," one administrator remembered. "He'd shoot students in a minute if you gave him the chance." Campus leaders knew that Harvey had introduced police dogs to control crowds and was known to walk around with a two-by-four during demonstrations. When Harvey arrived, he and his deputies started throwing tear gas. Law enforcement officers in riot gear chased people through campus. Students banged on Fleming's door, just steps from South University Avenue, trying to escape Harvey's forces.[70]

Fleming joined with city officials the next day to try to avoid another violent confrontation between demonstrators and police. The city and UM organized a rock concert on campus next to the Administration Building. Thousands attended the concert, while police in riot gear and an armored car mounted with a machine gun stood on South University Avenue. The concert proved successful in avoiding further conflict. Still, the incident proved a reminder to Fleming of what could happen when police met demonstrators. The violence stayed with Fleming and informed his future decisions regarding how to manage protest.[71]

When the fall semester began, Fleming's battle with SDS resumed. The organization had been leading a fight for a student-run bookstore on campus for several years. Fleming and the regents refused to meet all the organization's demands. On September 25, SDS led about one hundred students into the LSA building and refused to leave. The building takeover tested Fleming's fear of the police. He used the knowledge he had gained from the attorney over the summer and tried to control the police intervention as much as possible. When he finally felt that the Ann Arbor police wouldn't instigate violence, he allowed them to enter the building and arrest the students. Fleming watched from the roof of the Administration Building at 4 a.m. as a bus carried police officers to the LSA building. The students were arrested peacefully.[72]

When black students prepared for their own demonstration a few months later, Fleming's fear of campus violence was the greatest of his career. Fleming saw what could happen when he couldn't control law enforcement. Fleming's experience with SDS would hang over Fleming's response to black student activism during the 1969–70 academic year.

By fall 1969, the slow pace of change put stress on Fleming's managerial tactics to co-opt black campus activism. Fleming's techniques depended on black activists' faith that administrators were working on their behalf—faith that activists could win institutional change by working within the bureaucracy. By winter 1970, that faith had disappeared.

In January 1970, black activists from organizations across campus joined together in a mass meeting to craft a list of demands to present to the regents during their next meeting. Members of the BSU, the Black Law Students

Association, the Association of Black Social Work Students, and students from other departments without official organizations were present.[73] Fleming invited black activists to his home for dinner to discuss their concerns. It was one of Fleming's classic moves. He would listen to black student activists and show his sympathy with their concerns, hoping to show them that working for change within bureaucratic channels was still viable. It didn't work out that way. By the time they arrived, the student activists were calling themselves the Black Action Movement (BAM). BAM members didn't sit down for dinner. They knocked on Fleming's door and then read their demands in his front yard. The students' first demand created the most controversy. They insisted that black students represent 10 percent of the student body by the 1973–74 academic year. In the short term, BAM understood that much of the recruiting and admissions process was already complete for the following year. So they demanded that the incoming class in fall 1971 include 450 black first-year students, 150 undergraduate transfers, and 300 black graduate students. To fund this growth, the students insisted that the university increase financial aid for minority students. The students also believed that any new admissions program would have to be coupled with a robust supportive services program. They wanted the university to implement J. Frank Yates's Freshman Year of Studies proposal, which Fleming refused to fund in 1969. Black faculty hiring, students also demanded, must become a priority. Other demands focused on strengthening the connection between the university and the local black community. They wanted a black student center in a location that would link the university to Ann Arbor's black neighborhoods. They also wanted to ensure that African Americans in Ann Arbor would have a voice in the Center for Afro-American Studies, which was under development. Furthermore, the students demanded that all university administrators, faculty, and staff stop using the term "Negro" and begin using "Black" instead. Finally, the students called for the university to admit fifty Chicano students by the fall semester. This demand revealed an alliance black student activists had formed with Chicanos for Michigan, a small organization of seven UM Chicano students.[74]

The demands showed that students were learning from Fleming's methods. "We do not expect the university to procrastinate and sub-committee these demands," the document read. "They are for immediate and positive action." Black student activists saw committees as a management tool that administrators used to stall and eventually reject demands. Black student activists also recognized that abstract demands gave too much power to administrators to craft inclusion policies, which rarely fulfilled activists' goals. To address this issue, black students included a list of policies that could be implemented immediately. For example, rather than simply demanding that black students comprise 10 percent of the student body, they laid out a plan to increase black representation. The students asked for seven full-time graduate recruiters and nine new undergraduate recruiters. Understanding that OAP's exclusive focus on in-state students would hamper their 10 percent demand, they asked for an out-of-state recruiter to build networks in "Black population centers." The recruiter would also have the money to provide scholarships for out-of-state black students. Students' financial aid policy recommendations were even more specific. They suggested new ways to create more accurate estimates of parents' expected financial contribution; proposed a board composed of faculty, students, and administrators so that students' could contest their financial aid package; called for tuition waivers for all in-state black students admitted through special programs; demanded that administrators renew solicitations from businesses for donations to the Martin Luther King fund; and suggested that the Student Government Council (SGC) assess a $3 fee on each student to help fund minority enrollment.[75]

In justifying these demands, activists tried to teach the campus community new ways to understand racial disparities at the university. BAM introduced a term that hadn't been used at Michigan to frame the institution's problems: "institutional racism." UM's racial disparities didn't simply stem from individual prejudice, BAM concluded; institutional racism could be found in the university's "standards, goals, systems of measuring and operating procedures." Nobody at UM needed to act with malicious intent toward blacks to ensure the university's racial disparities—they only needed to carry out the university's established values and policies. In other words, racial disparities were part of "the bones and sinews of the place," BAM wrote. Perhaps no other words get to BAM's ideas about the university better than these. Institutional racism was so invasive and rooted in the university's practices and values that it made racial disparities seem logical, natural, even race neutral. Viewing UM in this framework rejected white officials' claim that UM was a benevolent institution operating in a racist society. Instead, black student activists wanted the UM community to see the university as an active part of a "structure" that "rob[bed] Black people of financial security, political sovereignty and human dignity."[76]

BAM outlined how institutional racism worked at UM. There was nothing natural about how university officials measured student quality or distributed financial resources. Instead, these decisions represented the university's underlying values and goals. According to BAM, the university's current function was "primarily to provide manpower for large corporations, government, and educational institutions." That explained why the University of Michigan measured student quality based on high school grades and SAT scores. These measurements, according to BAM, measured "a narrow range of skills connected with middle-class job performance." The university's financial commitments also reflected these priorities. "Only a white racist sense of spending priorities" that privileged subsidies for businesses and the military over racial justice, BAM activists claimed, explained UM officials' resistance to funding black students' demands. The fact that these values were so deeply embedded in the university's policies, incentives, and intellectual frameworks helped clarify why administrators' excuses seemed "ritualistic." This is what BAM members meant when they talked about the "bones and sinews of the place."[77]

The alternative was a new set of university values that served the interest of racial justice rather than the interests of business and the military. If those values were implemented, BAM contended, the university would help black communities become more autonomous from white people. UM's policies would help create black communities that no longer had to rely on white doctors, lawyers, business executives, teachers, and government officials. Empowering black communities, then, would become a central institutional priority. "It's not a question of whether the university will train people to do the tasks in the real world," BAM activists contended, "but what tasks, and whose needs determine the decision."[78]

These demands represented disruptive change, not reform. This vision would require a new institutional mission. It would require new priorities and values. The quality of the university would have to be measured differently, as the university's success in empowering black communities would be part of that calculation. Admissions and hiring decisions would change, as UM officials would need to build a university community that could help UM achieve its new mission. All the institutional rationales for racial disparities would no longer seem so natural.

More than any of BAM's demands, this disruptive vision challenged university administrators' priorities and values. Since 1963, UM leaders framed the purpose of affirmative action and other racial inclusion initiatives so that they fit within existing institutional priorities. BAM made it clear that they didn't simply want new policies; they wanted to change the university's mission. Conversely, administrators wanted limited reform.

Administrators' response to BAM revealed their persistent optimism in the discourse of racial innocence to stymie activism. Racial innocence had worked to resist some of Walter Greene's most ambitious recommendations. In 1970, though, administrators made serious errors in deploying racial innocence, which helped undermine their efforts to resist BAM's demands.

When the regents finally arrived on campus for their monthly meeting on February 19, BAM leaders learned that executive administrators would not push the regents to accept BAM's demands. Most of the meeting centered around the cost of BAM's proposed initiatives and the financial burden they would place on the university. Racial innocence and efforts to implement inclusion cheaply worked hand in hand. Stephen Spurr, vice president and dean of graduate studies, presented the university's financial position. Just to maintain OAP at its current level, UM would have to spend $1.5 million during the next year. Expanding the program to meet BAM's demands would prove unfeasible, according to Spurr. In other words, Spurr suggested that administrators' resistance to BAM's goals didn't represent a lack of sympathy for black activists; rather, the budget tied administrators' hands.[79]

The regents asked Fleming to submit a five-year plan to increase minority enrollment at their next meeting but refused to vote on BAM's demands. Unhappy, BAM members walked straight to the undergraduate library and began throwing books off the shelves. The next day, after a second regents meeting, BAM members went back to the library and repeated the action. On February 21, members continued their assault on the library, taking their actions a step further by setting off a stink bomb. Fleming responded by asking the Ann Arbor police to guard the building.[80] Over the next week, BAM members continued their tactics. Activists went to the university snack bar and stole food to protest the lack of "soul food." They also disrupted classes to read their demands.[81]

Racial innocence played a central role in crafting the five-year plan. After an executive officers meeting, William Haber—the former LSA dean who had stayed with the university to develop affirmative action hiring policies—wrote the initial draft. As was typical of racial innocence rhetoric, he claimed that racial inclusion was a core institutional priority before he explained that the university didn't have the resources to support black students' demands. Haber wrote that "we consider our obligation to provide a larger opportunity for minority students to study at the university as most important and assign toward this objective the highest priority." But then Haber made a serious misstep in employing racial innocence that wouldn't be corrected in revised drafts that became public. Rather than writing about costs abstractly, he decided to list all the things that took precedence over increasing funding for black students. All the university's "flexible funds," Haber contended, "were now heavily committed to such things as laboratory renovations, land purchases, badly needed equipment, library books, nominal capital improvements, and expansion of recreational facilities." Executive administrators didn't see the contradiction between claiming racial inclusion was the university's "highest priority" and explaining that there wasn't enough money for black students' demands because UM was building more recreational facilities.[82]

The draft also revealed the assumptions that Haber used to craft racial innocence. Administrators claimed that racial inequality outside the institution meant that the university would never be able to recruit enough "qualified" black students to meet BAM's demands. But it was clear that Haber took for granted that 10 percent black enrollment was unworkable and then looked for evidence to support his conclusion. For example, he had no idea what the pool of potential black applicants looked like, but he assumed it was small. Assuming that the percentage of black students who graduated from high school would likely support his argument, he wrote, "The State Board of Education reports that only _____ of those [black students] of college age have actually graduated from high school." He would find the data and fill that in later. The sections on the cost of black students' demands were filled with similar holes. Haber had no idea how much it would cost to fulfill the demands; he just knew it was too much.[83]

Haber did have one piece of data that administrators would continue to rely on in the early discussions of the BAM demands. OAP students' attrition rate was twice as high as that of non-OAP students. Pointing to black student attrition rates represented an important negotiating tool. Haber assumed that the attrition rates would explode if the university tried to pursue BAM's enrollment goal. The words he wrote next, though, would galvanize a small campus movement and help turn it into the most widely supported campus protest in the University of Michigan's history. The words he chose were so important they deserve a long quote:

> We know from our present experience that the attrition rate on [sic] Opportunity Awards students approximates twice the average of all students, but still tolerable in terms of what is being accomplished. We do not know how much deviation there can be from this standard and still accomplish anything. At some point it is clear that the student is far better off to enter a community college where the competition is less severe and where the course options are less academically oriented.

Haber didn't stop there. He claimed that to fulfill BAM's goals, the university would have to lower its admissions standards to the acquisition of a high school diploma. Because, in Haber's eyes, these students would almost certainly drop out when they were left to compete with the rest of the students admitted under selective admissions policies, the university would have to lower its admissions standards for all students just to make sure affirmative action admittees would graduate. "This would drastically change the character of the University," Haber concluded, "and adversely affect the position of academic preeminence which it has achieved over the years." In other words, the black high school students BAM was fighting for threatened the reputation of the university.[84]

None of this language raised concerns when the regents looked at the document. After all, believing that racial inclusion was an institutional priority and believing that most black high school students were threats to UM's quality were perfectly compatible ideas in 1970. What *did* raise the regents' concern was Haber's attention to race. Haber's original draft committed UM to double the number of black students within four years. The regents were more comfortable with the word "disadvantaged" than "Black" because, at least on the surface, "disadvantaged" was race neutral. Even though OAP's focus on "disadvantaged" led to a program that was 90 percent black, the word offered political and legal cover. So the final proposal stated that UM would "establish as a goal the availability of a University of Michigan education for double the present number of disadvantaged students by 1973–74." In an effort to satisfy black students, the document reminded BAM members that "Black students presently constitute a large majority of all disadvantaged students."[85]

All these discussions occurred during UM's spring break. On March 5, the Thursday of spring break, Fleming wrote to members of the Black Action Movement. He wanted students to know why the executive officers decided that the students' demands were unviable. Almost word for word, he repeated Haber's passage about the university's financial commitments in library books and capital improvements. Exactly word for word, Fleming copied Haber's passage about black student attrition rates. He chose to tell BAM members that many of the black high school students that activists were fighting for were better off at community colleges. He attached Haber's edited proposal in its entirety, including the offer to double the number of "disadvantaged" students by the 1973–74 academic year.[86]

The documents simply reinforced BAM's message that racial inclusion was low on the University of Michigan's list of priorities and gave the group important allies. When students returned from spring break, Fleming witnessed growing support for BAM.

Administrators' attempts to claim racial innocence failed to temper activism, and a more confrontational protest movement developed in the wake of Fleming's letter. The success of these protests reveals the power of disruption. The fear of violence caused administrators to change course and offer unprecedented concessions.

On March 18, BAM leaders again presented their demands at an open meeting of the board of regents. When the regents refused to accept BAM's 10 percent black enrollment demand, the group's leaders announced a one-day campus-wide boycott of classes. The potential for a prolonged campus strike finally led to the first major concession from the administration.[87]

The threat of protest proved to be a powerful tool. Some campus leaders reluctantly accepted policy changes in order to avoid further demonstrations. One of the regents fits this model. Gertrude Huebner called the concessions the regents made throughout the strike "overly generous," but she explained that "the alternative was worse." In her eyes, making concessions meant not "killing a lot of people." Her own perceptions of black students as intimidating and threatening likely added to her concerns about violence on campus. "Black people can really look big," Huebner recalled years later, when she was trying to convey the fear she had felt during a BAM demonstration.[88]

Protest could also create an environment in which powerful people began to rethink their assumptions. This is what started to happen to Fleming. Nobody within Fleming's administration had seriously considered whether the 10 percent goal was attainable. In other words, administrators' unwillingness to investigate the validity of black activists' demands helped sustain campus leaders' resistance to BAM. The fact that OAP students' attrition rate was twice as high as that of non-OAP students was all the evidence they needed to conclude that it was impossible. When black students called for a one-day strike, though, Fleming was suddenly willing to investigate whether the 10 percent goal was attainable. He started asking new questions about the pool of eligible black students who could graduate from the university. The numbers that came back suggested that the pool was probably bigger than everyone thought. Fleming would continue to be skeptical of the viability of the 10 percent goal, but for the rest of the strike he never again suggested that it was impossible to find enough "qualified" black applicants to meet BAM's enrollment demand.[89]

The next day, the regents voted on a new proposal that approved an admissions goal "aimed at 10 per cent enrollment of Black students and substantially increased numbers of other minority and disadvantaged groups" by the 1973–74 academic year. A goal, rather than a guarantee, might sound like a minor concession, but it was the first-time administrators had acknowledged that there might be enough "qualified" black students to increase black enrollment to 10 percent of the student body. It also created new openings that black students would soon exploit.[90]

The regents' concession looked less appealing to BAM when activists saw that the amount of money the regents were willing to spend remained the same. The regents proposed to pursue the 10 percent black enrollment goal with the funds administrators determined were necessary to raise enrollment to 7 percent. How would the university triple black enrollment with only enough money to double enrollment, BAM activists asked?[91]

About eight hundred BAM members and supporters waited outside the building as the regents discussed and voted on the proposal. Some of the supporters who stood there likely followed BAM's call the day before for students not to attend classes and for faculty and staff to refuse to work. When the regents' meeting ended, BAM leaders held a rally outside the building, then led a march through campus, walking through academic buildings and disrupting classes in order to convince students to join the strike.[92]

The protests revealed the failure of Fleming's strategy to stymie unrest. When it was clear that Fleming's management techniques wouldn't stop demonstrations, he turned to the police. Fleming had mobilized local and state police the day before, anticipating a potential confrontation with protesters. But Fleming, trying to avoid any contact between law enforcement and students, had asked the bulk of the police to stay on a "stand-by basis." They stayed that way until students reorganized at Regents Plaza. There, activists saw Fleming walking to the Administration Building with Arthur Ross, vice president for state relations and planning, and regent Robert Brown. The students surrounded the three university leaders, shouting insults but allowing them to walk to their destination. When they arrived at the Administration Building, a guard unlocked the door and let Fleming and Brown enter. When Ross walked across the threshold, students rushed the entrance. The guard struggled to push the door closed, but the students were too strong. One student took the keys to the building out of the guard's hand and about twenty demonstrators stood in the lobby. Within five minutes, forty-five police officers in riot gear arrived and took over the building. When the last officer entered, a brick soared through the air, crashing through the glass panel in the door.[93]

None of the police saw who threw the brick, but they soon claimed they saw a student throw a rock. Suddenly, Veronica Banks, a nursing student, was in the back of a police car. Five hundred protesters yelling "Let her go" surrounded the car. The riot sticks of twenty police officers emerged as the officers charged the crowd. Then debris started flying through the air as protesters threw bricks, rocks, and bottles. The twenty police officers retreated and regrouped with forty additional Ann Arbor police officers. Behind them stood another twenty-five state police officers. The melee was over. It had lasted less than thirty minutes. Four students were arrested. Two were charged with felony assault and another with misdemeanor assault and resisting arrest. Banks was charged with malicious destruction of property.[94]

BAM leaders didn't condone any of these actions. They struggled throughout the strike to control their supporters' actions and consistently advocated nonviolence. White-led protest groups often ignored black leadership. The Honors Convocation was the largest event scheduled for March 20. BAM leaders organized a protest outside the convocation with signs reading "The Regents Copped Out" and "Stop Racism." But SDS had different plans. SDS members marched into Hill Auditorium, disrupting the convocation and shouting "Open it up or shut it down." That afternoon, one hundred protesters blocked traffic at South University and South State Streets, a major intersection on campus. Some of the protesters smashed car windows and threatened drivers. In the midst of these protests, the university received four bomb threats.[95]

BAM leaders continued to try to control activists who advocated for physical violence and property damage. Some of the most radical activists were white students who had long criticized black activists as being too timid. Some went so far as to call BAM leaders "Uncle Toms." At one point, white activists offered BAM guns. BAM leaders refused. BAM struggled to control the actions of some black activists, too, who wanted more direct action. Black students were not a monolithic group. There were tense disagreements between BAM's leadership and some black student protesters. Reports flooded in to administrators about black students who entered the chemistry building and used fire hoses to spray water on the floors. Other reports documented students who entered the law library, smashing chairs, and then went through classroom buildings, banging garbage can tops.[96]

While BAM leaders worked hard to prevent these acts, they benefited from activists who disobeyed BAM directives and destroyed property. Again, the Detroit Rebellion hovered over black activism at UM. As Fleming later explained, "You cannot sit here 35 miles or whatever it is from Detroit . . . the huge city in which there had been in 1967 that very explosive incident, and not expect those people to get involved. And once you get outside groups involved, then you've got a lot of trouble on your hands. So we had to get the thing over with, and I think people realized that."[97] The impact of the Detroit Rebellion speaks to the power of violence, despite the fact that black protest at UM remained largely nonviolent. Yet even in their nonviolence, black student activists benefited from the images of fires and police cars with their wheels in the air. These images made the threat of violence real, made black student protests look more dangerous, and made the need for solutions look more urgent. Campus leaders feared that UM activists would turn to these tactics. Administrators also feared that activists from Detroit involved in the 1967 rebellion might come to campus. This was the reason why black student activism on a campus like Michigan can never be seen in isolation from other disruptions around the country in the late 1960s.[98]

BAM exploited these fears on March 25, when the Senate Assembly held a special meeting. The faculty wanted the strike to end, if only to start teaching their classes again. One estimate suggested that as high as 50 percent of LSA courses had been canceled. Other classes devoted all their time to discussing the strike. With final exams approaching in April, classes need to resume in order to finish the term.[99]

At the meeting, Daryl Gorman, a black student activist, and Gloria Marshall, a black untenured professor of anthropology, presented BAM leaders as the moderate group that faculty should support and work with. Gorman and Marshall also emphasized that they couldn't control the people who ignored BAM's directives and destroyed property. Marshall reminded the audience that "the longer the demonstrations continue the more likelihood that acts of violence will escalate." They sent a clear message: if faculty members wanted the violence to stop, they needed to support BAM's demands.[100]

Gorman and Marshall also used the meeting to reframe BAM's language to attract faculty support. Gone was BAM's focus on institutional racism, which focused on the unjust values of the university and the need to create a new institution that saw justice and access as its foremost mission. Instead, the two spent their time showing how their demands could coexist with university values. In particular, they focused on how the BAM goals wouldn't undermine the university's quality. They responded to questions about the pool of "qualified" black students and tried to alleviate concerns that pursuing the BAM goals would lower academic standards and, in turn, the status of the university.[101]

Their focus on preserving institutional quality again shows that the policies BAM demanded were less threatening than the disruptive intellectual framework some activists used. BAM's disruptive vision required changing the entire mission and priorities of the university. Because the movement depended on the faculty's endorsement, BAM activists faced a difficult decision. Connecting BAM's demands to deeply embedded institutional values represented the easiest path to gain faculty support, but it also meant sacrificing the revolutionary potential of the movement. The incentives rooted in framing their demands in the values shared by the majority—in this case, the overwhelmingly white faculty—were too great for BAM activists. BAM desperately needed faculty support to win concessions from Fleming.

The meeting proved to be the turning point of the strike. Getting faculty support was especially important because Fleming claimed that the funds necessary to support BAM were tied up in the schools and colleges across the university. The Senate Assembly approved a motion that urged faculty within each school and department to support the 10 percent black enrollment goal and work with the administration to achieve it. Within two days, almost every school and college on campus voted to support the BAM demands and agreed to reallocate the funds necessary to raise black enrollment to 10 percent of the study body. The political science department went even further, starting a private donation drive to support the funding necessary to reach the 10 percent goal.[102]

Thus far, the contest between BAM and the administration had focused almost exclusively on the admissions goal and the funding necessary to accomplish it. Once that was settled, negotiations moved to BAM's other demands. After seven hours of discussion on Saturday, March 28, and a full day of negotiations on Sunday, the two sides were close to a settlement. But one of the more pressing issues, how BAM supporters who committed campus code violations would be punished, was still on the table.[103]

Both BAM leaders and Fleming wanted to end the strike. BAM leaders feared that their support was waning. Fleming feared that if he didn't end the strike soon, violence would erupt. The final negotiations were long and grueling, finally ending around 4 a.m.[104] BAM lost some of its most coveted demands. There would be no tuition waivers for black students. Despite the fact that the SGC had passed a resolution to collect a $3 fee from students to support black enrollment, the university administration refused to collect the money. A black student center was also off the table. As the regents made clear in the final agreement, they were "opposed to the establishment of University financed special student centers on the basis of race." BAM also lost the battle over reprisals against demonstrators, although they did get a small concession from Fleming. Students could request an "outside impartial hearing officer," which Fleming would appoint, to oversee disciplinary hearings.[105]

Still, BAM scored significant concessions from Fleming and the regents. The final agreement committed the university to the goal of raising black student enrollment to 10 percent of the student body and guaranteed the funds necessary to reach that goal. The students also won seven new undergraduate and three graduate recruiters, as well as two financial aid counselors. Regarding black faculty, Fleming offered to convert an existing position to "the purpose of helping departments to become aware of prospective Black faculty candidates." Fleming also agreed to issue a statement to every department, urging them to "vigorously" recruit black faculty members. Furthermore, he would ask departments to turn in reports three times a year that outlined the efforts they had made to recruit black faculty members. Fleming committed $63,000 for a supportive services program and a base budget of $250,000 for a center to support the black studies program. Finally, black students kept their promise to Chicano students. Fleming agreed to hire a Chicano recruiter and pursue the goal of enrolling at least fifty Chicano students by the fall semester.[106]

The Black Action Movement strike represented the breakdown of Fleming's co-optation techniques. In 1968, after black students occupied the Administration Building, he set out to end future disruptions. He emphasized the university's commitment to inclusion in speeches, created a new inclusion bureaucracy filled with black officials, and employed the narrative of racial innocence, but these techniques didn't hide the slow rise in black enrollment and faculty representation. It also didn't hide the poor racial climate. Black activists wanted to see results.

During the BAM strike, administrators briefly lost control over inclusion, agreeing to goals and reforms that they believed were unviable and inconsistent with the university's priorities. In the years after the strike, Fleming focused on preventing another BAM and regaining control over the meaning and character of inclusion. Fleming spent the early 1970s considering new co-optation tactics that would make it more difficult for black students to change the institution. When students returned in fall 1970, they started to see signs of a new regime.

# CHAPTER 4

# Controlling Inclusion

When the BAM negotiating team arrived at the Michigan Ballroom on April 1, 1970, to a cheering crowd of twelve hundred, the frustration after a long battle with Fleming was evident in their speeches. "This wasn't the best agreement we could have settled on," Dave Lewis told the crowd, "but it was a first step, a first substantial step." BAM leaders knew that much of the hard work was still to come. BAM leaders explained that they were ready to help the university in the "long-range, day-to-day, tedious work of . . . implementing the programs that have now become part of the University policy." "Tedious" didn't do the task justice.[1]

The five-year period between 1970 and 1975 changed the University of Michigan. The university implemented the most ambitious affirmative action admissions policies in its history, increased the number of black officials on campus, and redistributed millions of dollars to inclusion initiatives. At the same time, UM administrators deployed new and old techniques to co-opt black campus activism. They added new disciplinary codes to deter confrontational activism; expanded the inclusion bureaucracy; and fought against black, Asian American, Chicano, and Native American activists who tried to build on the BAM concessions. By 1975, BAM's revolutionary vision that called for a new institutional mission was nowhere to be found. The university still hadn't reached the 10 percent black enrollment goal, and the racial climate was still creating obstacles for black students on campus. The fact that black campus activists weren't able to mobilize a campus strike that rivaled BAM's in response to these failures signaled that executive administrators had a firm grasp on racial inclusion once again.

Fleming went to work after the BAM strike to show the UM community how the concessions didn't disrupt the university's values and priorities. In fact, Fleming claimed that these new inclusion goals were perfectly compatible with the university's mission. Fleming had two objectives in framing the concessions this way. First, he wanted to protect the institution from BAM's revolutionary vision: to place racial justice at the heart of the university's mission. Second, as someone who was committed to affirmative action, he wanted to protect the university's racially attentive admissions practices from opponents. University leaders saw themselves as mediators, caught between student activists who could undermine the university's reputation and white backlash, which sought to undermine the university's commitment to affirmative action.

BAM offered a biting critique of the university. According to BAM, the university was part of a larger "white power structure" that "systematically rob[bed] Black people of financial security, political sovereignty and human dignity." The solution didn't involve simply eliminating individual prejudice on the part of administrators; it involved challenging a "structure" that "is embodied in the impersonal institutionalization of power that we find in the very standards, goals, systems of measurement and operating procedures." So for BAM, changing the university's "structure" didn't mean incorporating racial justice into UM's existing values. To them, racial justice was incompatible with the university's existing values. Nothing less than rethinking the entire university value system was going to work. And with a new value system would come new ways of measuring and defining institutional quality, which didn't see black students as impediments to the university's reputation.[2]

Fleming and other officials rejected BAM's portrayal of UM as a racist institution that needed to be rebuilt from its core. Maintaining control over the definition of racism continued to be a key tool in the university's racial innocence narrative. After the BAM strike, university leaders reframed the BAM concessions as an effort to address the problem of racism outside the university's walls. The university's admission tools weren't racist. The university's mission to preserve its elite status based on standardized test scores wasn't racist. In rejecting claims of institutional racism, UM leaders emphasized that the university could implement reforms without undermining established values and priorities.[3]

At the same time, university officials defended the concessions against white backlash. Richard Nixon's vice president, Spiro Agnew, used the BAM strike as a political football. At a Republican fund-raising event in Des Moines, Iowa, which was covered in major news outlets around the country, Agnew called the University of Michigan's concessions a "callow retreat from reality." The BAM strike played into two of Agnew's favorite political narratives: college campuses were too willing to give in to student protesters who did not represent the views of most Americans, and affirmative action was taking away jobs and admission slots from better-qualified white applicants. According to Agnew, by conceding to unruly protesters, UM was destroying the quality of the American higher education system. Because there were not enough "qualified" black students to increase black enrollment to 10 percent of UM's student body, Agnew argued, the university would have to lower its standards and, in turn, lower the quality of the university. Angry alumni, students, and Michigan citizens joined Agnew by flooding Fleming's office with letters of dissent. Others wrote letters to the editor in newspapers around the country, using UM's case to vent their anger over affirmative action.[4]

UM officials defended the BAM concessions against these attacks by showing how the concessions fit into the university's hierarchy of values, which privileged the university's elite status over inclusion. To challenge critics who argued affirmative action lowered institutional quality, university officials drew on the internal studies of the 1960s. The University Relations Office released a document stating, "There is considerable evidence that this group is not as accurately judged by test score devices which are generally applied to those who have both cultural and educational advantages in elementary and secondary schools." Furthermore, it claimed, "There is also evidence that their high school grades are less meaningful than their degree of motivation." Fleming would repeat these exact words in the *Detroit Free Press* the next month. Fleming also wrote back to disgruntled letter writers with a similar message: "We believe that there is evidence that testing devices do not as well reflect black as white aptitudes, and that high school grades do not have the same value."[5]

Fleming also reframed BAM's vision of racial justice to speak to the interests of business leaders. The university's reliance on donations created powerful interest groups that didn't share BAM's worldview. The BAM strike made an immediate impact on fundraising, adding to the university's financial problems as state contributions declined. In the year after the BAM strike, private donations to the university dropped by one-third.[6] Fleming needed to reverse this trend. That meant courting donors and alleviating concerns about the university's new commitments to an ambitious affirmative action plan. Here he relied on businesses' dependence on the university's affirmative action program to meet their own affirmative action goals. Fleming knew how important the University of Michigan was to businesses that wanted to comply with federal equal employment mandates. UM served as a recruiting ground for employers searching for potential black employees, and the university hosted special offices, such as the College of Engineering's Minority Projects Office, to help businesses find black students. A short list of the companies that came to UM to interview black undergraduate and graduate students during the 1970–71 academic year through the Minority Projects Office included General Motors, General Electric, and Gulf Oil. Looking for business leaders' continued financial support in the aftermath of BAM at the Economic Club of Detroit, Fleming claimed that when the university finally reached the 10 percent goal, it would not only substantially increase blacks' representation at the university but also "[pour] them into the job market." Fleming later confirmed that after an initial drop in donations, BAM did little to hurt the university's fund-raising campaigns in the long term. This was likely due, at least in part, to the fact that many businesses had a stake in increasing the number of black graduates in order to pursue their own affirmative action hiring programs.[7]

Fleming and other UM officials took control over the intellectual rationales of affirmative action from BAM in the early 1970s. Together, they co-opted BAM's rhetoric, stripping any reference to institutional racism. Instead, officials offered an argument for affirmative action that preserved the university's hierarchy of values, privileging the institution's status over inclusion. The efforts to use these same arguments to defend affirmative action against opponents, though, speaks to how administrators could undermine black students' vision and still feel as though they were champions of black students' access. Opponents of affirmative action became a convenient reference point for administrators in framing who was for and against racial inclusion. Their battle to preserve affirmative action in the face of white backlash allowed campus leaders to portray themselves as champions of racial inclusion even while undermining BAM's vision of racial justice.

"The University of Michigan operates within the general tenet that dissent is to be fostered rather than suppressed on a university campus but that disruptive dissent is incompatible with the purpose of an academic community," James Brinkerhoff, the university's vice president and chief financial officer, wrote in 1971. Brinkerhoff was preparing a document for the governor that described all the steps the university had taken since the BAM strike to prevent more campus disruptions. The document signaled a new era of discipline. In the late 1960s, Fleming tried to accommodate dissent, believing that repression would only lead to more problems on campus. But the BAM strike marked a turning point in UM's history. BAM's tactics forced UM administrators to make concessions that they thought were unviable and potentially compromised

UM's priorities. More than ever, Fleming tried to punish the types of dissent that made BAM successful. All the methods he defined as unacceptable would be met with a new disciplinary regime that handed out harsh consequences.[8]

Fleming wasn't just concerned with another strike that would lead to more concessions; Fleming was also concerned about controlling the implementation of the concessions already won in April 1970. There were still many details left to be worked out, and campus leaders wanted as much control over those details as possible. Confrontational activism represented a tool that black activists could use to influence the outcomes of the BAM concessions.

Disciplining BAM protesters represented the first step in controlling protests. The University of Michigan wasn't well prepared to punish tens, let alone hundreds, of students for nonacademic infractions after the BAM strike. There was no university-wide set of rules or disciplinary body that governed all students. The Student Government Council had its own set of rules governing undergraduate students and its own judiciary body. Each school and college within UM also had its own set of rules and disciplinary procedures. The problem with this decentralized structure for Fleming was that he had little control over the process. The rules and punishments also varied greatly. It wasn't an ideal structure for someone who wanted to deter future protests through discipline.[9]

Fleming had to work within these limitations to punish BAM supporters who broke campus codes. When he negotiated with BAM members, they agreed on a disciplinary process that allowed students accused of a violation to have their cases heard in front of their respective school's or college's administrative board or by a hearing officer from outside the university, selected by Fleming. In the end, professors brought charges against nine students. By November 1971, four had been found guilty, three were acquitted, and two cases were still pending.[10]

Fleming and the regents wanted more control over the definition of unacceptable dissent and the process of disciplining students who violated campus rules in any future protest. Just over two weeks after BAM members celebrated the concessions, the board of regents introduced a new set of university-wide rules and disciplinary procedures without faculty and student input. The rules prohibited the "use of force or violence" against anyone on campus, "disruption or unauthorized interruption of a class" or any "authorized university activity," "continued occupation of a university facility after being ordered to leave by the president or his agent," and "defacement, damage to or theft of university property." The regents outlined a variety of penalties, ranging from a warning to expulsion. Cases would be heard in front of a hearing officer employed by the president exclusively to hear these cases. The new rules clearly defined acceptable dissent. Not surprisingly, none of the most effective tactics of the BAM strike fell under acceptable dissent. The goal here was clear: limit the power of campus movements by threatening harsh consequences for any protest tactic that could force administrators into concessions that they thought were unviable. Under the rules, students who wanted to fight for institutional change were left to write requests to administrators and hold public demonstrations—as long as they didn't interrupt a class or a university function.[11]

The interim rules joined a growing disciplinary apparatus created in both Congress and Michigan's state legislature. In the late 1960s and early 1970s, federal and state legislatures passed laws that used financial aid to punish students involved in campus protests. In 1969, Congress passed two appropriations bills that affected student protesters. The 1969 appropriations bill for the Department of Housing, Education, and Welfare (HEW) included a provision stating that no HEW funds could be used to support a student convicted by a court "of the use of or assistance in the use of force, trespass, seizure of property under control" of a higher education institution "to prevent officials or students from engaging in the duties of pursuing studies." An amendment to the Higher Education Act of 1968 went even further, allowing schools to deny aid to students who violated the university's rules regarding disruptions. In January 1970, Michigan joined thirty-two other states in passing new laws regarding campus disruptions. The State Higher Education Bill prohibited state financial aid to students who were convicted in court of "disorderly conduct, violence to a person, or damage to property" while participating in a campus disruption. It also prohibited aid to any student convicted of the same violations by a university disciplinary authority.[12]

Michigan's state legislature added another layer of criminal codes for student activists. In the wake of the BAM strike, Michigan's governor William Milliken signed a law that allowed a judge to impose a jail sentence of up to ninety days and a fine of between $200 and $1,000 for acts so ambiguous that they could include almost any protest tactic. A protester could go to jail for presenting a "clear and substantial risk of physical harm or injury to other persons." Equally vague, a protester could be convicted of constituting a "risk of damage to or the destruction of property of the institution." Going further, the law prohibited the "unreasonable prevention of disruption of the customary and lawful function of the institution by occupying space necessary (for carrying to the institution's functions) by the use of threat of force." Finally, for any student who refused to leave a campus building when ordered to do so by the university president or a president's "designee," a court could impose a fine of up to $500 and a thirty-day jail sentence.[13]

UM's efforts to discipline students empowered these laws. Before the BAM strike, when university officials tried to limit police intervention on campus and the campus rules for nonacademic conduct were weak, these federal and state laws weren't great deterrents for student demonstrators. However, the regents' interim rules and judicial process made the possibility of a campus violation for demonstrating more likely. After the BAM strike, students were also more likely to come into contact with police on campus and face criminal conviction. When students returned to campus in fall 1970, they found two police officers stationed on campus, hired with federal money meant to improve police-community relations. The university had never assigned full-time police officers to the campus before.[14]

University officials also created the university's first director of safety position in fall 1970. The director wasn't a sworn police officer but was tasked with gathering information about potential campus disruptions by developing contacts within and outside the university in order for UM officials to prepare for, and potentially stop, campus demonstrations before they started. The director would also coordinate any police activities if law enforcement was called to campus. This represented an attempt to professionalize UM's responses to campus disorder. Before BAM, administrators tried to use their limited knowledge to anticipate and respond to campus protests. After BAM, they created new positions to deal specifically with activism.[15]

These measures didn't target faculty, but faculty allies of student activists still experienced retribution. Gloria Marshall was a key faculty ally for BAM. In 1970, she was a young black faculty member in the anthropology department coming up for tenure. In the aftermath of the strike, the regents were ready to exact revenge by denying her tenure. Only after the vice president for academic affairs, Allan Smith, pleaded with the regents not to use Marshall's role in the strike as a factor in their decision did the regents finally approve her tenure. However, it was still a warning to untenured faculty that their support of black campus activism could potentially undermine their future at UM.[16]

Administrators were more willing to exact revenge in other ways. UM's Center for Research and Conflict Resolution (CRCR) provided important resources for BAM in the early stages of the strike. BAM activists initially organized the strike out of a student's apartment with a single phone line. CRCR leaders offered the center's office to BAM, and it quickly became the strike's headquarters. BAM activists suddenly had access to multiple phone lines, printers, and meeting space—all important resources for a campus protest. A year after the BAM strike, administrators closed the center. Justifying the decision, one executive administrator explained, "When it comes to educational change, our faculty are mostly conservative. They want to make sure that strong academic discipline is kept." Faculty allies might not have experienced disciplinary hearings, but they still faced retribution after the BAM strike.[17]

This new disciplinary regime hung over the heads of student activists and their allies in the early 1970s. Students now faced a greater threat of arrest and conviction, campus code violations, and the loss of financial aid. They had to make more difficult calculations when deciding whether to participate in protests. Faculty members, too, had to worry about tenure and the future of academic centers. These disciplinary measures influenced how administrators implemented the BAM concessions. In an environment that limited the power of activism, administrators had more control over what the new inclusion programs would look like.

The new disciplinary codes made it more likely that black students would work for change with institutional bureaucrats. Fleming continued to place great faith in the inclusion bureaucracy to move dissent inside University of Michigan offices after the BAM strike. Executive administrators preferred to channel institutional change through the inclusion bureaucracy because campus leaders believed that they could control inclusion bureaucrats. Executive administrators could reject reforms coming from the inclusion bureaucracy that they thought were unviable or challenged institutional priorities and values. In the aftermath of the strike, executive administrators expanded the bureaucracy created in the 1960s, hiring new black officials across the university. Administrators moved to make some quick reforms to show activists that the institution could change without more protest. By 1972, activists saw black enrollment climbing, new supportive services, a new black studies center, an office devoted to affirmative action hiring, and racial sensitivity programs in campus housing.

Administrators believed that increasing black enrollment, in particular, was important in showing activists that the administration was committed to implementing the concessions. The 10 percent black enrollment goal represented the most visible concessions and the easiest for students to measure and evaluate. Thus, UM leaders turned to the inclusion bureaucracy to increase black enrollment quickly.

Executive administrators immediately fulfilled one of BAM's demands that they believed was vital to increasing and sustaining black enrollment. BAM wanted Fleming to fund J. Frank Yates's plan for a supportive services program. Before the strike, Yates had crafted an ambitious proposal while serving as assistant to the dean of LSA, but Fleming chose not to fund it. In the immediate aftermath of BAM, Yates suddenly received the funding and autonomy to create his supportive services program.

In fall 1970, just months after the BAM strike, Yates introduced the Coalition for the Use of Learning Skills (CULS). The program was open to students regardless of race but targeted black undergraduate students. The College of Literature, Science, and Arts, in which the vast majority of black students were enrolled, hosted the central branch of the program. CULS offered a variety of new services, including an orientation for Opportunity Program students to prepare them for the potential emotional and academic obstacles they might face once the school year began (Goodman dropped "Awards" from the program's title in 1970). CULS also improved the academic support black students received. For required first-year courses, CULS provided course-specific study groups led by specially trained upperclassmen, graduate students, or faculty members. In addition to helping students master the course material, the study sessions worked to improve the basic skills necessary to succeed at the university, including analytical reading and writings skills and test preparation. CULS also offered special sections of English 123, a required composition course for all first-year students, specifically set up for minority students—although technically open to all students—and taught by nonwhite teaching assistants. Yates developed the special sections with the "assumption that for minority students, a racially homogenous atmosphere is more conducive to the improvement of writing skills." Rather than reading Thoreau and Shakespeare, the course material revolved around literature produced by black writers. These courses incorporated the critiques of a Eurocentric curriculum that black students had been making at UM since 1966. Ten minority students took advantage of the special sections in 1970, but enrollment expanded quickly. In 1973, 192 black students and 10 other minority students enrolled in CULS's sections of English 123.[18]

There were, of course, other motivations behind administrators' support for CULS. The program helped address fears that increasing black enrollment would compromise academic standards. As much as Fleming and other administrators cited studies showing that traditional admissions tools didn't effectively measure black students' potential, they still feared that more aggressive affirmative action policies would produce skyrocketing attrition rates for black students. Improving academic support services, then, seemed to be the only alternative to ensure that attrition rates wouldn't explode.[19]

Some faculty members raised the same concerns and put pressure on executive administrators to build new academic support services to support the Opportunity Program (OP). These faculty typically supported more aggressive affirmative action practices but still saw those practices as a potential threat to the University of Michigan's elite status if not implemented properly. A professor of physics, for example, expressed concern that administrators were not discussing the "special programs of instruction" to prepare students from what he called "substandard ghetto schools" for the rigorous standards of the University of Michigan. Without academic support programs, he assumed the university would face a large number of frustrated black students "seeing their dreams for a better life crumbling. The resulting riots and destruction would far eclipse the present problems." He feared that the riots would force administrators to grant "soft degrees" and, in turn, lower the quality and reputation of UM.[20]

This professor's concern about granting soft degrees gets to the heart of the anxieties brought about by the BAM concessions. As much as the evidence suggests that the majority of UM's faculty supported affirmative action in principle, many still believed that the drive for racial equity, if taken too far, could undermine the university's status as an elite postsecondary institution. Some faculty members might have worried that UM would become the next City University of New York (CUNY). By 1970, CUNY's "open admission" plan had become the symbol of an inclusion program that went too far, threatening the institution's reputation. In spring 1969, a multiracial coalition of CUNY students successfully fought for an admissions system that would open the institution to any student who graduated from a New York City high school. Critics argued that CUNY represented a campus that stretched the delicate balance between equity and quality too far.[21]

Yates's supportive services program helped to win community members confidence that the university could pursue the BAM enrollment goal without lowering academic standards. That confidence empowered George Goodman, the admissions official who would carry out the affirmative action goals of the BAM concessions. Goodman began his career at the university in 1968 as the admissions official in charge of the Opportunity Awards Program. For the first two years of his career, recruiting black students was a one-person job. With few resources, he traveled the state trying to increase black enrollment. Everything changed when Fleming agreed to the BAM concessions.[22]

Goodman soon found the resources necessary to expand the program. An influx of financial aid dollars from the university's general fund proved particularly important in increasing black enrollment. Federal and state financial aid didn't cover the full cost of OP students' education. In 1971, for example, 40 percent of the financial aid for minority students came from the university's general fund. To meet BAM's goals, UM would have to devote an unprecedented amount of general fund money to black students' financial aid packages. Between the fall of 1970 and 1973, the university's general fund contribution to OP students' financial aid packages rose from $782,753 to over $5 million. The sum was so large that Fleming briefly considered prohibiting

Detroit OP students from living on campus. Fleming figured he could save the university money if it didn't have to pay for those students' room and board. UM instructors would go to Detroit to teach classes for OP students during their first year; UM would allow them to live on campus beginning in their sophomore year. Another plan would have sent buses to Detroit every weekday to transport students to their classes in Ann Arbor and then take them back home at the end of the day. Fleming never put these ideas into practice, and the university's contribution to OP students' financial aid exploded.[23]

The Opportunity Program also benefited from money to expand its staff. In the six months following the BAM strike, ten new staff members joined OP. Many of these staff members were African Americans who had worked in Detroit. The new staff allowed the admissions office to pursue an unprecedented recruiting campaign that brought more students into its special admissions process. The rising numbers of black applicants to OP reflects the success of their efforts. The fact that the BAM concessions came at the end of the 1969–70 academic year made it difficult for the admissions office to make major changes before the incoming class was solidified. Four hundred seventy-two students applied to OP for the fall 1970 class. The next year, though, after a full year of recruiting, 810 students applied to OP. By 1972, the number rose again to 842 applicants.[24]

Goodman also received the independence and support needed to create policies that could increase black enrollment. In these policies, SAT scores played less of a role in admission decisions. For OP applicants on the margins of the program's criteria, Goodman began using an alternative test, created by UM researcher Benno Fricke, that measured motivation. As a result, the OP admission rate went up, even as the number of black students applying skyrocketed. Between 1964 and 1968, the program's admission rate stood at 58 percent. By 1973, the OP admission rate had risen to 71.8 percent.[25]

These policy changes—increased funding, a larger staff, new academic support services, and new methods to measure "ability"—made an immediate impact on the program. Black enrollment in OP rose from 229 in 1970 to 362 in 1971 and 442 in 1972.[26]

As enrollment rose, students felt some optimism about working within the inclusion bureaucracy to address the university's racial climate. Complaints of racial tension only increased in the aftermath of the BAM strike. As black enrollment grew, so did reports of the word "nigger" on dormitory doors as well as other forms of verbal and physical abuse. Adding to the tension, one of the dormitory building directors reportedly called black students "monkeys" in a public meeting. When black students tried to create a space for themselves in dormitories, such as a black lounge, white students complained.[27]

Black students turned to the inclusion bureaucracy for help. Georgia Williams arrived at UM just before the BAM strike. She filled a new position in the housing office—director of special programs—created after John Feldkamp failed to find a solution to black students' demands for a separate living space in 1969. She became one of the many black officials who would spend their career at UM helping black students improve their experience on a predominantly white campus. One student described Williams as a mentor to black students and someone who saw her job as something more than a way to pay her bills. When black students came to her asking for help in addressing the racial climate in the dormitories, Williams assisted them in developing Race Awareness Workshops. About fifty to seventy-five people attended each of the five workshops intended to improve race relations.[28]

In the early years after BAM, then, there were positive signs that student activists might be able to achieve significant institutional change without more protest. Inclusion bureaucrats showed that they could implement important changes. Black enrollment almost doubled in just two years, as the university put an unprecedented amount of money into recruiting and financial aid for the Opportunity Program. CULS offered the academic support services that BAM called for. And activists found support from Georgia Williams in creating sensitivity training in campus housing.

As long as inclusion bureaucrats pursued programs and policies that executive administrators supported, black students witnessed institutional change, even if it didn't always fulfill their expectations. Black student activists began to experience the limits of working within the inclusion bureaucracy when they began pushing for changes that executive administrators opposed. The proposals that tried to improve black students' social experience on campus received the greatest level of scrutiny from campus leaders. The obstacles black officials faced in improving the racial climate demonstrate the power executive administrators wielded over the inclusion bureaucracy. The battles would test Fleming's co-optation strategy in the wake of BAM.

BAM activists wanted to continue to fight for initiatives left out of the 1970 concessions. In particular, they believed that white administrators had yet to take black students' social alienation seriously. The rising number of black students that would come to UM as a result of a more aggressive affirmative action program would help address this issue, but black students argued that a larger black student population alone wouldn't solve the problem. Activists wanted physical spaces on campus where black students could briefly escape the overwhelmingly white social and academic environments. University of Michigan president Robben Fleming and the board of regents rejected these appeals during the BAM strike, but black students held out hope that new inclusion officials could help implement these initiatives.

The quick implementation of the Center for Afroamerican and African Studies (CAAS) also likely gave BAM activists a sense of optimism. CAAS institutionalized black studies. As an academic center, CAAS wasn't part of the inclusion bureaucracy, but it clearly showed that black students could force the university to create spaces on campus devoted to serving black students' interests. During the 1970–71 academic year, 1,026 students enrolled in CAAS's degree program, while another 424 took classes offered by CAAS. The center also represented the BAM concession that most closely resembled what sociologist Fabio Rojas calls a "counter center," which he defines as "a formalized place inside mainstream organizations where alternative viewpoints are established." CAAS would serve as a home to faculty who would continue to fight for racial justice within the university. In future years, CAAS faculty produced new research on black students that challenged institutional knowledge and supported future black protests, helping black students organize and put pressure on the administration.[29]

Still, CAAS sheds light on the differences between the leaders of academic centers and inclusion bureaucrats. Although academic units still had to answer to executive administrators, they enjoyed a degree of autonomy from the administration that inclusion bureaucrats did not. Academic units also enjoyed independent budgets, which allowed them to pursue initiatives that administrators might have been uncomfortable with. Inclusion bureaucrats, in contrast, had to appeal to executive administrators to fund their projects. This gave administrators more control over the initiatives inclusion bureaucrats proposed.

When black student activists began calling for reforms to improve the racial climate, they realized just how little power inclusion bureaucrats held. Black activists wanted a black student center. The center had been part of BAM's demands, but the regents refused to make it part of the concessions. Black student activists went to Gilbert Maddox for help. Stephen Spurr, vice president for student affairs, hired Maddox as the special assistant of academic projects after the BAM strike. Maddox's main task was to create new programs to improve black retention rates. Maddox's support for the black student center represented another example of a black official who brought an interpretation of attrition that challenged prevailing assumptions. The leading interpretation of the period continued to see attrition as the product of academic deficiency. In contrast, Maddox believed that black students' social environment on campus helped explain their higher attrition rates, making a direct connection between black students' academic success and the university's racial climate. He believed that the black student center would build a strong sense of cultural identity and help improve retention rates.[30]

Maddox's background likely informed his analysis of attrition and the emphasis he placed on strengthening black students' cultural identity to improve retention. Maddox graduated from Wayne State University in 1951, but only after almost failing out during his first year. After teaching in the Detroit Public School District, Maddox entered graduate school and received his doctorate degree in speech in 1970. Throughout the 1960s, he spent much of his professional life promoting the value of black history and culture. Maddox produced and hosted an eighteen-week black history television and radio series. He also directed plays at the Concept East Theatre, a Detroit theater that targeted a black audience, and hosted and produced *Profiles in Black*, a Detroit public television series that profiled important black leaders.[31]

Maddox went to Spurr, his direct supervisor, to try to get support for the center. Spurr thought Maddox's idea had "a great deal of merit" and endorsed the project as long as black students could still use "conventional services," so that participation in a "racially segregated center" did not become compulsory for black students.[32]

What happened next reveals the degree of oversight campus leaders exercised over the inclusion bureaucracy. Spurr's support, even though he was an executive administrator, wasn't enough. Fleming and the board of regents scrutinized new student services for black students more than other programs. The problem was that Maddox's proposal for a black student center violated one of the prevailing assumptions behind racial inclusion policies at UM since World War II: that interracial contact was vital to improve race relations, as segregation reinforced prejudice. Fleming and the regents still placed great value in this ideal in the early 1970s.

In a world where many campus leaders divided programs into the neat categories of integration and separatism, Maddox faced the burden of showing how a black student center was compatible with the goal of improving race relations between white and black students. To Maddox, the center would give black students a space to develop the racial pride that was necessary to build an integrated society. One racially exclusive space, then, wouldn't prevent meaningful interracial contact at UM. In fact, Maddox suggested, it would improve interracial relationships in all other spaces. Maddox's rationale showed how black officials tried to accommodate white administrators' goals of improving race relations through interracial contact to gain the necessary support for their programs. In the end, improving black students' experience on campus—and, in turn, black retention rates—wasn't enough to justify Maddox's program.[33]

Executive administrators still didn't see the racial climate as a leading cause of black student attrition. CULS, which offered tutoring and special courses, best reflected administrators' understanding of attrition. Academic deficiency led to attrition, administrators thought. A year later, social scientists on campus would provide new studies that supported Maddox's claims about the connection between the racial climate and attrition. Before those studies were available, though, Maddox fought a losing battle in getting administrators to see the student center as a black retention initiative. The hard truth was that black perspectives often needed the support of white social scientists. Black voices needed data, data, and more data. Maddox didn't have any data to support his claims; consequently, he was never able to change the discussion over what was at stake in the student center.[34]

Campus leaders also refused to reconsider their hierarchy of priorities. Building a model multicultural community remained more important than addressing black students' social alienation. Despite Maddox's efforts to show how one racially exclusive space would improve interracial interaction in all other spaces, campus leaders continued to believe that any racially exclusive space—no matter how small—would harm race relations. For the regents, there was no grey area in defining integration and segregation. President Fleming added that Maddox's proposal represented the "kind of separatism which we thought was undesirable." Fleming contended that "gradually, as their numbers increase, I think Black students will feel more comfortable here." "I would hope our Black students would recognize the good faith effort on the University's part," Fleming continued, "and understand that we can't change everything overnight." Fleming recognized that black students faced social problems and that a black student center might help mediate some of those issues. But for Fleming, improving relations between white and black students was more important.[35]

Fleming's comments invited criticism from black students, who were not willing to wait for the gradual change that the president called for. One student called Fleming's argument "alarmingly simplistic." For black students, she contended, coming to the university was like coming to a "foreign, unfriendly country." Like foreign visitors, a variety of social and cultural characteristics, including speech patterns and social conventions, set black students apart at a predominantly white university. African Americans' unique position, the student argued, meant that the university needed to recognize them as a distinct group with different needs. Black students also expressed frustration with the slow pace of institutional change to effectively address their feelings of alienation. "When the University decides to change itself," the black student commented, "it moves like a huge, tired animal. Departments and offices . . . are shaken up a bit and put back a few yards ahead. Old policies and old attitudes slowly peel off like dead skin."[36]

This was the struggle of black officials in the early 1970s, who tried to implement programs that challenged administrators' priorities and preconceptions about improving race relations. Maddox faced an administrative structure that offered him little power and support. As he realized these limitations, Maddox began to question whether campus leaders were committed to any fundamental changes. In 1971, frustrated with the administrative obstacles he faced in supporting black students, Maddox resigned from his position. He then joined with J. Frank Yates, director of CULS, and Charles Kidd, a black professor in Michigan's School of Public Health, to write a scathing opinion piece in UM's student newspaper. The group accused the university of hiring black officials without giving them any power, which represented a "calculated attempt to fool" people "into thinking that great progress is being made." In reality, they argued, black administrators were pawns that only hid executive administrators' apathy for black students' struggles.[37]

Making such a strong accusation might not seem like a pathway into an administrative position, but incorporating dissent into the inclusion bureaucracy became a tool to try to show that campus leaders were committed to addressing black students' concerns. Six days after the letter was published, Charles Kidd accepted the position of assistant vice president for student affairs. Suddenly, Kidd was the highest-ranking black official at UM. Kidd had spent the late 1960s and early 1970s as a student activist at UM while working toward his PhD in environmental engineering. In 1971, he was a newly minted faculty member in the School of Public Health and planned to leave the university for a better job.[38] But the offer to implement the victories of the BAM strike, a strike that he had been a part of, convinced him to stay. Over the objections of his family, Kidd "succumbed to my desire to get further involved because I believed I could affect some change."[39]

Despite Maddox's experience with the regents, building a black student center became one of Kidd's primary goals. Kidd didn't think he could get the regents to change their position. He knew, if given the chance, the board would squash the project, so creating the center became an exercise in political maneuvering. The regents had ruled that university funds couldn't be used to create the center. Kidd thought that this left open an opportunity to establish a black student center with private funds. As he searched for alternatives, he came across the Martin Luther King Memorial Fund, a private scholarship fund set up in 1968 after black students chained the doors of the Administrative Building shut. In order to circumvent the regents, Kidd received a grant from the MLK fund to purchase a building and finance UM's first black student center.[40]

In the summer of 1971, students learned about the new Trotter House, a three-story, fifteen-room building on Michigan's campus. Kidd named the house after William Monroe Trotter. Trotter was one of the most vocal and famous civil rights activists of the late nineteenth and early twentieth centuries. In 1901, he founded the *Boston Guardian*—a newspaper that focused on the battle for black equality. He was a cofounder of the Niagara Movement, an ardent opponent of Booker T. Washington, and an uncompromising writer and activist. Kidd didn't advertise Trotter's background. In fact, when one executive officer asked him who William Monroe Trotter was, Kidd didn't tell him because he feared that Trotter's background might undermine the house.[41]

The building eventually housed counselors for black students; meeting rooms for black student organizations; and spaces for social events, exhibits, and lectures. Without the need to get funding and approval from executive administrators, he didn't need to reframe the purpose of the Trotter House to appeal to campus leaders' priorities and values. Instead, Kidd focused on the value of the center for black students, rather than emphasizing how the center could improve race relations. The Trotter House, Kidd stated explicitly, was for black students to create a central location to hold social and cultural events relevant to African Americans. Kidd hoped the Trotter House would foster "better unity amongst the Black community." The house did not accommodate members of other racial groups because, according to Kidd, "different groups would demand different things to create a home-like atmosphere."[42]

The obstacles Kidd had to maneuver to win the Trotter House highlights executive administrators' efforts to control the inclusion bureaucracy. Even when an inclusion official successfully circumvented executive administrators, the victory still felt fragile. The Trotter House occupied a tenuous position on campus, dependent on private funds and operating without the full support of executive administrators.

Black student activists trying to work within the inclusion bureaucracy to change housing policies never found a solution like the Trotter House, which circumvented executive administrators. Black students identified campus housing as a principal contributor to the poor racial climate. These were spaces where black students experienced regular incidents of racism and feelings of social isolation, as some black students lived on floors without another black student in sight. In other spaces, there were ways to create informal black communities. Black students might eat together, for example, in a campus cafeteria filled with white students. But housing spaces felt more fixed, harder to transform. Students were assigned to a space with another person, after all.[43]

Black students initially turned to Georgia Williams, the housing official who had helped black students create racial sensitivity training. Black student activists saw few positive results from the sensitivity training. They found that the white students who had shown up to the voluntary sessions weren't the ones who needed it the most. When students lost faith in racial sensitivity training, they called for more ambitious reforms, which led to another showdown between black officials and the board of regents. In December 1971, not long after the Trotter House opened on campus, a group of black women living in Stockwell Hall, led by Gayle Nelson, and members of the South Quad Minority Council, led by Lee Gill, began a campaign for an all-black living corridor within a UM dormitory building. They justified the living unit by citing "gross inequities," "dehumanizing" conditions, and "double standards" within Michigan's student housing. The university's color-blind housing policies, Nelson claimed, impeded black students' "psychological, sociological and intellectual development" by forcing them to live with white students. An all-black corridor would offer a form of protection against the realities of living in a predominantly white dormitory.[44]

Gill later called the original proposal for a racially exclusive living unit "part of being naïve and not understanding the political process" at UM. Gill and Nelson soon understood that the board of regents would not approve racially exclusive spaces in university dorms. Getting around this problem would not be as easy as Kidd's solution for a black student center, which took advantage of private funds to purchase a building for black students' use. Gill and Nelson were dealing with spaces in university-owned buildings, where first-year students were strongly encouraged to live. They also faced an important legal obstacle. In 1969, the Department of Health, Education, and Welfare sent a memo to universities receiving federal funds, clarifying whether university housing allotted by race was compatible with Title VI of the Civil Rights Act of 1964. The simple answer was no. The memo concluded, "All housing which is owned, operated or supported by the institution . . . must be made available to all students without regard to race."[45]

Williams helped students carefully craft their new proposal in order to avoid claims of intentional segregation while still fulfilling their goal of living in a community with other black students interested in cultivating racial pride. They proposed Afro-American and African Cultural Living Units, which they described as spaces with "an educational, cultural, and social identity with Afro-American and African life-styles," leaving open the possibility that white students could also live there. For a model, they used existing housing communities at UM where students chose to live together because of common interests, such as learning a foreign language. Anticipating claims that the students would only choose other black students to live in the units, drafters of the proposal created selection methods that they saw as being color blind.

To live in the units, applicants would have to meet at least three of five requirements:

1. Participation in Afro-American and African courses.
2. Participation in educational, social, or cultural activities designed to promote better multi-ethnic sensitivity and understanding.
3. Participation in experiences, which were designed to promote more positive race relations.
4. Living experience in a multi-ethnic environment.
5. Human relations skills for the implementation of the goals and objectives of the Afro-American and African Cultural Living Unit, namely designing and implementing activities which will promote educational, cultural, and social identity with Afro-American and African life styles.

Williams and the students believed that the criteria provided a color-blind method for selecting students that would help avoid claims of intentional segregation.[46]

It's unclear whether Williams and the students found inspiration for this proposal from other institutions. Northwestern University, for example, had come up with a similar solution when HEW told the university that its plan to create a racially exclusive housing unit violated civil rights laws. Also, recall that John Feldkamp's 1969 proposal took a similar approach, emphasizing cultural affinity, not race. Organizing housing spaces around a shared interest in black culture offered a way around claims that the university violated the law by taking race into account in allotting housing space.[47]

Georgia Williams and the staff of the housing office started the application process to prove that white students would live in the corridor. They found that many white students wanted to live in the space. The housing office accepted 103 students to live in the unit, of which 30 were white. Williams and the students used this evidence to show that black students had no intention of segregating themselves.[48]

The university's legal counsel, R. K. Daane, still wasn't convinced that the units would comply with civil rights laws. Daane believed that the living units were actually intended only for black students, and that de facto segregation would emerge despite the color-blind language of the proposal. He warned that if the units did become segregated, then the university would face "an entire galaxy of legal problems ranging from equal protection and freedom of association to the more arcane questions arising under the 1964 and 1968 Federal Civil Rights Acts and the Fair Housing Act." Daane feared that using race as a factor in the selection process offered the only way to ensure that the units would be multiracial; otherwise, the units had the potential to become entirely black. But Daane warned that using race as a factor in selection, even to create a multiracial unit, could invite potential lawsuits. The regents, then, would have to weigh Daane's interpretation of the law and his assumptions about the intentions of black students against Williams's evidence that the units could sustain their multiracial character.[49]

If Fleming and the regents were looking for a legal opinion that countered R. K. Daane's, they could find support from the Michigan Civil Rights Commission. The commission, created in 1963 as part of the state's new constitution to investigate claims of discrimination based on "religion, race, color or national origin," endorsed the legal merits of the living unit.[50] The ACLU joined the Michigan Civil Rights Commission, as did the Detroit Urban League and the Michigan Democratic Black Caucus.[51]

Civil rights laws represented just one obstacle. Williams and the students also needed to show that the living unit was compatible with the administration's goal of creating a model multiracial community. An early rationale suggested that the units were necessary to protect black students from the psychological damage they experienced when forced to live in and occupy white-majority spaces. But students eventually realized that in order to gain support from UM's executive administrators, they needed to show that the living units would lead to better race relations. Lee Gill wrote in UM's student newspaper that if black students wanted to segregate themselves, they would have chosen a facility on the outskirts of campus. Instead, they chose a space on the middle floors of the South Quad complex in the heart of campus, "because we did not want to be isolated or segregated, but wanted to be in a place where interaction and involvement was guaranteed." According to Gill, after black students developed a "Black consciousness," students and staff in the housing unit would lead "outreach activities," which "would bring minority people into interactions with the majority to promote greater understanding and more livable co-existence with each other." This justification mirrored Maddox's rationale for a black student center.[52]

The final proposal in March showed how executive administrators' priorities, which privileged addressing white prejudice over addressing black students' social alienation, continued to influence black students' proposal. Williams and the black students were more explicit about how the living units would support the model multiracial community. They didn't abandon the language of their original proposal, which laid out the benefits the units would offer to black students. But they also proposed programs that they hoped would address the board of regents' interest in improving relationships between black and white students. The proposal included weekly race awareness workshops, forums, and seminars for students living in the units, designed to build "racial understanding, individually and culturally." It pitched the living units as a place where white and black students could learn to live with "different races and cultures."[53]

The new rationale for the living units appealed to administrators' interests by bringing the ideal of cultural diversity—which suggested that learning to value cultural differences could lead to better race relations—into the conversation about the meaning and purpose of racial inclusion. This rationale also resonated with many students on campus. Michigan's Student Government Council, for example, supported the living units by arguing that the administration's color-blind housing policies more closely resembled segregation than did black students' proposal. "Black and White students," the council reported, "eat at separate tables, use separate lounges, have separate governments, attend separate parties, and, in short, live separate, segregated lives." Two African American students in a corridor dominated by white students "is hardly a real integration of the two cultures." In contrast, the council thought that black students' proposal represented a more legitimate attempt at integration, in which white and black students would live together and "work out the difficult problems of mutual racism and cultural difference."[54]

However, Williams and the black students quickly found a problem with using diversity as a rationale for the living spaces. The members of the Michigan community who were attracted to this new language focused exclusively on diversity's potential to improve race relations, ignoring the fact that black students were using diversity language to justify programs that addressed their feelings of social alienation and to gain more power over the spaces they inhabited. Throughout spring 1972, the black students who advocated for the living units continued to remind administrators and fellow students that one of the purposes of the living units was for African Americans to "gain a greater knowledge of themselves," which would "increase [black students'] psychological, sociological and intellectual development." But it was clear that black students were losing control and ownership of the meaning and purpose of diversity.[55]

Black students also found that one of the unintended consequences of this language was that it offered a new intellectual framework to those white students who opposed black spaces. Before the introduction of the diversity framework, most students and administrators at UM saw segregation as a problem because it perpetuated white prejudice, harming African Americans. Diversity rhetoric, which promoted the benefits of interracial interaction for white and black students, helped some white students see themselves as the victims of racially exclusive spaces. A group of female students living in Bush House of South Quad, for example, argued that the black students promoting the living units were actually trying to create a segregated living unit. The Bush House contingent viewed this as a problem because they saw contact with members of different ethnic and racial groups as part of the educational experience provided by dormitory living that allowed the student to "grow as a person." They emphasized the fact that few students had had much contact with members of different racial groups before coming to Michigan. So part of the valuable educational experience offered by dormitory living, they argued, was "to provide the student with the opportunity to come into contact with other people from a variety of cultural, racial, and religious environments and backgrounds." These students used diversity language to communicate a new value in interracial contact: that white students' interaction with students of different racial and ethnic groups was an important experience that they were entitled to. Diversity language, then, helped white students see any attempt to take their access to students of color away as harmful to whites' education.[56]

As white students shifted their attention away from how the living units would benefit black students, one black official tried to refocus the discussion to get administrators to see the connection between the racial climate and black student retention. In March 1972, as the board of regents was set to rule on the proposal, Kidd suggested that it would be wise to remember that academic failure did not explain the high attrition rates of black students. Like Maddox, Kidd argued that black students' "inability to adjust to the university environment" due to the "drastic change from urban ghetto life to a large predominantly white university" explained the attrition rates. Kidd was trying to frame the living units as a retention initiative rather than a program that had to prove whether it would improve race relations. Just like Maddox, Kidd faced administrators who were reluctant to change their assumption that academic deficiency represented the key explanation for attrition. The first internal social science data that supported Kidd's argument was still eight months away. Black officials rarely overturned the long-held assumptions of white administrators without the help of social scientists.[57]

The proponents of the living units still saw some hope by late spring 1972. Their proposal pushed Fleming to modify his understanding of separatism. Just a year earlier, Fleming had called a black student center the "kind of separatism which we thought was undesirable," but the efforts of Williams and the students to guarantee that the units would be multiracial made Fleming stop and think. The proposal didn't fit neatly into what seemed to be the simple categories of integration and segregation. He struggled with the decision for months. He read the opinions of the various civil rights groups who wrote to him with advice. In the end, despite the fact that the units would be predominantly black, Fleming decided to support the living units. He pointed out that many of the housing units on campus were overwhelmingly white, but none of the critics of the proposal questioned whether they were segregated. "Is 95 per cent white segregated?" Fleming asked. "Or is it 90 per cent or 70 per cent? We don't really know. When our dorms are 95 per cent white . . . we haven't called it that." He suggested that critics of the proposal were applying a different standard of integration to the black students' proposal, since most white students were able to live together on campus without any questions from the university's legal counsel.[58]

What happened next further reveals the obstacles inclusion bureaucrats faced in implementing initiatives. Williams and the black student activists had gained the support of the president of the university, but even that wasn't enough; the regents would still have to vote on the living units' fate. Few initiatives on campus received this type of scrutiny, but the volatile issue of race and campus space ensured that inclusion initiatives had to run the gauntlet of the university bureaucracy.

The regents voted unanimously against the living units. Although the housing office had already completed the application process for the living units and could show board members that 103 students—73 black and 30 white— were accepted, several regents argued that the housing office could not guarantee that the living units would not become de facto segregated in the future.[59] Regent Gerald Dunn made it clear that he "didn't want us as a public body to go on record in support of segregation of any kind." Regent Lawrence Lindemer went further in calling the proposal "among the most counter-productive moves suggested on the University campus in a long time." The regents then unanimously supported a resolution recognizing that although "there are serious academic, counseling, and living problems for minority students on campus," the "Regents do not approve the proposal for Afro-American and African Cultural Living Units."[60]

In place of the living units, the regents approved the African American Cultural Lounge in South Quad. Stocked with books about black history and adorned with African-themed murals painted by CAAS instructor and professional artist Jon Onye Lockard, the lounge became an important space on campus for black students to socialize and hold meetings. But the lounge was still a far cry from the living units.[61]

Georgia Williams continued to argue that the living units represented the best way the housing office could support black students, but the resistance of the board of regents limited the solutions Williams could pursue. In the end, Williams abandoned the fight for new living units and created a diversity training program in the dormitories—the same type of program black students had initiated with Williams and abandoned because they were ineffective. Williams described Project Awareness as a sensitivity training program developed for "students and staff to gain a knowledge of dealing with different races and cultures" and the "problems . . . arising because of differences." Project Awareness included a variety of programs meant to introduce students to different cultures and to teach students how to live in racially integrated spaces. For example, students in Mosher-Jordan Hall, one of Michigan's dormitories, watched *Black History: Lost, Stolen or Strayed* narrated by Bill Cosby. The film explained the importance of racial identity to African Americans and showed the lengths that they went through to assimilate into the white world. Students in Couzens Hall attended the talk "Black Language—Fact or Fiction," in addition to participating in an interracial dance and events organized around black art, food, and beauty.[62]

The frustration black officials felt in trying to improve the racial climate led to turnover within the inclusion bureaucracy. Fighting to change an institution from low- and mid-level positions without the support of campus leaders proved taxing. Black officials, like Williams, often came into the institution with grand ambitions and optimism that they could transform UM to meet the needs of black students. But they soon found out that most of their grand visions would be met with strong resistance and left their positions frustrated and disillusioned. Williams soon resigned. Regular turnover among black officials proved problematic in trying to advance black students' goals over the long term. Some of the black students' strongest allies left within a year of taking a management position; others didn't last much longer. Students would struggle in the future to find a stable set of black allies in staff positions who could help lead institutional reforms.[63]

The problem didn't stop there. In the aftermath of the living unit struggle, administrators implemented a new hiring strategy that helped executive administrators gain tighter control over the inclusion bureaucracy. Many of the black officials hired in the late 1960s and early 1970s tried to help black students advance initiatives that made executive administrators uncomfortable. This led some administrators to become more careful in vetting the views of future black officials. As the students fought for the living units, the university was searching for a new vice president for student affairs. The university hired Henry Johnson, the first African American to hold a position in the president's executive cabinet. But Johnson was no great victory for black activists. In Johnson, the university hired a black administrator who supported the regents' vision of inclusion. Johnson immediately stated his opposition to the living unit. "There is no future for Blacks in the area of separatism," he stated.[64]

Henry Johnson also helped administrators co-opt black students' vision of cultural diversity. "A diverse Black population within the predominantly white institution," Johnson contended, "can offer a mutual learning experience—of great value to the Black student community" and "of great value to the white community as well. The interchange of experience can benefit us all." Johnson's comments shed light on what black students lost in the early 1970s. Diversity became a central framework for university administrators in their efforts to improve race relations, but missing in the diversity language was how it would address black students' social alienation on campus. What began as a tool for black students to gain more control of their social environment was transformed into a new administrative vision to create the multiracial community. Diversity in administrators' hands helped officials take control of the meaning of inclusion.[65]

Despite all that black students had lost in addressing social alienation and gaining some control over living spaces, there were no signs of a renewed black protest movement in 1972. For Fleming, the absence of disruptive protest represented the measure of co-optation's success. Campus leaders managed to retain control over campus priorities and values, ensuring that the model multiracial community remained more important than reforms that would address black students' social alienation on campus. Black students might have been unhappy about that, but the fact that Fleming came to work every day without having to call the police to arrest protesters was a sign that co-optation was working.

In spring 1973, black students received more bad news. Enrollment projections for the 1973–74 academic year showed that black enrollment would fall well short of the BAM concessions. The university had agreed to the goal of raising black enrollment to 10 percent of the student body by fall 1973. As admissions officials began sending out rejection and acceptance letters, they projected that black students would comprise between 8.5 and 9 percent of the student body.[66]

University officials rushed to explain the university's innocence in failing to meet the BAM enrollment goal. Declining resources became a favorite explanation. State appropriations to UM declined in the early 1970s, which made it more difficult to fund supportive services programs and generous financial aid packages. According to the admissions office, the funding shortage also made it more difficult to compete with other in-state institutions that began to offer generous merit-based packages for black students with high standardized test scores.[67] Others blamed the pool of "qualified" black students. In explaining the failure to meet the 10 percent goal, Pat Wilson, an undergraduate admissions counselor, explained that UM "is a selective institution. . . . We cannot and will not take every minority student who applies." Here Wilson suggested that the admissions office was innocent because it was protecting the university's elite status. There simply weren't enough "qualified" black students to admit. The alternative, according to Wilson, was admitting "unqualified" black students and compromising the university's selectivity. Admissions officials didn't simply see themselves as gatekeepers; they saw themselves as protectors—protectors of the university's reputation.[68]

The assumption that black students left UM before graduating because of academic deficiency supported the narrative of racial innocence. This assumption only led to the conclusion that straying even further from the traditional admissions tools to admit black students would simply increase attrition rates. The university had put an unprecedented amount of money into academic support services for black students after the BAM strike. CULS offered tutoring and even separate introductory courses for minority students. If black students couldn't succeed with these resources, the popular argument went, what else could the university do?[69]

As officials tried to explain the university's innocence, Fleming revealed how racial disparities also offered a tool to show potential donors that BAM didn't compromise the university's elite status. Standing in front of a crowd of four hundred spectators at the Economic Club of Detroit, he claimed that coming up short of the BAM goal revealed that the university "did not, as some people thought, abandon all admissions standards." One way to view Fleming's speech is as a response tailored to a key constituency in order to defend affirmative action. The university relied even more on donors, many of whom opposed or were skeptical of affirmative action, especially as state appropriations declined. Clearly black campus activists weren't the only constituency that Fleming had to respond to in the early 1970s. But this perspective overlooks how university officials contributed to donors' perspective that few black students were academically prepared to compete at Michigan University.[70]

As university officials rushed to explain why UM didn't meet the BAM enrollment goal, they kept vital information from the public about why black students left the university before graduating. Missing from university officials' assessment of attrition was new internal evidence that showed that most of the black students who left before graduating were in good academic standing. These studies began circulating internally in November 1972 and social scientists continued to find similar results in 1973. One study, conducted by Ruth Eckstein, found that half of the OP students who dropped out were in good academic standing (2.0 GPA or above). Even among black OP students who had earned a GPA of 3.0 or above, 22 percent still left the university without a diploma.[71] Eckstein's study made an immediate impact on administrators' views of attrition. Her research reached the top levels of the university, with university president Robben Fleming expressing alarm at the fact that 50 percent of OP students who left the university were in good academic standing. Mirroring Maddox's claims, Fleming now argued that the university's counseling services, "which have concentrated largely on students having academic problems, have not adequately addressed non-academic problems." As executive administrators admitted that their long-held assumptions were probably wrong, they commissioned more studies on attrition. Chuck Woodward, who conducted one of these studies, agreed that nonacademic factors were primarily responsible for OP attrition. After interviewing twelve staff members who worked with OP students, he concluded that "below-the-surface" factors better explained the high attrition rates of OP students than did academic failure.[72]

Another researcher found that social alienation was especially important in understanding why minority women left the university before graduating. The researcher found that 50 percent of minority women in the Opportunity Program and 73 percent of those enrolled outside the program left UM voluntarily before graduating—meaning that their academic records hadn't forced them out of the university. In comparison, 36 percent of minority men in the program and 46 percent enrolled outside the program withdrew voluntarily. Despite these findings, the unique struggles black women faced on campus remained outside the scope of most studies. The striking fact about administrators' understanding of race is that while they often recognized the intersections between race and class, they rarely recognized the intersections between race and gender in evaluating black students' experiences on campus. Still, studies like this continued to show administrators that the racial climate played an important factor in black student attrition.[73]

Despite the fact that Fleming admitted that the university's assumptions about attrition were likely wrong, UM officials never used these studies to explain to the public why the university failed to meet the BAM enrollment goal. The public continued to receive messages about black student deficiencies. UM officials likely worried about the consequences that the new attrition data would have on their co-optation strategy. Racial innocence had long been a strategy in deflecting criticism and curtailing disruptive protest with broad campus support. Highlighting black student deficiencies worked seamlessly with the narrative of racial innocence, while studies that blamed the university's racial climate held UM officials responsible for racial disparities. That knowledge could have sparked a new campus strike. It could have also provided ammunition for a new fight for black living units.

This lack of transparency had serious consequences for black students and the future of affirmative action. UM officials talked openly about the fact that black students scored lower on standardized test scores and suggested that black student attrition rates were twice as high as whites because of black students' academic deficiency. These public comments and data added fuel to the fire of white backlash and anti-affirmative action forces. In contrast, the data and social science reports that vindicated black students' academic performance at UM found a place in office file cabinets and internal memos. Officials never communicated the new findings to the public. University officials can never be seen as the victims of white backlash when evaluating the limits that white resistance placed on affirmative action programs. They contributed to this backlash and then saw themselves as champions of racial inclusion when they defended the merits of affirmative action against critics.

If Fleming measured the success of co-optation by the lack of confrontational protest, then hiding attrition data paid off. The administration had failed to meet the most important and visible BAM concession. Even worse, the projections for black enrollment for fall 1973 were too generous. When students arrived on campus, black enrollment stood at 7.3 percent, more than a percentage point below early projections. And yet Fleming could look calmly outside his office window and see no sign of another campus uprising. That was more important to Fleming than telling the public the truth about black student performance.[74]

If the failure to meet the BAM concessions disappointed black students, the outcomes of affirmative action hiring further revealed the limits of the inclusion bureaucracy in changing the institution. Black students had long connected the small number of black faculty members to the poor racial climate. Affirmative action hiring didn't make it into BAM's demands, but mention of the small number of black faculty members filled activists' critique of the institution. Perhaps that's why Fleming included affirmative action hiring in his plan to implement the BAM concessions. Fleming, though, didn't create a full-time director position immediately after the strike. Instead, he planned to hire a part-time staff member to help departments find prospective black faculty, issue a statement urging departments to "pursue [Black faculty] vigorously," and ask departments to create reports on the efforts they made to recruit and hire black faculty. Still, there was no plan to create incentives or consequences to motivate departments to improve affirmative action hiring efforts.[75]

Fleming didn't create a full-time position to oversee affirmative action hiring until black students received help from white women, who pushed university leaders to make more significant reform. A month after BAM final-ized negotiations with Fleming, FOCUS on Equal Employment for Women—an Ann Arbor group that included many UM faculty and staff—filed a sex discrimination complaint against the university with HEW. In previous years, the civil rights victories of the 1960s had frustrated many feminist activists working in higher education. Title VI of the Civil Rights Act of 1964, which precluded discrimination in educational institutions receiving federal con-tracts, did not cover sex discrimination. Title VII, which dealt with hiring practices specifically and *did* protect women, excluded certain employee clas-sifications, making it difficult for faculty members to use it. But new opportu-nities arose in January 1970 when Bernice Sadler, an activist working with the Women's Equity Action League, used Executive Order 11375 to file a com-plaint with HEW arguing that there was an industry-wide pattern of sex dis-crimination within higher education and requesting that the agency conduct compliance reviews of all universities and colleges receiving federal contracts. The executive order amended Executive Order 11246—President Johnson's previous order prohibiting federal contractors from discriminating based on race, religion, and national origin—to include sex discrimination. The strategy quickly spread. Not long after Sandler's complaint, the National Organization for Women filed a sex discrimination complaint against Harvard University under Executive Order 11375, which resulted in the first HEW investigation into a university's discrimination against women.[76]

Just a month after the conclusion of the BAM strike, FOCUS brought this strategy to Ann Arbor, when the group filed a discrimination complaint against the University of Michigan. The Chicago HEW office sent a team of investiga-tors to UM at the end of August. Two days later, Don Scott, who headed the investigation, informed Fleming that the university was engaged in discrimi-nation against women and offered a plan to address that discrimination. The plan included back pay for lost wages due to discrimination and a salary equity plan in all job categories. It also called for an affirmative action promotion plan for women in the university. Fleming resisted these changes, which culmi-nated in HEW's decision to withhold new federal contracts from UM, resulting in the loss of $7.5 to $15 million. Fleming continued to resist until January 1971, when a slate of UM's federal contracts was set for renewal. Finally, Fleming settled with HEW, which resulted in several commitments, including salary equity between male and female employees in the same classification, pay-ment of back wages lost to discrimination since October 1968, and priority con-sideration for women in clerical or nonacademic positions for promotions.[77]

The threat HEW posed to UM's federal contracts represented a new era of federal compliance at UM. University officials saw HEW bureaucrats as more of a nuisance than a threat in the 1960s. But when HEW strengthened its enforcement, losing federal contracts suddenly became real, and UM officials began taking federal compliance more seriously. Even so, it would take another year and a half for the university to create a special position to help the university comply with federal discrimination laws, including racial discrimination. Nellie Varner, who created the university's first black studies program, became the university's first director of affirmative action in September 1972.[78]

Varner's position, though, didn't come with the authority necessary to transform hiring practices at Michigan. She never had the power to hold the people who made hiring decisions accountable for following affirmative action hiring guidelines. Executive administrators never intended to take any power away from individual departments in making hiring decisions, even if that meant few women and minorities were hired in faculty positions. Just as administrators believed the university's status was tied to bringing the "best" students to campus, they also believed UM's status was tied to hiring the most accomplished faculty. Therefore, the admissions office was supposed to protect the university's status, much like individual departments were supposed to protect the university's reputation through their hiring choices. The same types of fears about affirmative action admissions, then, framed executive administrators' resistance to holding people accountable for affirmative action hiring. Given those constraints, Varner went to work improving data-gathering mechanisms and educating departments about their affirmative action responsibilities. By 1974, Varner could claim little success. Between 1972 and 1974, female minority representation on the faculty stayed stagnant. Male minority faculty representation showed small gains, rising at the assistant professor rank from 4.6 to 5.7 percent, at the associate professor rank from 6.2 to 7.4 percent, and at the professor rank from 3.1 to 3.4 percent.[79]

In January 1975, Jewell Cobb's nomination as dean of LSA represented the ultimate test of Nellie Varner and her affirmative action office's efforts to educate the university community on their affirmative action duties. When Frank Rhodes was promoted from LSA dean to vice president for academic affairs, a black woman rose to the top of the applicant pool to replace him. At the time, Jewell Cobb was dean at Connecticut College, where she had developed a reputation as a strong advocate for black students. The problem was that Cobb wasn't Fleming's first choice. Fleming preferred Billy Frye, who had become associate dean of LSA two years earlier and was currently serving as interim dean.[80]

Despite Fleming's preference for Frye, the search committee recommended Cobb. The regents quickly approved the committee's decision. However, the zoology department refused to give her tenure. Although administrators, such as deans, don't typically teach courses, they still expect tenure in an academic department. The reason is obvious: tenure in a department gives an administrator job security. If Cobb's contract as dean wasn't renewed, she could stay at UM and teach in the zoology department.[81]

Zoology faculty claimed that they denied her tenure because of deficiencies in her scholarship. The truth was that the zoology department had a long history of resisting affirmative action. Recall the 1966 survey of departments' affirmative action hiring and graduate student recruiting practices covered in chapter 2. The survey offended a few department chairs so much that they attached letters opposing affirmative action. One of those letters came from the chair of the zoology department, who wrote that special recruiting practices for black students and faculty were "contrary to my own ideas as well as those of my colleagues." To add to the problem, zoology was also Billy Frye's home department.[82]

The case showed how executive leaders at UM enabled departments, such as zoology, to resist black candidates. The decentralized management structure gave individual departments the power to hire and nominate faculty for tenure. Fleming claimed he had no authority over academic departments' decisions, but it was a constraint he created for himself. No thought went into how to overcome decentralization. During the Fleming administration, decentralization was taken as a given, even if that meant affirmative action hiring goals were rarely fulfilled. In the future, UM presidents would commit to hiring more black faculty, and administrators would find that there were many tools they could use to push departments to fulfill affirmative action goals. In the 1970s, though, Fleming used decentralization as an excuse. He was trapped by the decision of the zoology department. In other words, decentralization supported executive administrators' narrative of racial innocence and helped hide the fact that Fleming's preference for a different candidate likely aided his inaction.[83]

Fleming called Cobb with the news, offering her a two-year contract without tenure. It was another disappointing experience at UM for Cobb. She had first come to the University of Michigan as an undergraduate in 1941. She quickly learned about the university's poor racial climate after being assigned to live in a racially segregated league house off campus. She recounted that once she arrived, she "was never allowed in the mainstream of social life on campus." Cobb transferred to Talladega College after her first year. Now, more than thirty years later, she found herself again feeling unwelcome at the University of Michigan.[84]

Word quickly circulated about the university's offer to Cobb. Betty Morrison, a black education professor at UM, told a reporter, "To call [the offer] insulting is almost too mild."[85] George Goodman, who began his career at the university as the Opportunity Program's admissions counselor and by 1975 was the program's director, called the administration's offer to Cobb a "personal affront to every responsible minority person."[86] Anonymous sources began telling *Michigan Daily* reporters that Fleming was deliberately derailing Cobb's appointment in order to support his first choice, Billy Frye. Two hundred students, faculty members, and university officials protested outside the Administration Building.[87]

Fleming wouldn't budge. Nobody in the executive administration tried to get the zoology department to reconsider. Cobb finally declined the offer after negotiating for about two weeks. To no one's surprise, Fleming's top choice, Billy Frye, got the job.[88]

In the aftermath, an internal investigation committee blasted Fleming and the zoology department. The committee reported that the zoology department's process of reviewing Cobb's merits and denying her tenure took only twenty-four hours. Zoology faculty only had some of Cobb's publications, and Cobb was never consulted about which publications she felt were most significant. The department never invited her to give a presentation of her research. In fact, nobody in the zoology department ever contacted Cobb to ask her anything. The committee concluded that the zoology department's decision to deny Cobb tenure simply allowed Fleming to move ahead with Frye's candidacy. Regional HEW officials tried to withhold a large federal grant in response to the university's unusual offer to Cobb, but the agency's top leaders overturned the decision.[89]

The incident represented a great loss for Varner, demonstrating the limited impact she had made in her time at UM. To add insult to injury, her office had to refocus on convincing the federal government that UM was in full compliance with affirmative action laws. HEW still hadn't approved the university's affirmative action plan. Finally, in February 1976, Varner's plan gained HEW's approval. It must have been a pyrrhic victory for her. She successfully accomplished what her supervisors most wanted from her—the federal government's approval of an affirmative action plan so that the university's federal contracts were secure. But she failed to make the type of impact on hiring practices that she had hoped for when she took the position. Like so many black administrators, she left her position in frustration, resigning the month after HEW accepted the affirmative action plan.[90]

The demonstration outside the administration building in response to Fleming's offer to Cobb was brief and unorganized. Again, Fleming must have thought that co-optation was working. Black discontent over affirmative action hiring didn't translate into disruptive protest that could challenge Fleming's inclusion policies. A month later, though, he saw the first sign that another campus movement might be brewing that could undermine his control of inclusion.

By February 1975, Fleming's co-optation strategy had survived for years without another black campus strike. Despite failing to meet the BAM enrollment goal, resisting black students' efforts to address the racial climate, and playing a visible role in undermining Cobb's candidacy, Fleming didn't see the signs of an emerging black campus protest. But suddenly in February 1975, he found a large group of student activists occupying the Administration Building, calling for new ambitious racial justice reforms. But this time, the students in the building looked different. Alongside the black students, Chicano, Asian American, and Native American students filled the rooms of the building.

The BAM strike had ignited activism among nonblack minority groups who wanted to build on black students' victories. Chicano, Native American, and Asian American students believed that black students were reaping the rewards of racial inclusion, while other minorities were left behind. As black student organizing began to decline after BAM, these minority groups provided the energy behind a new wave of activism that eventually led to the 1975 building occupation.

Especially concerning to nonblack minority groups were their small numbers in the Opportunity Program. From fall 1964 to 1969, 669 new black students entered UM through OP. In the same period, 8 Chicano, 6 Asian American, and 2 Native American students gained access through the program. To put this into perspective, 124 white students were admitted as Opportunity Program students in the 1960s. This meant that the vast majority of nonblack students entered UM through the traditional admissions process and without the financial and support services of OP. For example, in fall 1968, about 99.4 percent of Native American students, 96.2 percent of Asian American students, and 68.8 percent of Spanish-surname students gained admission to UM without the benefits of OP. In contrast, only 40 percent of black undergraduates were enrolled outside OP in 1968.[91]

Chicano students were in the best position to gain better access to OP in the aftermath of the BAM strike. Second to African Americans, they were the best organized group on campus and the only nonblack minority group to win any concessions in the BAM strike. Recall that Fleming agreed to hire a Chicano recruiter and pursue the goal of enrolling at least fifty Chicano students by the fall semester of 1970. After the strike, to fulfill the concession made to Chicano students, the admissions office hired Raymond Padilla—the leader of the campus protest group Chicanos of Michigan—as an admissions counselor.

According to Padilla, admissions officials didn't know about his activist past when he was hired, and Padilla certainly didn't offer the information in his interview. Once he got the job, he tried to advance the concessions he had won as an activist from within the admissions office.[92]

Padilla went to work establishing connections with Chicano communities in Michigan. Thus far, OP recruiters had focused on predominantly black high schools. Now Padilla started traveling to predominantly Chicano high schools and distributing bilingual recruiting pamphlets about OP across the state. He also created a program that reclassified the children of migrant workers as in-state students, broadening the number of Chicano students who could access the Opportunity Program. To qualify, an applicant's parents had to have worked in the state of Michigan during three of the previous five years. These initiatives had an obvious impact. Between 1964 and 1969, only 8 OP students had Spanish surnames. In 1972, under Padilla's direction, 70 students with Spanish surnames were enrolled in the program. By 1974, that number had jumped to 124.[93]

Administrators put up more obstacles for groups not included in the BAM concessions. The BAM concessions, in administrators' eyes, had already stretched the university's budget too far. Now they tried to ensure that demands from other minority groups would not stretch the budget even further. Native American and Asian American students faced an uphill battle.

The small number of Native American students made it difficult to exert pressure on the administration. During the 1970–71 academic year, there were 41 Native American undergraduate students on campus. That meant that they constituted 0.2 percent of the undergraduate student body that year. In comparison, 732 black undergraduate students (3.8 percent) walked onto campus in fall 1970. Yet that didn't stop Paul Johnson from making demands on UM administrators to improve Native Americans' access. Johnson was a UM graduate student in the early 1970s and the associate director of the Great Lakes Indian Youth Alliance—an organization that fought for educational opportunities for Native Americans. He found a part-time job as a graduate assistant in the admissions office to help fund his graduate work and was able to use some of his time recruiting Native American students. But Johnson knew that the little time he was allowed to spend on recruiting efforts was woefully inadequate to improve access for Native Americans.[94]

In May 1971, Johnson submitted a proposal to the regents that made a series of recommendations to improve the university's commitment to Native Americans. First, he wanted a full-time Native American recruiter in the Opportunity Program. Second, because Johnson believed that OP's focus on in-state students limited Native Americans' opportunities, he wanted the university to fund out-of-state recruiting. There were only thirty thousand Native Americans in the state of Michigan, which made for a small recruiting pool. But the issue of out-of-state recruitment meant more than expanding the pool. "Not only is the limited number of Indians a rationale for out of state recruiting," Johnson argued, "but Indian people did not draw any state or territorial boundaries; non-Indians did after stealing the country from its original inhabitants." Limiting the OP program to in-state students, he suggested, only served as another tool whites used to take power and access away from Native Americans.[95]

Johnson's proposal didn't lead to quick institutional change. As was often the case, university officials cited budget concerns when explaining why university officials had yet to act on any of Johnson's recommendations. In other words, the BAM concessions had already taxed the university's resources. At the end of July, when university administrators hadn't made any attempt to fulfill Johnson's requests, he threatened the university with legal action. When the university again failed to respond, Johnson filed a lawsuit in August in Washtenaw County Circuit Court. The case hinged on an interpretation of the 1817 Treaty of Fort Meigs, in which Chippewa, Pottawatomie, and Ottawa tribes gave land for what would become the University of Michigan. Article 16 of the treaty stated, "Some of the Ottawa, Chippewa, and Potawatomy tribes . . . believing they may wish some of their children hereafter educated, do grant . . . to the corporation of the college at Detroit" 1,920 acres of land that officials could use or sell. Officials did eventually sell that land and use it to fund the university's development in Ann Arbor. The lawsuit claimed that the treaty required UM to provide educational opportunities to Native Americans, and the university had failed to fulfill this obligation. As a remedy, Johnson wanted the court to order UM to pay 3 percent compounded interest on $1 for each of the 1,920 acres. Johnson hoped the university would pay $1 million toward Native American education at UM.[96]

University officials promised to contest the lawsuit. By the mid-1970s, the lawsuit that Johnson filed in 1971 continued to move slowly through the court system. Roderick Daane, the university's lawyer, fought for a narrow interpretation of the 1817 treaty, which gave the university no responsibility to provide new funds or admissions practices that would expand Native Americans' access. The case wasn't resolved until 1981, when the court finally ruled in the university's favor. The university made only one small concession after Johnson filed the lawsuit. The Undergraduate Admissions Office hired one Native American recruiter, but he was hired only half time. He also had to work within the constraints of the Opportunity Program. Despite Johnson's recommendations, OP continued to serve only students living within the state.[97]

Asian Americans faced a different problem: how they would convince the university that they were a "disadvantaged" group and maintain access to the Opportunity Program even as their representation on campus grew to historic numbers. Since the university began reporting racial and ethnic data to HEW, Asian American students represented the second largest minority group on campus. In the late 1960s and early 1970s, Asian American undergraduate enrollment stayed steady, holding at 0.7 percent. By 1974, an additional fifty Asian American students were on campus, as their numbers reached over two hundred. For the first time, Asian American students represented 1 percent of the student body.[98]

Asian Americans' growing representation on campus raised concerns about their status as "disadvantaged" minorities. The 1970 census—although flawed in many ways—showed that Asian Americans represented about 0.7 percent of the U.S. population. For the first time in UM's history, a minority group's representation on campus exceeded its share of the U.S. population. In January 1974, George Goodman, now director of the Opportunity Program, decided that Asian Americans could no longer qualify for OP solely through their minority status. Asian American applicants could still qualify, just as whites could, if they could prove they were socioeconomically "disadvantaged."[99]

The decision helped spark an Asian American student movement at UM. While other groups formed protest organizations along ethnic lines in the late 1960s and early 1970s, Asian American students did not do so until 1974. In that year, a group of Asian American students, who would eventually form East Wind, organized to preserve their status as "disadvantaged" minorities. The university had failed, in the students' words, to provide "equal minority treatment."[100]

According to Asian American activists at UM, the problem was that university officials mistakenly saw Asian Americans as the "model minority." In historian Ellen Wu's words, the stereotype came to signify "a racial group distinct from the white majority, but lauded as well assimilated, upwardly mobile, politically nonthreatening, and *definitely not-Black*." This stereotype took hold by the mid-1960s. Asian American student activists tried to challenge the "model minority" image by highlighting a long history of discrimination against Asian American groups, which resembled the discrimination that other minority groups faced.[101]

The students also hinted at a critique that would become much more prominent among Asian American student activists in the late 1970s and early 1980s. The term "Asian American" itself hid the fact that large disparities existed in economic status among Asian Americans who emigrated from different nation-states. Using the term, student activists claimed, gave UM officials an excuse to ignore the most disadvantaged groups, such as Filipinos. The fact that only Canada sent more international students to UM than China and India only exacerbated the "model minority" stereotype and kept officials from recognizing disadvantaged Asian American groups. UM kept careful records concerning which minority students were U.S. citizens in order to report figures to the federal government. Thus, the numbers the university released concerning Asian Americans didn't include international students. Nevertheless, the number of Asian international students, activists argued, made it appear to people walking around campus that Asian American students were even better represented than they actually were. In 1973, for example, there were 853 graduate and undergraduate students of Asian descent, but only 322 were American citizens. Despite their efforts, OP continued to exclude Asian Americans—except those who could prove economic disadvantage—from the program.[102]

More than any minority group on campus in the mid-1970s, Asian American activists responded to this situation by calling for a broad coalition of minority students. They suggested that the university was trying to divide minority students by not allocating enough resources to support all the minority groups on campus. As each group fought over limited resources, minority students often saw one another as obstacles to overcome, not potential allies. Asian American activists suggested that "minority groups seem to forget that what brought them together was a common history of racist oppression. Instead of working together, they have often engaged in comparative oppression which is, at best, a counter-productive activity." For a brief moment in 1975, it looked like minority students could overcome these obstacles and form a multiracial coalition to challenge the university.[103]

"We're here because we want to turn the University upside down," a student protester told a reporter in late February 1975 while sitting on a faux Mahogany desk outside Robben Fleming's office. Fleming's secretary usually sat at the desk, but a group of two hundred students had stormed the Administration Building and sent personnel scrambling. In some respects, the protest looked similar to past building occupations for racial justice. Sleeping bags and food covered the orange carpet. Students talked about nonnegotiable demands. But a quick look inside the building showed reporters that something new was unfolding. This was a multiracial student protest calling for demands that spoke to the needs of all minority groups. Although the protest would later be remembered as the second black action movement, or BAM II, the students called themselves the Third World Coalition Council (TWCC).

The TWCC made six nonnegotiable demands that the group's leaders said had to be met before the students would leave the Administration Building.

1. Recognition of the Third World Coalition Council as the official negotiating team of minority students.
2. Immediately reinstate Cleopatra Lyons (a black nursing student who had been expelled for allegedly administering insulin to a patient without a doctor's approval).
3. Establish an Asian American advocate.
4. Establish a Chicano Cultural Center.
5. Raise the appointment of the Native American advocate from half time to full time.
6. Total amnesty from reprisals for all demonstrators.

The TWCC also called on Fleming to begin negotiations on a series of other demands. One of these demands called for the university to increase the percentage of Chicanos, Native Americans, and Asian Americans at UM to match their composition in the U.S. population. Thus far, administrators avoided any nonblack enrollment goals tied to a specific percentage of the student body. The BAM concessions, which established the 10 percent black enrollment goal, put black students in a unique position. Other minority groups wanted the university to make similar commitments.[104]

The rest of the TWCC's supplemental demands concerned only African Americans. Black students wanted to hold the university accountable for not meeting the 10 percent black enrollment goal within the established time frame. The 1970 BAM concessions originally gave the university until the 1973–74 academic year to reach the 10 percent goal. In fall 1973, black enrollment stood at 7.3 percent. A year and a half later, the university still hadn't reached the enrollment goal. Now activists put even more pressure on university officials, demanding that the university raise black enrollment to 13 percent of the student body by September 1976 and a percentage equal to or greater than African Americans' share of the state population by September 1977. They made similar percentage demands for black faculty.[105]

The administration's failure to fulfill many of the BAM concessions also influenced the demands. The students were no longer willing to entrust the implementation of protest victories to administrators and staff members. Black activists wanted more control over the power mechanisms of the university. The Black United Front, the major black activist organization of the period, wanted control of the admission, financial aid, and recruitment of black students. The group also wanted control of 25 percent of UM's budget and all university services for black students. Black activists saw the value of black administrators in implementing demands and thus called for an immediate increase in black officials. But they also saw that not all black administrators worked in the interest of black activists. The Black United Front wanted the power to hire and fire black administrators.[106]

Fleming didn't grant any of these demands. The students tried to hold out, forcing the university to concede or use the police to physically remove the students. But after nearly sixty hours, the students left the Administration Building with only a simple promise from Fleming that he would continue to talk to them. It was a great failure for the most significant coalition of minority groups in the university's history thus far.[107]

There were early signs, however, that the coalition wouldn't be able to hold together long enough to force Fleming into action. The imbalance in the demands among minority groups—with black students' interests dominating the list—suggested tension. Even more telling was the lack of socialization among groups when they got inside the building. Black students occupied one room, other minority groups sat in a different room, and white students congregated in yet another room.[108]

Interracial tension, though, explains only part of the TWCC's failure. The fact was that building takeovers were poor tools to create change in 1975. In the late 1960s, building occupations looked threatening to administrators, who hadn't seen that type of protest before. But subsequent protests changed that. The 1970 BAM strike might have led to unprecedented concessions, but it also made protests that didn't make physical threats or destroy property appear tepid and nonthreatening. Staff and administrators described the 1975 protesters as mild, even polite, in comparison to the 1970 activists. Dorothy Parker, a secretary in the Administration Building, compared the two protests, suggesting that the 1970 strike "was much more threatening. Any of us who were here could tell the difference." The 1970 protesters, she continued, "let you know that they were going to be violent right from the start and they were." Richard Kennedy, UM's vice president of state relations, told a reporter, "The mood was entirely different." "The hostility, the vehemence," he continued, "I can't describe it. The tenor was totally different." Levi Cash, the assistant to the president, called the 1975 building takeover "just another routine event."[109]

The routineness—the feeling that the takeover was easy to manage—revealed the consequences of the new disciplinary laws and codes implemented after the BAM strike. The multiracial coalition of 1975 faced a different environment than had the BAM protesters. The grand bargain Fleming eventually struck with students in the early 1970s was that he was willing to accommodate protest, even building takeovers, as long as students didn't destroy property or make physical threats. Any protests that used BAM's more confrontational tactics would face the full consequences of UM, state, and federal disciplinary codes and laws. The goal was to create demonstrations that were, in Cash's words, "just another routine event."[110]

As the TWCC demonstrators found in 1975, most routine events didn't create significant change—or any change at all. The failure of the TWCC had long-lasting consequences. It would take more than a decade for another multiracial protest coalition to emerge at the University of Michigan. The small 1975 protest was a sign that Fleming's tactics were working. Even as UM failed to meet minority students' expectations, Fleming avoided another major demonstration that shut down the university.

In the years after the BAM strike, campus leaders wrestled control of inclusion from activists. While black enrollment rose to historic heights, it never reached the 10 percent goal. Administrators carefully controlled initiatives to address the racial climate, rejecting attempts to create intraracial spaces. Black students saw an unprecedented number of black officials on campus, but those officials struggled to implement activists' vision of justice. Other minority groups joined black students in activism, but these groups failed to create a multiracial movement that could challenge the administration to implement new demands.

The fear administrators shared regarding the black campus movement was gone by the mid-1970s. It's no coincidence that an era of racial retrenchment emerged as black campus activism waned. In the late 1970s and early 1980s, university officials implemented new policies that reversed most of the enrollment gains black students had won over the course of the late 1960s and early 1970s.

# CHAPTER 5

# Affirmative Action for Whom?

If the student activists who took over the Administration Building in 1975 knew what was going to unfold in the second half of the 1970s, they might have risked the disciplinary codes and returned to the tactics of the Black Action Movement. It would have been difficult in 1975, though, to imagine the racial retrenchment that was about to come. After all, even though black enrollment still fell short of the BAM concessions, black students' share of the student body was still close to record numbers. Over the next eight years, almost all the enrollment gains made since BAM were reversed. During these years, black enrollment fell from 7.25 percent to 4.9 percent of UM's student body by 1983.[1] Just as important, the economic backgrounds of black students at UM changed, as UM officials shifted their recruiting, admissions, and financial aid policies to focus on bringing middle-class black students from suburban areas around the country. Even as black enrollment began to rise again in the mid-1980s, UM would never again craft its affirmative action policies to target working-class students in Detroit.

The policies administrators introduced in the late 1970s revealed that the co-optation of racial justice was a long-term project that evolved to protect the university's priorities as conditions changed. New fears about the future of the university's elite status helped usher in new interpretations about the fate of cities and the merits of black students living within them. The declining power of black student activists also gave administrators more control over how the university would respond to the changing environment. By the end of the 1970s, the character of affirmative action looked nothing like BAM's vision of racial justice.

Two university officials crafted and pitched new affirmative action policies, which ultimately led to the racial retrenchment of the late 1970s and early 1980s. Cliff Sjogren and George Goodman had only recently taken over important offices on campus. Sjogren became the director of undergraduate admissions in July 1973. Still, he was no novice. The forty-six-year-old director came to UM as an admissions counselor in 1964; the same year UM inaugurated the Opportunity Awards Program. He quickly moved up to assistant director, and then, when his mentor Clyde Vroman retired after almost twenty-five years at the helm, Sjogren took over. Goodman was another longtime university employee. He joined the admissions office as the admissions counselor for the Opportunity Program (then called the Opportunity Awards Program) in 1968. In 1973, he became the director of the program. The position brought him outside the admissions office for the first time. As director, he oversaw the supportive services for OP students and crafted the policies that governed the program.[2]

Goodman and Sjogren aren't the actors that scholars typically associate with the backlash to the victories of the black freedom movement. Both UM officials believed that the university had a responsibility to address racial inequality through affirmative action admissions. Both took steps in their positions to advance affirmative action. Sjogren took a leadership role, using his resources when he became director to increase the number of minority admissions counselors. In Goodman's case, he spent the first years of his career at UM as the only black admissions officer, taking on the responsibilities of recruiting and admitting OP students. No UM admissions official was more responsible for the boom in black enrollment in the late 1960s and early 1970s.[3]

Nevertheless, these were the two university officials most responsible for the racial retrenchment of the late 1970s and early 1980s. While both officials supported affirmative action, they were uncomfortable with the BAM concessions. Both were skeptical that UM could find enough "qualified" black students through OP—which focused primarily on Detroit students—to raise black enrollment to 10 percent of the student body. Goodman, in particular, took black students' attrition rate more personally than others. As the OP admissions officer in the late 1960s and early 1970s, the attrition rate wasn't a number; it represented the names and faces of black students. He wondered whether he was letting these students down. What were their lives like after they left UM? Would they have been better off at another university?[4]

Sjogren and Goodman had their own ideas about how to reform affirmative action admissions. Sjogren wanted to raise the admissions criteria for affirmative action while still raising black enrollment. He believed that he could do this by expanding affirmative action to include out-of-state students. The exclusion of out-of-state students was especially problematic in meeting the BAM goals because in the 1960s and 1970s, out-of-state undergraduate enrollment in LSA often fluctuated between 20 and 30 percent of the student body. This meant that the university had no affirmative action admissions process for a large contingent of its students, putting even more pressure on the in-state Opportunity Program to admit enough students to reach the BAM enrollment goal. Sjogren believed that this limitation forced his admissions office to recruit and admit too many black students who were academically underprepared and would likely leave UM before graduating. Expanding the pool of black students who were eligible for affirmative action, he thought, would allow UM to admit more black students who presented lower risks of attrition.[5]

Sjogren didn't want just any out-of-state black student from any location and socioeconomic background. Although he never said it in public meetings in the mid-1970s, he wrote in internal correspondence about "a potential applicant pool of middle and upper income Blacks," especially those outside the state of Michigan, that he would like to recruit if he had the funds. Sjogren saw potential in the growing population of black families living outside cities that escaped the harshest effects of the economic recession of the late 1970s and moved into suburban areas. In the early 1960s, when the university first implemented affirmative action admissions, only 2.5 million African Americans lived in suburban areas nationwide. By 1980, that number leaped to 6.1 million. Sjogren wanted to take advantage of that growth because he believed urban school districts were deteriorating and suburban districts better prepared black students for UM's competitive environment.[6]

To recruit these students, who he believed were better prepared to compete at UM, Sjogren thought the university needed to devote more money to merit aid. OP offered generous financial aid packages, but the packages were based on financial need. Sjogren wanted to redistribute the university's resources to recruit the black students with the highest standardized test scores and the most college preparatory coursework. Many of these students, he understood, were from middle- and upper-income families, who wouldn't benefit as much from need-based financial aid.[7]

Sjogren's ideas worked in harmony with Goodman's vision for the future of OP. As director of the Opportunity Program, Goodman wanted to reform OP to improve retention. To Goodman, the program was too big to offer the type of support necessary to reduce academic attrition. Many of the OP students didn't need or want academic counseling. But to reduce attrition rates, Goodman thought he needed to make academic counseling mandatory for all OP students. Goodman's solution involved purging all students who didn't need academic support and remaking OP into a program exclusively for students who he thought were at risk of leaving the university before graduation. He also wanted to create a Summer Bridge program for the OP students he thought posed the highest risk of leaving UM due to academic underpreparation. OP, then, would become smaller, and many black students would have to find a different admissions and funding mechanism. Goodman's proposed changes benefited Sjogren, because reducing the size of OP, and the money needed for its generous financial aid packages, freed up funds for Sjogren's merit-based scholarships.[8]

Still, there were clear obstacles in Sjogren's and Goodman's way. First and foremost, these policy changes required new affirmative action tools. If the number of OP students declined, the Opportunity Program could no longer represent the only affirmative action admissions mechanism for in-state students. And if Sjogren wanted to expand affirmative action to include out-of-state students, new tools for identifying and evaluating black students outside Michigan had to be put in place. Essentially, they needed ways to identify students' race when counselors evaluated applications. The problem was that UM leaders had long resisted racial identification on applications. They were more comfortable with OP's process, which allowed UM to claim that admissions officials focused on "disadvantaged" students, not black students. That changed in 1976, when university leaders agreed to add questions about racial and ethnic identity to admissions applications.[9]

Richard English, the associate vice president for academic affairs, was responsible for creating support for racial identification on admissions applications. English was one of the few African Americans in UM's administration in the mid-1970s.[10] It's unclear whether English supported placing questions about racial identity on applications in order to implement Sjogren's and Goodman's policies. Richard English, though, was also a strong advocate of Sjogren and Goodman's proposed policies. By 1976, English believed that the admissions office had exhausted the pool of in-state black students who could graduate from UM. He knew that if the admissions office wanted to increase black enrollment, UM had to enroll more out-of-state black students. English advocated for more merit aid to recruit these students. Adding racial identity to applications proved vital to fulfilling these policy initiatives.[11]

In internal correspondence, though, English framed the decision to place questions about race and ethnicity on applications as a federal compliance measure. Since the mid-1960s, administrators had been collecting data on the racial identity of students and employees. Throughout those years, administrators expressed great concern that by leaving racial identification off applications, they were providing incomplete and inaccurate racial data. The federal government's pressure for data only increased in the mid-1970s. HEW began demanding data on the degrees the university conferred, broken down by students' race, which required the university to track students throughout their time at UM.[12] At the same time, the consequences for not complying with HEW grew by the mid-1970s. As noted in chapter 4, losing federal contracts for not following federal affirmative action guidelines had become a real possibility by that time. This reality likely helped push UM officials to put racial identification on applications.[13]

Whatever pushed UM leaders to add racial identification to admissions applications, the decision meant that the admissions office would no longer have to rely on OP to pursue affirmative action admissions. Admissions officials could now identify the race and ethnic background of any student while making an admissions decision. Now admissions counselors could evaluate students who identified themselves as black, Hispanic, or Native American—not just the in-state students who checked the Opportunity Program box—with special admissions criteria.

As important as adding racial identification to applications was to carrying out Sjogren's and Goodman's policies, the two officials still needed to convince executive administrators and enough faculty members to support their larger vision. Although the university's decentralized structure gave Sjogren and Goodman much independence, they still had to deal with oversight. The admissions office had to answer directly to the vice president for academic affairs. Further, the Undergraduate Admissions Office was supposed to carry out the admissions goals of the College of Literature, Science, and the Arts, along with those of other, smaller colleges that admitted undergraduates. So any major admissions policy changes needed broad support.

To pitch their policy changes, Goodman and Sjogren led an intellectual assault on black students, especially those from Detroit—UM's primary recruiting ground for black students. Goodman and Sjogren offered a new institutional knowledge that saw standardized tests as viable prediction tools for black students, viewed attrition solely as a sign of academic deficiency, and claimed that all but two public Detroit high schools poorly prepared black students for study at UM. Goodman summarized the situation bluntly. Although some Opportunity Program students enrolled in the Honors Program and graduated with distinction, "the average grades earned at the University during the freshmen year are generally below the University average," and "an alarming number are below 2.0 [grade point average]." Goodman concluded, "To the extent that the rising attrition rate is due primarily to academic survival, a new approach is needed."[14] Sjogren agreed with Goodman. The admissions director argued that attrition presented the most significant obstacle to increasing minority enrollment. Just pointing out that attrition was a problem, of course, did not necessarily mean that Sjogren believed that academic deficiency was the culprit. Nevertheless, the solutions Sjogren presented for the attrition problem identified academic deficiency as the sole factor behind attrition. Sjogren claimed that executive administrators had two choices: raise admissions standards to admit minority students who were better academically prepared, or substantially increase academic support services.[15]

These claims flew in the face of a decade of institutional knowledge about the academic proficiency of black students. In the 1960s and early 1970s, in order to counter concerns that affirmative action would not hurt institutional quality, social scientists offered data that showed that traditional admissions tools poorly predicted black students' performance and that black students' higher attrition rates didn't suggest that affirmative action brought poorly prepared black students to campus. Early 1970s research on black students at UM showed that half of OP students who left before graduation were in good academic standing. Social scientists also revealed that nonacademic factors, such as social alienation, were more responsible for attrition than was academic underpreparation. A 1975 internal study showed that academic underpreparation continued to be a poor explanation for black student attrition rates. In that year, 62 percent of black students who left before graduating were in good academic standing—an even higher percentage than the early 1970s studies reported. Despite all this research, Goodman and Sjogren framed black student attrition exclusively as a problem of academic underpreparation.[16]

Any plans to decenter Detroit in UM's affirmative action efforts also challenged ten years of institutional practice and the common understanding of the purpose of affirmative action. For a decade, UM officials and activists had emphasized a vision of social justice rooted in addressing racial inequality in cities. But now Sjogren and Goodman were suggesting that cities could no longer be the primary recruiting grounds for affirmative action admissions. In the mid-1970s, Sjogren and Goodman didn't publicly mention Detroit or highlight the fact that they wanted to focus on recruiting black students from outside the state's cities. Nevertheless, when the two talked about getting "better" students and looking at new areas of recruitment, it was clear that they weren't referring to new neighborhoods in Detroit, Flint, or Grand Rapids. The critique of the current pool of black students was a thinly veiled attack on black students in Michigan's cities. But as much as these attacks on cities were veiled, there was at least one obvious sign that Sjogren planned to decenter cities in recruitment. In 1976, Sjogren closed the Grand Rapids Adjunct Admissions Office. While Detroit had always been the university's primary recruiting ground for black students under OP, Grand Rapids served as a secondary site, much like Flint. The adjunct office allowed students to access admissions officers and get information and advice on the admissions process. Those services were no longer available once Sjogren began focusing on middle- and upper-income black students in the nation's suburban areas.[17]

The lack of transparency clearly helped Sjogren and Goodman. As mentioned in chapter 4, UM officials didn't release to the public the social science studies that showed most of the OP students who left UM before graduating were in good academic standing. These social scientists found that UM's racial climate was more to blame for black student attrition than any lack of academic preparation. Consequently, UM faculty and students didn't know that all of the available data contradicted Sjogren and Goodman's claims.

Still, the claims that Sjogren and Goodman were making about black students represented an unprecedented attack from officials who were supposed to carry out affirmative action. What's especially striking about this period is the relative ease Sjogren and Goodman enjoyed in attacking the quality of urban schools and suggesting that academic underpreparation explained black student attrition rates. Between 1975 and 1978, nothing in the historical record reveals a single person who questioned Sjogren's and Goodman's claims. Not in the faculty meeting minutes, where Sjogren and Goodman unveiled their policy proposals and critiques of black students' preparation. Not in communications with executive administrators. Not in the student newspaper, which often pushed admissions officials to explain low black enrollment numbers in the past. All the evidence supports Sjogren's claim that faculty had sent him a clear message in the mid-1970s: "Give us more minorities and smarter minorities."[18]

To so radically change the characterization of black students, one might assume that Sjogren and Goodman must have commissioned numerous studies. Surely they must have found evidence that the academic preparation of Opportunity Program students had declined dramatically. Surely they must have found enough evidence to counter ten years of social science data on black students at UM. But they didn't. There is no evidence that Sjogren and Goodman commissioned any new studies that suggested poor academic preparation explained black student attrition in the mid-1970s. They certainly didn't present any new evidence from studies to faculty and administrators. In fact, they presented no evidence to support any of their claims. Nothing.[19]

And still, nobody raised their voice against Sjogren and Goodman. Nobody asked for evidence.

Notice how easily Goodman and Sjogren took over as the legitimate knowledge producers about black students. In a climate where social scientists' research conflicted with the policy goals of university leaders, social science studies about black students' performance on campus disappeared. There was a great imbalance in the types of evidence necessary to argue for and against the qualifications of black students. The people who fought against negative assumptions about black students' academic capabilities needed data, data, and more data from social scientists. But in the mid-1970s, Sjogren and Goodman made arguments as if the declining quality of black students from the state's cities was self-evident. No evidence was necessary.

Sjogren and Goodman also experienced little resistance when they proposed to redistribute need-based aid to support an ambitious merit-based program that would allow the university to attract out-of-state students. Putting money into merit-based programs represented a philosophical shift at UM. Before the mid-1970s, the prevailing assumption that guided recruitment was that while the university should aid students who could not afford to attend, the university should not "purchase good talent," in financial aid director Thomas Butts's words. In the eyes of UM officials, the quality of the faculty and the university's overall reputation would attract the best student talent. In this formula, the only obstacle to getting the "best" students was making sure the brightest low-income students could afford to attend.[20]

Sjogren and Goodman understood some of the consequences of their new policies before they went into effect. Before the two administrators made any decisions, Goodman investigated the potential impact his policy recommendations would have on OP. It was clear that the new criteria would force those low-income black students who scored too high on the SAT or graduated too high in their high school class, designating them as students who didn't need OP's academic services, to pay as much as $1,550 through loans and work study. These were low-income students who would have previously benefited from the Opportunity Program's financial support, which typically covered expenses that a student's financial aid package failed to cover. One staff member, Pat Wilson, raised the key question: "Will we lose bright, but poor minority students (who will not be coded as Opportunity Program applicants) because they will receive less grant funds from the University?" Wilson answered her own question: yes, but the "new procedure cannot be avoided, nor can we revert to the old procedure, at this point in time." Sjogren and Goodman didn't share this information with faculty when they proposed the policy changes, but it's difficult to imagine that the faculty and other officials believed that redirecting need-based aid into merit-based scholarships wouldn't hurt low-income students.[21]

Goodman and Sjogren didn't propose these policies with the intention of lowering black enrollment. They believed that, at worst, their policies would maintain black enrollment because out-of-state black students would rise dramatically and make up for the decline in OP enrollment. At best, they believed their plan would finally fulfill the 10 percent enrollment goal. Still, their policies revealed that they were offering a new concept of racial inclusion that disconnected affirmative action from the working-class black students in the state. They wanted to use affirmative action to recruit middle-class students.

Explaining why Sjogren and Goodman received so little resistance offers an opportunity to explore the type of institutional environment that was especially ripe for racial retrenchment. In what moments were UM faculty members willing to accept new negative portrayals of the state's black students? In what environments were they willing to take important resources away from students most in need of financial support?

Any explanation must begin with the university's perceived crisis of quality that emerged in the mid-1970s. Beginning in 1974, Sjogren presented a gloomy picture of the university's student body that would soon help change the character of affirmative action at the University of Michigan. He told the faculty that the average SAT scores of all admitted students—not just black students—were declining. When Sjogren surveyed the scope of the problem and reported to the faculty, he revealed that declining SAT scores were a national trend. Sjogren suggested that the pool of students ready to compete at an elite institution was declining and that it would decline even further in the future, when the last of the baby boomers graduated from high school. He sent the message that there would soon be a war among selective universities for this shrinking pool of "good" students, and only a handful of selective institutions would survive. The rest would lose their elite status.[22]

The crisis of quality created an environment ripe for new critiques of black students' preparation. For much of OP's history, officials presented information about black students in an era when faculty members and administrators celebrated the overall quality of the university's student body. It might seem counterintuitive to argue that affirmative action enjoyed its greatest support during moments when average SAT scores were rising. Nevertheless, challenges to the qualifications of black students were weakest when the UM community felt most confident that the university's elite status was secure. The faculty's support of—or at least complicity in—Sjogren's and Goodman's attacks on the qualifications of black students during a perceived crisis of quality, then, shouldn't come as a surprise. Historically, when faculty members and administrators at UM believed that the future of the university's elite status was in question, there was a well-supported effort to purge the most vulnerable students to solidify the university's position. Recall from chapter 1 that a similar crisis in the 1950s resulted in a successful effort to paint previously "qualified" students as "mediocre" and threats to the future of the institution.[23]

The political economy of the 1970s exacerbated these concerns. Beginning early in the decade, conservatives used the national recession and rising inflation to attack the costs of public institutions and social services. The cost of liberal policies, they argued, undermined businesses' competitiveness in domestic and global markets. A new era of austerity was necessary. Public universities felt the consequences. In the 1960s, the state government provided 80 percent of the University of Michigan's general fund operating budget. By the mid-1970s, state appropriations accounted for 66 percent of UM's general fund operating budget. That number would only continue to decline.[24]

UM officials raised tuition and fees to cover the funding gap. Rising tuition costs helped bring a market ethos into admissions logic. Sjogren claimed that UM was in a poor position to maintain its elite status in this environment. In the past, UM could compete with Ivy League schools for students without offering merit scholarships because generous state funding kept tuition at UM less than half the price of places like Harvard. UM didn't need active recruiting programs for the "best" out-of-state students because of the university's reputation and cheap tuition. But now, because of declining state appropriations, UM's out-of-state tuition was approaching that of the Ivy League, and other elite universities were offering substantial merit scholarships. As Sjogren's assistant director explained, UM now faced an "increasingly competitive marketplace for students" because schools offering merit scholarships for the limited pool of high-quality students had created a "buyer's market."[25] Sjogren suggested in faculty meetings that he could lower minimum SAT scores required for admission in order to sustain UM's enrollment numbers. Essentially, Sjogren gave the faculty two options: lower admissions criteria and give up the university's elite status or support his plan to use merit scholarships and out-of-state recruitment to fight for the "best" students in the country.[26]

Essentially, generous state funding, which kept tuition low, allowed UM to focus its general fund financial aid resources on low-income students. When tuition was cheap enough for middle-class families to afford—and much lower than UM's elite private competitors—UM officials never thought they had to choose between middle- and working-class students when determining how to distribute general fund financial aid resources. But declining state appropriations and rising tuition costs created questions about who was more deserving of financial resources. When tuition prices created obstacles for middle-class students' access to UM—the students whom officials had long seen as essential to sustain UM's quality—redistributing need-based aid to support merit aid found widespread support.

The changing political economy also made it easier to attack the credentials of black students living in Detroit. Critiques of black OP students took hold as the political economy of the 1970s revealed its devastating consequences for cities, especially those in the Northeast and Midwest. Deindustrialization and white flight moved the economic and political power centers to new locations in America. As cities became blacker and African Americans began winning important political races, whites went to great lengths to keep their beachheads of power and privilege autonomous from African Americans in cities. In this environment, Detroit became the symbol of urban decline narratives.[27]

Two court cases in particular protected the educational privileges that white families created for their children.[28] *Milliken v. Bradley* directly concerned the city of Detroit. In 1970, the Detroit NAACP, along with parents of Detroit children, sued the state of Michigan, challenging policies that led to racial segregation in the city. The district court judge ordered an ambitious desegregation plan that reached outside Detroit's borders into the surrounding suburbs. The desegregation plan included 53 suburban school districts and Detroit, requiring 295 school buses to transport students around the area. The plan would have pierced the beachheads of privilege that whites had created outside Detroit, giving black students in the city access to the resources of suburban schools at a time when Detroit's resources were crumbling. White parents in these suburbs challenged the plan. In 1974, the Supreme Court finally ruled that the district court's plan was unconstitutional. The court's majority ruled that suburban districts had not engaged in racial discrimination and were not required to remedy racial inequality.[29]

The year before, the Supreme Court ensured that states had no obligation to make sure that schools in places like Detroit had the same financial resources as those in suburban areas. The case originated in San Antonio, where the school district challenged school funding methods based on a city's local property taxes. Property tax–based schemes simply meant that schools in wealthy areas were well funded, while schools in poor districts struggled financially. The school district wanted a state funding scheme in which all children, no matter the local property tax base, would receive equal funding. In *San Antonio Independent School District v. Rodriguez*, the Supreme Court ruled that the "Equal Protection Clause does not require absolute equality or precisely equal advantages." Disparities in school funding were perfectly compatible with the Fourteenth Amendment, the court ruled, because they were not "so irrational as to be invidiously discriminatory."[30]

The two cases created a perfect recipe for a conservative state government in Michigan to implement new financial policies. These policies further protected the white beachheads of privilege that surrounded Detroit, as white parents guarded their children and tax dollars from the city's school district. By 1973, Detroit's schools were in financial trouble, as the school system faced a $70 million deficit. Rather than redistributing the tax dollars of wealthy suburban areas to help fund Detroit's school system and avoid future deficits, as the *Rodriguez* case would have mandated, the state government provided loans to cover the deficit and appointed a financial officer to ensure that Detroit would learn to fund its schools within the limited city tax resources available. Managers of the Detroit school system made tough choices. Class sizes grew, and schools ran short of basic school resources, such as paper and textbooks. Some high schools cut college-preparation courses, such as advanced calculus. These cuts unfolded just as Sjogren began to place even more emphasis on advanced placement courses in UM's admissions decisions.[31]

The fact that industry, tax dollars, and increasingly whites were moving outside city lines in the 1970s helped change what was at stake in addressing urban problems. When Detroit was no longer a political and industrial power base for whites, the social problem of large numbers of young, unemployed African Americans took on a different narrative. Young African Americans were simply seen as a threat to individuals' security—not threats to the future of a place vital to the nation's economic and political future. Rather than focusing on the policies that threatened the economic security of Detroit's residents, pundits marked Detroit as a dangerous place that couldn't be saved. The city found state and federal resources to bulk up its police force but found few resources to improve the education and employment opportunities for residents. As historian Julilly Kohler-Hausmann argues, the tough-on-crime policies that emerged in the 1970s "helped absolve government of responsibility for marginalized people's well-being and accountability to their voices."[32]

Growing attention to crime in urban America captured much of the press's attention just as UM officials and faculty were debating the fate of policies that would affect black students. On August 15, 1976, almost two hundred young African Americans attacked concertgoers at Cobo Hall in downtown Detroit. Hundreds reported that they were assaulted and robbed. Then stories of gang members breaking store windows downtown were reported. The Cobo Hall incident came on the heels of other nationally publicized incidents of violence in Detroit, including a woman who was abducted and raped after her car suffered a flat tire on the highway, and thirty-two bus passengers who were held hostage and robbed during rush hour. Crime also framed portrayals of Detroit's public schools: A teenage girl suffered a gunshot wound at the front door of Denby High School. A janitor was raped in a classroom at Cody High School. A Northeastern High School student was shot in the buttocks as he approached the school's entrance. "The schools, like the city they serve, are learning to live with violence," a *Detroit Free Press* journalist concluded.[33]

The message in national media outlets was that although crime plagued many cities, Detroit was unique. By 1974, Detroit took on the unwanted reputation as the "murder capital of the world." "I am outraged," one Detroit writer concluded in the *New York Times*. "Young Black hoodlums control the streets. People are held up. Homes are broken into. People are murdered." Detroit "may, in a real sense, be dead," he concluded. "The first dead large city in the nation."[34]

Dead. Not broken. Dead.

This, of course, was an unfair characterization of Detroit. The city was filled with people fighting against the headwinds of a new political economy. Nevertheless, those people didn't get to define national perception—and they didn't get to influence the perception of officials at the University of Michigan.[35]

These were the popular images of Detroit as UM faculty and administrators listened to Goodman's and Sjogren's policy proposals, which would change the character of affirmative action. The Detroit school system was cutting advanced preparation courses as it dealt with a budget shortfall. Students were getting shot in front of schools. All these images could have been justifications for a renewed commitment to Detroit students. But as the UM community feared the loss of elite status in a new, more competitive environment, faculty and administrators again chose to privilege status over racial justice.

If perceptions of Detroit helped support Sjogren's and Goodman's policies, the declining power of black campus activism also made it easier to attack the academic merits of black students. The TWCC/BAM II protest represented the last gasp of the well-organized student protests for racial justice that emerged in the late 1960s and early 1970s. UM's history reveals a clear difference in the way university officials handled racial inclusion when they feared black student protest and when they didn't. The threat of black student activism made officials think—not always successfully—about the consequences of the words they used to characterize black students and the initiatives they proposed. The lack of resistance Goodman and Sjogren experienced shows what could happen when university officials no longer feared the consequences of black campus protest.[36]

Sjogren's and Goodman's intellectual assaults on UM's black students gave opponents of affirmative action an opportunity to join in mainstream debates about racially attentive policies. One of these opponents was Carl Cohen. The philosophy professor was one of the only UM faculty members who publicly denounced affirmative action. Cohen must have known that his views about affirmative action were unpopular at UM. Even as faculty members supported Sjogren's and Goodman's policies, which would hurt Detroit students, faculty meeting minutes suggest that most faculty members believed these new policies would allow Sjogren and Goodman to increase black enrollment. The faculty's message to Sjogren to "give us more minorities and smarter minorities" hardly represented Cohen's anti–affirmative action views. But the environment of the 1970s still offered him opportunities to shape affirmative action practices.[37]

While the new discussions that questioned black students' academic capabilities energized Cohen, he was still a political realist. He wasn't going to convince his colleagues and UM officials to eliminate racially attentive practices. Cohen was a regular at faculty meetings in the 1970s and was even on the LSA admissions committee in the late 1970s. He had plenty of opportunities to raise his voice against affirmative action. Only once, in a Senate Assembly meeting in 1976, did Cohen raise his voice against affirmative action, suggesting that merit scholarships should be based on ability, not race.[38]

Instead, Cohen made a conscious choice to try to curtail affirmative action practices at UM rather than try to eliminate them. The debates over quality in the mid-1970s gave him the perfect opportunity to limit affirmative action. Cohen fanned the flames of the university's declining status and the poor quality of students entering the university. Cohen let his colleagues make demands for more minority students without objection, but he continued to push them to call for "better" students. Sjogren and Goodman probably never needed Cohen's help; there were enough faculty members who wanted minority students with higher standardized test scores to support the new policies. Nevertheless, the fact that Cohen was such an ever-present voice in these discussions showed that the mid-1970s offered space for affirmative action opponents to join mainstream discussions about the future of affirmative action. The absence of rhetoric calling for the end of affirmative action in UM's faculty meetings, then, hides some of the anti–affirmative action sentiment that drove new affirmative action practices.[39]

Cohen must have seen the mid-1970s as a moment of possibility. As he worked to modify UM's affirmative action practices, he worked with Allan Bakke's lawyer in the most important anti–affirmative action case of the decade. Allan Bakke, a white student, didn't gain admission to the University of California–Davis Medical School and was suing on the grounds that the medical school discriminated against him on the basis of race. After the California Supreme Court ruled in Bakke's favor, the United States Supreme Court agreed to hear the case. At that moment, Bakke's lawyer, Reynold Colvin, came across Cohen's published writings on affirmative action and was impressed. They exchanged phone calls and letters about the case. Cohen tried to modify Colvin's strategy as the attorney prepared his briefs for the Supreme Court. Cohen worried about Colvin's emphasis on the perniciousness of racial quotas. The University of California–Davis Medical School reserved 16 out of 100 seats in each incoming class for minority candidates. Cohen didn't want Colvin to differentiate quotas from any other selection process that took race into account. They were all equally pernicious in Cohen's mind. Emphasizing the problem of quotas, Cohen worried, would give the Supreme Court the opportunity to rule narrowly, striking down quotas but allowing other forms of affirmative action, such as UM's system.[40]

Of course, that's exactly what happened. In a divided decision, Justice Lewis Powell broke the deadlock by finding a middle ground. His opinion struck down racial quotas but allowed other forms of affirmative action, as long as race was used as one of many factors in the admissions decision. Powell went further, concluding that universities could not use affirmative action to correct a long history of societal discrimination. Instead, they could use race as a factor in admissions to create the educational benefits of a diverse student body or to correct specific policies of discrimination within an institution.[41]

The *Bakke* decision didn't frighten officials at the University of Michigan. UM officials interpreted the decision narrowly and paid little attention to the nuances of Powell's opinion. All of their attention focused on the mechanisms of using race to select students. Quotas were clearly unconstitutional. Since UM didn't use quotas, the ruling didn't produce much concern among UM officials. As Theodore St. Antoine, dean of UM's Law School, said after the ruling, "Affirmative action is still alive and kicking."[42]

Soon after the decision, UM's admissions office created the most racially attentive affirmative action admissions system in the university's history. By 1979, admissions officials evaluated students using a separate admissions grid for underrepresented minority applicants. Using only applicants' grade point averages and standardized test scores, admissions officers found the appropriate box in the grid that gave them an initial recommendation to admit, reject, or delay an application. When the admissions office received an undergraduate application from a black, Hispanic, or Native American applicant—Asian Americans weren't part of the affirmative action program—the admissions counselor placed an orange dot on the application, so they would know which grid to use. If an underrepresented minority student's grades or SAT scores were lower than the minimum SAT score or high school grade point average that Sjogren identified as acceptable for admission, the admissions counselor placed a "Y" on the application, which indicated that the student might be eligible for the Opportunity Program. Generally, any minority student with a grade point average of 3.0 or above and an SAT score of at least 850 were admitted. Students with GPAs between 2.9 and 2.7 and SAT scores between 850 and 750 were evaluated to see if they were good candidates for the Opportunity Program and the Bridge Program. The grid offered only an admissions recommendation, which an admissions officer would evaluate more closely, so minority students could still receive a rejection letter even if their scores fell into an admission category. For example, if counselors determined that the students' high school curriculum didn't prepare the student for UM's coursework, counselors could still reject the applicant. Nevertheless, when UM officials decided to place questions about race on applications, it gave Sjogren an opportunity to create a new system that evaluated all underrepresented minority applicants with a separate admissions grid.[43]

The 1970s must have left Carl Cohen frustrated. Helping to raise admissions criteria at UM represented his only victory. As someone who felt that affirmative action was morally unjust, he now worked at a university that employed the most race-conscious affirmative action program in its history.

"Who Won?" asked a *New York Times* article in the aftermath of the *Bakke* decision. The case didn't lend itself to easy analysis. There was no clear victor, and no clear loser. But the article tried to simplify the answer. The proponents of affirmative action won. Allan Bakke might have been admitted to medical school and quotas might be unconstitutional, but proponents of racially attentive admissions policies "gained the blessing of the Supreme Court."[44]

What didn't appear in the *New York Times*'s report of the case was the struggle over affirmative action unfolding at places like the University of Michigan. Black enrollment started to decline slowly at institutions nationwide in the late 1970s. Despite the national attention he received, Allan Bakke didn't turn out to be the greatest threat to racial equity at the University of Michigan in the 1970s. Some of the most important threats to racial equity at UM were sitting in the boardrooms and offices on campus.[45]

As reporters flocked to the Supreme Court, UM officials and faculty members were about to face a new challenge. In the mid-1970s, when faculty and UM officials contemplated changes to affirmative action, the outcomes of Sjogren's and Goodman's policy changes were still uncertain. In fact, faculty members and high-level officials showed some optimism that these policy changes could sustain—and maybe even raise—black enrollment, even if those students might come from different places and socioeconomic backgrounds.

But by the late 1970s, the policy outcomes were clear. Black enrollment was plummeting.[46]

Part of the problem came from the decision to raise the minimum SAT and high school grade point average required for admission, while also placing more emphasis on a college preparatory curriculum in evaluating applicants. This had an immediate impact on admission rates. In 1973, the admission rate for first-year applicants to OP was 71.9 percent. Between 1978 and 1982, the admission rate for all black first-year applicants hovered between 38.2 and 41.7 percent. This isn't a direct comparison, as not all black students applied through OP in the early 1970s, but about 70 percent of black students did gain admissions through OP in that era. Black enrollment, not surprisingly, fell as admission rates declined. In the fall of 1976, before the admissions policies took effect, 965 black undergraduate students enrolled in LSA. A year later, that number dropped to 872. In 1978, black enrollment rose slightly to 877, only to plummet to 805 in 1979. African American enrollment in LSA dropped every year thereafter until it reached 660 in 1983. A similar trend was unfolding across the university. In 1983, black enrollment at UM represented 4.9 percent of the student body, the lowest percentage since 1971.[47]

The drop in black enrollment revealed that recruiting what Sjogren called "high quality" black students was more difficult than he had originally thought. In the late 1970s and early 1980s, Sjogren entered into a national recruiting battle for the black students with the highest standardized test scores. Just identifying these students presented a formidable obstacle. Sjogren put new resources into national databases. By 1977, the admissions office started buying from the College Board the names and contact information of minority students who self-reported grade point averages of 3.5 and scored at least 45 on the verbal section and 50 on the math section of the Preliminary Scholastic Aptitude Test (PSAT). The university also used the National Scholarship Service and Fund for Negro Students, which linked universities with "highly qualified" black students through organized interview sessions in different cities. During the 1979–80 academic year, the university attended six of these sessions around the country, which gave recruiters about six hundred prospective students.[48]

If finding "high quality" black students represented an obstacle, getting them to enroll at UM proved even more difficult. It wasn't hard to figure out why. Sjogren knew that he needed merit aid to recruit these students. By 1978, the admissions office used three merit-aid programs to recruit minority students: the Academic Recognition Scholarship, the Regents-Alumni Scholarship, and the Michigan Annual Giving Program. None of the programs were exclusively for minority students, but each were supposed to give special consideration to black, Hispanic, and Native American students. Nevertheless, these programs largely benefited white and Asian American applicants. In 1979, of the 1,300 students nominated for the Academic Recognition Scholarship, 19 (1.4 percent) were underrepresented minorities. Of the 626 students nominated for the Regents-Alumni Scholarship, 43 (6.8 percent) were underrepresented students. And of the 1,400 students nominated for the Michigan Annual Giving Program, 18 (1.3 percent) were underrepresented students.[49]

These numbers reveal that Sjogren initiated the new affirmative action admissions practices before adequate financial aid policies were in place to support his focus on "high quality" black students who usually didn't qualify for generous need-based financial aid packages. When an admissions staff member called twenty-eight black students from Illinois, Ohio, and Indiana, who were admitted to UM but did not enroll, he found out who Michigan was competing with: Yale, Duke, Stanford, Cornell, Brown, and Northwestern. When the staff member asked the students why they chose those schools over UM, most of the students responded that those schools offered more scholarship money.[50]

Even as Sjogren's efforts to recruit black students with high standardized test scores from outside the state stumbled, Goodman had initiated and still maintained policies that limited the size of the Opportunity Program. In 1971, 70 percent of the university's black students enrolled in OP. By 1977, the ratio of black OP to black non-OP students was 63 to 38. By 1978, the ratio was 53 to 47. Together with Sjogren's policy failures, Goodman's reforms to OP caused black enrollment to plummet.[51]

Goodman's policy changes effectively severed ties between the University of Michigan and its primary recruiting pool: working-class black students from Detroit. Reducing OP's size not only threw many of these students into Sjogren's new affirmative action admissions program, with its stronger emphasis on SAT scores and a college preparatory curriculum, but also cut those students off from important need-based aid at a time when federal financial aid was declining. Since its inception in 1972, the Pell Grant program had been the most important piece of federal funding for low-income students at UM. Between 1975 and 1990, the purchasing power of the maximum Pell Grant award declined dramatically. Other federal grants did not fill the gap. Instead, federally backed student loans filled in to help students pay for college.[52]

Still, the Opportunity Program's story reveals the problem with focusing too closely on federal financial aid in explaining why low-income students struggled to gain access to higher education institutions. Even before these cuts, federal grants never completely paid for working-class black students' education at UM. With money from UM's general fund, the Opportunity

Program filled in the gap between federal dollars and the cost to attend UM. When Goodman cut the size of the program, the university's general fund contributions to OP students' financial aid declined from $2,861,924 in the 1974–75 academic year to $1,775,039 in 1978–79. Given the university's changing priorities, the money the university saved on OP likely went into merit aid programs. Now with Goodman's policy changes, low-income students who scored too high on the SAT to gain entrance to the Opportunity Program but not high enough to qualify for a merit scholarship did not have access to OP's generous need-based package, taken in part from UM's general fund. By 1982, more minority students from families making less than $6,000 (equivalent to the buying power of just over $16,000 in 2018) were enrolled outside the Opportunity Program than within it, forcing them to find other ways to finance their education. The fact that this happened at the same moment that Pell Grants were declining made the gap between federal grants and the cost of tuition even greater.[53]

Ironically, Goodman's policy changes helped finance a large number of middle-class students who enrolled in OP. It turned out that many of the students who applied to UM and scored low enough on the SAT to gain entrance into OP were actually middle-class black students from Michigan. In 1982, five students from families making over $52,000 ($138,964 adjusted for inflation); four students from families making between $46,000 and $51,999 ($122,930 and $138,961); eleven students from families making $40,000 to $45,999 ($106,895 to $122,927); nine students from families making $36,000 to $39,000 ($96,206 to $104,233); and twenty-four students from families making $30,000 to $35,999 ($90,172 to $96,203) took advantage of the financial benefits of the Opportunity Program. This meant that low-income black students who scored too high on the SAT to gain entrance through OP received less generous financial packages than middle-class OP students with lower SAT scores.[54]

All these policy changes helped transform the makeup of black students at the University of Michigan. UM officials never exclusively recruited black students from working-class backgrounds, but the working-class black community in the state's cities reaped most of the benefits of OP in the 1960s and early 1970s. In 1968, for example, 71 percent of the fathers of OP students held unskilled or semi-skilled jobs. When Sjogren and Goodman shifted affirmative action admissions policies, the socioeconomic character of the black student body changed. In 1983, after five full classes of black students were recruited and admitted under the new admissions and financial aid policies, the median parental income of black students was $31,400 ($80,909 adjusted for inflation). Clearly, this wasn't the same black student population that walked onto campus in 1968.[55]

Co-optation was a long-term process that adapted to changing circumstances in order to align inclusion with the university's more important values and priorities. As campus leaders perceived new threats to the future institutional status of the University of Michigan in the mid-1970s, officials created new inclusion practices that they argued would preserve UM's elite reputation. In this context, UM officials transformed the purpose of affirmative action. No longer seeing affirmative action as a tool to address inequality in the state's cities, officials crafted new admissions and financial aid policies that sought to recruit and admit largely middle-class black students from the nation's suburbs. In the process, they led an intellectual assault on working-class black students living in cities like Detroit.

The declining power of the black campus movement provided the backdrop for these attacks. In a period in which administrators no longer feared organized protests, they had more power to shape the meaning and character of inclusion. Chapter 6 documents administrators' efforts to sustain these policies as black students once again tried to organize and push for more equitable practices. Administrators turned to the language of diversity to justify and maintain the racial retrenchment.

# CHAPTER 6

# Sustaining Racial Retrenchment

By 1979, the devastating impact of Goodman's and Sjogren's policies were clear. Black enrollment was plummeting, and the preferred affirmative action recruiting grounds were shifting away from the state's cities. The remaining vestiges of the black campus movement tried to push back. Black activists expressed their frustration and called on administrators to recommit to addressing the racial inequities rooted in urban areas. UM leaders weren't willing to return to the affirmative action practices of the past, and they were ready to fight to preserve the new policies.

In this context, diversity—the idea that a racially heterogeneous student body improved education and prepared students for a multiracial democracy and global economy—became a tool to defend and sustain George Goodman's and Cliff Sjogren's policies. Diversity helped sever the purpose of affirmative action from addressing the inequality rooted in cities, offered ambiguous goals that helped officials avoid accountability, and advanced administrators' interests in introducing a corporate model for the university. The diversity ideal, in other words, didn't spark racial retrenchment. Instead, diversity became a tool to sustain the university's policies of retrenchment.

Administrators still had to work to retain control over the meaning of diversity and ensure it supported Sjogren's and Goodman's policies. When diversity took hold among administrators, black students and their allies tried to employ diversity language to undermine the policies of retrenchment. Administrators ensured that never happened.

A twenty-one-year-old black psychology student from Detroit was the first to call attention to the consequences of Sjogren's and Goodman's policy changes. Pam Gordon could see the demographic shifts unfolding. In 1979, Gordon and some of her peers began raising their voices. The new test was whether faculty and UM leaders were willing to stay committed to these policy changes despite their disastrous consequences for black students' access.

Gordon served as the student government's vice president for minority affairs. When she decided to challenge Sjogren's and Goodman's policies, she stood in front of the university's budget committee. Her speech represented a strong rebuke of the university's desertion of the state's cities and its commitment to racial justice. In her eyes, by abandoning the most vulnerable students in Michigan's cities, UM was "perpetuating the poverty and ignorance which stifles our urban communities and causes them to deteriorate." She laid out a vision that harked back to BAM's idea of justice. Gordon also argued that the University of Michigan had a responsibility to admit students who would return to serve the state's urban black communities. This was central to BAM's goal of empowering black communities in Michigan. Gordon felt that the university failed to support this goal when admissions officers focused on black students living outside cities. In Gordon's eyes, these weren't the students who would use their training at UM to help the most vulnerable black communities. "One cannot realistically expect that minority students who were not raised in poor communities," Gorman suggested, "who have not dealt with the complexities and insufficiencies that are part of day-to-day existence in them, will be willing to devote their skills to uplifting them." In perhaps her most powerful statement, she told the budget committee that "any so-called affirmative action program which does not include human beings from these kinds of environments, where a brilliant mind has a greater chance of ending up in a penal or mental institution, than it does of reaching an institution of higher learning, is a superficial and fundamentally useless affirmative action program."[1]

Gordon also attacked Goodman's and Sjogren's interpretation of attrition. She understood that university officials were using attrition rates to justify admissions policies that excluded most black students in Detroit. Goodman and Sjogren offered an interpretation of attrition that focused on academic deficiency, while ignoring black students' social alienation and the poor campus services available. Gordon had more faith in the academic potential of black students educated in discriminatory environments. A black student with a C average who attended "a low-rated public school like Central High in Detroit" didn't leave the university before graduating because of academic deficiency, as Goodman and Sjogren claimed. Students like these experienced higher attrition rates, Gordon argued, because the university wasn't committed to changing the social environment on campus and providing the proper resources for these students to succeed. Rather than addressing these issues, she implied that university officials wanted to admit students whose success didn't hinge on institutional reform and hundreds of thousands of dollars in academic resources.[2]

The Black Student Union (BSU) shared Gordon's concerns. In April 1979, soon after Gordon gave her speech in front of the budget committee, the BSU presented a proposal to the regents to review the university's affirmative action policies. Chief among the BSU's suggestions was that affirmative action practices should "attempt to attract a minority student body more representative of minority communities, especially that of inner cities." The BSU asked how university officials expected to maintain the number of black students on campus "when it overlooks the majority of predominantly Black Detroit area high schools and concentrates on the more elite schools such as Cass Tech and predominantly white schools with only a few Black students." Like Gordon, they were concerned that UM's affirmative action policies ignored students from low-income backgrounds and were creating a black student community dominated by the middle class.[3]

The BSU also challenged Sjogren's and Goodman's efforts to blame black student attrition on academic deficiency. Like Gordon, the BSU offered an interpretation of attrition that focused on the negative impact of the university's racial climate. If the university was serious about addressing these problems, the BSU contended, it might have reached BAM's 10 percent goal.[4]

The Black Student Union's presentation highlighted the changing power dynamics on campus in the late 1970s. The BSU wasn't in a position to lead another BAM strike to challenge the university's policies. Instead, BSU activists asked for a task force to investigate their critiques and hopefully make policy recommendations that would address their concerns. Given their weak position on campus, the BSU hoped to find allies within the university who could help their cause. The regents agreed to create a task force to address the BSU's concerns. Black activists would have to wait almost two years for the task force's report.[5]

George Goodman and Cliff Sjogren went on a public relations campaign to defend their policies in light of declining black enrollment. Goodman outlined what was at stake in challenging the BSU's critiques. He started a line of argument that university officials had managed to keep just below the surface when they first presented plans to redistribute resources and focus on "good" black students. Goodman and Sjogren had also managed to avoid direct references to Detroit in the mid-1970s, when presenting their policy ideas. Gordon and the BSU's critiques, though, pushed Detroit into the center of the conversation.

Goodman suggested that it would be unfair to admit students from most Detroit schools. He argued, "The quality of the Detroit schools has declined during the past ten years, and we can only still legitimately predict a high probability of success from students coming from Cass Tech." He also added a new wrinkle to arguments about the small pool of "qualified" black students. As Goodman explained, bringing too many low-income black students created stereotypes of African Americans, marking all black students as poor and academically deficient. By recruiting "high ability," often middle-class black students, the university could help change those stereotypes.[6]

This type of argument about stereotypes could have been taken directly out of the anti–affirmative action strategy book. It was the type of argument that allowed affirmative action opponents to appear as if they opposed affirmative action in black students' interests, not because they wanted to preserve white privilege. It was one of Carl Cohen's favorite arguments. In his writings, he argued that affirmative action stigmatized black students, injuring those who could gain admission without affirmative action.[7]

When Goodman gave a public talk about the state of black enrollment, he continued his attack on Detroit. He told the crowd that if he had to give advice to Detroit parents who wanted their children to go to the University of Michigan, he would tell them to get their kids ready by eighth grade to attend Cass Tech or Renaissance, which just recently joined Cass as the city's second special-admit high school. UM still admitted at least four students each from other Detroit high schools, including Immaculata, Northwestern, Mumford, Central, Henry Ford, and Highland Park. Nevertheless, Goodman was confident that even these small numbers would continue to decline. Outside of Cass Tech and Renaissance, Goodman argued that there was "a whole lot of slippage" in academic standards. For Detroit students who applied to UM from other high schools, the "statistics clearly would not be in the student's favor," Goodman explained.[8]

Goodman repeated these same accusations to Steve Raphael, a journalist for *Detroit News* who was investigating the university's declining commitment to recruiting black students from Detroit. Raphael challenged the OP director to explain the declining opportunities for black students at UM. "We owe it to the faculty not to admit dumb kids," Goodman explained. "Dumb kids" was a harsh description that wouldn't have been acceptable at UM just a few years before. A comment like that might have brought protests or a reprisal from an executive official. But the fact that Goodman could say this without consequences spoke to the new environment of the late 1970s and early 1980s, in which officials didn't fear black protest, and much of the UM community believed that the university's status as an elite institution was at stake.[9]

Sjogren echoed these statements when he defended the policies in front of the Task Force on Minority Concerns—the task force appointed to review the BSU's criticism of declining black enrollment.[10] Sjogren claimed that the "deterioration of education in our major pool—the Detroit public schools" was largely responsible for declining black enrollment. Perhaps seeing the committee as a potential threat, Sjogren finally presented some evidence to back up his claims about the pool of "qualified" black students. He told the committee that Detroit offered no more than four hundred to five hundred minority students prepared to graduate from the University of Michigan. Of that number, he was able to enroll about ninety.[11]

The data Sjogren drew on was problematic. To figure out the pool of potential black students in Detroit, UM's admissions office used data gathered from a survey sent to black graduates from Detroit public high schools and Preliminary Scholastic Aptitude Test (PSAT) scores gathered from the College Board. The PSAT is essentially a preparatory SAT exam that students can take earlier in their high school career—a test that isn't free and requires the necessary financial resources. From the survey data, Sjogren found that about 38 percent of the students were taking what he considered an "academic curriculum," and 60 percent had a grade point average between 2.64 and 4.0. From the College Board, Sjogren found that 37 percent of black students in Michigan took the PSAT and scored at least 80 (equivalent of 800 on the SAT). He made the assumption that 37 percent of black Detroit students, then, would receive at least 80 on the PSAT. This meant that only 438 black high school graduates in Detroit were eligible for admission at UM. Sjogren offered no evidence that there was a strong correlation between black students' PSAT and eventual SAT scores or that the black students who took the PSAT were representative of those who took the SAT.[12]

Sjogren also told the task force that his office raised admissions criteria for black students because of retention problems. Here he continued to claim that attrition was due solely to academic underpreparation. These arguments showed how easily he and Goodman eliminated the institutional knowledge on black student attrition, which showed that nonacademic factors, such as social alienation, caused attrition. He still offered no evidence to support the claim that academic failure represented the leading cause of attrition.[13]

The task force would spend the rest of 1980 evaluating affirmative action policies. Meanwhile, Sjogren and Goodman gained an important ally.

On January 1, 1980, Harold Shapiro became the University of Michigan's next president. The nationally renowned economist with executive-level experience seemed like a logical choice to the regents. An economic downturn, coupled with declining state appropriations, put many of the university's priorities in question. Shapiro was confident that he could maintain the university's reputation through tough economic times. In choosing Shapiro, though, the regents empowered someone who had overseen the declining number of black students at the University of Michigan. Shapiro had served as vice president for academic affairs—the executive position that oversaw the admissions office—from 1977 to 1980.[14]

In his time as vice president for academic affairs, he showed that he had a high tolerance for racial disparities. He refused to hold the admissions office accountable, even when one of his assistants questioned the office's commitment to affirmative action and pushed Sjogren to create new policies. It's no surprise, then, that Shapiro sided with Goodman and Sjogren over the BSU when Shapiro became president. Shapiro outlined his position on affirmative action in front of an audience gathered to talk about the legacy of the BAM strike of 1970. It had been ten years since black student activists had shut down the university. Prominent BAM activists, faculty participants, and former administrators involved in the strike had gathered in Ann Arbor at the request of the Center for Afroamerican and African Studies to remember the strike and to chart a new way forward to improve black students' opportunities at UM. If any of these participants thought Shapiro's administration represented a moment of opportunity, his speech showed otherwise.[15]

Shapiro offered a new intellectual framework for racially attentive admissions that would help support Goodman's and Sjogren's policies. Shapiro told the audience, "I think it would be desirable if no one here had any concept of affirmative action or any commitment to affirmative action." Here he didn't mean that it would be desirable if the university no longer used racially attentive admissions practices. Instead, he wanted to change how the university community understood the purpose and value of those policies. Shapiro explained that affirmative action policies were intended to "create an environment here on campus which reflects a good deal more cultural diversity and historical experience than has been the case in the first 150 years or so of the university's existence." This environment, Shapiro explained, would enrich the "intellectual experience of all students" at UM.[16]

Shapiro's speech marked an important turning point for the University of Michigan. While the diversity ideal—the idea that a racially and ethnically heterogeneous student body produced educational benefits—had been used to support programs to improve race relations, it had been used sparingly to justify racially attentive admissions policies at the university. But beginning in the 1980s, the language of diversity began to consume discussions about affirmative action admissions.[17]

The increasing popularity of diversity so close to the *Bakke* decision makes it tempting to attribute the diversity rationale's rise at UM to Powell's famous written opinion in the case. Yet nothing suggests that Shapiro and other UM officials adopted the diversity rationale in response to *Bakke*. Nobody in the late 1970s and early 1980s suggested that UM needed to emphasize the educational benefits of diversity in order to comply with the ruling. As noted in chapter 6, administrators' attention was focused on the mechanisms of using race to select students. Quotas were clearly unconstitutional. Since UM didn't use quotas, the ruling didn't produce much concern among UM officials.[18]

Instead, diversity became popular at UM because it helped support Goodman's and Sjogren's policies. Diversity helped sever the purpose of racially attentive admissions from addressing the inequality rooted in cities. Shapiro made it clear in his speech that the university no longer saw Detroit as the central recruiting ground for affirmative action. Instead, the purpose of diversity was to get black students who could serve the interests of the university. In this formulation, black students didn't need to come from a particular place or social class. They simply needed high enough standardized test scores to preserve the quality of the university and be present on campus to improve white students' education.[19]

Diversity also helped Shapiro modify how the university would measure racial inclusion. Shapiro shared Goodman's and Sjogren's pessimism about the pool of "qualified" black students. He told the audience gathered on the tenth anniversary of the BAM strike, "I don't know . . . what realism there was in the ten percent goal." The statement wasn't a slip of the tongue. He later reiterated this claim in the same speech: "I don't think if anyone thought about it that the 10 percent enrollment objective was realistic. I don't know what is realistic in the next few years." Shapiro saw the 10 percent black enrollment goal as a problem. It had hung over the administration like a black cloud since 1970. Every year, black enrollment numbers came out and officials had to explain why they had failed, yet again, to meet the BAM enrollment concession. No matter what new policies administrators implemented, no matter how much money they devoted to recruitment, the message was still the same: they had failed.[20]

Shapiro thought that this assessment was unfair. He didn't think that UM's commitment to racial inclusion should be measured by a standard that he considered unrealistic. Rather than measuring the university's commitment to inclusion against the 10 percent goal, Shapiro told the audience, "I think we've simply fallen short of what is a desirable goal for a great university." It's no coincidence that Shapiro never attached numbers to this statement. How many black students were necessary for a great university? Diversity became valuable because it wasn't supposed to answer that question. It was supposed to be ambiguous. It was supposed to relieve the university of the inconvenient accountability of the BAM concessions.[21]

Diversity was also valuable because of its racial and ethnic ambiguity. The new language represented an effort to decenter black students in UM's vision of racial inclusion. Shapiro rarely used the word "black" in his speech, preferring "minority" instead. At one point, he suggested that the BAM concessions created a 10 percent minority, rather than black, enrollment goal. This wasn't simply the result of years of activism on behalf of Asian American, Hispanic, and Native American students to be recognized as legitimate beneficiaries of affirmative action. Instead, it represented an opportunity for UM officials to take credit for the growing numbers of Hispanic, Native American, and Asian American students on campus.[22]

UM officials were desperate to tell a story of racial progress on campus in the early 1980s, and it was almost impossible to do that if black students were at the center of the story. A black story was a story about the university's retrenchment, but a story about minority students looked different. Every year, the total number of nonblack minority students was on the rise. A combination of conscious and accidental practices led to rising numbers of Hispanic, Native American, and Asian American students in the late 1970s and early 1980s. Although Asian Americans weren't part of UM's affirmative action admissions program, their rising numbers were partly due to conscious policy efforts. Privately, Sjogren wrote about his desire to create new resources for out-of-state recruitment and merit aid to enroll, in his words, "middle and upper income . . . Asian Americans." It's no surprise, then, that Asian Americans disproportionately benefited from the merit-based aid Sjogren introduced. Sjogren intended merit aid to work that way. Between 1975 and 1980, Asian American undergraduate enrollment rose from 245 to 556. Native American and Hispanic student numbers, in contrast, rose by accident. The admissions office didn't introduce new programs that targeted these students in the late 1970s. But when the admissions office placed racial identification on applications, it gave Hispanic and Native American students access to affirmative action like they had never had before. When the Opportunity Program represented the university's only affirmative action admissions tool, UM never devoted the same resources to in-state Hispanic and Native American recruiting as it did to recruiting black students. Hispanic and Native American communities within Michigan were also much smaller than they were in many other states. With the new application system, Hispanic and Native American students' access to affirmative action no longer depended on their residential status and their knowledge of OP's complicated admissions process. As a result, despite the policies that led black enrollment to plummet, undergraduate Hispanic student numbers rose from 157 in 1975 to 248 in 1980. During the same period, Native American enrollment rose from 38 to 107. A story of minority enrollment, then, allowed UM officials to tell a story of racial progress.[23]

Finally, diversity helped Shapiro frame inclusion to fit into his new corporate model for the university. Shapiro was hired to lead the university through tough economic times. Declining state appropriations continued into the 1980s. Shapiro wanted to create an institution built for an era when the university couldn't depend on the state for the majority of its budget. Even before he took office, he started talking about the possibility of major cuts—possibly the elimination of entire departments, offices, and initiatives. He sold this plan as "smaller but better." Introducing budget cuts within the university wasn't new. The university had seen tough economic times in the past and enforced sharp budget cuts. It was the market-based logic that Shapiro used to decide what to cut that represented a significant turning point for UM. As Donald Deskins, an associate dean of the Rackham Graduate School, noted, "The University is being run much more like a business. . . . The question is, what is the place of minorities in this businessman-like view of the University."[24]

This "businessman-like view" influenced the way Shapiro envisioned social problems. Recall that historically, rationales for special admissions programs included a two-step process. First, administrators defined a social problem that the university could address. Since the early 1960s, university officials justified racially attentive policies as an effort to address racial and socioeconomic inequalities, especially in urban America. Addressing racial inequality didn't represent one of Shapiro's core issues. Instead, Shapiro wanted to focus on an entirely different problem: he believed that the United States was unprepared to compete in an era of globalization. This problem, to him, was more pressing than racial inequality. Shapiro fit the purpose of racial inclusion into this framework. He saw a multiracial student body as a tool to train students in the racial and ethnic sensitivity necessary to do business in a global marketplace. Racial inclusion, then, became a tool to help the economic interests of the United States.[25]

Shapiro's modification to the second prong of the affirmative action rationale represented an even more dramatic transformation. Historically, the second piece of the affirmative action rationale showed how racially attentive policies didn't harm the university's status. But under Shapiro's new formula, showing that racially attentive policies didn't harm the university's status wasn't good enough. To justify racially attentive policies, proponents had to show how affirmative action added value to UM.[26]

On the one hand, value could be measured based on whether academic units and program initiatives were vital to the quality and status of the University of Michigan. Diversity language helped show that racially attentive admission policies improved the quality of UM. As Shapiro explained, there were educational benefits in cultural diversity on campus and in the classroom. In Shapiro's corporate model, though, value also meant the economic revenue that units or programs contributed to university coffers. As the university faced a world where it could rely less on state support, Shapiro looked for ways to substitute government funds for private money. He knew he would have to rely more on alumni donations. Still, donations would make only a small dent in the funding shortfall. Shapiro had his sights on corporate money. He wanted to turn Ann Arbor into the next technology hub—the next Palo Alto. Stanford University, which had created a thriving research park that linked the university to businesses, provided the model. Diversity fit into this campaign because the university was also selling access to a future workforce—a student body prepared for a new era of globalization. Educated in a diverse environment, these students were ready to help businesses compete in the global economy.[27]

When Shapiro finished his speech, he didn't receive a warm reception from a crowd ready to talk about and remember the BAM strike of 1970. One audience member immediately questioned his use of diversity as a rational for affirmative action. "I certainly take issue with your perspective that it is desirable for the university to admit minorities specifically for the reason of cultural diversity," he told Shapiro. "I think the important reason we should have minority students at the university is precisely because it is an important social responsibility[,] not merely having a blend of cultures and mixtures of races." Shapiro stepped back from his earlier statements and told the audience that he didn't reject social justice as a reason to increase minority representation on campus. Instead, Shapiro claimed he was simply adding an additional justification.[28]

Diversity, though, was clearly the rationale Shapiro preferred. In the years that followed, diversity began to eclipse social justice as the favored rationale of university administrators. Social justice never went away, but to keep social justice in line with admissions policies, social responsibility took on a different meaning in order to work seamlessly with diversity rhetoric and to support admissions policies that increasingly looked away from low-income black students living in cities.

"We should be attempting to increase the ethnic diversity of our campus," the committee report read. It was 1981, and the committee appointed to evaluate the concerns of the Black Student Union had finally returned with its conclusions. The committee's findings spelled bad news for black students attending high schools in Detroit. The committee recognized that the BSU was especially concerned about the declining enrollments of "inner-city Detroit residents." But while task force members agreed with the BSU that the university should serve students "of all social classes," they concluded, "it is our impression that students from lower social classes are less likely to be adequately prepared for academic work at this University." Thus, the university "should do a better job with [the low-income students] it already admits before it seeks to recruit and admit students who are greater academic risks." After a two-year investigation, the task force vindicated the practices of the admissions office and the Opportunity Program.[29]

The committee report showed the impact of Sjogren and Goodman, who changed the way the university saw black student attrition. Fundamental to portraying black students from Detroit as risky and black students from suburban areas as talented was ignoring all the attrition data from the late 1960s and early 1970s that showed that Detroit students were not dropping out because of academic failure. Seeing attrition exclusively in academic terms was essential in juxtaposing smart middle-class students with risky low-income students.[30]

The report also showed how officials preserved social justice rhetoric in the early 1980s, modifying it to fit with Shapiro's diversity ideal. The report recognized that increasing the number of minority students on campus was important "because social justice demands that ethnic minority groups have the same access to higher education as does the majority and because such diversity" enriched the "educational opportunities of the majority." To blend social justice and diversity, the report used an abstract definition of racial justice that was disconnected from geography. Throughout the 1960s and the first half of the 1970s, officials focused on the need to address inequalities embedded in cities. But now officials focused more broadly on racial inequities—the national racial disparities in income, high school graduation rates, and college-going rates. This focus represented an understanding of inequality that grouped all African Americans together, ignoring the different experiences based on social class and place. Racial inequality existed. It was bad. And the university should admit more minority students to do something about it. This was the type of ambiguous social justice vision that melded easily with diversity rhetoric. Both diversity and social justice language could serve as tools to justify the university's decision to limit access to working-class black students in Detroit.[31]

Still, the problem remained that black student enrollment was plummeting. By the time the committee issued its report, black undergraduate enrollment had fallen to 1,058 students (4.8 percent). By fall 1982, black enrollment fell by another 14 students. Administrators again turned to merit aid as the solution. The problem was that the existing merit aid programs didn't serve black students well. Recall that in 1979, underrepresented minority students won 1.4 percent of Academic Recognition Scholarships, 6.8 percent of Regents-Alumni Scholarships, and 1.3 percent of Michigan Annual Giving Program scholarships. Robert Seltzer, assistant director of undergraduate admissions, thought he knew the answer to this problem. The university could fund one hundred (fifty in-state and fifty out-of-state) full-tuition merit scholarships specifically for underrepresented students. The university wouldn't have to worry about attrition, he argued, because these students weren't "risky." Using the market ethos that Shapiro introduced, he sold the program by arguing that it "would not involve a significant increase in support service costs," since these students had "better academic credentials." In short, "good" minority students were especially attractive because they cost less to manage. The marketplace ethos helped to see low-income black students as too costly.[32]

Seltzer's vision finally found support in fall 1983, when black enrollment hit its lowest point since 1971. For the first time in a decade, fewer than one thousand black undergraduates had registered for classes at the University of Michigan. Seltzer's Michigan Achievement Awards offered merit scholarships to in-state and out-of-state students. Data shows how the program shifted aid away from students in Detroit's public schools. Of forty-nine students in LSA who were offered the award, five were black students from Detroit. Two of these students went to private high schools and two others went to Renaissance, one of Detroit's special-admit high schools. Only one student went to a public Detroit high school that wasn't a special-admit institution.[33]

In 1984, another task force on undergraduate student aid discussed the consequences of devoting more of the university's resources to merit-based aid rather than need-based aid. Again, the committee vindicated the practices initiated by Sjogren and Goodman. At the center of its analysis was an interpretation of low-income students as academic risks who hurt the quality of the university. "It is not easy," the task force concluded, "to choose between" funding low-income and middle-income black students. But increasing merit aid was vital to "attract[ing] large numbers of good students . . . and the value of these students in preserving overall academic quality levels at UM will be important." "The numbers of high ability undergraduates at UM are slipping at a noticeable rate," the task force went on. "There is . . . an unusual risk in doing nothing."[34]

Even as black enrollment continued to plummet in the early 1980s, UM task forces defended Sjogren's and Goodman's policies. "Bad" and "risky" became acceptable descriptions of Detroit's black students, and university officials found a way to make diversity and social justice work in harmony to justify racial retrenchment.

For administrators, diversity was an intellectual rationale designed to sustain policies already in place. The ideal would have become useless to administrators if it became a justification for policies they disagreed with. Campus leaders, then, had to work hard in the 1980s to stymie efforts by black student activists and their allies to appropriate the diversity ideal in order to challenge the policies of retrenchment and advance a different vision of racial justice in higher education.

In February 1984, Niara Sudarkasa (formerly Gloria Marshall) joined the administration as associate vice president for academic affairs, a new position created to stem the tide of declining black enrollment and address the poor racial climate on campus. A decade earlier, the board of regents would have balked at giving Sudarkasa a position of influence. She had been one of the most vocal black faculty members during the BAM strike and had played an important role in the protest and negotiations. Sudarkasa almost lost her job as the result of her participation.[35]

University leaders created Sudarkasa's position as black student activists began to reorganize in the early 1980s. By fall 1982, the Black Student Union reemerged after having dissolved in 1979. The campus chapter of the NAACP also resurfaced after a seven-year hiatus. BAM III didn't develop during the 1982–83 academic year, but administrators could see an emerging threat. In November 1982, BSU members held a teach-in on racism at the university. They invited Ed Fabre, a leader of the 1970 BAM strike, who called the teach-in "déjà vu." Black students and professors discussed turning the teach-in into direct action. As black enrollment continued to decline and black student organizing gained strength, administrators eventually brought Sudarkasa into the administration.[36]

It was a classic co-optation strategy. Not only were campus leaders trying to get black student activists to work for change within the inclusion bureaucracy, but they were also bringing a faculty ally, experienced in organizing student protest, into the administration. Executive administrators didn't employ this tactic to allow activists to capture the institution and remake it in student activists' vision. Rather, they invited activists into the bureaucracy because they believed that they would have more control over reform. The alternative was dealing with disruptive dissent, which could lead to concessions that administrators believed were unviable and violated the university's priorities and values.

Sudarkasa knew as well as anyone the university's long history of using black officials to stymie dissent. She had become an astute observer of university practices as she worked to reform the university with black students in the 1960s and 1970s. She knew that the university rarely gave black officials any power. Her position wasn't any different. Associate vice president might sound powerful, but it was essentially an advisory position. She had no budget with which to implement programs. She had no power to fire anyone who didn't implement her policy recommendations. But she still believed that she had the skills to work within these limitations and create significant institutional reforms that could stem the tide of declining black enrollment and faculty hires at the University of Michigan. More than that, she envisioned creating successful programs that universities across the country would emulate. It wouldn't take long to realize that her optimism was misguided.[37]

Just as many black officials had in the past, Sudarkasa challenged campus leaders. She was a harsh critic of the ambiguity of Shapiro's diversity framework. She came into her position during a period when Shapiro and other officials doubted the probability of BAM's 10 percent black enrollment goal. Shapiro suggested that the university should do away with the goal altogether and instead pursue a fuzzy ideal of a diverse student body, which included no numerical goals. Sudarkasa refused to accept Shapiro's vision. She quickly made it clear that she would use her position to reach the BAM enrollment goal. Not only was the goal attainable, but she wanted to reach it within three to four years. In effect, Sudarkasa was trying to outline a new era of accountability. Racial inclusion efforts would be judged against the numerical goals that were supposed to be achieved within a defined timeline.[38]

Sudarkasa also challenged Shapiro's efforts to decenter black students in the university's vision of racial inclusion. She didn't ignore the rising number of nonblack minority students, but she was concerned that administrators were using Asian American enrollment, in particular, to hide the declining number of black students on campus. When discussing affirmative action, she emphasized that Asian American students were overrepresented, and their numbers shouldn't be used to measure the success of racial inclusion programs.[39]

In challenging administrators' use of Asian American students, she brought the university into a new era—one that could see African Americans as unique while still acknowledging the challenges that Hispanic and Native American students also faced. She used the term "underrepresented minority"—a term that had been used in the past but still wasn't widely adopted at UM. Black, Hispanic, and Native American students all held a special position because their share of the student population didn't reflect their share of the state population. Still, according to Sudarkasa, even among underrepresented students, black students held a special place. No group was more underrepresented at UM than black students; thus, they deserved more resources and attention.[40]

Her most difficult challenge, though, was restoring the university's confidence in the academic capabilities of black students from Michigan's cities. In Sudarkasa's eyes, the only way to achieve the 10 percent black enrollment goal was to make Michigan's cities the key recruiting grounds for black students again. To do this, she knew that she had to challenge Sjogren's claims about the academic merits of black students in the state. When Sjogren finally presented some evidence to support his claims about the capabilities of black students in Michigan's cities, the evidence came in the form of pool studies—in other words, studies that outlined the number of qualified black students that the admissions office could recruit. He used PSAT scores and high school grades to argue that few black students in the state qualified for admission at UM. Sudarkasa tried to counter Sjogren's claims by producing her own pool study of Michigan's black high school students. She started with the premise that "more weight should be given to the independent predictability of grade point averages and written evaluations by teachers." To justify this conclusion, she tried to revive some of the institutional knowledge about black students' performance that supported affirmative action in the 1960s and 1970s. In particular, she emphasized that the SAT represented a poor tool to predict whether a black student could graduate from UM. The admissions office no longer commissioned social scientists to analyze the utility of standardized tests in predicting black students' performance, so Sudarkasa looked to scholarship produced outside UM, citing two social scientists who called the SAT a "third-rate predictor of college performance" and concluded that the test was particularly unfair to minorities and low-income students. Their findings mirrored internal studies at UM completed in previous decades.[41]

When Sudarkasa created her pool study, then, she deemphasized the importance of standardized tests to identify potential UM students. Not surprisingly, Sudarkasa presented a much larger pool of qualified black students than had Sjogren. Using data on high school graduates in 1984, she found that of the 5,466 black students who took the ACT—a standardized test UM accepted as an alternative to the SAT—4,211 didn't score high enough to qualify for admission at UM. The ACT made only 15 black students eligible as honor students, marked 254 as "qualified," and deemed another 986 as "qualified with reservation." That meant that test scores alone made 77 percent of the potential pool of black applicants unqualified. It was by far the highest rate of any racial group. The ACT deemed 53 percent of Hispanic and Native American students unqualified, as well as 28 percent of Asian Americans and 31 percent of whites. But if admissions officers looked at high school performance, a different picture emerged of the academic proficiency of black students. If admissions officers ignored standardized test scores, 389 black students became honor students, 1,348 became "qualified," and another 1,741 became "qualified with reservation." The "students apparently get the message that test scores are much more important admission criteria than grades," Sudarkasa concluded, because of the 1,348 students whose grades put them in the "qualified" category, only 178 (13 percent) actually applied to UM. Of the black students whose grades put them in the "qualified with reservation" category, only 3 percent applied.[42]

Rather than doing away with the diversity ideal, she believed she could use diversity to justify new policies that recommitted the university to the BAM goals and black students in Detroit. For Sudarkasa, arguing that "our pursuit of academic excellence is enhanced by the diversity of our student body" didn't prohibit arguments about the university's responsibility to working-class black students in Detroit. She never ruminated on diversity, offering a detailed definition of the word that included the diversity of socioeconomic backgrounds and geographic locations. Instead, she adopted administrators' abstract language of diversity along with strong statements about the university's social responsibility to suggest that UM should recruit black students from Detroit.[43]

Campus leaders, of course, didn't want people to think about the university's commitment to Detroit when they heard the word "diversity." Thus, to preserve their meaning of and purpose behind diversity, they had to limit Sudarkasa's power to undermine Sjogren's and Goodman's policies. They did so by protecting Sjogren from Sudarkasa's criticism.

Sjogren openly mocked Sudarkasa's goals. In a special LSA Blue Ribbon Commission meeting organized to review admissions policies, Sjogren continued to question whether Detroit was a viable recruiting ground for minority students. Sjogren told the committee members that the pool of in-state minorities was small because of the poor quality of the Detroit school system.

Initially, Sudarkasa thought she could get Sjogren to change his stance. Sudarkasa was sitting in that meeting with Sjogren. As she sat silently waiting to confront the admissions director, she didn't understand how little power she actually had over Sjogren. She knew that her role, despite the powerful sounding title of associate vice president, was merely an advisory position. She had no power to fire Sjogren. Her power came from Billy Frye, the vice president for academic affairs, and his willingness to support her and discipline the director of admissions. Sjogren needed to fear Frye in order for Sudarkasa to have any power over the admissions director. But Sjogren didn't fear Frye, and Sudarkasa didn't know it yet.[44]

Recall that Frye began his rise up the administrative ranks after he was hired over Jewell Cobb as dean of LSA in 1975. Cobb was the black candidate who was initially offered the position, but Fleming and other administrative officials effectively undermined her selection in order to hire Frye. Frye proved a poor advocate for racial justice. He failed to create any consequences for officials, like Sjogren, who were responsible for racial retrenchment. Instead, he accepted tepid plans from the admissions office to reverse declining black enrollment.[45]

This was the environment that Sudarkasa stepped into at the 1985 meeting where Sjogren was offering his analysis of the Detroit school system. After the meeting, she challenged his statements, questioning his assumptions about the lack of talented students in Detroit. Sjogren would have to expand his efforts to admit more students beyond Cass and Renaissance if the admissions office planned to meet the black enrollment goals, she told him.[46]

Sjogren wasn't accustomed to this type of attack from anyone in the administration. Sjogren fired back in a strongly worded letter to Sudarkasa. Her criticism was "unwarranted" and "unfair," Sjogren contended, and made increasing black enrollment much more difficult. He suggested that she make an effort to understand how the admissions office actually functioned. He listed the recruiting initiatives that took place in every Detroit high school to show Sudarkasa that he had not given up on Detroit students. But then he repeated the same message that he had been spreading for a decade: Cass and Renaissance enrolled "high ability, serious students from Detroit," while students from other schools had a history of attrition at UM.[47]

Sudarkasa fired back. Sjogren could list as many Detroit recruiting events as he wanted, she told him, but "the record of declining Black enrollment from 1977 to 1983 speaks for itself." In response to Sjogren's "disappointment" over Sudarkasa's remarks, she wrote that "if there is anyone who should be disappointed, it is I, who have been charged with providing leadership to the University in the area of increasing minority enrollment . . . and who found reason to believe . . . that the Director of Admissions espouses views that might be viewed as counterproductive to these efforts." The last statement was supposed to remind Sjogren that she held an executive position on campus and that his job was to follow her leadership—not challenge it.[48]

Sudarkasa expected Frye's full support. What happened next surprised her. Frye did inform Sjogren that his letter to Sudarkasa was unacceptable and that the director of admissions shouldn't talk about Detroit schools in that manner. But then Robert Holmes, Frye's assistant vice president, worked with Sjogren to compose a letter of reconciliation to Sudarkasa. Sjogren wrote the original draft. He said that he would increase his efforts in Detroit, but he still wasn't willing to let go of his original comments about "ill-prepared" students. For example, he wrote, "I am sure that you will agree with me . . . that the admission of ill-prepared students will not only be counterproductive to our goals, but will adversely affect the future lives of a great number of young people." Holmes told Sjogren to strike this sentence from the draft because he wasn't "hearing any more about 'lowering standards.'" But then Holmes wrote that "I obviously agree with your statement," but "I suggest that we keep it in reserve for a time, if ever, that it might be needed." In essence, Holmes told Sjogren that the executive administration agreed with his analysis of "ill-prepared" Detroit students but simply asked him to stop saying it in public. This was hardly the type of change that Sudarkasa was looking for.[49]

Frye also scolded Sudarkasa. He suggested that her communication with Sjogren threatened to undermine the administration's relationship with the admissions office and, in turn, efforts to increase minority enrollment. If Sudarkasa couldn't challenge the director of admissions, what power did she have to hold anyone accountable? What impact would any of her reform recommendations have if university officials could flaunt their opposition—in this case, with Sudarkasa in the audience—without any consequences?[50]

Sudarkasa realized that she also wouldn't get Shapiro's support to push Sjogren to reform his policies. Sudarkasa had contact with Shapiro, as the president consulted her to craft public messages about black enrollment efforts and racial climate issues. Sudarkasa wrote statements for Shapiro that embraced diversity and tried to get Shapiro to reconsider his views about the Detroit school system. Rather than blaming Detroit schools for falling black enrollment, she wanted Shapiro to focus on the impact of the economic recession, which more than doubled black unemployment in the state, and decisions by legislators that cut federal and state financial aid. Essentially, she gave Shapiro the popular narrative of racial innocence that allowed UM to escape culpability for racial disparities without blaming the quality of the Detroit school system. But Shapiro ignored her counsel and continued to focus on the Detroit school system in public statements to explain low black enrollment. It represented the failure of all the work Sudarkasa had done to change perceptions of Detroit. Here was the president of the university repeating the same lines that Sjogren and Goodman had offered him in the late 1970s and early 1980s.[51]

Sudarkasa finally realized the true limits of her power. She wrote to Frye complaining that she was "not in charge with carrying out the programmatic initiatives to reach the minority enrollment goal." She lamented that without the authority to hold anyone accountable, her role was basically to advise executive officers on ways to increase minority enrollment and assess the effectiveness of the university in those efforts. But Sudarkasa felt that she was "being put in the position of having to take personal responsibility for accomplishing the goals which the University has set, whereas this is not my role." "I don't have the authority to bring" Sjogren and other important policymakers on board, she continued. She made clear that only Frye and Shapiro could do that. Sudarkasa knew all these limitations when she took the position. Still, she believed that she would act with the support, and thus authority, of Frye. That didn't turn out to be the case. Sudarkasa's complaints echoed the sentiments of black officials in the early 1970s that accused the university of using black administrators as scapegoats and giving them no power.[52]

When Sudarkasa ran into problems with Sjogren, she turned her attention to the university's racial climate, which she knew posed problems for black student recruitment and retention. If Sudarkasa believed that initiatives to repair the racial climate would receive less resistance than her efforts to change admissions policies, she would be sorely disappointed. She soon found that she would face similar limitations on her power to lead institutional reform, despite her attempts to accommodate diversity rhetoric.

Sudarkasa took her position during another struggle over how to interpret the connection between the racial climate and black student attrition. A young black professor of sociology at UM, with a dual appointment in CAAS and sociology, tried to revive the institutional knowledge of the early 1970s that contended that the racial climate was to blame for black student attrition rates. Walter Allen arrived at the University of Michigan in fall 1979. His appointment speaks to the role of CAAS in bringing black professors to campus who would challenge institutional knowledge about black students. Allen immediately went to work, studying the experiences of black students on campus. During the winter term of 1980, he sent questionnaires to black undergraduate students. Allen concluded from the survey evidence that black student attrition at UM was rooted in "culture shock" and "social alienation," not lack of academic preparation. This type of interpretation mirrored the social science studies of the early 1970s and challenged the administrative knowledge that dominated institutional decision making in the late 1970s and early 1980s.[53]

Black students also told their stories to other researchers and journalists. Barry Beckham, a professor at Brown University, released *The Black Student's Guide to Colleges* in 1982. UM's profile included a quote from one black student who called relations between white and black students "the pits." The 1984 edition of the book went even further, warning black students thinking of attending Michigan that they should be "prepared to combat possible culture shock and social alienation." The *New York Times* offered a similar message, giving UM undergraduate Veronica Woolridge an opportunity to present her view of the institution. After three years at Michigan, she reported that she had only taken one class with a black instructor—a visiting professor from Detroit's Wayne State University. There were so few black students, she continued, that black students had an "unwritten code" that they greet each other on campus, even when they didn't know each other. She also described a flyer that appeared on campus the week before the article ran declaring April as "White Pride Time," featuring "counciling [*sic*] sessions on how to deal with uppity niggers." Publicity like this was particularly concerning for UM officials, who were trying to raise black enrollment.[54]

Still, UM officials remained committed to the views about black student attrition that Sjogren and Goodman had created in the latter half of the 1970s. They continued to downplay the importance of black students' social alienation by claiming that academic deficiency represented the key factor explaining attrition. Vice president of student services Henry Johnson made this clear when he told a reporter, "I'm concerned with what (Black) students need more than what they want." "What they need," he explained, "is a good academic support service." "The key issue for keeping students here," he continued, "is keeping them here academically. What keeps you here is not how comfortable you are outside of class, it's whether you can cut it in class." The fact that Johnson made these comments was all the more significant because he was the executive administrator who was supposed to oversee programs that addressed black students' social alienation. If he didn't see the connection between the university's racial climate and attrition, who was going to address the issue?[55]

Black student activists hoped that they would find a more receptive audience in Sudarkasa. Her early reports suggested that she would challenge the prevailing views of administrators. She argued that the poor racial climate at the University of Michigan contributed to black student attrition and declining black enrollment. The problem for black students was that Sudarkasa believed that increasing black enrollment and creating a "critical mass" of black students represented the best way to improve the racial climate. In order to recruit enough black students to create a "critical mass"—she never defined how many black students were necessary for "critical mass"—she believed that she needed to repair the image of the university as a hostile place for black students. In the short term, that meant suppressing black students' public complaints about the racial climate.[56]

Sudarkasa's efforts to repair UM's image put her at odds with black students who publicly testified about their experiences on campus. A 1985 *Detroit Free Press* article particularly irked administrators, including Sudarkasa. Cheryl Jordan, a black political science major in her senior year, told the reporter that "a lot of them (Whites) are very open about" racism, as "there are swastika signs on doors." Another student reported that someone had written "kill niggers!" on a library carrel. Roderick Dean, president of the Black Student Union, added that he was "shocked" when he arrived at UM. "The first thing I noticed when I arrived on campus was the graffiti," which was "much worse than the graffiti I saw in the South."[57]

Sudarkasa, along with other administrators, were furious when they read the *Detroit Free Press* article. Sudarkasa believed that the school was being unfairly targeted, since the racial climate on UM's campus reflected a problem that existed on all predominantly white campuses across the country.[58] She didn't reserve her criticism for the *Detroit Free Press*. Once the paper published the article, Charles Holman of the NAACP brought some of the black students interviewed for the article to meet with UM administrators, including Sudarkasa. Holman thought the meeting represented an opportunity to discuss institutional reform. Instead, Holman reported that Sudarkasa verbally attacked the black students. "She even attacked me verbally for bringing up the problem," Holman explained. Then "she stormed out [of] the room."[59]

As much as campus leaders shared Sudarkasa's concerns that negative portrayals of the racial climate hurt efforts to raise black enrollment, they also feared that these articles would hurt the university's larger recruiting efforts. By the mid-1980s, UM officials began using diversity as a recruiting tool for white students. As officials fought for the "best" students in a competitive environment, they pitched UM as a place where students could get the unique experience of living with people of different backgrounds. They offered idyllic images of a contentious-free environment. Newspaper portrayals of a contentious racial climate threatened to compromise diversity as a marketing tool. Administrators' lack of support for concrete proposals to improve the racial climate shows that they were more invested in positive portrayals of the racial climate than putting the necessary resources forward to improve black students' experience on campus.[60]

Despite her hopes that the media would stop covering black students' experience on campus, press attention only increased. In the final months of 1985, Sudarkasa began meeting with minority students. Students accused the administration of not "paying enough attention to retention" by ignoring the university's racial climate. They wanted Sudarkasa to create programs that would address campus racism and black students' social alienation.[61]

In the aftermath of these meetings, Sudarkasa called for a program to improve the university's racial climate that she called the Year of Understanding the Value of Diversity at the University and in Society. In the initial proposal, she framed the need for such a program as a minority student retention initiative. "My perception," Sudarkasa concluded, "is that we urgently need to take the initiative in addressing this concern on the part of students." "If we do not," she stressed, "all the other initiatives we are taking in the area of minority student enrollment will be compromised."[62]

Again, Sudarkasa had faith that she could use diversity language to justify a program that addressed black students' concerns. She pitched the Year of Understanding as an opportunity "to explore, understand, and reaffirm the value of diversity for strengthening the intellectual and cultural life of our campus." The proposal harked back to 1972, when black students used diversity language to address social alienation and advocate for a living space dominated by black students. As with the 1972 proposal, Sudarkasa was trying to use diversity language to speak to administrators' interests while addressing black activists' concerns.[63]

Because Sudarkasa had no budget or power to create student programming on her own, she had to get the support of Henry Johnson, the vice president of student services. Johnson headed the Committee on Diversity, which evaluated proposals like Sudarkasa's. Johnson had long been critical of the idea that the university's racial climate affected black student attrition rates. Not surprisingly, the final committee draft of the Year of Understanding stripped any reference to black students' social alienation from the final proposal. Rather than framing the benefits of the program as a retention initiative, the committee recast the benefits as an opportunity to "celebrate the rich racial, ethnic and cultural diversity of our campus and society-at-large." Framing the problem of the university's racial climate in this way further severed the relationship between the racial climate and academic attrition.[64]

Sudarkasa still tried to implement the program. She sent the proposal to Shapiro, hoping he would provide the money for the project. He didn't. "I find the proposal thought provoking and instructive," he wrote, but "I have decided to delay the full consideration of the proposal until the winter term." He was already funding other projects, he wrote. Since Shapiro planned to go on sabbatical for much of the winter term, his letter didn't give Sudarkasa much hope.[65]

The fact that Sudarkasa failed to attain funding speaks to the power of administrators in resisting efforts to make diversity language serve black activists' goals. Sudarkasa had faith that she could convince administrators to support new policies as long as she adopted their preferred intellectual framework. Diversity, however, wasn't as malleable as Sudarkasa thought. It was only useful to administrators as long as it supported particular policies. Administrators fought hard to preserve their intended meaning and purpose for diversity.

When Shapiro rejected her proposal for the Year of Understanding, she once again reflected on the constraints placed on her. "My position is essentially an advisory one," she wrote again, "with no direct responsibility for, or accountability from, units responsible for implementing policies that I recommend." There were great expectations among minority officials when a senior black official was hired with what they thought was the authority to bring about change. "Given these expectations, it is no wonder then, that some staff have expressed disappointment over the dearth of programs being developed and administered from my office." A one-person office without "any built-in authority" was destined to fail. She hinted that perhaps that was administrators' intention when they created the position.[66]

Sudarkasa offered her resignation in September 1986. She took a position as president of Lincoln University, a historically black institution in Pennsylvania. Shapiro wouldn't have the opportunity to reconsider Sudarkasa's Year of Understanding in the winter. When Sudarkasa left, Shapiro didn't understand the level of discontent among the black students who remained at the university. He went on a scheduled sabbatical in January 1987 and left his temporary replacement with a powder keg that was ready to explode.[67]

The diversity framework often gets blamed for the persistent inequality in higher education. This chapter clearly supports these critiques in showing that diversity contributed to racial retrenchment. But it also serves as a reminder that focusing too closely on diversity language can hide the underlying factors behind inequality. Diversity didn't lead to racial disparities. It didn't spark the policies that changed affirmative action practices and led UM recruiters away from Detroit. Diversity, instead, served as a tool to sustain the devastating policies for black students that were already in place. For those interested in challenging the policies of inequality, then, combating the diversity framework is only a first step. The motivations behind the policies for inequality are more deeply rooted and difficult to challenge than diversity language.

This chapter also questions critics who suggest that diversity disconnected social justice from inclusion. This is only partly true. Cleary administrators favored the diversity rationale over social justice beginning in the 1980s. But social justice language never disappeared. In fact, administrators found it easy to bend the meaning of social justice to fit the goals and purpose behind the diversity rationale. Again, for those interested in challenging inequality, the solution isn't as easy as forcing universities to reframe affirmative action as a social justice initiative.

# CHAPTER 7

# The Michigan Mandate

"You talk to the average man on the street and their image of the university is that it's filled with all these radical, liberal folks, right?" Doug Houweling, the university's vice provost for information technology, told a reporter. "You talk to the average university administrator and they'll tell you the university is highly resistant to change, that it's a very conservative organization. Well, what's the truth?" Houweling gave this interview in 1989, not long after James Duderstadt took the reigns as UM's eleventh president. Duderstadt was in the process of laying out the Michigan Mandate, one of the most ambitious racial inclusion initiatives in UM's history. The initiative responded to black student activists who, in 1987, led a campus-wide protest that threatened to shut down university operations. The Michigan Mandate allocated unprecedented resources to repair UM's racial climate and increase underrepresented minority students, faculty, and staff. Was the Mandate a sign of "radical, liberal folks" or a sign of a "conservative organization"?[1]

Conservative pundit Dinesh D'Souza would have provided a quick answer to the question. Writing just a few years after Duderstadt announced the Mandate, D'Souza identified UM as part of the "vanguard of the revolution of minority victims," along with universities like the University of California–Berkeley, Harvard University, and Howard University. What struck D'Souza most was that he believed the leaders of these institutions didn't need much prodding from activists to support ambitious affirmative action and multicultural initiatives. The "victims revolution," D'Souza thought, was a top-down revolution led by administrators, not a reluctant response to student activists. The University of Michigan was clearly a radical institution in D'Souza's eyes.[2]

D'Souza, of course, greatly downplayed the importance of activist pressure and administrators' resistance to student demands in the late 1980s and early 1990s. He also missed the purpose of the Michigan Mandate. The Mandate didn't represent an institutional revolution; the Michigan Mandate represented a deliberate attempt to co-opt the student movement for racial justice on campus and gain administrative control of racial inclusion.

Although the Mandate raised black enrollment and redistributed millions of dollars to inclusion initiatives, it sustained some of the most important pieces of co-optation. UM officials continued to protect the admissions policies that targeted middle-class black students living outside cities. Officials also continued to privilege the goal of combating white students' prejudice through interracial contact over addressing black students' social alienation. Diversity continued to serve as a key intellectual foundation in sustaining these priorities.

The Michigan Mandate evolved out of black student protests that began during the winter of 1987. In January, Shapiro left on sabbatical, and James Duderstadt took over as acting president of the university. Duderstadt didn't have a long background in the executive administration, only accepting the position of provost and executive vice president for academic affairs seven months earlier. The interim president didn't worry, though. January and February were usually routine months for a president, he thought. Duderstadt told a reporter that he hoped no "earth shattering issues" unfolded before Shapiro returned in March. Duderstadt didn't make it a month before the earth shattered.[3]

On January 27, a group of black women were meeting in a lounge in Couzens Hall, a campus dormitory, when they saw a piece of paper slide under the door. It was a facsimile of an Ohio hunting notice, which read, "Be it known that due to severe drought and fire this past season, and to decreased animal populations; the hunting of DEER, RABBIT, QUAIL and POSSUM, has been prohibited. . . . The government has provided by special decree for a substitute animal to be hunted so that no hunter will lose his skill during the season . . . there will be an OPEN SEASON ON PORCH MONKEYS. (Regionally known as: Jigaboos, Saucerlips, Jungle Bunnies and Spooks.)" The flyer then went on to list the rules and suggestions for how to hunt African Americans.[4]

The women in the lounge ran out into the hallway. The perpetrator had disappeared. "I read the letter and it hurt; it hurt deeply," Leteshian Kennebrew recounted. Weeks later they learned that a nineteen-year-old white, first-year student and fellow resident in Couzens had produced the flyer.[5]

The flyer appeared in an environment ripe for another major black campus protest. Organizations with strong membership and leadership were already mobilized. And these organizations had spent years trying to push the administration to institute reforms through traditional channels. They had met with Niara Sudarkasa. They had appeared at regents meetings to air their grievances. Traditional channels led to little success. Duderstadt also faced an environment in which national media outlets were on high alert for individual acts of prejudice in higher education. In late 1986 and early 1987, national media outlets reported upswings in incidents of racism around the country. National coverage caught fire in October 1986, when a rash of racist incidents attracted reporters to the issue. At the Citadel, a South Carolina military academy, white cadets dressed as Ku Klux Klan members broke into a black cadet's room and yelled racial slurs. Students at Smith College defaced the school's minority cultural center with the phrases "Niggers, chinks and spics stop your complaining" and "Niggers go home." Later that month, two black students at Smith found a note attached to their door that read: "We don't want niggers on our floor. Leave tomorrow or die." But the most reported story of the month involved a fight between white and black students at the University of Massachusetts at Amherst following game seven of the World Series—a fight that left one black student unconscious. Because universities didn't develop systems to record and report incidents of racism, it is difficult to measure whether racist incidents actually increased during the late 1980s. Nevertheless, the perception that the number of these incidents were rising made racial prejudice on college campuses the trending news story of the time. UM activists, then, wouldn't have to work hard to bring the nation's attention to Ann Arbor. If all these environmental factors were kindling, the Couzens flyer provided the first spark that led to a powerful student protest movement at UM.[6]

Barbara Ransby was ready to lead a campus protest when students found the flyer. The Detroit native and future history professor, renowned for her work on the black freedom movement, came to UM in 1984 to begin her graduate work. Since then, her name appeared in just about every antiracism initiative on campus. She became best known, though, for her fight to get the regents to divest from businesses profiting from South African apartheid. She founded the Free South Africa Coordinating Committee (FSACC) with fellow student Hector Delgado in 1985. It would have been difficult for any UM community member to avoid Ransby's work. Her group built a large wooden shanty on the Diag, meant to bring attention to the housing conditions black families endured under apartheid.[7]

After the flyer incident, Ransby stood on the steps of the graduate library and told an audience of three hundred, "We want to embarrass Vice President Duderstadt for not taking a stronger stand against racism." Connecting the university's racial climate to black students' academic performance, she told the audience that the cumulative effect of racist incidents at UM made it almost impossible for black students to get an education. Within a week, Ransby brought together a coalition of groups, including the FSAAC and the university's NAACP chapter, into an organization called the United Coalition Against Racism (UCAR).[8]

Duderstadt tried to move quickly in order to limit UCAR's momentum before its leaders could organize a powerful protest movement. The typical administrative response in these situations included forming a committee, hiring a new black administrator, or announcing funds for a new racial inclusion initiative. Duderstadt reached into the administrative toolbox and pulled out cash. He announced a $1 million initiative that he claimed would help increase minority employees and address campus racism.[9]

Any hope Duderstadt had that the new funds would limit UCAR's support ended by mid-February. A tape of a radio show on UM's WJJX—the "station that storms the dorms"—surfaced. The show aired just a few days after the Couzens incident, but the tape recording of the program didn't circulate around campus until weeks later. The weekly program featured host Ted Sevransky, a sophomore who called himself "Tenacious Slack." On February 4, a listener phoned in calling himself "Miami Mike." The conversation that followed gave UCAR the momentum it needed:

MIAMI MIKE: What happens when you mix a Black and a groundhog?
SEVRANSKY: What?
MIAMI MIKE: Six more weeks of basketball season.
SEVRANSKY: That's a pretty bad one. Hang on a second, let me go find the laughter soundtrack. Meanwhile you can go ahead and tell another one.
MIAMI MIKE: Why do Blacks always have sex with their mind. Because all of their pubic hairs are on their head. [laugh track plays] Oh, they loved that one.
SEVRANSKY: Yeah, they sure did. Alright. Here, try it again.
MIAMI MIKE: Ok hold on. I got to find a good one.
SEVRANSKY: Why? Are you looking at a book for this?
MIAMI MIKE: Ted. Me? Tenacious, come on!
SEVRANSKY: Oh. Silly me for even asking." [Caller laughs] Any more?
MIAMI MIKE: Yeah. Who are the two most famous Black women in history?
SEVRANSKY: Who?

MIAMI MIKE: Aunt Jemima and motherfucker.

SEVRANSKY: Oh no. That was a bad thing to say. We'll have to edit. Edit that please. Edit that. Edit that, please. Wait, we got to get the tapes. For those of you that heard that out there, remember that this is a family radio station. This is a phone caller. We did not personally . . . WJJX endorses none of the products. You know, the whole disclaimer thing.

MIAMI MIKE: This is funny.

[inaudible]

MIAMI MIKE: Why do Black people smell?

SEVRANSKY: Why?

MIAMI MIKE: So blind people can hate them too. [laugh track plays]

SEVRANSKY: This is disgusting ladies and gentlemen.

MIAMI MIKE: One more. One more. Wait.

SEVRANSKY: No. no. no. Racism is a bad thing.

MIAMI MIKE: What do you call a Black smurf?

SEVRANSKY: What?

MIAMI MIKE: A smigger. [laugh track plays]

SEVRANSKY: This is disgusting. This is a radio station. I can't even listen to this. . . . . This is disturbing. This institutionalized discrimination within the university. Here we have a radio station, a family radio station, and people call up and make racial jokes. I mean yeah, how many white people does it take to screw in a light bulb. I mean, you never hear that or anything like that. I mean, we are all a family here; this is supposed to be some type of bonding between fellow students at the university. It's just so hard for me to comprehend; so hard for me to understand. It really kind makes me upset, you know, that this type of thing has to happen at a university as liberal and liberated as this. And I, Tenacious Slack, I am speaking out against racism. I say no racism in the classroom. Brothers and sisters we all can be one together.

Sevransky's sarcasm at the end of the conversation showed more than an ignorance of the problems of racism. Sevransky actively mocked black student activists by using their concepts, such as "institutionalized discrimination."[10]

On March 4, vowing to bring UM "kicking and screaming into the 20th century," UCAR members read a list of twelve demands to two hundred people on the Diag:

1. Create an honorary degree for Nelson Mandela.
2. Increase Black enrollment and retention substantially.

3. Create an Office of Minority Affairs with a Supervisory Commission elected by the minority campus community.
4. Create a Financial Aid Appeals Board so that no student is excluded from Michigan for economic reasons.
5. Create a mandatory workshop on racism for all incoming students.
6. Create an orientation for incoming minority students.
7. Create tuition waivers for underrepresented and economically disadvantaged minority students.
8. Create a minority lounge and office in the Michigan Union.
9. Create a required course on racism and diversity for all University students.
10. Create a full, public and immediate investigation of all reported incidents of racial harassment and a publicized mechanism for reporting such incidents.
11. Full observance of the Martin Luther King Holiday[,] including closing the University.
12. The immediate removal of all those perpetrators of racist incidents from the dorms.[11]

Then the demonstrators marched from the Diag to the Administration Building, where they read the demands in unison to Duderstadt. The six-foot, five-inch interim president towered over many of the demonstrators. He gave the students the type of well-worn response that they had heard many times before: racism was "not appropriate for this nation," Duderstadt told UCAR members. "We have got to take actions and educate the majority in particular about the importance of respecting pluralism and diversity on campus." UCAR was tired of this type of response, as it was usually a sign that administrators weren't going to take any steps to make institutional reforms. "We did not come here to hear this," one student told Duderstadt. "We made our statement here, we don't want to hear anymore of this administrative jibberish. Either act now or you are going to see us in a different form." Another student threatened a new Black Action Movement— alluding to the protest organization that shut down much of the university in 1970—if the demands were not met. UCAR gave Duderstadt two weeks to fulfill their demands.[12]

The threat black student activists posed in 1987 was new to the people in charge at UM. None of the university's leaders were in administrative positions during the 1970 BAM strike. Executive leaders had become accustomed to weak and often unorganized black activism, which felt more like a nuisance than a threat. For the first time in seventeen years, administrators were looking at a protest organization that might be able to shut down university operations.[13]

UCAR's cause gained national attention the next day. Representatives of the *New York Times*, the *Chicago Tribune*, the Associated Press, and WDIV—Detroit's NBC affiliate—found seats among eight hundred people in the Michigan Union's Grand Ballroom. Morris Hood, a state representative from Detroit and chair of the state's higher education appropriations committee, was on campus to hear the testimony of black students about UM's racial climate. Hood organized the hearing after the recording of Sevransky's show emerged. Sixty-one people testified, including President Shapiro, who had returned from his sabbatical. Over the course of the hearing, Hood listened to story after story of racism. One black female student endured mammy jokes while she worked in the campus kitchen and was told on another occasion that she would be lynched if she didn't pay housing fees. A black graduate student recounted an incident in which a white student physically attacked her young son and called him a "Black motherfucker." A professor asked the same student, "Who are you calling yourselves this year?" The hearing lasted for four and a half hours.[14]

UCAR members likely would have appreciated the hearing years before, when testimony about racism represented a vital tool for a small, emerging movement that didn't yet have the collective power to force change. Now UCAR was ready to move beyond testimony and deploy the tactics of a protest organization capable of shutting down university operations. In the weeks before the hearing, black activists were mindful that in the past, their meetings often became forums to tell stories of racism. "We don't want to turn this into another testimonial of the racist incidents," one student activist reminded participants. "Now we need to propose motions to the administration to decrease (racism)." Three hundred UCAR members stood up at the hearing and in unison read the twelve demands they had presented to Duderstadt.[15]

As administrators were sorting out how to respond to UCAR, another group emerged, calling themselves the Black Action Movement III (BAM III). The group felt that UCAR's demands didn't focus enough on the specific challenges and needs of black students. Although black students dominated UCAR, the group was multiracial, and the demands reflected the group's composition. So BAM III made its own list of demands, which focused exclusively on black students:

1. We demand the establishment of a permanent and completely autonomous yearly budget of $35,000 for the Black Student Union.
2. We demand the immediate endowment of $150,000 for the William Monroe Trotter House to insure that the integrity of African-

American culture will be preserved in spite of the vile climate of racism that persists at the University of Michigan.

3. We demand the University immediately grant tenure to all presently hired Black faculty, and develop an accelerated tenure program for all newly hired Black faculty. Furthermore, we demand an increase of Black faculty members, such that every department of the University has tenured Black professors.

4. We demand that the University's Board of Regents and administration adopt a plan that appoints Blacks as department chairpersons or heads of 30 percent of all academic departments of the University's schools and colleges.

5. We demand the immediate addition of a racial harassment clause in the University rules and regulations to punish institutionally those who perpetuate, motivate and participate in any type of racist activity.

6. Full participation of the Black Student Union executive board in the formulation and implementation of any reform, program or policy that implicitly or explicitly affects the Black community of the University or our community at large.

7. We demand President Shapiro's $1 million initiative to improve the recruitment and retention of Black students be extended to a $5 million five-year initiative. At the end of the five-year period, the initiative will be evaluated and possibly extended indefinitely.

8. We demand the development of a permanent Black music program and Black affairs program at the University-owned, student-run, stations. These programs shall be produced, programmed and operated by Black students.

9. We demand that all University publications cease degrading and insulting the integrity of Black people by the use of lower case "b" when referring to the Black race.

10. We demand the uncompromised ratification of UCAR's anti-racism proposals.

11. We demand total amnesty for all reprisals incurred by students during BAM III.[16]

By UCAR's March 19 deadline, Shapiro had made only one concession: an honorary degree for Nelson Mandela. That night, UCAR and BAM III activists occupied the first floor of the Administration Building. Security officials scrambled to lock the stairwells and elevators so that students couldn't access the upper floors. One hundred students prepared to stay overnight. They ordered pizza and listened to speeches of Martin Luther King Jr. and Malcolm X. Some discussed whether they would lose their summer jobs if the police arrested them.[17]

Despite the threat that UCAR and BAM III posed, Shapiro refused to concede to more demands. The stalemate signaled the beginning of a prolonged battle. But student leaders knew they couldn't keep up a long fight. It was already late March. The university's term ended in April, and final exams were quickly approaching. UCAR and BAM III would lose much of their mobilizing force as students focused on finals and then left campus for the break. They looked to Jesse Jackson to speed up the negotiating process.

Jackson, the longtime civil rights activist, was just beginning his presidential campaign. UCAR had a direct connection to Jackson because the father of one of its members was Jackson's lawyer. The presidential candidate arrived in Ann Arbor on March 28 and spent the day meeting with student activists and faculty to learn what was most important to them before the negotiations began. The next day, Jackson brought about twenty people with him—each representing different community and student groups—to meet with Shapiro, Duderstadt, and John D'Arms, dean of the graduate school. Jackson began the meeting by stating that he wanted the university to agree to a goal to increase black enrollment at UM to 24 percent of the student body within five years. Jackson chose that number because African Americans made up 24 percent of southeastern Michigan's population. He then asked the representatives he brought with him to announce their demands. One black student announced that he wanted $35,000 for the Black Student Union. Another announced that he wanted an Office of Minority Affairs. Shapiro, Duderstadt, and D'Arms waited as all the people around the table announced their demands.[18]

The administrators had one advantage in the negotiations. The meeting started at 10 a.m., and Jackson had scheduled a rally on campus at 4 p.m., with the national media in attendance. If Jackson wanted to celebrate his skills in reconciling racial tensions on national television, he could not show up to the rally blaming racist white administrators for undermining negotiations. The administrators formed a plan to hold out for more favorable terms. The goal of 24 percent black enrollment was especially worrisome. Black enrollment hadn't topped 7 percent in over a decade. In fact, Shapiro, Duderstadt, and D'Arms did not want to commit the university to a target percentage at all. They thought that was one of the major mistakes administrators made during the original BAM strike. However, members of Jackson's entourage objected to any agreement that did not include a target for black enrollment. As the clock clicked closer to 4 o'clock, Jackson convinced them to go along with concessions that did not include specific targets. Instead, they allowed Shapiro to leave out a numerical target from the written concessions and simply announce in the press conference the university's "aspiration" to increase black enrollment to reflect African Americans share of the state population— although left unstated, it was about 12 percent. Just as important, the statement left out any reference to socioeconomic status. UCAR's original demands pressed for new financial aid policies that would broaden access of low-income underrepresented students. Clearly, Shapiro and Duderstadt didn't want to reverse the affirmative action policy changes of the late 1970s that privileged middle-class, underrepresented students. The negotiations, in this respect, represented a clear victory for administrators.[19]

Jackson and the administrators agreed to six concessions, which administrators later referred to as the "Six-Point Plan." The concessions included the establishment of a vice provost for minority affairs; $35,000 for the Black Student Union; funds for minority faculty development; plans and eventual targets for minority enrollment and faculty and staff hiring; development of a racial harassment policy; and the creation of an advisory committee on minority affairs to advise the university president. At the scheduled rally, Jackson brought Shapiro on stage with him, praising him for agreeing to their demands. Just minutes before, he was a villain on campus. Suddenly, he was standing before a large gathering of students, faculty, and Ann Arbor community members while Jackson and others involved in the negotiations praised him for his leadership.[20]

One month later, Shapiro announced that he would leave UM to become the president of Princeton University. The events surrounding the UCAR/BAM III protest were not the only factors that pushed Shapiro to leave Michigan. Princeton had been courting Shapiro for a year, and he had been contemplating the move. The protest, though, did make him think seriously about whether Ann Arbor was the best place for him and his family. Criticism of his leadership from black politicians and radio hosts in Michigan made him question whether he could be "a good representative of the university anymore." He later recounted, "'You know, I don't need to do this, I don't have to put up with this.' I viewed myself as trying to provide a social product for the state," and he thought the black legislators' efforts "to take advantage of a difficult ongoing situations to lay the burden of all the social pathology of this country on the university and on my shoulders" were unfair.[21]

As much as Shapiro liked to see himself as a victim of unfair critiques, he oversaw one of the worst periods of racial retrenchment in UM's history. After a decade of policies that gutted many of BAM I's victories, Shapiro left the university at the start of a new era of black student activism. Administrators learned from Shapiro's failures when they again tried to wrestle control of inclusion from activists in the aftermath of the UCAR/BAM III concessions.

When Shapiro announced his resignation in April 1987, the weight of implementing the Six-Point Plan fell to Duderstadt. The provost saw the plan's implementation as part of a much bigger strategy to co-opt activism. His initial strategy was to make highly visible policy changes that would demonstrate to the UM community that he was serious about addressing UCAR and BAM III's concerns in order to minimize the groups' support. Duderstadt's general strategy section in his 1987 Diversity Agenda read, "Keep enough activities moving ahead to neutralize disruptions and provide the time for more comprehensive strategic action." Only then, when Duderstadt didn't have to worry about confrontational protest, could he implement his own vision of inclusion.[22]

Duderstadt's primary goal was to take back control of the racial inclusion agenda. Duderstadt believed that administrators should govern the purpose, details, and goals of inclusion programs. The alternative worried Duderstadt. The problem with letting students control the agenda, Duderstadt believed, was that it often led to concessions that administrators didn't think were viable. There were many consequences when administrators conceded to goals that they believed were unfeasible, he thought. First, administrators were reluctant to hold people accountable for not meeting goals that the administrators believed weren't attainable in the first place. Second, failing to meet unachievable goals only led to more student protests that demanded, in administrators' eyes, more unachievable goals. Duderstadt wanted a plan that he believed in—a plan in which every agenda item, in his eyes, was attainable. Only then could he get people to buy in to his goals; only then could he hold people accountable.[23]

The initiatives Duderstadt proposed greatly limited the vision of racial justice proposed by UCAR and BAM III. In student protesters' eyes, there were consequences in allowing administrators to define what types of goals and programs were viable. At one point or another, administrators had considered almost every racial inclusion goal and program unfeasible before activism forced officials' hand. Part of activists' role was to push people in power to rethink what was possible. UCAR and BAM III activists weren't willing to step aside and let Duderstadt define what racial inclusion would look like and what the university could achieve. Duderstadt, then, would have to work hard to limit activists' power in shaping his racial inclusion plans.

Limiting UCAR and BAM III's power was easier said than done. The group's influence came from a widespread feeling on campus that racial justice was not a priority for university administrators. So Duderstadt went to work to fulfill the Six-Point Plan quickly. Just one month after the concessions, he announced that he had already responded to the first concession by creating the Office of Minority Affairs. He hired Charles Moody as vice provost to run the office with a $1.25 million independent budget. Creating a new office fit neatly into co-optation techniques, as expanding the inclusion bureaucracy represented a typical administrative response after protest. The $1.25 million independent budget, though, signaled that Duderstadt was going to go well beyond past administrations. Inclusion bureaucrats usually came into their positions with little to no money, which required them to write program proposals and ask for money from executive administrators. By fall 1987, Duderstadt also created a base budget line of $35,000 for the Black Student Union, made affirmative action efforts a part of the merit evaluations of deans and directors, and formed a presidential advisory committee on minority affairs.[24]

Duderstadt saved his most visible policy innovation for faculty hiring. One of the UCAR/BAM III concessions read that a "budget incentive will be provided to attract and retain Black faculty and administrators." Duderstadt created Target of Opportunity (TOP) funds, which made available a pool of money to recruit senior minority faculty members to the university. Departments, then, wouldn't have to wait for a new faculty line to open up to recruit and hire minority faculty. Duderstadt told departments to search for senior minority faculty members at other universities, and he would provide the money to hire them at Michigan. Charles Moody wasn't shy about the implications of this type of recruiting policy. "Raiding is natural. . . . Don't be bashful," Moody told a group of faculty members at a scheduled fireside chat.[25]

Duderstadt was also mindful that administrators often announced ambitious programs and pools of money to solve problems, but they rarely produced results. Duderstadt wanted to show that TOP would produce the outcomes that students were looking for. So he made a pool of funds available immediately, and by the fall, three departments had used the money to make senior hires. During the 1987–88 fiscal year, Duderstadt announced that he would commit $1 million to TOP.[26]

Duderstadt knew that UCAR, in particular, would return in the fall semester ready to press the administration to fulfill the organization's demands that weren't part of the Six-Point Plan. UCAR was the best organized group on campus in 1987. When the fall semester began, Barbara Ransby and her co-leaders began holding meetings, organizing new students, and developing their strategy. But Duderstadt felt he was in a good position, having introduced new inclusion policies during the summer.

As UCAR tried to influence the implementation of the 1987 concessions, one final piece of the Six-Point Plan compromised the organization's broad support and helped Duderstadt gain control of inclusion. High on UCAR's agenda was a racial harassment policy that held students accountable for racist speech. Shapiro had begun to craft a policy in his final months as president. The new interim president, Robben Fleming, finished and then introduced an early draft of the racial harassment policy at the regents meeting in January 1988. The proposal sparked outrage among some of UCAR's strongest allies. Fleming's code would penalize students who made "discriminatory remarks which seriously offend many individuals beyond the immediate victim" and gave the power of enforcement to the deans of each college. Critics of the policy claimed that the definition of harassment was so broad that it could be used to punish any student with whom the deans disagreed. The *Michigan Daily* editorial board published a front-page editorial on the subject, something that rarely happened in the history of the student newspaper. To the editorial board, the code represented a "cheap power grab" that threatened First Amendment rights and was designed to discipline student dissent, not end racism. The Michigan Student Assembly, a strong ally of UCAR on other issues, used similar arguments to oppose the policy. The regents sent Fleming back to work, asking for a policy that better protected First Amendment rights and took punishment power away from deans.[27]

In April, the regents finally approved a revised racial harassment policy. The revised code didn't temper critics. Opponents were so vocal and confrontational that the regents moved the meeting upstairs in the Administration Building, open only to the press. Security guards blocked the hallways and elevators as students tried to shove their way into the stairwells. The policy that the board approved created physical spaces and forums where the "broadest range of speech and expression will be tolerated," short of physical violence and property destruction. These included the Diag, Regents Plaza, and the *Michigan Daily*. The policy also created protected spaces, where discriminatory harassment interfered with "an individual's academic efforts," such as "classroom buildings, libraries, research laboratories, [and] recreation and study centers." In these spaces, a student could be punished for "any behavior, verbal or physical, that stigmatizes or victimizes an individual on the basis of race, ethnicity, religion, sex, sexual orientation, creed, national origins, ancestry, age, marital status, handicap or Vietnam-era veteran status." The new rules fell well short of UCAR's vision of an effective racial harassment policy. Punishing people in power was as important to UCAR as disciplining students, but the policy neglected to include administrators and faculty members. The policy also failed to guarantee minority participation in the disciplining process. A year later, a court struck down the racial harassment code. An even weaker code replaced the rules that black activists were already unhappy with.[28]

University housing officials also went to work on strengthening their own policies, as housing wasn't a protected space in the board's racial harassment policy. The housing office created a definition of harassment that was much broader than the policy approved by the regents, including anything that "creates a hostile or demeaning environment." A student could violate the harassment code by excluding someone from a study group because of their racial or ethnic identity, displaying a confederate flag, or making racist comments. It included not only making discriminatory jokes but also laughing at them.[29]

Duderstadt benefited from these speech codes. Of all the concessions included in the Six-Point Plan, it was clear that the racial harassment code was the most controversial. It worked against UCAR, peeling away its broad support and allowing Duderstadt to take back control of the racial inclusion agenda and avoid making additional concessions to protesters. The racial harassment code was also the only concession he played no part in crafting. This was especially important for Duderstadt, as he hoped to be UM's next president. Fleming, the interim president, absorbed the criticism while Duderstadt interviewed for the job.

On June 10, 1988, the regents voted unanimously to appoint Duderstadt as the eleventh president of the University of Michigan. This represented a sad day for UCAR. On September 1, one of its main adversaries during the 1987 protest would officially take the reins of the University of Michigan. Duderstadt was the last person that UCAR believed could transform UM to the benefit of minority students.[30]

Duderstadt, though, believed he was exactly the right person for the job. Ever since Shapiro had announced his resignation, Duderstadt had been working on a plan that represented his vision of inclusion. The plan, which started out as the Diversity Agenda and then the Michigan Plan, finally evolved into the Michigan Mandate. Duderstadt explained that he would pursue four objectives over the next five years. First, he wanted to "substantially increase" underrepresented minority tenure-track faculty members. Second, he wanted to increase the number of underrepresented students and improve retention. Third, he wanted to increase the number of underrepresented minorities in staff positions, especially leadership positions. Finally, he wanted to "foster a culturally diverse environment," which could "significantly reduce the number of incidents of racism and prejudice."[31]

The Michigan Mandate would prove to be the most ambitious centralized plan for racial inclusion in the university's history. It also bore most of the marks of the co-optation techniques developed over the past thirty years.

Just as campus leaders had in the past following displays of activism, Duderstadt made clear that the university's new inclusion programs would protect the university from activists' disruptive vision of racial justice. Duderstadt made the diversity rationale the centerpiece of the Michigan Mandate to demonstrate how the Mandate would advance the university's values and priorities. According to Duderstadt, the educational benefits of diversity made the heterogeneous student body that the Mandate would create vital for preserving the university's excellence. Moreover, a diverse student body offered an opportunity to create a model multiracial community, which would serve the university's interests in improving race relations and helping the United States to compete in a global economy. In UM's hierarchy of priorities, preserving the university's status and building a model multiracial community continued to trump expanding access and addressing black students' social alienation.

Where Shapiro used the diversity rationale to justify declining black enrollment, Duderstadt used it to argue that a more aggressive affirmative action program would serve the university's interests in preserving UM's elite status. The Michigan Plan, an early draft of the Mandate, began with a "Fundamental Premise: Diversity is a necessary condition for the achievement of excellence." "Our ability to achieve excellence in teaching, research, and service, in a future increasingly characterized by its pluralism," the plan continued, "will be determined by the diversity of our campus community." Duderstadt eventually put this point into the title of the Michigan Mandate, adding the subtitle "A Strategic Linking of Academic Excellence and Social Diversity." The Mandate made the message clear: Duderstadt's efforts to increase underrepresented minority students was in service of preserving UM's elite status.[32]

The Mandate also used diversity to show that new programs would help build a model multiracial community. As university presidents had been arguing for decades, he suggested that the university could be a site where students would learn to live and work in a multicultural world. Like Shapiro, he thought the model multiracial community could serve business interests, looking for students prepared to interact with clients across the globe. Duderstadt also thought the model multiracial community could help preserve a functional democracy in a nation that was becoming increasingly heterogeneous.[33]

While Duderstadt showed more commitment to affirmative action than Shapiro, the diversity rationale continued to suppress black students' greatest concerns. In Duderstadt's public speeches and documents, affirmative action wasn't about addressing inequality. Further, the model multiracial community wasn't intended to address black students' social alienation and reduce attrition rates. In this respect, the Mandate's use of diversity fit well into the legacy of retrenchment.

But Duderstadt didn't see the diversity rationale as a tool of retrenchment. The racial retrenchment of the late 1970s and early 1980s was all the evidence Duderstadt needed to believe that social justice was no longer a driving principle within the UM community. With the exception of UCAR and a few other activist organizations on campus, declining black enrollment was met with apathy. Duderstadt believed that diversity language held the key to showing the UM community that ambitious racial inclusion programs were in the institution's best interest. Even given the value Duderstadt placed on diversity in taming resistance, he believed he was acting in black students' best interest in deemphasizing social justice and focusing on diversity to frame affirmative action.[34]

Experts on institutional change reinforced Duderstadt's ideas about the value of the diversity rationale. Early in his presidency, he surrounded himself with people who understood how to transform institutions. This informal group—which he called the "change group"—included officials like Charles Moody, Duderstadt's vice provost for minority affairs. Moody brought almost two decades of experience working for more equitable institutions. After a career as both a teacher and an administrator in public schools, he earned his doctorate in education from Northwestern University. In 1970, UM hired him to take a new position as director of the Program for Educational Opportunity within UM's School of Education, which UM created with federal funding to help public schools with desegregation. Others with expertise in institutional change joined Moody in the change group, including Mark Chesler, a sociologist who wrote extensively about how to transform organizations. Change group members warned Duderstadt about the internal resistance that would rise up against the Michigan Mandate. While they thought that diversity language wouldn't solve resistance by itself, members of the group believed diversity's ability to frame change in the self-interest of the university and its community was an important tool in gaining support.[35]

Experts outside UM also confirmed Duderstadt's views about the utility of diversity. In June 1987, Bailey Jackson and Edith Seashore arrived in Ann Arbor to lead a series of sensitivity training retreats for UM executive officers and selected faculty. The two consultants headed New Perspectives, Inc., a company that specialized in organizational change and diversity training. Duderstadt brought them to campus to help UM officials develop a long-term strategic plan for racial inclusion that would allow administrators to control the meaning and implementation of inclusion. These consultants sent UM officials a clear message about how to gain support for new racial inclusion initiatives: they needed to frame inclusion in the self-interest of everyone in the institution.[36]

The strategy Jackson and Seashore presented to UM executive officers relied on assumptions about how universities functioned in the 1980s. They assumed, correctly, that corporations and universities increasingly looked similar. The advice they gave UM had developed out of institutional change techniques that diversity consultants had perfected in businesses, which brought assumptions about the limited power of social justice arguments in the 1980s. Jackson and Seashore suggested that institutional change came only when people within the institution believed it was in the best interest of the institution. They also came with an argument tailored to respond to the white backlash against affirmative action within businesses. According to Jackson, many whites would see inclusion initiatives and "fear they are losing their rights." Whites at UM needed to believe racial inclusion would benefit them personally.[37]

Despite Duderstadt's belief that the diversity rationale held the key to gaining broad support for the Mandate, he reluctantly added tepid statements about social justice to the Mandate. He understood that there were constituencies on campus that wouldn't respond favorably to the diversity rationale. When he laid out his initial plans for institutional transformation, he listed UCAR and the Black Student Union as constituencies that he needed to satisfy. To do this, he mixed diversity and social justice language. Early on, though, Duderstadt's social justice message looked like an afterthought. An early draft included a weak social justice rationale, suggesting that "as a public institution, the University has a responsibility to increase the participation of underrepresented racial, ethnic, and cultural groups." Statements like this weren't enough to avoid criticism from black students and faculty. Shortly after Duderstadt released the Michigan Plan, UM's Association of Black Professionals and Administrators sent Duderstadt a biting critique. "Diversity and pluralism," the group wrote, "are terms that obscure the ethical and moral issues that underlie the causes of social inequality." The group concluded that the plan needed to stress "justice" and "equality."[38]

This critique clearly had an impact. Duderstadt slowly included a stronger emphasis on social justice until the social justice rationale filled two pages of the Michigan Mandate. Those pages explained that "first and foremost, the University of Michigan's commitment to affirmative action and equal opportunity is based on our fundamental social, institutional, and scholarly commitment to freedom, democracy, and social justice." "Equity and social justice," the Mandate continued, "are fundamental values of this institution and integral to its scholarly mission. They are the basic reasons for making a commitment to promoting diversity."[39]

Nevertheless, Duderstadt showed that he could maintain ambiguity while adding stronger social justice language—an important tactic of co-optation. The initial Michigan Mandate sought to, "in each of the next five years, achieve increases in the number of entering underrepresented minority enrollment." The Mandate did reference plans for future concrete minority enrollment targets but concluded that these targets would eventually be set within each school and college. This brought ambiguity to the concessions Shapiro made to end the UCAR/BAM III protest. Although not part of the Six-Point Plan, Shapiro had verbally agreed that the university would aspire to increase black enrollment so that it matched African Americans' representation in the state, which was about 12 percent in the late 1980s. Now Duderstadt replaced that agreement with a statement about vague "increases" in minority enrollment. Duderstadt also used "minority" strategically. Shapiro used the term in the 1980s to decenter black students when discussing enrollment. It represented a tool to avoid talking about the declining number of black students while celebrating the growing representation of other minority groups, such as Asian Americans. Duderstadt used the term "underrepresented minority," which excluded Asian Americans, but he was still signaling to the university community that Hispanic, Native American, and black students were a coherent group. Black students had been fighting against this perspective for a decade. Measuring progress based on the number of underrepresented students meant that black student enrollment could decline as long as Hispanic and Native American enrollment rose.[40]

Diversity and social justice, then, continued to work in harmony to administrators' benefit. Stronger social justice statements never took the ambiguity out of diversity. In all the discussion about the importance of a diverse student body, there was no effort to define what a diverse student body looked like. How many black students were necessary to improve "teaching, research, and service"? How many Hispanic students? How many Native American students? There was also no discussion of social class or place. Did diversity require a mix of low-income and middle-class students? Did it require minority students from cities and suburbs? Historically, discussions of numerical representation and socioeconomic justice accompanied social justice language. But the ambiguous social justice statements allowed diversity to avoid these subjects.[41]

"I'm an individual that likes achievement," Duderstadt told the regents just before they voted to hire him as president. "I'm results oriented." Duderstadt often called himself a stereotypical engineer who focused on getting things done. He became the first president in UM's history to hold an admissions director accountable for poor performance on affirmative action. But as much as Duderstadt valued accountability, he still took advantage of the ambiguity of diversity. Ambiguity kept discussions of social class and geography out of admissions discussions. It also meant that activists couldn't hold Duderstadt accountable for failing to meet enrollment commitments. Duderstadt, then,

strategically mixed accountability and ambiguity, allowing him to push officials to implement the Mandate's policies while making it easier to tell a story
of racial progress to the public.[42]

Duderstadt's change group advised him that framing the Mandate in diversity language was important but not enough to get university officials to
carry out his initiatives. People at the top of the organization also needed to
provide incentives and consequences for the people who would be carrying
out the policy initiatives. This was what had been missing from all the past
administrations. In order to get decision makers throughout UM to place the
Mandate's goals high on their list of priorities, Duderstadt created consequences for people who wouldn't implement his vision. In the months before
he became president, he sent a message to UM officials by removing people
who he believed were obstacles to his ambitious plans. Cliff Sjogren stood at
the top of his list. The great decline in black enrollment unfolded during Sjogren's reign as undergraduate admissions director, and he put up a fight when
senior administrators pushed him to change his policies. The difference between Duderstadt and his predecessors was that they were willing to accommodate Sjogren's resistance. Duderstadt pushed him out, giving Sjogren the
option to retire or be fired. Sjogren chose to retire.[43]

Duderstadt replaced Cliff Sjogren with Richard Shaw. Shaw had been the
associate director of admissions at the University of California–Berkeley since
1983. Duderstadt believed the California university had done a better job admitting underrepresented students than UM had, and he hoped that Shaw
would bring some of Berkeley's commitment to affirmative action to Michigan.[44] Shaw immediately hired Ted Spencer—a black admissions official who
would eventually take over UM's admissions office when Shaw left for Yale in
1992—to help him with his affirmative action efforts. Spencer came to UM
from the Air Force Academy, where he oversaw minority recruitment and retention for more than a decade. During the period of UM's struggle with affirmative action admissions, Spencer helped raise minority representation at
the Air Force Academy—from 3.8 percent in 1976 to 17 percent in 1988.[45]

While Duderstadt's new mission to hold people accountable removed Sjogren and brought Shaw and Spencer to campus, the ambiguity of the Mandate helped co-opt UCAR's vision. Recall that UCAR wanted the university to
reaffirm its commitment to low-income, underrepresented students through
new generous need-based financial aid policies. Duderstadt had no intention
of returning to the affirmative action and financial aid practices of the 1960s
and early 1970s. He didn't bring Shaw and Spencer to UM to raise the number
of low-income black students from Detroit. The Mandate called for an increase
in black students; it gave no attention to the students' social class or neighbor-

hood. The singular focus on race, then, offered important ambiguity concerning the socioeconomic background and neighborhoods of students who would benefit from a more aggressive affirmative action program.

Not surprisingly, then, Shaw and Spencer kept most of the policies introduced in the late 1970s that put black students from urban areas at a great disadvantage. The two officials kept Sjogren's grid system, which evaluated white and Asian students with one grid and underrepresented minority students with another. Using only applicants' grade point averages and standardized test scores, admissions officers found the appropriate box on the grid that gave them an initial recommendation to admit, reject, or delay an application. In 1986, Sjogren decided to create a more systematic formula to calculate students' credentials. He introduced the "SCUGA Factor." Basically, SCUGA created different factors that readjusted an applicant's high school GPA. For years Sjogren had considered a student's high school curriculum and other factors to evaluate applicants' high school performance. The new system simply created a rigid formula that counselors could use to take these factors into account and produce a high school GPA that had more meaning for admissions evaluations. The "S" in SCUGA stood for the "school factor." An admissions counselor could raise a student's high school GPA from 0.1 to 0.3 point, depending on whether a student went to a "very good," an "unusually good," or a "superior school." "C" stood for the "curriculum factor," in which counselors could raise a student's GPA 0.1 or 0.2 point depending on the number of Advanced Placement and International Baccalaureate courses the student took. "U" stood for "unusually distinguishing characteristic factor," which could lead a counselor to add 0.1 point to a GPA if a student published a written work or showed "unusual contribution to a social cause." Initially, underrepresented minority students were not awarded the benefits of the unusual factor automatically. "G" referred to the "geographic factor," which gave 0.1 point to students from underrepresented areas, such as northern Michigan, rural central and western Michigan, and some states in the South and West. Finally, "A" referred to the "alumni factor," which added 0.1 point to the GPA of out-of-state students who had a grandparent, child, sibling, or spouse who was a UM alumnus.[46]

A later study showed that all these factors, expect for the "U" category once underrepresented students were included, placed black, Hispanic, and Native American students at a disadvantage. Underrepresented applicants were disproportionately in schools that didn't qualify for points in the "S" factor and didn't offer enough advanced placement courses for students to win points in the "C" factor. For Michigan residents, the "G" factor gave points to students in overwhelmingly white areas. Finally, few underrepresented students qualified for the "A" factor, because UM's alumni were overwhelmingly white. To compound these problems, standardized test scores of students usually correlated strongly with the type of curriculum offered in a school. So students who went to schools with a demanding, college-preparatory curriculum generally scored much higher on the SAT. In sum, by looking at both the SAT and the "S" and "C" factors, UM compounded the disadvantage that black students, especially those living in urban areas, faced in the admissions system.[47]

Shaw and Spencer didn't make many changes to Sjogren's admissions policy. Both in-state and out-of-state underrepresented students continued to be evaluated using the same admissions grid. Much like Sjogren's grid, Shaw's system allowed underrepresented students who didn't fall into the recommended admission or rejection grids additional time to prove their academic merits. Admissions officers called this a delayed decision. Essentially, admissions counselors waited for new standardized test scores or the student's fall high school grades to make a final decision. One of the biggest changes that Shaw and Spencer initiated regarded these students who fell into the delayed category. The grids offered admissions counselors a tremendous amount of discretion in evaluating these students. Shaw and Spencer created more tools that could help students who fell into the delayed category prove their academic merit. First, they added an essay option. Second, they gave underrepresented students the opportunity to interview with an admissions counselor. Shaw and Spencer also modified SCUGA's "unusual" category, raising all underrepresented students' grade point averages by 0.1 point. Surprisingly, though, at least one important aspect of Sjogren's grid was actually more generous to underrepresented students, allowing students to score lower on the SAT. Under Shaw's system, the lowest SAT score that an underrepresented student could submit and still receive an admissions letter was 850. Under Sjogren, it was 750.[48]

The most significant changes Shaw and Spencer introduced had nothing to do with admissions criteria, though. None of the minor modifications they made to the admissions grid reversed the policy changes that Sjogren implemented in the mid-1970s, which placed great weight on SAT scores and a college preparatory curriculum. The biggest difference between Sjogren and the new admissions leadership was the effort Shaw and Spencer put into expanding the pool of black applicants. They went to work transforming minority recruiting practices. In the past, the admissions office designated particular counselors to oversee minority recruiting. That meant that a small number of counselors had the burden of traveling the entire state—and the country once the admissions office emphasized out-of-state minority recruiting. All the other counselors were assigned to particular geographical areas without any minority recruiting responsibilities. Under Shaw and Spencer, every admissions counselor took on the responsibility of recruiting minority students. Importantly, they held admissions counselors accountable for the outcomes of their recruiting practices. Admissions leaders kept data on the minority enrollment of every school in each counselor's geographic area and used that data to evaluate the minority applicant pool each counselor created. A counselor's performance in persuading minority students to apply was incorporated into merit evaluations and could influence pay raises and promotions.[49]

The Mandate also offered the resources necessary to carry out an ambitious recruiting campaign. The admissions office needed scholarship money and the financial resources to travel and recruit students. Duderstadt ensured that those resources were available to meet the Mandate's goals. Unlike Sjogren, who often complained that he lacked the resources to increase underrepresented minority enrollment, Spencer and Shaw never felt that money was an obstacle to their affirmative action efforts.[50]

The admissions office also benefited from the visibility of the Michigan Mandate. In recruiting efforts, admissions officials emphasized the university's efforts to improve the racial climate for underrepresented students. Shaw remembers that the university's minority faculty hiring initiative was especially important in making the university attractive to minority students. The close link between affirmative action hiring and admissions continued in the 1990s.[51]

Finally, Shaw and Spencer put new resources into repairing the university's relationship with Detroit, which had been damaged during Sjogren's tenure as admissions director. The university used the Wade H. McCree Jr. Incentive Scholarship Program as a tool to provide access for Detroit students. The scholarship program, which came from the President's Council of State Universities, offered four-year scholarships to underrepresented minority students in the state who maintained a 3.0 grade point average in college preparatory courses. UM committed money from its general fund to support the program. The university also provided special recruiting visits to Ann Arbor for McCree scholarship winners, where prospective students attended UM classes and toured the campus.[52]

Still, these new practices didn't significantly improve access for Detroit's low-income black students. A researcher later looked at all of UM's admissions applications from 1995 to 1998. Despite efforts to improve UM's relationship with Detroit, few students who attended predominantly black Detroit schools with high poverty rates applied to UM. At Northwestern High School, where over 99 percent of students were black and 50 percent qualified for free lunches, only 27 of 656 graduates applied to UM. At Cooley High School, where over 99 percent of students were black and 55 percent qualified for free lunches, only 17 of 866 graduates applied to UM. At Central High School, where over 99 percent of students were black and over 60 percent qualified for free lunches, only 2 of 407 graduates applied. At Kettering High School, where 98 percent of students were black and 56 percent qualified for free lunches, only 3 of 685 students applied. Not surprisingly, most of the Detroit public school applicants came from two high schools: Cass Tech and Renaissance. These two schools hosted far fewer students eligible for free lunch. Ninety-two percent of Renaissance students were black, but only 18 percent were eligible for free lunch. Black students represented 89 percent of Cass's student body, and only 30 percent qualified for free lunch. One hundred thirty-seven Renaissance students sent applications to UM, and 121 were admitted. Three hundred sixty-four Cass students sent applications to UM, and 320 received acceptance letters. As much as UM hoped to repair its relationship with Detroit, Shaw and Spencer continued to recruit and admit students from the same two special-admit high schools in the city.[53]

The ambiguity of the Mandate still allowed administrators to celebrate the outcomes of Shaw and Spencer's efforts. Their practices led to unprecedented increases in black enrollment. By 1995, for the first time in UM's history, over 10 percent of UM's first-year class was black.[54] The next year, black students constituted over 9 percent of the entire undergraduate student body for the first time. With no attention to who these black students were, the Mandate appeared to reverse the racial retrenchment of the late 1970s and early 1980s. All the celebratory articles, however, missed how the Mandate preserved key pieces of retrenchment. Working-class black students living in Michigan's cities still had little chance of admission and were still seen as threats to the quality of the institution.[55]

Duderstadt's vision of a model multiracial community also furthered the co-optation goals of the 1960s and 1970s. Black student activists wanted programs that would address their social alienation on campus. But the Mandate never saw black students' social alienation as the most pressing priority in improving the racial climate. Instead, the model multiracial community wanted to address individual prejudice through interracial contact.

The Mandate's model depended on long-held administrative views about challenging individual prejudices. Since the 1970s, administrators accepted the idea that cultural pluralism was compatible with racial and ethnic harmony. But UM administrators concluded that pluralism could only succeed under certain conditions. Most important, interracial contact was central to improving race relations. Most of these assumptions challenged the solutions to racism that black student activists proposed to improve the racial climate. Black activists didn't oppose the idea that cultural expression could improve social relations, but that wasn't their most important goal. For activists, addressing their social alienation on campus should take precedence over improving race relations. That's why black students sometimes called for intraracial spaces and social gatherings despite the fact that administrators believed interracial contact held the key to improving race relations. If administrators wanted to improve race relations, black activists suggested, officials should take on the burden of training and disciplining white students to overcome their prejudice.[56]

These same divisions played out in the Michigan Mandate. Duderstadt made clear that improving racial harmony was more important than addressing black students' social alienation on campus. Like administrators before him, he saw interracial contact as the key component to making pluralism work. Duderstadt critiqued black students for what he called "self-segregation," putting some of the blame for racial tensions on minority students. The only difference between Duderstadt and past administrators was the amount of money he was willing to devote to putting these ideas in place.[57]

Despite Duderstadt's commitment to solving prejudice through interracial contact, black student activists had some success in influencing efforts to improve the racial climate. These activists agreed that addressing white students' prejudice was important, but they didn't want to feel as though they had the primary burden to teach white students about racism. Activists wanted the university to take on that burden through a mandatory antiracism course. Because faculty oversaw the curriculum, students could circumvent Duderstadt. LSA faculty finally approved a mandatory course in 1990. To fulfill the requirement, a course needed to cover the "meaning of race, ethnicity, and racism"; "racial and ethnic intolerance and resulting inequality as it occurs in the United States or elsewhere"; and "comparisons of discrimination based on race, ethnicity, religion, social class, or gender."[58]

Duderstadt, though, implemented his vision of a model multicultural community by funding new programs that sought to show the harm of intraracial spaces. Claude Steele, a UM psychologist, ran one of these initiatives. Steele and his brother Shelby became famous in the 1990s for their starkly different views about racial justice. Shelby found his public voice as a conservative critiquing "political correctness," white guilt, and affirmative action, while Claude offered important evidence that supported the need for affirmative action. Claude Steele's research focused on the negative impact of stigma on black students, and he was trying to develop environments that could counter that stigma on campuses. He worked with the presumption, as he wrote in his proposal to Duderstadt, that in an interracial educational setting, black students faced a "vulnerability to the judgment of racial inferiority." This negative stigma, he hypothesized, led black students to "dis-identify with school as a protection against this vulnerability." Essentially, stigma caused black students to underperform in the classroom.[59]

Claude Steele's research fit well with Duderstadt's vision of a model multicultural community because it critiqued minority-specific support programs and ethnocentrism as contributors to the stigma attached to black students. Minority-specific programs offered the message that minority students were likely to struggle at UM, Steele suggested, while whites were not. He also saw ethnocentrism as a contributor to stigma. Importantly, though, this wasn't just an issue for whites. In Steele's proposal, black students bore some of the blame for isolating themselves and not breaking down white students' assumptions about African Americans' capabilities through social interaction. The proposal, then, critiqued black students' efforts to create intraracial social spaces—spaces black students had formed, in part, as retention initiatives. Steele believed that these types of intraracial spaces actually fueled stigma and, in turn, fed black attrition rates.[60]

As a solution, Steele proposed a living-learning community situated in a UM dorm to test his hypothesis. He wanted about 350 students—300 white and 50 black—to live and take some of their classes together. He chose this racial breakdown because it reflected the reality of a predominantly white campus while also providing a large enough black sample to offer statistically significant results. All the students would come from the same academic background—students who showed potential but would likely need academic support services to graduate. White students, then, were carefully selected so that they didn't show stronger academic preparation than black students in the program, which Steele believed would mediate against stigma. Once in the program, the students would participate in intergroup relations courses and workshops that were supposed to create a "sophisticated social environment in which students are exposed to the contributions of diverse groups, the cost of ethnocentrism, and the advantages of open relations between groups." Steele planned that students would stay in the program through their first two years at the university.[61]

Steele received Duderstadt's financial support, and the program began in fall 1991 as the 21st Century Project. Two hundred sixty-seven LSA first-year students filled a wing of Mary Markley Hall. It became one of Duderstadt's prized programs, which he used to show what a model multicultural community could look like.[62]

Duderstadt funded another program with some of the same assumptions about intraracial spaces. The Program on Intergroup Relations, Conflict, and

Community (IGRCC) began in 1988 with Duderstadt's financial support. The program brought together social scientists and student affairs personnel to address prejudice on campus. IGRCC was voluntary, offering two credits to first-year students living in the university's residence halls who wanted to participate.[63]

IGRCC's theoretical principles seemed tailored for the Michigan Mandate, as the program stressed the value of interracial contact. In a small room in Alice Lloyd Hall's basement, small groups of twelve to sixteen students of different racial groups came together in weekly intergroup dialogues mediated by a facilitator. The dialogues were designed to expose conflicts between groups that led to prejudice and allow students to work through those conflicts.[64]

This, too, became one of Duderstadt's favorite examples of UM's efforts to build a model multiracial community. Still, the IGRCC's theoretical principles called into question many of the Michigan Mandate's programs. The programs' creators recognized that not all interracial contact was productive. One of the premises of the program was that "contact between members of different social identity groups . . . may be helpful in reducing prejudice . . . , but contact may also increase prejudice and discrimination." To be productive, interracial contact needed to be carefully controlled and managed under a particular set of environmental conditions. This perspective never made it into Duderstadt's centralized plans to improve race relations. The Mandate, in contrast, assumed that any interracial contact was productive for improving race relations.[65]

Studies of the impact of the Mandate revealed the poor outcomes for black students. Social scientists developed a longitudinal study that measured the evolution of undergraduates' racial attitudes over the course of four years. In 1990, UM first-year students would fill out the survey when they arrived on campus and then fill out the same survey four years later.[66] The Michigan Student Study, as it came to be known, showed that UM's programs had a transformative impact on white students. For black students, though, social alienation continued to be a serious problem. Fifty-five percent of black students in the survey reported that it was difficult to feel "comfortable in the campus community—feeling as though I *belong* here." In contrast, only 34 percent of Latinos, 22 percent of Asian Americans, and 21 percent of whites responded the same way.[67]

These numbers confirmed black students' critiques. The Mandate wasn't designed to address black students' social alienation.

There was much for UM officials to praise about the Mandate's inclusion efforts. Black enrollment exploded. By 1995, for the first time in UM's history, over 10 percent of UM's first-year undergraduate students were black. The next year, black students constituted over 9 percent of the entire undergraduate student body for the first time. The Mandate, despite its flaws, reversed some of the racial retrenchment that marked Harold Shapiro's presidency.[68]

Nevertheless, the Michigan Mandate clearly fit into the legacy of co-optation. The Mandate sustained affirmative action policies that allowed few working-class black students from Michigan's cities into the university. Moreover, the Mandate continued to privilege addressing white students' prejudice over black students' social alienation. Even as black enrollment numbers rose, some of the policies of retrenchment persisted.

# CHAPTER 8

# *Gratz v. Bollinger*

"Dad, can we sue them?" Jennifer Gratz asked her father. It was April 1995, and the young white UM applicant from the Detroit suburbs had just opened her rejection letter. She immediately thought about her Hispanic classmate who was admitted to UM and Gratz concluded that affirmative action was to blame for her rejection. It would take a couple of years for Gratz to get her wish, but she eventually became the lead plaintiff in *Gratz v. Bollinger*, which challenged the racially attentive undergraduate admissions practices of the College of Literature, Science, and the Arts. *Grutter v. Bollinger*, which challenged the Law School's admissions practices, was filed soon thereafter. These cases put UM on a crash course with the Supreme Court.[1]

Since the 1960s, UM leaders hadn't faced a viable legal or political challenge to their affirmative action admissions practices. They watched as other universities went to court or battled with their state legislature. But the 1990s brought the University of Michigan into a contentious national battle over affirmative action. Suddenly, UM was at the center of the most important legal challenge to affirmative action admissions since *Bakke* (1978).

This chapter follows *Gratz* and the university's efforts to defend the undergraduate admissions policies in LSA. *Gratz* and *Grutter* have received their fair share of scholarly treatment. Countless books and articles have offered legal analyses and narratives of the cases. My goal here isn't to provide a round-by-round recitation of *Gratz* from the district court to the Supreme Court. Instead, I shed new light on UM's defense of affirmative action by showing how the university's co-optation of racial justice aligned with the rightward shift of the Supreme Court since the 1980s. UM leaders' preference for diversity over the social justice rationale, their discomfort with enrollment targets, their efforts to make affirmative action serve business interests, and their selective incorporation of social science that promoted the benefits of interracial contact all made UM's chances of swaying at least one conservative justice more likely.

*Gratz* emerged in a new political and legal climate. The 1990s witnessed another wave of backlash against racial inclusion initiatives that emerged directly from the national campaign for racial justice waged on college campuses across the country. The minority student protests of the late 1980s weren't isolated in Ann Arbor. While the Michigan Mandate became one of the nation's most ambitious and visible responses to campus activism, universities and colleges across the country put new inclusion policies in place. The outcomes of these policies received widespread attention, as Americans were reading about the sudden reversal of a decade of declining black enrollment. "We frankly don't know all the reasons for this," Richard Rosser, president of the National Institute of Independent Colleges and Universities, said of the sudden increase in black enrollment. Aggrieved whites thought they knew the answer: new, more aggressive affirmative action programs. By the early 1990s, journalists were documenting what they saw as a renewed backlash movement against racially attentive admissions policies in higher education.[2]

New efforts to transform the curriculum also brought news headlines. None were as popular in the press as Stanford University's decision to revise its core curriculum, replacing a required course on Western culture with the class Culture, Ideas, and Values. In 1988, the new course required a few readings produced by women and people of color. The decision came on the heels of student pressure and with the help of Jesse Jackson, who held a rally chanting, "Hey hey, ho ho, Western culture's got to go." The usual conservative pundits of the late 1980s made Stanford the symbol of multiculturalism gone awry. Charles Krauthammer of the *Washington Post* warned that if other universities followed suit, "we will be firmly embarked on another round of cultural destruction." George Will called the course emblematic of "special-interest scholarship," in the same vein as Black Studies and Women's Studies. Dinesh D'Souza called it "force-fed multiculturalism."[3]

California became ground zero for the political backlash against higher education's renewed racial inclusion efforts. In 1995, California's Republican governor Pete Wilson used his influence with the University of California Board of Regents to ban affirmative action policies in all University of California (UC) institutions. The next year, Wilson and UC Board of Regent member Ward Connerly led a fight to ban racially attentive practices in all state institutions through a state ballot initiative. In 1996, California voters approved Proposition 209, an amendment to California's constitution that banned "racial preferences" in all public institutions. Two years later, Washington joined California as the second state to ban affirmative action through a state initiative. Conservative columnist Charles Krauthammer announced that conservatives might not have to worry about fighting affirmative action in the Supreme Court anymore. "Affirmative action is dying," Krauthammer wrote in an opinion piece that was published in newspapers across the country, "and the cause of death will be legislative not judicial."[4]

Krauthammer's prediction overlooked the changing legal environment that opened new opportunities for the opponents of affirmative action. Despite the political victories that opponents of affirmative action scored in the 1990s, a group of conservative lawyers were ready to test their luck in court. The cause of affirmative action's death would be judicial, they thought.

Much had changed in the federal court system since *Bakke*. By the late 1980s and early 1990s, the opportunities to use the courts to advance conservative interests expanded as Ronald Reagan and George H. W. Bush made their marks on the federal judiciary. Reagan alone appointed 368 federal district and appeals court judges and 3 Supreme Court justices. He also raised William Rehnquist to chief justice. No president in history had appointed so many federal judges. Bush pushed the court even further to the right, replacing the court's strongest civil rights advocate, Thurgood Marshall, with the conservative black justice Clarence Thomas. It didn't take long for opponents of affirmative action to take advantage of these appointees.[5]

In 1989, even before Thomas took his seat, the Supreme Court changed the landscape of affirmative action law. The most important case, *City of Richmond v. Croson* (1989), centered on the constitutional merits of a Richmond, Virginia, program that mandated that 30 percent of public contracts awarded by the city go to minority contractors. Until *Croson*, the Supreme Court hadn't agreed on the proper standard of review for racial classifications used by states. Proponents of affirmative action had long argued that the standard of review should depend on whether the racially attentive program in question represented invidious discrimination—practices meant to oppress minority groups—or whether the program represented benign discrimination—practices meant to rectify racial discrimination against minorities. Opponents of affirmative action didn't see a difference between invidious and benign discrimination. Race represented such a dangerous and suspect category, they argued, that any racially attentive program should be held to the highest standard of judicial review, called strict scrutiny. Under strict scrutiny, an affirmative action program needed to represent a "compelling government interest" and be "narrowly tailored" to meet the purpose of that program.[6]

*Croson* transformed affirmative action law because, for the first time, a majority of judges agreed that the strict scrutiny standard must be applied to all racially attentive practices created by state and local entities. Another case in 1995 applied this standard to the federal government. In *Croson*, Sandra Day O'Connor, a Reagan appointee and the new swing vote in affirmative action cases, outlined just what strict scrutiny would mean for local and state entities trying to defend their affirmative action programs. O'Connor divided a compelling government interest, the first prong of strict scrutiny, into a two-step evaluation process. In legal scholar Goodwin Liu's words, the first test of compelling interest determined "whether a particular government interest is sufficiently important . . . to justify a racial preference." The second step in determining compelling interest evaluated whether "a government actor has produced sufficient evidence to substantiate its alleged interest." Essentially, it asked whether the "stated interest is the *actual* interest motivating the government actor in the particular case." A government entity, for example, couldn't simply state that it was trying to remedy its own discrimination. It faced the evidentiary burden to show that it had discriminated, and remedying that discrimination was the driving motivation behind its affirmative action program. O'Connor's interpretation of narrow tailoring, the second prong of strict scrutiny, placed even more burdens on government entities. She suggested that any state actor would have to show that no "race-neutral" means could fulfill the same purpose as its affirmative action program.[7]

*Croson* gave opponents of affirmative action new confidence that they could challenge racially attentive programs in court. It was just a matter of time before conservative lawyers tested the limits of *Croson* by asking the court to apply the same standards to affirmative action admissions in higher education.

Three years after *Croson*, journalists expected that Cheryl Hopwood would be the next Allan Bakke. Hopwood represented the ideal plaintiff for an anti–affirmative action case. She fit the narrative pushed by conservatives that affirmative action punished disadvantaged whites. Raised in humble circumstances by her mother, Hopwood had to pay her own way through college. After she graduated from California State University–Sacramento, she established residency in Texas and achieved a respectable LSAT score, but she received a rejection letter after she applied to the University of Texas (UT) Law School.[8]

When she decided to sue UT, Hopwood found support from an emerging force in the United States: the conservative public interest law firm. The first of these firms emerged in the 1970s at the same time that conservative think tanks, such as the Heritage Foundation, found a place in American politics. These conservative firms sought to challenge the liberal political and legal victories of the past decades. The number of conservative public interest firms only increased in the 1980s, as former Reagan staffers looked to build on the administration's work. One of the newest of these conservative public interest firms, the Center for Individual Rights (CIR), took Hopwood's case.[9]

In 1996, the Fifth Circuit Court of Appeals ruled in CIR's *Hopwood v. Texas*. The judges decided that diversity didn't meet the compelling interest standard set in *Croson*. Diversity, in other words, wasn't a constitutionally permissible justification for affirmative action. The Supreme Court decided not to take the case, limiting the impact of *Hopwood* to Texas, Louisiana, and Mississippi, but the case gave CIR new confidence and struck new fear in the hearts of affirmative action supporters. There were signs that the University of Michigan might be CIR's next target.

"Cordial greetings," the letter began. "Under the provision of the Michigan Freedom of Information Act [Sec.4.1801] I request, hereby, the following information, stated separately for the College of Literature, Science & the Arts, the Law School, and the Medical School of the University of Michigan." The letter went on to request a series of data points broken down by race, including standardized test scores, grade point averages, and admissions offers for the entering class of 1995. The letter put UM on a path to the Supreme Court.[10]

Carl Cohen, the same UM professor who advised Allan Bakke's lawyers in the famous 1978 anti–affirmative action case, submitted the document request. He found what he was looking for in March 1996. The university sent him the admissions policies for the College of Literature, Science, and the Arts. He found the grids that evaluated white and Asian American applicants differently than underrepresented minority applicants. Hoping to create pressure on UM to end affirmative action, Cohen immediately made these documents public.[11]

Cohen's findings came at an opportune time for some of the state's staunchest affirmative action opponents. The outcomes of the Michigan Mandate, which raised black enrollment in the early 1990s, sparked white backlash in Michigan. State representative David Jaye had been trying to follow California's model to make Michigan the next state to ban affirmative action in public institutions. Despite Republican control of Michigan's legislature, Jaye and like-minded colleagues found little success. They managed to pass only one ineffective anti–affirmative action bill, which amended the state's Elliot-Larsen

Civil Rights Act of 1976. The amendment prohibited state employers and universities from "adjusting test scores, using different cut-off scores, or otherwise altering the results of a test on the basis of religion, race, color, national origins, or sex." UM officials were not worried about the bill because they believed that the university didn't technically alter test scores or use different "cut-off" scores for white and minority applicants.[12]

When political efforts failed to eliminate affirmative action, Jaye saw Cohen's FOIA documents as an opportunity to bring a court case against the University of Michigan. He and Deborah Whyman, another state legislator, contacted CIR, hoping the organization would use Cohen's documents and sue UM. Jaye and Whyman told Michael Greve, a co-founder of CIR, that they would find the plaintiffs. On May 1, without any firm commitment from Greve, Jaye and Whyman, along with two other colleagues, announced that they were looking for potential plaintiffs for an anti–affirmative action court case against UM. Jaye alone received information about 450 potential plaintiffs. In total, the legislators received letters identifying 1,500 potential plaintiffs. Most of the complaints came from parents or grandparents, claiming that their child or grandchild didn't get into UM because they were white. The politicians forwarded the complaints to the Center for Individual Rights. By September 1997, CIR was interviewing potential plaintiffs. It found Jennifer Gratz and Patrick Hamacher. The next month, CIR filed the lawsuit, claiming that LSA's undergraduate affirmative action practices violated the Fourteenth Amendment.[13]

After CIR filed *Gratz*, the university hired the law firm Wilmer, Cutler, & Pickering. John Payton took the lead on the case. Payton was a nationally renowned lawyer with experience in defending affirmative action. He argued on behalf of the city of Richmond in front of the Supreme Court in *Croson*. Payton faced a difficult decision in *Gratz*. There were two constitutionally permissible defenses for an affirmative action admissions program. Despite the *Hopwood* decision, *Bakke* was still the law of the land outside the three states covered by the Fifth Circuit. *Bakke* made clear that universities could take race into account in order to achieve the benefits of a diverse student body. Further, although the case ruled that universities couldn't use affirmative action to correct societal discrimination, *Bakke* also offered a constitutionally permissible remedial rationale. UM could argue that affirmative action was necessary to correct the university's own discrimination. These defenses weren't mutually exclusive; in fact, the University of Texas offered both in *Hopwood*.[14]

Payton, though, believed that diversity offered UM its best defense. This is where the legacy of co-optation likely influenced Payton's legal strategy. UM officials had long used racial innocence to avoid culpability in the university's racial disparities. As a result, top-level white administrators didn't publicly admit that affirmative action intended to address institutional discrimination. *Croson* made clear that lawyers couldn't develop a constitutionally permissible justification for an affirmative action program after an institution had already been sued. The justification offered in court had to reflect the institution's driving motivation behind its affirmative action program. The popular institutional narrative of racial innocence, then, made it difficult to show that addressing institutional discrimination motivated UM's affirmative action policies. Payton, though, saw references to diversity in many of the official documents produced since the Michigan Mandate.[15]

As Payton went to work, UM leaders didn't leave the institution's legal defense to lawyers. University officials offered support for Payton's legal argument about the university's commitment to diversity by addressing one of the potential problems that the Michigan Mandate posed for lawyers. To satisfy activists, Duderstadt had filled Mandate documents with social justice language. This was especially problematic, as it wasn't the type of social justice language that offered a constitutionally permissible rationale for affirmative action. There were no references to institutional discrimination. In the Mandate, social justice referenced the institution's responsibility to rectify societal discrimination outside UM's walls—the type of social justice rationale that *Bakke* prohibited. Even worse, this rationale didn't appear as a passing reference. The Mandate included six full pages that explained its motivations. Two of those pages explained that "first and foremost, the University of Michigan's commitment to affirmative action and equal opportunity is based on our fundamental social, institutional, and scholarly commitment to freedom, democracy, and social justice." "Equity and social justice," the Mandate continued, "are fundamental values of this institution and integral to its scholarly mission. They are the basic reasons for making a commitment to promoting diversity."[16]

Duderstadt resigned in September 1995, two years before *Gratz* was filed. By the time Lee Bollinger replaced Duderstadt in January 1997, the former UM Law School dean could see a lawsuit coming. Bollinger instructed staff to stop using the term "Michigan Mandate." In his inauguration speech, he never mentioned the Mandate or affirmative action. University officials also rushed to strip social justice references from all the university's official documents, ensuring that diversity represented the single documented driving influence behind affirmative action. In 1997, for example, the university's admissions office made it clear that it sought "students who meet the spirit of contributing to a diverse class." The office later added to its admissions guidelines a clear statement that "admissions is based on several factors that combine to produce a freshman class that provides a mixture of attributes and character-istics valued by the University." It's the university's "sincere belief," the guide-lines continued, "that this mixture contributes to the education of our students, as well as fulfills the University's mission to prepare society's future citizens and leaders." In 1998, the university's Senate Assembly released a statement on the "Value of Diversity." The National Board of Directors of UM's Mich-igan Alumni Association did the same. Nancy Cantor and Lee Bollinger also gave speeches and wrote op-eds espousing the university's commitment to diversity. All these documents that purged references to social justice were introduced as evidence that diversity, and diversity alone, motivated the uni-versity's affirmative action practices. Importantly, they were presented as sim-ply the continuation of policies and ideals introduced during the early years of the Michigan Mandate, not as a significant break from the Mandate's state-ments on social justice.[17]

To support the diversity defense further, campus leaders wanted to rewrite the history of inclusion at UM. They wanted to show that diversity represented a priority deeply rooted in the university's core values. Much of this work fell to Nancy Cantor, the university's new provost and one of the nation's preemi-nent social psychologists. At the time, though, none of the high-level officials knew anything about the history of diversity as a core value at UM; they had to create this history for the case. Cantor heard about Laura Calkins, a young historian who was helping UM's Center for the Education of Women identify documents in its basement that should be preserved in the university's insti-tutional archives. Cantor called Calkins into her office just a couple of months after CIR filed the anti–affirmative action cases. The provost asked her to look for documents in the university's archives that could establish diversity as a keystone institutional principle.[18]

Calkins went to work, looking through the early records of UM presidents. She struggled to find something Cantor could use. Not a single president in the nineteenth or early twentieth centuries mentioned any educational value in a diverse student body. That shouldn't be a surprise. UM officials didn't reg-ularly begin promoting the education value of students from different back-grounds until the 1940s and 1950s, when officials defended admissions policies for international and out-of-state students. And university officials didn't reg-ularly promote the value of diversity in justifying affirmative action until the early 1980s.[19]

The only document Calkins could find that might help Cantor was in the records of James Angell, the university's third president. In 1879, Angell gave a speech titled "The Higher Education: A Plea for Making It Accessible to All." Nothing in the document suggested that contact between students of different backgrounds improved education or prepared students to participate in democracy. Instead, the speech defended low tuition rates in order to make higher education accessible to students of all social classes. His justification looked more like the social justice rationales proposed by black student activists than any diversity argument developed later by university administrators. Angell began by suggesting that universities had an obligation to provide education to people of all classes because it was "just." Then he turned to more utilitarian arguments. It's here that Angell came closest to contemporary diversity arguments by suggesting that providing education equity had implications for American democracy. But again, this argument resembled that of black student activists, who argued that the university had a responsibility to empower black communities, more than that of contemporary diversity advocates. Angell was worried that higher education exclusively for the wealthy would create an "aristocracy of wealth" that would "endow the rich alone with the tremendous power of trained and cultivated minds." It would "consign the control of all intellectual and political life to the hands of the rich," creating bitter class hatred with "no stable equilibrium." No democracy could survive such turbulence, he suggested. Moreover, he assumed that most of the wealthy segregated themselves in cities. But for democracy to work, he argued, small towns and rural areas needed well-educated individuals to serve in government, schools, and medical facilities. He envisioned universities educating students from these places, and those students returning to serve their communities. For Angell, higher education was a tool to empower the poor and counter the power of the wealthy.[20]

In Cantor's hands, though, the document became evidence of the university's long-standing commitment to the value of diversity. Soon after she received the document from Calkins, Cantor wrote an article in the *Michigan Alumnus* claiming that Angell's speech showed a clear connection between the values the university was defending in court and the values of late nineteenth-century university officials. Cantor stretched Angell's arguments well beyond their intended meaning. She claimed that through affirmative action, the university was "building, as Angell predicted, a lively democracy in which students can challenge each other by virtue of the variety of life experiences." Nothing in Angell's speech suggested that students could learn anything from contact with peers from a "variety of life experiences." Furthermore, she took Angell's arguments out of context. Cantor claimed that Angell and contemporary officials saw the university as the "essence of democratic living." It's true that Angell saw higher education as "the most democratic atmosphere in the world." But to him, the definition of a democratic atmosphere was a college that gave the highest social status to the smartest individuals, not those with the largest family estates. He never thought about the democratic atmosphere as a place where students learned to get along with people from different backgrounds. Thanks to Cantor's interpretation, the speech appeared in a footnote in the university's Supreme Court brief. Although the document never became a core piece of evidence in the university's legal argument, Cantor's efforts to find the diversity rationale—and only the diversity rationale—in Angell's speech represented an important strategy in the case—stripping social justice from UM's ideals and replacing it with a long-standing commitment to the benefits of diversity.[21]

UM officials also rewrote the origins of the Michigan Mandate. The history of the Mandate posed problems because the initiative was a direct response to black campus activism that demanded a more aggressive affirmative action program to combat institutional racism. Nobody within UCAR or BAM III claimed to be fighting for the educational benefits of a diverse student body. University lawyers needed to silence this activism. James Duderstadt gave lawyers what they needed. In his deposition, Duderstadt claimed that the Michigan Mandate "was stimulated by a growing realization of the importance of the diversity of our campus, our students, our faculty and our staff, to the quality of our academic programs and to the educational experience of our students." Duderstadt offered little recognition to the students who facilitated that realization or the social justice arguments that became so central to the Michigan Mandate. Lawyers used this statement from Duderstadt's deposition to show that the educational benefits of diversity drove the university to adopt the affirmative action policies in question.[22]

To present diversity as the exclusive motivation behind affirmative action, UM's legal defense also had to ignore the history of black officials who saw affirmative action as a tool to address the university's racist practices. The black official who crafted the university's first affirmative action admissions program, Leonard Sain, had suggested that racially attentive policies were necessary because UM's admissions and financial aid system identified and supported only middle-class white students. He called the university's racially exclusionary practices "sins of omission." J. Frank Yates, who served as the director of CULS and CAAS in the 1970s, explained that the BAM strike and its affirmative action demands were necessary responses to the university's value system, which was "racist and exclusionary." Niara Sudarkasa, when she served as associate vice president for academic affairs, called for new affirmative action practices to combat Sjogren's and Goodman's policy decisions, which led to the drop in black enrollment in the late 1970s and early 1980s. Charles Moody, a key figure in developing the Michigan Mandate, suggested that the Mandate intended to counter UM's "corporate culture" of racism. "The first things people have to come to grips with," Moody told a reporter, "is that racism is still alive and well on this campus." These statements never appeared in *Gratz* because UM lawyers chose not to make the constitutionally permissible argument that UM used affirmative action to address institutional discrimination.[23]

Silencing these statements was also significant because groups of minority students wanted to intervene and make institutional discrimination an important part of the case. Richard Shaw represented seventeen high school students—sixteen black and one Hispanic—who planned to apply to the University of Michigan. Shaw wanted the court to hear the one remaining remedial defense available to universities: that an institution could pursue affirmative action in order to address its own discrimination. The University of Michigan refused to make this argument, Shaw contended, because confessing to discriminating against minority students would open the university up to potential civil lawsuits. Nevertheless, the remedial defense would be essential in winning the case and preserving underrepresented students' access, Shaw contended.[24]

UM's lawyers fought against Shaw's intervention in the case. Payton filed a motion against intervention, arguing that UM was well prepared to defend the interests of the prospective minority applicants. The district court judge agreed with Payton and quickly rejected Shaw's motion to intervene. CIR and UM continued to prepare for the case, taking depositions and moving through the discovery process without Shaw. Shaw, though, took his case to the Sixth Circuit Court of Appeals. In August 1999, just over a year after the district court rejected intervention, the Sixth Circuit ordered the district court to accept the intervenors as a party in the case. Despite the ruling, UM continued to fight against the intervenors' access to institutional documents, and the university refused to give the intervenors time in oral arguments when the case eventually reached the Supreme Court.[25]

Still, when given the opportunity, Shaw challenged the university's claim of racial innocence embedded in the diversity defense and offered a different history of institutional change. To show that affirmative action was necessary to combat UM's institutional racism, he hired education historian James Anderson to investigate UM's long history of discrimination. Anderson uncovered a history (pre-1960s) of segregated dormitories and policies that allowed campus organizations to discriminate. He also showed that black activists, not benevolent administrators, were responsible for institutional change. Administrators never pursued dramatic institutional changes—like the Michigan Mandate—because of a deep commitment to diversity. Anderson portrayed UM officials as reluctant supporters of racial inclusion after BAM I, BAM II, and BAM III. Despite the institutional changes that unfolded after these protests,

Anderson argued that administrators tolerated, even accepted, racial disparities and a poor racial climate.[26]

Shaw also wanted to show that all the "color-blind" criteria in UM's admissions system harmed underrepresented students, making affirmative action a necessary remedial tool to rectify the institution's discrimination. To do this, Shaw hired a group of social scientists to look at UM's admissions practices. William Trent, a sociologist in the University of Illinois's Department of Educational Policy Studies, analyzed UM's admissions tools. After CIR filed the case, UM eliminated the grid system and introduced a unified point system to evaluate all students. Students were awarded points for various factors, including grade point averages, essays, recommendation letters, extracurricular activities, and SAT scores. Underrepresented students received twenty automatic points in order to get results similar to the grid evaluations. Many of the basic components of the grid system and the point system, though, remained. For example, the point system continued to use the SCUGA method to evaluate a students' high school GPA and calculate point totals. The "S" factor evaluated the quality of a students' high school. Trent found that no more than two predominantly black high schools in Michigan received an "S" factor score, which would benefit an applicant in the admissions process. The "C," or curriculum, factor, which gave students points for taking AP and IB courses, also disadvantaged black students. Trent found a strong correlation between students' racial identity and the number of advanced courses offered in students' high schools. The more black students in a particular school, the fewer AP and IB courses were offered. He also found a strong correlation between standardized test scores and the number of AP/IB courses a student took. This meant that when UM took the SAT and the "C" factor into account, underrepresented students were "doubly disadvantaged."[27]

Trent pressed further, looking at the final two factors in SCUGA. In the areas where students could benefit from the "G," or geography, factor, less than 1 percent of the population was black. Finally, few black students benefited from the "A," or alumni, factor. Between 1995 and 1998, 75 percent of the applicants reporting an alumni connection were white, whereas 4 percent were black. The only factor that benefited black students was the "U" factor, but it didn't overcome the disadvantages imposed by the other factors.[28]

All this showed, according to Shaw, that affirmative action was necessary to redress the university's discriminatory "color-blind" admissions practices. In doing so, he asked the court to reconsider O'Connor's standard, set in *Croson*, that argued that any rationale presented in court needed to reflect the driving purpose behind an institution's affirmative action program. That standard asked institutions to implicate themselves in discrimination, Shaw argued—

something that institutions would almost always avoid because it put them at risk for civil rights lawsuits. The standard in *Croson*, then, placed an undue burden that prohibited an important constitutionally permissible rationale for affirmative action.[29]

The university's lawyers did eventually incorporate a history of discrimination into its argument, just not in the way the intervenors preferred. UM lawyers needed to show why the experience of diversity on college campuses was a compelling government interest. Part of this argument depended on showing that students came to UM without much experience with interracial contact and how the experience with diversity would improve U.S. democracy. The university contacted Thomas Sugrue, one of the preeminent historians of race and urban inequality in the United States. In his expert report, Sugrue revealed that segregation in Detroit was worse in 1990 than it had been in 1960. The state of Michigan didn't fare much better. Michigan's schools were the fourth most segregated in the nation—more segregated than any state in the South. In *Gratz*, university lawyers used this history of discrimination outside campus walls to show the necessity of creating spaces of interracial contact at UM. "Americans tend to enter college without having had meaningful and sustained contact with people from races other than their own," the lawyers concluded using Sugrue's report. "This lack of contact with one another fosters misconceptions and mistrust on all sides and affords little or no opportunity either to disrupt the perpetuation of racial stereotypes or to experience the richness of different racial and ethnic communities." Inequality was only useful when it served UM's diversity argument.[30]

The empirical evidence used to support the diversity defense revealed another legacy of co-optation in *Gratz*. UM leaders selectively incorporated social science to advance their interests. UM's lawyers relied on social science evidence produced in previous years to offer an idyllic picture of race on UM's campus, where diversity improved educational outcomes and taught students how to interact positively with different groups.

Patricia Gurin, professor of psychology and women's studies at UM, wrote the expert report that showed the benefits of a diverse student body. Gurin was a renown social psychologist who wrote extensively about intergroup relations. She drew on three studies that began before the *Gratz* case was filed in district court. Two of these empirical studies were conducted at the University of Michigan during the Michigan Mandate era—the Michigan Student Study, covered in chapter 7, and a similar study on students by the Program on Intergroup Relations, Conflict, and Community. Gurin also used a national database provided by the Cooperative Institutional Research Program, which surveyed over nine thousand students nationwide on topics related to race relations.[31]

Gurin's analysis of these studies provided the empirical foundation for Payton's claims that a diverse student body represented a compelling government interest that justified using race as a factor in admissions. Gurin claimed that the studies showed that diverse student bodies led to positive learning and democracy outcomes. Without diversity, the quality of higher education and universities' efforts to prepare students for a heterogeneous democracy would be in peril.[32]

To show how diversity improved learning outcomes, she drew on decades of psychological literature on critical thinking and studies of students' academic growth. Scholars had long questioned whether providing a college-level education, without any attention to the larger environment, produced "deep and complex thinking." Students often came to college campuses, Gurin wrote, in a state of "mindlessness"—a commitment to particular ideas that had become so routine that thinking had become unnecessary. They hadn't been taught the value of critical thinking and instead followed scripts that repeated information and values taught to them before they arrived on campus. Students couldn't easily break out of this "mindlessness." Gurin argued that racial and ethnic diversity represented an essential tool in getting students to question and evaluate the ideas they brought to campus. Because most UM students came from homogeneous communities, diversity created a new and unfamiliar environment, while classes encouraged students to see the world from multiple perspectives. In the end, Gurin analyzed the data of the three studies and found a positive relationship between the degree of students' interracial contact and the growth of students' critical-thinking skills. She concluded that diversity got students to "think deeply and effortfully to take into account multiple points of view, evaluate evidentiary claims, and draw conclusions based on conceptual soundness."[33]

Gurin also claimed that the data revealed positive democracy-related outcomes. *Gratz* worked its way through the court system in the midst of a contentious national debate about the future of American democracy as whites' share of the national population decreased. Pat Buchanan's presidential runs in the 1990s, for example, stoked fears about the incompatibility between democracy and diversity. Gurin placed high stakes on affirmative action in higher education, offering evidence that a diverse educational experience was vital for the future of a heterogeneous democracy. On a diverse campus, where students met each other as equals and participated in civil discourse, students gained the necessary skills to lead and participate in a twenty-first-century American democracy. Those fundamental skills included accepting conflict as a normal part of life, valuing difference, and taking other perspectives into account. Gurin revealed that a diverse campus changed students. They were more likely to live in heterogeneous communities and discuss racial and social issues across racial lines after they graduated.[34]

Evidence that didn't fit UM's legal argument never found a prominent place in Gurin's report. Instead, Gurin offered a positive portrayal of the university's racial climate. Only a small section of her report documented black students' negative experiences on campus. The survey evidence Gurin relied on didn't show that black students experienced positive educational and democracy-related outcomes from their contact with white students. Black students' survey responses revealed the importance of relationships with other black students. Gurin tried to downplay these results by suggesting that the data didn't show positive learning and democracy-related outcomes for black students because of the smaller pool of survey responses. Still, Gurin discussed the potential consequences of ending affirmative action and the subsequent decline in the number of black students on campus. The evidence suggested that there was a correlation between black attrition and the number of black students on campus. The university could expect black student attrition to rise if black enrollment went down, she argued. Relegated to the appendix, though, none of this was part of Gurin's key arguments in the expert report. It never became part of the university's legal briefs, either.[35]

These efforts to downplay black students' survey responses fit neatly into the university's long-standing practice of discounting black students' social alienation. Since the 1960s, university leaders had prioritized changing white students' behaviors over addressing black students' social isolation. Since the mid-1970s, officials had often ignored the issue of social isolation altogether.

The intervenors offered an alternative portrayal of the university's racial climate. Rather than arguing that affirmative action was necessary to create the type of student body that created positive educational and democracy-related outcomes, Shaw argued that affirmative action was necessary to help mediate against the impact of the university's poor racial climate—a racial climate produced and maintained by institutional racism. Shaw's experts showed that declining underrepresented student numbers would negatively affect the university's racial climate and, in turn, the success of underrepresented students on campus.[36]

Walter Allen, former UM professor and then sociologist at the University of California–Los Angeles, and Joe Feagin, a sociologist at the University of Florida, served as Shaw's experts. Recall that Allen was the UM social scientist in the 1980s who presented evidence that connected black students' attrition at UM with the racial climate. Campus leaders didn't listen. Here was his opportunity to present that information in court. Feagin and Allen concluded that UM's racial climate—and the climate at HWCUs more broadly—was detrimental to the success of underrepresented students. Unlike Gurin's report, Feagin used words like "horrible" to describe the university's racial climate. Black and Hispanic students endured racist jokes, stereotypes, exclusion from social groups, and heavier policing. The two social scientists highlighted the racist graffiti in campus dorms, racist literature on campus buildings, and racial epithets that black and Hispanic students saw and heard during their time at UM. A "critical mass" of black students, the scholars' argued, was vital for black students to succeed in a racial climate like this. In Feagin's words, "the anxiety and fear generated by being a Black person in a mostly White university are mitigated by the presence and support of other Black students."[37]

Their research represented one of the only moments in *Gratz* where underrepresented students' actual voices entered the case. Allen conducted focus groups with undergraduate students at UM in April 2000. He submitted quotes from students of color who questioned the university's commitment to diversity. One student, identified as a woman of color, said in a focus group: "The university promotes this image of being diverse and interested in multiculturalism but I think it's problematic because a lot of times we don't take direct action in doing so." A Hispanic student noted that the "environment is such that it's hostile for minorities to succeed because there are, let's say, fifty people and then there's one minority. And it's very hard for minorities to succeed in that position because it's hard for him to relate to the people." One black woman said, "I can't stand this school and I'm ready to leave." The focus groups revealed a hostile racial climate that undermined underrepresented students' academic performance and made them feel socially isolated.[38]

"Critical mass" eventually made it into the University of Michigan's argument, just not in the way the intervenors would have hoped. When the case made its way to the Sixth Circuit and then the Supreme Court, Payton began arguing that the absence of a critical mass of minority students caused harm. A critical mass was necessary, according to Payton, to "ensure that minority students do not feel isolated or pressured to 'represent' their racial or ethnic group." Here Payton sounded like the intervenors. But he departed from the intervenors when he explained why social isolation was problematic. It wasn't a problem because it would lead to black student attrition; it was a problem because black students wouldn't "feel comfortable acting as individuals" and interacting with white students, all of which was necessary to produce the learning and democracy outcomes the university wanted. In other words, without critical mass, minority students' presence on campus wouldn't serve the educational interests of the institution. Payton transformed critical mass to make the university the victim of low minority enrollment numbers, ignoring the harm minority students' faced on a campus that was overwhelmingly white.[39]

Ambiguity was at the heart of the University of Michigan's defense. Payton tried to avoid referencing an enrollment goal or target for underrepresented minority students. Instead, Payton preferred to use ambiguous terms like "meaningful numbers" and "more than token numbers." Clearly, this was part of a legal strategy that tried to appease the moderate conservatives on the court. But this ambiguity was already embedded in the university's co-optation strategy. Since the 1980s, university administrators resisted efforts to use numerical goals for affirmative action admissions. Again, UM's co-optation strategies worked in harmony with its legal defense.

UM administrators had long preferred ambiguous affirmative action goals. Since the 1960s, UM leaders tried to resist efforts by activists and federal officials to make specific enrollment and hiring targets, and hold people accountable if those targets weren't met. Administrators favored ambiguous goals because they preferred to measure the university's commitment to inclusion based on the amount of effort UM officials devoted to inclusion, not by the outcomes of those efforts. It was easier to tell a story about UM's commitment to inclusion when officials could point to all the money, programs, and staff members devoted to inclusion. Numerical targets led to annual stories of the university's failure to create the types of outcomes administrators promised.

BAM's 10 percent enrollment concession represented a brief period in which administrators reluctantly agreed to enrollment targets. But by the early 1980s, Shapiro used diversity to return to the university's preferred position of ambiguous enrollment goals. Even when protesters again fought for numerical targets during the UCAR/BAM III protests in 1987, Shapiro offered only verbal support. These enrollment goals never made it into the Six-Point Plan. When Duderstadt took over and crafted the Michigan Mandate, he also resisted enrollment targets, leaving goals up to individual units.

This co-optation strategy worked to Payton's benefit. Powell's opinion in *Bakke* constricted Payton's choices. Powell left uncertainty about how much attention universities could pay to the number of underrepresented students on campus in making admissions decisions. Clearly, *Bakke* made quotas illegal. But Powell's endorsement of goals and targets were left to interpretation. Powell stated that diverse student bodies "cannot be provided without some attention to numbers," and he went further in arguing that "there is some relationship between numbers and achieving the benefits to be derived from diversity." But that only led Powell to conclude that admissions committees had to pay "some attention to distribution among many types and categories of students" to create a diverse student body. What did "some attention" mean?

Payton took a conservative approach when he answered that question. When pushed about the university's attention to numbers, he argued that Powell allowed the university to consider black enrollment numbers when crafting admissions policies. But given the rightward shift of the court, Payton was never willing to suggest that UM officials were trying to achieve a specific numerical black enrollment goal. "Meaningful numbers," "more than token numbers," and "critical mass"—all used interchangeably—became popular tools to preserve the ambiguity of the university's goals. And UM officials' resistance to specific targets meant that Payton didn't have to explain away numerical goals in internal documents. Deploying ambiguity in court did require some legal skill. In oral arguments at the Supreme Court, the ambiguity of critical mass came to a head. When Payton suggested that critical mass required "meaningful numbers," Chief Justice William Rehnquist pushed Payton for a more specific definition.

> REHNQUIST: Mr. Payton, what is a meaningful number?
> PAYTON: It's what we've been referring to as critical mass.
> REHNQUIST: Okay, what is critical mass?
> PAYTON: Critical mass is when you have enough of those students so they feel comfortable acting as individuals.
> REHNQUIST: How do you know that?
> PAYTON: I think you know it, because as educators, the educators see it in the students that come before them, they see it on campus.

Payton danced around any definition of critical mass that tied affirmative action to numerical goals or targets. According to Payton, educators at UM could simply tell when affirmative action successfully created a critical mass. When pushed further, Payton suggested that the university had been able to achieve the benefits of diversity when underrepresented students constituted between 12 and 17 percent of the student body. Still, Payton refused to argue that the university was committed to a fixed percentage range.[40]

This was an area where Payton and the intervenors agreed. Likely because Shaw, too, saw the legal problems in attaching numbers to affirmative action, the intervenors avoided defining critical mass. While Feagin and Allen disagreed with Payton about the purpose of critical mass, the two social scientists were just as vague about how many minority students were necessary to achieve it. For them, the university achieved critical mass when underrepresented "students are able to form the necessary community and social support networks associated with success." The way the university would measure that was just as vague as Payton's definition.[41]

The university's argument against so-called race-neutral alternatives to affirmative action were rooted in UM's attack on working-class black students in Detroit, which began in the mid-1970s. UM officials opposed race-neutral alternatives primarily because they would force the university to return to inclusion practices that focused on working-class black students living in cities. UM was trying to defend its co-optation of affirmative action, which allowed officials to recruit and admit mostly middle-class students living in the nation's suburbs. The way UM crafted this argument fit well with the court's shift away from remedial rationales.

"Race-neutral" alternatives became an important part of the case because of *Croson*. The second prong of strict scrutiny required any affirmative action program to be "narrowly tailored" to achieve the stated "compelling government interest." In *Croson*, O'Connor suggested that affirmative action hiring programs needed to show that "race-neutral" alternatives couldn't produce similar results compared to the racially attentive program in question. Gratz's lawyers tried to hold UM's admissions program to the same standard.

Gratz's lawyers argued that UM put little consideration into the available race-neutral alternatives that could provide similar outcomes as UM's point system. By the time the case reached the Supreme Court, Texas, California, and Florida had created race-neutral plans in response to court decisions, referendums, or executive orders that banned racially attentive admissions policies. Texas's plan, for example, gave in-state students who graduated in the top 10 percent of their high school class automatic admission to the state's top institutions. The architects of the plan took advantage of the state's segregated schools. Since black students often went to schools that were overwhelmingly black, the system would continue to produce a sizable pool of black students who were eligible to attend the state's top public universities.[42]

Payton made clear what was at stake in rejecting race-neutral plans. UM's lawyers argued that the race-neutral percentage programs would force the university to admit underrepresented students with poor academic credentials to pursue a diverse student body. Without saying so directly, they suggested that race-neutral policies would bring too many black students from Detroit to UM. The university's lawyers tried to make this argument more subtly by stressing the importance of geographical diversity within the underrepresented minority student population. Lawyers argued that a percentage plan, like Texas's 10 percent plan, would force UM to admit black students from a small geographical area—meaning Detroit—which would frustrate "the interest in geographic and other diversity within all sections of the student body." Of course, when Sjogren and Goodman crafted admissions and financial aid policies that moved affirmative action recruiting and admissions away from Detroit, administrators were concerned about getting what they called "better" black students. At no time did administrators suggest that they were interested in the benefits of a black student population from all corners of America. Geographic diversity served as a benevolent cover for the university's interest in rationalizing the exclusion of low-income black students in the state's urban areas.[43]

Lawyers made further claims that harked back to university administrators' resistance to black activism. According to Payton's team, a race-neutral alternative would require selective universities to "radically alter their missions," as they would no longer be able to "enroll a highly qualified, broadly diverse student body." UM's lawyers argued that such a plan would undermine the university's "character, reputation, and educational excellence." Black students were important, in other words, but elite universities could only have a certain type of black student to be inclusive and excellent. Even if a race-neutral plan could sustain black enrollment numbers, "the University would be an entirely different institution," Payton argued. These statements resembled William Haber's memo during the BAM strike in 1970. Haber concluded that BAM's enrollment demands would "adversely affect the position of academic preeminence which it has achieved over the years" and "drastically change the character of the University." When these words circulated around campus in 1970, they helped BAM gain widespread support for a campus strike. In the early twenty-first century, Payton hoped these words would save UM's affirmative action practices in court.[44]

In the mid-1970s, UM officials didn't have any internal evidence to support their attack on working-class black students from Detroit—and they still didn't have any evidence twenty years later. Thus, Payton turned to William Bowen for expert testimony. Bowen provided evidence from his recent book, *The Shape of the River*—a widely read defense of affirmative action, which he wrote with Derek Bok. The two authors were former Ivy League presidents in the 1970s and 1980s. Examining decades of data on minority students at the nation's most selective institutions, Bowen and Bok challenged the most popular conservative arguments against affirmative action, namely that black students weren't prepared for study at elite universities and would be better served by less selective institutions—an argument popularly known as "mismatch theory."[45]

A small section of the book that Bowen relied on in his expert report proved especially important for UM's defense. Bowen and Bok argued that alternatives to race-based affirmative action could never sustain minority enrollment as long as UM wanted a student body that was both "academically excellent and diverse." Bowen and Bok were more explicit than UM's lawyers about the background of these black students, who would preserve the academic excellence of the university. Affirmative action allowed selective universities, like UM, to recruit middle-class black students with the academic credentials that could sustain the academic standards of elite schools, the two authors submitted. Alternatives to affirmative action, such as class-based selection tools, were flawed because there were simply too few low-income black students who could meet the admissions criteria of selective universities. They went even further, suggesting that current affirmative action admissions practices bring in minority students with future leadership potential in politics and business. The assumption here was that only middle-class black students had the potential to serve in these positions. It shouldn't have surprised anyone that Bowen and Bok would make this type of argument. These were two Ivy League presidents who served during the era of racial retrenchment in higher education. Just like UM administrators, they were unapologetic about shifting affirmative action practices that focused on middle-class black students outside cities.[46]

In *The Shape of the River*, Bowen and Bok used SAT scores and grades to show that few low-income black students could meet selective institutions' academic criteria. This reflected shifting assumptions in the mid-1970s that institutions could successfully use the SAT to predict black students' performance effectively. The most problematic evidence showed that over 70 percent of black students at selective institutions came from middle-class families. To Bowen and Bok, this again showed that only middle-class black students were prepared for elite study. What it really showed was the outcomes of practices at elite universities that excluded low-income black students who had performed well in previous years. They offered no data that revealed that low-income black students had begun to perform poorly. Their argument about race and social class represented selective universities' version of mismatch, which relied on evidence that was as incomplete and problematic as the evidence in conservatives' mismatch theory. Nevertheless, Bowen's expert report became key evidence for UM's attack on race-neutral alternatives in the *Gratz* case.[47]

Other universities came to UM's defense, echoing some of the same arguments Bowen offered in his expert report. Four public universities joined together to submit an amicus brief. Two Pennsylvania universities included in the brief—Temple University and the University of Pittsburgh—showed that they were especially concerned about the prospect of depending on low-income black students from the state's cities if they were forced to adopt a percentage plan similar to Texas's 10 percent plan. They used the Philadelphia school district as an example. Temple and the University of Pittsburgh pointed to the fact that the state of Pennsylvania had recently assumed supervision over the Philadelphia school district because "the education provided . . . was deemed to be so inadequate in preparing students." Given the state of Philadelphia's schools, the two universities argued that an admissions plan that offered admission to the top 10 percent of each high school's graduating class would force them to admit Philadelphia students who weren't as prepared to compete at selective universities as black students outside the city who didn't finish at the top of their high school class. While the brief never mentioned middle-class black students, it was a thinly veiled argument that these schools preferred middle-class black students educated outside the state's cities.[48]

Private universities rang in with similar concerns in their own briefs, as opponents could still argue that private universities could adopt a class-based program. A group of the nation's most prestigious liberal arts colleges, including Amherst College, Williams College, and Swarthmore College, argued against class-based alternatives to affirmative action by suggesting that "it is precisely the 'middle class' students from minority backgrounds who, research and experience shows, are most likely to succeed." There were no code words in this statement.[49]

The issue of social class, of course, wasn't the only issue that drove universities' resistance to race-neutral alternatives. Race-neutral plans were anything but race neutral. They were simply another form of race-based affirmative action that conservatives preferred. While these plans didn't take race into account at the point of selecting students, they were clearly race conscious. Consider Texas's 10 percent plan, which the state implemented in the aftermath of *Hopwood*. Legislators consciously created the plan with the racially attentive motivation to try to preserve the underrepresented minority enrollment in the state's most selective institutions. They knew that the 10 percent plan would continue to produce a sizable pool of black students who were eligible to attend the state's top public universities because much of the state's public school system remained racially segregated. Since black students often went to schools that were overwhelmingly black, legislators knew that a significant number of black students would qualify for admission. The fact that these plans took race into account meant that they would be open to future lawsuits.[50]

The percentage plans also wouldn't work well for public universities in many states. UM's lawyers pointed out that the percentage plans couldn't work in the state of Michigan because the state's small Hispanic population wouldn't support a diverse student body, as the vast majority of Hispanic students at UM came from outside the state. Private universities offered another layer of criticism to race-neutral alternatives. Because their student enrollments were small and they served a national population, they could never guarantee admission to even the top 1 percent of high school graduates.[51]

All these arguments served UM's goal of preserving an affirmative action program that focused on middle-class underrepresented students living outside cities. Even the intervenors never critiqued the university's socioeconomic and geographic preferences. Their argument suggested that all underrepresented students suffered from the university's discriminatory admissions practice equally, regardless of social class and geography. UM and their allies, then, advanced a critique of low-income black students in cities without any rebuttal in *Gratz*. The legacy of co-optation, again, found a prominent place in UM's legal defense.[52]

Finally, UM's co-optation practices made it easy for lawyers to make an argument about the corporate interests in affirmative action admissions. UM had long tailored its affirmative action defense to the interest of corporations. Beginning in the early 1960s, when Hobart Taylor intervened on behalf of the PCEEO, UM officials saw affirmative action admissions as a tool to help companies fulfill their federal affirmative action hiring responsibilities. UM leaders would go on to emphasize that relationship in order to get more funding for the Opportunity Program from companies. In the 1980s and 1990s, diversity helped sustain that relationship, as UM officials suggested that diversity-trained students could compete in a global marketplace. At every turn, UM leaders found ways to reframe the goals of activists to serve the interests of businesses.

When CIR filed the case, UM courted businesses to write amicus briefs to support the university's affirmative action practices. Given UM's long history of connecting affirmative action admissions to business interests, it should be no surprise that corporations came to UM's defense. It also helped that diversity became a corporate strategy to improve competitiveness beginning in the 1980s and early 1990s. When the threat of federal equal employment lawsuits declined during the Reagan administration, human resources officials began to use diversity to reframe affirmative action hiring so that it served the profit-driven interests of businesses.[53]

Companies submitted four separate amicus briefs that supported the University of Michigan in *Gratz*. General Motors, operating less than an hour drive from Ann Arbor, was the first to lend its support. Sixty-five other major corporations, including 3M, Nike, Microsoft, and Boeing, joined together in another brief. The MTV Networks (MTVN), which included popular television stations such as MTV, VH1, Nickelodeon, and Country Music Television, submitted its own brief. Finally, eighteen media companies, representing television, radio, print, and cable media, joined to support UM's affirmative action practices. Together, the briefs argued that businesses depended on selective universities' affirmative action practices to produce a diverse workforce trained in cross-cultural understanding.[54]

One of the popular arguments in the briefs suggested that diversity produced innovation. These companies found that a diverse workforce brought new approaches to problem solving and new ideas that produced a creative tension within companies that avoided the type of group thinking that kept companies stagnant. They worried that ending affirmative action admissions would harm their ability to cultivate a diverse workforce and subsequently stymie the innovative thinking that was essential to their market competitiveness.

These briefs also explained how diversity helped companies serve customers and clients. GM and the sixty-five leading businesses emphasized the necessity of diversity to compete in a global marketplace. GM and 3M sold products in about two hundred countries. Boeing sold 70 percent of its commercial aircrafts outside the United States. These companies wanted more employees of color to serve international clients and customers. All the companies submitting amicus briefs also argued that diverse workforces made them more competitive in serving minority communities in the United States. The media companies understood that communities of color wanted to see and read the perspectives of other people of color. Minority journalists and whites trained in cross-cultural understanding could also get better stories in these communities because they understood how to talk to people of color, one brief argued. MTVN argued that a diverse workforce was vital in cultivating its multicultural brand, which it wanted to sell to all communities in the United States.[55]

Finally, these companies argued that access to a diverse workforce trained in cross-cultural understanding was essential to improving employee relations. Racial tension inside companies was bad for business. It made it difficult for companies to retain valuable employees, leading to turnover and costly recruiting and hiring initiatives. It also led to costly discrimination lawsuits. Companies made it clear that they didn't want to take on the responsibility of training employees in cross-cultural understanding. As GM explained, businesses were "commercial enterprises, not educational entities." Universities had pedagogical resources that businesses lacked, which made campuses the ideal location to teach future employees cross-cultural skills. Businesses made it clear that they now expected employees to get those skills on college campuses. Eliminating affirmative action admissions would hinder that training and shift a costly burden onto businesses, the argument went.[56]

On June 23, 2003, the Supreme Court released its ruling in *Gratz* and *Grutter*. The court upheld the University of Michigan's interest in using race as a factor in admissions to create a diverse student body, but it struck down LSA's specific affirmative action practices. *Gratz* ruled that the old admissions grids based on race and the new system that automatically assigned the same number of points to all underrepresented minority students violated the Fourteenth Amendment. Instead, the court identified the Law School's holistic admissions system in *Grutter*—which evaluated each minority applicant individually and didn't assign a specific weight to underrepresented status—as an example of a constitutionally permissible affirmative action program.[57]

On the surface, *Gratz* might look like a disastrous loss for undergraduate affirmative action admissions at the University of Michigan. The College of Literature, Science, and the Arts, after all, would have to scrap its entire admissions system and create new affirmative action practices to comply with the ruling. But, taken with *Grutter*, *Gratz* represented a victory for University of Michigan leaders. The rulings allowed UM to continue to use race as a factor in admissions without disrupting any of the co-optation tools of the past decades. The court endorsed diversity's racial innocence narrative and its ambiguity—both of which the university used to wrestle control of inclusion from campus activists. The court endorsed the university's hierarchy of values, which saw the university's interest in maintaining its elite status as more important than its interest in creating a diverse student body. The ruling praised the model multiracial community's goal to improve relationships between white and minority students, while ignoring the persistent problems black students faced within UM's racial climate. Finally, the court embraced a brand of affirmative action that focused on recruiting and admitting middle-class black students outside cities.[58]

Because the court ruled on *Gratz* and *Grutter* at the same time, and UM presented almost identical arguments in both cases, the court didn't outline diversity's "compelling government interest" in both opinions. Instead, Chief Justice Rehnquist used the majority opinion in *Gratz* to explain why UM's specific admissions practices violated the Constitution. He referred readers to Justice O'Connor's majority opinion in *Grutter* for the court's decision that explained why diversity represented a constitutionally permissible justification for affirmative action in higher education. O'Connor made clear that she was overwhelmed by the evidence that diversity produced important benefits inside and outside higher education. Gurin's report convinced O'Connor that diversity was vital in producing the best educational outcomes and in preserving democracy. The support from businesses also impressed her, as she contended that a diverse student body was essential to the United States to compete in a global marketplace.[59]

In embracing diversity, she ignored the intervenors' remedial argument and endorsed the university's racial innocence narrative. She praised the university for its interest in pursuing the benefits of diversity. These benefits improved education and helped the nation. Despite the university's long history of discrimination and racial disparities in its student body and workforce, the university had become a well-intentioned institution with the best interests of all its students in mind. By ignoring the intervenors' brief, O'Connor's decision gave the university even more support for its preference for the diversity framework over social justice.[60]

Important for the preservation of UM's co-optation techniques, she embraced the ambiguity of diversity. Powell's decision in *Bakke* granted universities the ability to pay attention to numbers, but UM lawyers pitched a concept of diversity without any numerical goals. "Meaningful numbers" and "critical mass" were ambiguous goals without any coherent measuring tools. This was the type of ambiguity that UM administrators preferred, as they had long tried to avoid numerical targets in order to avoid accountability. It was also the type of ambiguity that O'Connor preferred. In celebrating UM's vague concept of diversity, with no numerical targets or measurable criteria, O'Connor further eroded the ability of activists to push for enrollment targets.[61]

O'Connor also endorsed the university's hierarchy of values. UM had always seen maintaining its elite status as its most important priority. UM leaders accepted inclusion initiatives only so long as they didn't disrupt the institution's status. O'Connor preserved this hierarchy of values when she embraced the university's argument against race-neutral alternatives. She argued that UM shouldn't have "to choose between maintaining a reputation for excellence or fulfilling a commitment to provide educational opportunities to members of all racial groups." In other words, UM should be able to keep a value system that prioritized its elite status over racial equity.[62]

While *Gratz* struck down LSA's specific practices, then, the *Gratz* and *Grutter* decisions allowed LSA to create a more holistic admissions system that preserved the fundamental principles of co-optation put in place since the mid-1970s. Neither decision paid any attention to the socioeconomic background or location of underrepresented minority students who gained access to UM. The majority opinions paid no attention to the fact that the weight

UM placed on standardized tests produced racial disparities and put low-income minority students at a special disadvantage. None of the justices raised concerns about the amicus curiae who stated explicitly that they didn't want to create an alternative affirmative action system that brought low-income minority students from cities to their schools. Only one liberal justice, Ruth Bader Ginsberg, addressed social class at all. In her dissent in *Gratz*, she outlined the persistent inequality in the United States in defending the constitutional merits of UM's undergraduate admissions system. "African-American and Hispanic children are all too often educated in poverty-stricken and underperforming schools," she wrote. But she never recognized that UM's affirmative action program didn't serve those students. In the aftermath of the rulings, UM could simply reconstruct an undergraduate affirmative action program that focused on the same middle-class underrepresented students going to high schools outside cities. This represented a huge victory for UM leaders.[63]

Ironically, Clarence Thomas provided the only argument that even came close to the claims of the intervenors. In his dissent in *Grutter*, Thomas offered a stinging critique of standardized testing. According to Thomas, the University of Michigan chose to use admissions tests that officials understood would produce racially skewed results. These were "self-inflicted wounds" of UM's "own choosing," Thomas argued.[64]

Thomas also took issue with the idea that admitting students with high standardized test scores was the only way to preserve a school's elite status. This mind-set, he argued, was the product of choices that higher education leaders had made over the last century. If university leaders created a system that produced racial disparities, they had the burden to create a new elite system that didn't require affirmative action to offer access. At times, Thomas's dissent looked even closer to UM's Black Action Movement of 1970 than that of the intervenors. The intervenors argued that discriminatory standardized tests required an affirmative action program. Thomas seemed to be calling for an entirely new system that didn't measure status by the standardized test scores that produced racial disparities.[65]

Still, Thomas didn't disappoint conservatives. Even after his critique of standardized tests, he turned to mismatch theory to argue that affirmative action brought too many minority students who weren't prepared to succeed at elite schools. Mismatch proponents argued that many minority students at elite universities would be better served at less selective schools. Most of these proponents used standardized test scores—the same scores that Thomas criticized—as evidence that minority students weren't capable of performing at selective institutions.[66]

This was the type of argument UM had set itself up for since the 1960s. UM leaders had created and sustained an admissions system that produced racial disparities. Just as importantly, this system produced an institutional knowledge about black students that played into the hands of conservatives. The knowledge that UM released to the public showed how black students scored lower on SAT scores and left the university before graduating at higher rates than did whites, giving mismatch theorists ammunition. UM officials made the situation worse when they withheld from the public important data from the early 1970s that showed that academic deficiency didn't explain black students' attrition rates.[67]

In defending an admissions system that produced racial disparities, UM leaders also gave conservatives like Thomas the opportunity to claim that they were the true champions of black students. Affirmative action has always been a tool of co-optation—an attempt to make only minor modifications to a discriminatory system. By preserving a discriminatory system and never offering a new admissions process built on justice and equity, UM leaders gave conservatives an opening to offer alternatives built on conservative principles. These conservative alternatives never matched black campus activists' vision for a revolution of values and priorities in higher education. Nevertheless, UM's reluctance to ever question an admissions system that had long produced racial inequality made Thomas's dissent appear, at times, closer to black activists' speeches and writings than UM's defense of affirmative action.

The day the Supreme Court released its opinions in *Gratz* and *Grutter*, Students Supporting Affirmative Action held a celebration on UM's campus. They held signs that read "DIVERSITY SAVED at UofM" and "AFFIRMATIVE ACTION IS RIGHT." On the steps of the Supreme Court, the university's president, Mary Sue Coleman—Bollinger accepted the president position at Columbia University in October 2001—sported a bright smile as she began holding press conferences.[68]

For students worried that the end of affirmative action would lead to even greater racial disparities, the Supreme Court's decision represented an important victory. But the Supreme Court's decision also represented a clear victory for UM's co-optation of racial justice. LSA might have to create a new affirmative action admissions system, but the admissions office could do so using all the principles of co-optation. The new affirmative action system could continue to focus on middle-class black students living outside cities. It could continue to use the ambiguity of diversity to avoid numerical goals and accountability. Affirmative action wasn't the only thing that survived in *Gratz* and *Grutter*. Co-optation survived in 2003.

# Epilogue
## The University as Victim

In 2006, Michigan voters approved an amendment to the state Constitution that banned affirmative action in public institutions. It was a devastating blow to the University of Michigan's efforts to preserve affirmative action. UM had just spent millions of dollars defending racially attentive admissions in court. The political arena, though, proved to be the university's most formidable obstacle.[1]

One way to read Proposal 2 is as the culmination of a conservative backlash to affirmative action at the University of Michigan. There is no doubt that these anti–affirmative action efforts have made racial inclusion more difficult at UM. But this book has shown that focusing blame on conservative court cases and political efforts to ban affirmative action misses the role institutional officials have played—and continue to play—in the persistence of racial inequality at UM. University of Michigan officials have long crafted visions of inclusion that accommodated and defended racial inequality. Proposal 2 didn't create racial disparities and a poor racial climate at the University of Michigan—it simply exacerbated existing problems.

In the wake of Proposal 2, black enrollment began to decline, and the racial climate worsened. Battles on campus since 2006 have revolved around the university's culpability in racial retrenchment. University officials have deployed racial innocence, blaming the constitutional amendment for any problems on campus. Black students, though, have tried to hold the University of Michigan accountable for its part in new era of retrenchment, despite Proposal 2.

One month after Michigan voters passed Proposal 2, University of Michigan president Mary Coleman announced the Diversity Blueprints Task Force, headed by Provost Teresa Sullivan and Senior Vice Provost for Academic Affairs Lester Monts. Coleman, who replaced Bollinger in 2002, asked the task force to recommend new policies that would comply with Proposal 2 but still further the university's goal of diversity. Sullivan and Monts took advantage of the fact that postsecondary institutions in other states had already faced similar bans on affirmative action. By the time Michigan voters passed Proposal 2, public postsecondary institutions in California, Washington, Georgia, and Florida had all crafted "race-neutral" alternatives. Administrators in Texas also had experience in dealing with a court-ordered ban on affirmative action before *Gratz* and *Grutter* overturned *Hopwood* and allowed public universities in Texas to use race as a factor in admissions again. Sullivan and Monts organized a two-day workshop with representatives from the University of California–Berkeley, the University of Texas-Austin, and the University of Washington—all flagship public universities—to discuss how they responded to bans on affirmative action admissions practices in their own states.[2]

UM's admissions office implemented many of the proposals that came out of the workshop. To evaluate students' contribution to campus diversity, admissions officers created essays about identity and life experiences. One essay, which was required of all students, asked applicants to respond to a prompt: "Everyone belongs to many different communities and/or groups defined by (among other things) shared geography, religion, ethnicity, income, cuisine, interest, race, ideology, or intellectual heritage. Choose one of the communities to which you belong, and describe that community and your place within it." An optional prompt asked students to "describe an experience that illustrates what you would bring to the diversity in a college community or an encounter that demonstrated the importance of diversity to you."[3]

The university also purchased a new program that offered proxies for race. The admissions office paid $15,000 per year to use Descriptor Plus. The College Board developed the program to help schools "shape [their] class profile" and "[t]arget hard-to-attract populations," including minority students. The tool used College Board and U.S. census data to divide high schools into 180,000 different geographic neighborhood clusters, which have, what the College Board called, "unique behavior profiles." In short, the program divided high schools into neighborhood clusters with students that share similar SAT scores, college acceptance rates, incomes, and racial backgrounds. Using an applicant's information, University of Michigan admissions officers could search for whether an applicant went to an underperforming high school or lived in a neighborhood marked by "limited access to educational opportunities." The assumption, of course, is that a higher percentage of underrepresented minority students attend underperforming schools and, thus, could serve as a proxy for race.[4]

The University's Alumni Association also tried to help UM mitigate the impact of Proposal 2. Before 2006, UM's affirmative action strategy depended on racially attentive scholarships to attract what officials thought were the "best" black students. When Proposal 2 eliminated those scholarships, the Alumni Association stepped in to provide similar funding resources. The association was a private organization, so it wasn't covered by the state's new constitutional amendment.[5]

Despite these efforts, underrepresented minority students' share of Michigan's student body began to decline. In 2006, underrepresented minority students composed 12.2 percent of incoming first-year students. In 2010, their share of incoming first-year students stood at 10.8 percent. Proposal 2 affected black enrollment even before Michigan voters passed the initiative. Applications from black students dropped dramatically during the contentious debate over Proposal 2. As a result, black students' share of incoming first-year students dropped from 7.2 percent to 6.1 percent between 2005 and 2006. Between 2007 and 2009, black undergraduate enrollment held steady between 6.19 and 6.58 percent. After that, the University of Michigan changed its applications, allowing students to check more than one race and ethnicity identification box. The university placed students who checked more than one box in a separate category, making it difficult to tell how many of those students might have identified only as black if the university had preserved its past application form. Since UM created this separate multiracial category, the percentage of students who identified only as black has hovered between 4.4 and 4.78 percent.[6]

When black enrollment began to decline in 2006, officials faced pressure to explain why racial disparities were increasing. They turned to a common technique: blaming external factors for the drop in black enrollment. Proposal 2 was to blame. The university was innocent of any wrongdoing.

Coleman and other officials tried to get critics to focus on the university's inclusion efforts in order to claim racial innocence. They emphasized that black enrollment didn't decline as much at UM as it had at the University of California–Berkeley and the University of Washington after those universities faced similar bans. Coleman stated that she was "pleased with holding our own with regard to underrepresented students." When Coleman made similar arguments at a Trotter House fireside chat, Walter Lacy, an undergraduate student, responded, "This is the response you get about race. That is, 'we're doing the best we can.'"[7]

Coleman initially signaled that the university might challenge Proposal 2 in court, but UM's lawyers never filed a lawsuit. Instead, the Coalition to Defend Affirmative Action, an activist group fighting against anti–affirmative action measures, filed the case against the state of Michigan and the board of regents of UM, Michigan State University, and Wayne State University. The case hinged on a complicated legal argument that claimed Proposal 2 violated the Equal Protection Clause of the Fourteenth Amendment. Coleman placed some hope in the lawsuit.[8]

The University of Michigan's racial innocence narrative found a place in the case. Although UM was a named defendant in a complicated case, UM officials wanted the court to rule in the plaintiff's favor and strike down Proposal 2. UM officials challenged Michigan's attorney general, who defended the merits of Proposal 2 in court. They claimed that the state's public universities couldn't maintain underrepresented enrollment through race-neutral means. Ted Spencer, UM's director of admissions, testified at the trial court about the difficulties he experienced in maintaining underrepresented enrollment in the wake of Proposal 2. UM also filed a brief in the case, claiming the decline in underrepresented minority enrollment after the passage of Proposal 2 clearly showed that UM couldn't create a diverse student body with race-neutral admissions policies. UM argued that it was a victim of the constitutional amendment. In 2008, the district court ruled against the Coalition to Defend Affirmative Action, but in October 2013, the Sixth Circuit reversed the decision, offering new hope to UM officials that they could soon return to old affirmative action practices. But when the Supreme Court agreed to hear the case on appeal, university leaders would have to wait.[9]

As UM officials waited for the high court's decision, black student activists were ready to mount a campaign against a new era of racial retrenchment. Black students had a low tolerance for administrators' excuses. They understood that Proposal 2 closed some of the most effective means of offering access to black students. Still, black activists refused to accept the idea that administrators were victims of Proposal 2. They refused to believe that university officials had exhausted all the available tools to raise black enrollment and improve the racial climate. Well publicized incidents of racism helped fuel a new protest movement. In perhaps the most highly publicized incident, Theta Xi, a fraternity on campus, advertised a "Hood Ratchet Thursday" party.[10]

As happened so often throughout the University of Michigan's history, the new protest movement began with black students' testimony. In November 2013, UM's Black Student Union launched #BBUM—a Twitter hashtag that stood for Being Black at the University of Michigan. The BSU asked students to go onto the social media site and testify about their experience on campus. The Twitter campaign caught national attention. Many of their testimonies could have come from any of UM's black students in previous decades:

@angel_crisstina: I look around to see how many stares I get after the instructor says Racism is the topic . . . since I'm the only Black person in class #BBUM

@TheSenCity: #BBUM being the one of the 5 Black males in the largest freshman dorm on campus

@Tiaraevelynn: Knowing more about other cultures than they know about ours #BBUM

@Cjeremya: That first class when Black culture become the topic and you suddenly become the voice of all Black people #BBUM

@JENNxoxo_: That pause that a person has when you say you're from Detroit. & you're just thinking "Yes, I made it here too." #BBUM

@LavashiaJM: #BBUM having to be extremely cautious of the tone of my voice because ill be seen as loud or ghetto.

@Larealkay: Being Black at umich means that I am accepted, but not necessarily welcomed. #BBUM[11]

The Black Student Union turned #BBUM into an organizing tool. By the time students returned from the winter recess, the group was ready with a list of demands for the administration. After Harry Belafonte spoke as part of the University's Martin Luther King Jr. Celebration, BSU representatives were standing on the steps of Hill Auditorium ready to announce their demands.

We demand that the university give us an equal opportunity to implement change, the change that complete restoration of the BSU purchasing power through an increased budget would obtain.

We demand available housing on central campus for those of lower socio-economic status at a rate that students can afford, to be a part of university life, and not just on the periphery

We demand an opportunity to congregate and share out experiences in a new Trotter [Multicultural Center] located on central campus.

We demand an opportunity to be educated and to educate about America's historical treatment and marginalization of colored groups through race and ethnicity requirements throughout all schools and colleges within the university.

> We demand the equal opportunity to succeed with emergency scholar-
> ships for Black students in need of financial support, without the
> mental anxiety of not being able to focus on and afford the university's
> academic life.
> We demand increased exposure of all documents within the Bentley
> (Historical) Library. There should be transparency about the university
> and its past dealings with race relations.
> We demand an increase in Black representation on this campus equal to
> 10 percent.

The students adopted a tone that administrators hadn't heard from a black student group since the late 1980s. They gave the university a seven-day deadline
to meet the demands or the BSU would respond with "physical action."[12]

Coleman agreed to meet with the group. While UM officials were willing
to take some responsibility for the racial climate, Coleman and UM officials
were unwilling to take responsibility for black enrollment. It was clear that she
didn't think the university could reach the BSU's 10 percent black enrollment
goal, and she didn't believe that the BSU should fault UM leaders for that. The
next month, she gave a speech that addressed the BSU's demands and emphasized the limitations that Proposal 2 placed on the university. "We have struggled in the wake of Proposal 2 and the ban on affirmative action. We know
that," she told the audience. "Our commitment [to diversity] has never waned.
The environment in which we operate, however, has changed." She emphasized all that the university had done to try to limit the impact of the constitutional amendment. She claimed the university had implemented the "best
practices" available to give underrepresented minority students access to UM.[13]

UM officials developed a favorite metaphor to describe why the university
struggled with inclusion in the face of Proposal 2. "It's like having your hands
tied behind your back," Provost Martha Pollack said of the constitutional
amendment. UM officials used it to deflect accountability. Much like officials
before them, they asked the UM community to recognize the constraints they
worked within and give them credit for all their efforts to advance inclusion.[14]

If Coleman had been holding out hope that the Supreme Court would solve
some of the university's problems, she was sorely disappointed. In April 2014, the
court rejected the Coalition to Defend Affirmative Action's arguments. In a 6 to
2 decision, the court upheld Proposal 2. Two months later, Coleman retired.[15]

"I firmly believe that we cannot achieve true excellence without leveraging the
experiences and perspectives of the broadest diversity of students, faculty, and
staff," Mark Schlissel told the audience at his inauguration as president of the

University of Michigan in September 2014. Clearly responding to the pressure from black students on his predecessor over the last year, he emphasized that "students of all experiences and backgrounds should feel they have a place in this community. We must continue to reach out to the most promising students, from our state and from across the nation and around the world."[16]

Just two months before he gave his inauguration speech, the Provost's Committee on Diversity, Equity, and Inclusion released a report on achieving inclusion at UM. Provost Martha Pollack created the committee in the midst of #BBUM. The problems the committee identified looked the same as those uncovered by committee after committee during the previous fifty years. Minority students experienced a hostile racial climate. Minority students needed more academic support services. The university didn't do enough to recruit and retain minority faculty. The university's decentralized structure made it difficult to coordinate inclusion efforts. The university didn't do enough to hold people accountable and create consequences for failing to achieve inclusion. The recommendations, too, looked like stock administrative responses to student pressure. The committee recommended the formation of yet another committee to make recommendations on improving the racial climate and another task force to study academic support services. It also suggested an aggressive public campaign "reaffirming the University's commitment to diversity as a core value." The committee did offer one stinging critique of the university's response to Proposition 2. "Many in the University community have used the passage of Proposal 2 as an inappropriate excuse for inactivity around diversity issues," the committee concluded.[17]

The committee report didn't stop the university from using Proposal 2 to advance a narrative of racial innocence. As UM formulated a strategic inclusion plan, university officials saw another opportunity to tell the university's struggles to the Supreme Court. In 2012, the University of Texas found itself in front of the nation's highest court. Abigail Fisher, a white undergraduate applicant, sued UT, claiming its affirmative action admissions practices didn't meet the narrow tailoring test of strict scrutiny. The majority remanded the case to the lower court, deciding that the district court didn't interpret strict scrutiny properly. When *Fisher* returned to the Supreme Court in 2015, UM officials decided to put their narrative of racial innocence to use to help UT.[18]

UM filed an amicus brief in the case, trying to show what would happen if the court ruled in Fisher's favor. Proposal 2 took away the University of Michigan's successful affirmative action programs, the brief claimed. University officials exhausted all the race-neutral options they had available, but these options failed. The university couldn't sustain minority enrollment. "The University's nearly decade-long experiment in race-neutral admissions," the brief read, "is a cautionary tale that underscores the compelling need for selective universities to be able to consider race as one of the many background factors about applicants."[19]

The university's brief, much like its legal arguments in *Gratz*, misrepresented institutional history to tell a story of racial innocence. #BBUM suddenly became the result of "student dissatisfaction with persistent low Black enrollment" caused by Proposal 2. The brief quoted students who wrote on Twitter about feeling isolated and being the only black student in a class. These weren't problems the university was responsible for, according to the brief. Proposal 2 caused these problems. Black activists on campus didn't support Proposal 2, of course, but they weren't using Twitter to protest the constitutional amendment. They were using Twitter to combat the university's narrative of racial innocence. They were trying to bring attention to the failures of university policy.[20]

As UM officials continued to invoke their racial innocence, Schlissel unveiled his strategic plan to improve inclusion. The plan included many of the hallmarks of past co-optation techniques, which attempted to quell activism while offering few systemic changes. The plan tried to move black students' #BBUM testimony on Twitter onto a university-controlled website called Diversity Matters. Second, the plan offered an influx of money into inclusion programs—a consistent feature of co-optation. In the past, that money often didn't last long and rarely fixed systemic problems. Time will only tell how long the money will last in coming years. Third, the plan expanded the inclusion bureaucracy, creating yet another administrative position to oversee diversity programs.[21]

As of 2018, the Go Blue Guarantee represents the most significant reform to come out of Schlissel's strategic plan. The program covers undergraduate tuition and fees for in-state students with family incomes of less than $65,000. It's UM's most important commitment to low-income students since the mid-1970s. Recall that UM undermined access for low-income black students when officials redistributed the university's general fund resources used for need-based aid to support merit aid. The Go Blue Guarantee comes closer to the Opportunity Program's original financial aid policies than any program since the mid-1970s.[22]

Removing financial barriers are meaningless, though, if underrepresented students can't gain admission. UM hasn't crafted new admissions practices to match the ambitious Go Blue Guarantee financial aid commitment. Wolverine Pathways, introduced in 2015, represents the university's most significant admissions initiative. It's a UM-community partnership that offers a supplemental education program to prepare students for UM's competitive admissions process. The program started in two small school districts with large percentages of underrepresented students and expanded to include Detroit in 2017. Students enter the program in seventh or tenth grade and are expected to remain in the program until they graduate from high school. During the academic year, students participate in sixteen Saturday courses, which involve project-based learning to enhance math and communication skills. During the summer, they participate in another sixteen daylong sessions. The program also offers standardized test preparation.[23]

Wolverine Pathways is an admirable program that will improve education opportunities for a select group of underrepresented students. But the program isn't a substitute for changes to the admissions system. The outcomes reveal the Wolverine Pathways' small impact it on UM's student body. The first class of students who spent four years in the program entered college in fall 2018. Of the eighty-nine students, forty-one gained admission and planned to enroll at the University of Michigan. The university hasn't reported the racial and socioeconomic background of these students. Nevertheless, even if all forty-one students are black, they still represent only 0.6 percent of the incoming class.[24]

In fall 2018, even with the Go Blue Guarantee and Wolverine Pathways, black students made up 5 percent of the first-year class. That represents a 1 percent increase from fall 2017. A 1 percent increase is nothing to scoff at, but it's also nothing to celebrate. A September 2018 study made that clear. The University of Southern California's Race and Equity Center released a report card grading public universities in all fifty states based on criteria that included black students' share of the student population in relation to young blacks' (18 to 24 years old) share of the state population. The University of Michigan received an F, finishing in the bottom quintile of all public universities. The Go Blue Guarantee and Wolverine Pathways aren't programs that will lift UM out of the bottom quintile. Neither program will come close to raising black enrollment to match blacks' (18 to 24) share of the state population—17 percent.[25]

The University of Michigan isn't alone. In the same University of Southern California study, other highly selective public universities received poor scores for black students' representation on campus. The University of Virginia received an F. The University of North Carolina-Chapel Hill received an F. The University of Texas-Austin received a D. The University of California–Berkeley received the highest grade of any elite public university with a C. It was a generous grade considering that black students at the Berkeley campus represent 1.9 percent of the student body and African Americans represent 6.6 percent of California's eighteen to twenty-four year old population. Grade inflation has extended to our universities' inclusion efforts.[26]

If the nation's elite private universities were included in the study, they would have also received dismal grades. At Stanford University, black students represent 3.8 percent of the student body. Black students at Bryn Mawr College represent 5 percent of the study body. At Harvard University, black students represent 6.7 percent of undergraduate students. The fact is that despite the protests for racial inclusion that enveloped universities and colleges nationwide in recent years, racial disparities persist at the nation's most selective institutions. Only 7 percent of black college students attend highly selective colleges and universities in the United States. Sixty-four percent of black students attend four-year and two-year schools for which a high school diploma is the only admissions requirement. In contrast, 23 percent of white and 36 percent of Asian American students attend the nation's most selective universities and colleges.[27]

Since UM's dreary black enrollment numbers are part of a larger national story, it shouldn't be a surprise that some of the university's recent responses to protest mirror popular reforms around the country. The Go Blue Guarantee, for example, represents a national trend. Columbia University, Cornell University, Duke University, and Brown University cover tuition for students whose families make less than $60,000. At Harvard University, Stanford University, Yale University, and Rice University, students from families making less than $65,000 don't pay tuition. Programs at Princeton University, Dartmouth University, and the Massachusetts Institute of Technology are even more generous, covering tuition expenses for students with family incomes ranging from $90,000 to $140,000.[28]

Some selective colleges and universities have gone further than the University of Michigan in reforming admissions. This book has shown the negative impact standardized tests have had on racial inclusion. While UM continues to require these tests as part of its admissions process, other universities are now removing these exams from the selection process or making them an optional requirement. In 2018, more than one thousand four-year institutions no longer require the SAT or ACT as part of their admissions process. Most of these institutions aren't selective, but some of the nation's most prestigious institutions have modified their standardized test requirements. Among selective institutions, the nation's top liberal arts colleges are leading the way. Bowdoin College, Bates College, Smith College, Bryn Mawr College, and Wesleyan University no longer require standardized tests, and are all ranked among the top thirty liberal arts colleges according to *U.S. News and World Report* rankings. Even more top liberal arts colleges are now "test flexible," which varies widely among institutions, but the policy generally gives students the ability to submit different types of test scores as a substitute or supplement to the SAT or ACT. For example, Hamilton College gives applicants the option to submit three exams of their choice, which could include an individual section of the SAT, the ACT writing score, an SAT subject test, an advanced placement exam score, or an International Baccalaureate final exam. In all, ten of the top thirty ranked liberal arts colleges have test-optional or test-flexible admissions policies. In fact, over half of the top one hundred liberal arts colleges have these policies. The nation's most selective research universities, though, lag behind. In June 2018, the University of Chicago became the first top ten ranked research university to make the SAT an optional admissions requirement. Only three of the top thirty and twelve of the top one hundred national research universities have test-optional or test-flexible policies.[29]

Recent studies show that test-optional policies, in particular, raise underrepresented minority enrollment at selective institutions. In one study that compared test-optional institutions to peer institutions that required the SAT or ACT, the researchers found two-thirds of test-optional colleges and universities saw their underrepresented minority populations grow at higher rates than their test-mandatory peers. Still, these jumps in underrepresented enrollment haven't fully closed the racial gap at selective institutions. A few test-optional universities and colleges have reported an impressive rise in their underrepresented minority enrollment of 3 to 4 percent, but most have reported more modest increases.[30]

It's too early to evaluate the full impact of test-optional policies for racial inclusion. While Bowdoin adopted the policy in 1969, most of these selective institutions have only a few years of experience in selecting students without standardized test scores or with alternative scores. There are promising signs that test-optional policies could eventually lead to greater growth in underrepresented enrollment than researchers have seen thus far. Selective institutions with test-optional policies have seen applications from underrepresented students, including low-income students, skyrocket. These developments are a reminder that the SAT and ACT have taught black students to discipline their ambitions. For more than half a century, universities and colleges have used standardized tests to signal to black students where they "fit" in higher education. Removing this requirement has clearly sent a message to more black high school students that they might now fit at the nation's most prestigious institutions.[31]

These reforms offer a glimmer of hope that black student enrollment for students of all socioeconomic backgrounds will rise in coming years. But these reforms are too limited to produce the type of access that black student activists have called for. The problem is that these reforms share the hallmarks of co-optation that filled this book, as they protect elite universities' hierarchy of values. They preserve a system that largely evaluates institutions' quality by the academic credentials of their students at the moment students apply. These credentials are better predictors of wealth and race than anything else. Even if universities reject the SAT, there are plenty of other credentials, such as the number of advanced placement courses students take, that will continue to produce racial and socioeconomic disparities at the nation's most selective colleges and universities.

The problem with celebrating reform is that it often helps people forget all the discriminatory policies still in effect. University of Chicago officials' celebration of their recent reforms serves as a case in point. When the University of Chicago announced UChicago Empower, which made the SAT an optional admissions requirement and offered applicants the opportunity to present alternative materials, such as a two-minute video, the dean of admissions suggested that the program "levels the playing field, allowing first-generation and low-income students to use technology and other resources to present themselves as well as any other college applicant." Reform doesn't level the playing field. Overlooking all the exclusionary admission methods still in play at the University of Chicago will support narratives that white and Asian American students are just more deserving of admissions slots when UChicago Empower doesn't dramatically increase underrepresented student enrollment. This reality should give us pause before we start celebrating the new test-optional or need-based aid initiatives.[32]

One of the lessons of this book is that it's important not to confuse reform with disruptive institutional change. Reform preserves elite universities' hierarchy of values and the measurement tools they use to define "elite." Inclusion initiatives, then, have only been acceptable as long as they don't disrupt these values. The problem is that institutions can't reform their way out of a value system that produces and defends racial inequality. Disruptive institutional change for racial equity is different. It sees the university's core values as the root of the problem. The goal, then, is to rethink the entire purpose and structure of elite institutions in order to create a truly inclusive university.

Some of the most disruptive ideas come from people who believe that advances in technology will revolutionize access by making the prototypical four-year college experience—that is, one confined to a campus—a relic of the past. The disruptive part isn't that students will learn online—that's already part of the higher education landscape. The disruptive piece of the vision is that new technology will end the monopoly colleges and universities have over what constitutes a degree. As universities and colleges put more of their coursework online and new technology offers better ways to evaluate and advise huge numbers of students in a single course, students will be able to tailor their own coursework, building a curriculum across multiple institutions that best serves each student's life goals. Rather than living on a campus, students with similar goals or interests might join together in their own learning communities. They might live in places that offer experiences that will advance their goals. Employers will look at the list of courses taken—and the institutions that provided the courses—in determining the qualifications of prospective employees.[33]

The prospect that advances in technology will allow postsecondary institutions—even the most elite institutions—the opportunity to add thousands, if not hundreds of thousands, of students to their courses has the potential to advance accessibility. The most optimistic foresee the end of admissions offices. As Kevin Carney writes, people won't apply to colleges in the future, they "will *join* colleges and other learning organizations for as long or as little time as they need." In that case, the main obstacles will be whether a student can pay tuition and complete the rigorous coursework.[34]

While some of these ideas, if implemented properly, have the potential to disrupt a historically discriminatory admissions system, the writers who advocate for technological disruptions are largely blind to race. They overlook a world where access to the types of technology necessary to participate in this new educational system is poorly distributed across racial and socioeconomic lines. The worst of this literature imagines a higher education industry where students will choose courses à la carte from nonprofit and for-profit and accredited and non-accredited institutions. Given the fact that for-profit and non-accredited institutions have preyed on low-income people of color, taking their money and leaving them without a meaningful education, should give us all pause about the future disruptions that new technology might bring. These writers also admit that the nation's elite colleges will be the last to make transformative changes.

I only hope that writers envisioning how technology can disrupt higher education will start thinking more about race and equity.[35]

Less disruptive, but more attuned to racial inequality, are writers who advocate for transforming the purpose of elite institutions. An institution's purpose drives admissions decisions. Legal scholar Lani Guinier argues that "universities have drifted away from their public mission to create active citizens in a democratic society." While elite universities like the University of Michigan place high-minded democratic ideals in their mission statements, their primary mission has been to preserve their status by admitting students with the highest test scores. According to Guinier, if universities were serious about training students to contribute to the future of democracy, standardized test scores and advanced placement scores wouldn't play such a large role in admissions. Instead, universities would need to craft a new vision of merit that she calls "democratic merit." This form of merit would require an admissions system that assesses students based on their potential ability to "serve the goals and contribute to the conditions of a thriving democracy for both their own good as well as for the collective good."[36]

However elite institutions redefine their purpose, Guinier's vision shows the power in redefining the mission and priorities of an institution. Doing so offers opportunities to reconsider the concepts and mechanisms that perpetuate inequality—concepts and mechanisms that many institutional leaders have taken for granted and that can even seem natural. Disruptive change, then, doesn't just call into question the SAT; it calls into question our entire understanding of who deserves access to elite institutions.

A key piece of this type of disruptive change would create new methods for measuring institutional quality and prestige. In Guinier's formula, universities' prestige would be measured by the degree to which they contribute to democracy. Clearly, this isn't the only way to redefine the purpose of elite institutions in order to promote access and equity, but it's important that any redefinition disconnects institutional prestige from the academic credentials of students the moment they apply. Imagine if we rated hospitals by the health of patients when they enter the door. We wouldn't ask about the care patients received. We would simply give the hospitals who admitted the healthiest patients the highest rankings, while giving hospitals who admitted patients in critical condition the lowest rankings. This probably sounds like a useless rating system that should never be used to grant prestige to any medical institution. But it's essentially the system we use to rank universities and colleges. Institutions achieve prestige by their admissions decisions, and we assume that great educational outcomes follow. It's hard to imagine a truly inclusive higher education system without eliminating this ranking procedure, which continues to provide incentives for institutions to perpetuate the educational inequalities at the primary and secondary levels.[37]

There are some recent positive signs that our ranking systems are beginning to change to encourage equity. *U.S. News and World Report* has started placing less weight on admissions selectivity and has introduced new social mobility categories—including schools' Pell Grant recipients and graduation rates—in the rankings. *U.S. News and World Report* is still a long way from offering a ranking system that helps create disruptive change, but it's creeping at a snail's pace in that direction. More encouraging are alternative ranking systems. The *Washington Monthly*, for example, tries to rank colleges and universities "based on what they are doing for the country." The ranking methodology places more weight on Pell Grant recipients, graduation rates, affordability, and the percentage of students who join service institutions, such as the Peace Corps.

The *Washington Monthly* doesn't include racial equity in its method—it should—but alternative ranking systems like this come much closer to Guinier's vision.[38]

As I write the final words of this book, anti–affirmative action cases against Harvard University and the University of North Carolina-Chapel Hill make the urgency for disruptive change even more pressing. It's possible that the Supreme Court will ban affirmative action in all American universities, public and private, in the next five years. It's a sobering thought. It's even more sobering when you consider that affirmative action in higher education has been a tool of co-optation that preserved the institutional values that continued to privilege white middle- and upper-class students. If anti-affirmative action forces put this much effort into challenging practices that preserve racial disparities, imagine the forces that will coalesce to resist efforts to disrupt institutional values and create a truly fair and equitable system.

Disruptive change won't be easy. The forces behind these anti–affirmative action cases will be the same forces that resist disruptive change in the name of inclusion. They will find allies in higher education leaders who have supported affirmative action but want to preserve the current hierarchy of values and criteria that measure institutional status. Disruptive change, then, will require a student movement, with allies outside the campus walls, that rivals that of the late 1960s and early 1970s. It will also have to offer ambitious visions for a new system. Activists won't be able to simply call for more students and faculty of color. Activists will have to demand disruptive change, not more inclusion reforms that eventually lead to small increases in representation.

Disruptive change will also likely require pressure on politicians to provide financial incentives and consequences to help spark and maintain disruptive change. Political scientist Suzanne Mettler has highlighted how elite universities benefit from federal subsidies while helping to perpetuate inequality in the United States. Most of us understand that the federal government provides billions of dollars to universities in grants and student loans every year, but postsecondary institutions benefit from other government policies. The federal government allows our richest nonprofit universities to pay nothing in taxes, including on capital gains from their lucrative investments. Federal tax policy also incentivizes charitable donations to our already wealthy universities through individual tax breaks. These policies have allowed America's top universities to accumulate enormous wealth. Harvard's endowment grew 10 percent in the 2018 fiscal year to $39.2 billion. Yale's endowment grew 11.3 percent to $29.4 billion. The University of Michigan's endowment stands at $11.9 billion. It grew by $1 billion in the 2018 fiscal year. Colleges and universities benefit from these tax breaks and direct federal money under the assumption that these institutions provide a public good. Given the uninterrupted stream of federal money and tax breaks, the persistence of racial and socioeconomic inequality seems well within Congress's definition of serving the public good. It shouldn't be. The federal government has shown some resolve in providing consequences for for-profit institutions that take federal money and leave students in insurmountable debt with few job opportunities. Nonprofit public and private institutions that enroll few low-income and underrepresented students of color, though, haven't received the same scrutiny. The federal government should offer incentives for institutions that implement disruptive change that advances inclusion through additional federal aid and grants. The federal government should also consider ending tax breaks, federal aid, and grants for institutions that continue to perpetuate racial and socioeconomic inequality. While tying aid to socioeconomic status is well within the Constitution, courts won't accept a funding standard based on the number of underrepresented students on campus. Still, there are other, although less effective, ways of measuring inclusion. Racial climate studies, for example, could offer a useful tool to tie funding to institutions' inclusion efforts. Whatever the standard, Congress must play a role in redefining the purpose of our elite colleges and universities.[39]

All of this likely sounds too hard and unrealistic. But if black student activists have taught us anything, it's to fight for what's right even when that cause will likely fail. Sometimes we forget that failure is one of the most consistent features of activism. Forgetting that fact generates frustration and sometimes leads activists to give in to calls to be "realistic." It's important to remember that the job of activism isn't simply to fight for what's possible; it's to get the world to reimagine what's possible. Failure comes with the territory. The most important social movement victories in U.S. history haven't come from activists who were "realistic."

If there is a place to start disruptive change, it must start with the understanding that inequality is a choice. Elite universities use racial innocence to try to convince us otherwise. But if we agree that inequality is a choice, then we can hold universities accountable. We can demand choices that lead to equality. We can root out the values and mechanisms that University of Michigan activists called part of the "bones and sinews of the place." It's time for some new bones and sinews.

# ACKNOWLEDGMENTS

I've never liked asking for help. I grew up in a small Oregon logging town, where you were supposed to figure out everything on your own. That approach doesn't work for writers. I don't think it ever worked for anyone in my hometown anyway. I only regret that I don't have room to thank everyone who made this book happen.

Money matters. When I was a graduate student, my credit card provided some of the funding for this project. I'm still paying it off. Thankfully, I eventually found the necessary institutional support for research travel. I received a Dean's Travel Grant while at the University of Mary Washington. Start-up funds from Texas Tech University allowed for long trips to Michigan. A fellowship from the Humanities Center at Texas Tech provided a course release that gave me time to write for a semester.

At the University of Michigan's Bentley Historical Library, archivists and staff pulled countless boxes and put many miles on their cars while retrieving boxes from an old Ann Arbor fire station. Thank you for putting up with me when I returned year after year.

The *Journal of Policy History* allowed me to use part of an article I wrote in 2017. Thank you to Donald Critchlow and the peer reviewers who gave me important feedback that improved that article and this book.

I never anticipated the importance of choosing the right publisher. I'm glad I met Michael McGandy at Cornell University Press. Michael supported this project long before it looked anything like a book and continued his support as I struggled along. Jonathan Zimmerman provided the right balance of enthusiasm, humor, and constructive criticism to keep me going. They also chose peer reviewers who took the time to provide pages of thoughtful feedback. Thank you for making this book better.

At Texas Tech University, I found a rare group of colleagues who went out of their way to support me. I wish I could thank all my friends in the department, but a few people, in particular, read drafts of chapters: Emily Skidmore, Jacob Baum, Erin-Marie Legacey, Benjamin Poole, Karlos Hill, Paul Bjerk, Zachary Brittsan, and Sarah Keyes. As luck would have it, another colleague, Laura Calkins, was involved in the famous affirmative action lawsuits at the University of Michigan and lent her insight whenever I needed it.

At the University of Mary Washington, I learned how to be an academic through trial and fire. Thank you, Jeffrey McClurken, Will Mackintosh, Jason Sellers, Nora Kim, and Marion Sanford for your friendship and guidance.

This book began more than a decade ago at Temple University. I'm thankful for the people I met in Philadelphia. Abigail Perkiss, Alessandra Phillips, Timothy Cole, and Ben Brandenberg read my clumsy writing over coffee. The fellows at Temple's Center for the Humanities offered support and important feedback on my earliest drafts. Heather Ann Thompson helped organize my ideas into a coherent narrative at a critical moment. Bryant Simon asked hard questions, many of which I didn't find answers to until years later.

David Farber and Beth Bailey deserve much of the credit for this book. They saw something in me that I didn't see in myself. Thank you for teaching me what it means to be a historian. I'll spend the rest of my career paying your generosity forward.

Finally, thank you to my partner, Lindsay. She gave me the love and support I so desperately needed during the hard times, when I struggled to find my voice. Just a few months ago a baby entered our lives. Avery is sleeping on my chest as I write this. I can only hope that she grows up in a world better than the one I write about in the preceding pages.

# NOTES

## Introduction

1. I'm drawing on a classic definition of "co-optation" that has its origins in Philipp Selznick's "Foundations of the Theory of Organizations," *American Sociological Review* 13, no. 1 (1948): 25–35.

2. Verta Taylor and Nella Van Dyke, "'Get Up, Stand Up': Tactical Repertoires of Social Movements," in *The Blackwell Companion to Social Movements*, ed. David A. Snow, Sarah A. Soule, and Hanspeter Kriesi (Oxford: Blackwell, 2004), 262–93.

3. Ibram H. Rogers, *The Black Campus Movement: Black Students and the Racial Reconstitution of Higher Education, 1965–1972* (New York: Palgrave MacMillan, 2012); Martha Biondi, *The Black Revolution on Campus* (Berkeley: University of California Press, 2012); Joy Ann Williamson, *Black Power on Campus: The University of Illinois, 1965–1975* (Urbana-Champaign: University of Illinois Press, 2003); Stefan Bradley, *Harlem vs. Columbia University: Black Student Power in the Late 1960s* (Urbana-Champaign: University of Illinois Press, 2009); Wayne C. Glasker, *Black Students in the Ivory Tower: African American Student Activism at the University of Pennsylvania, 1967–1990* (Amherst: University of Massachusetts Press, 2002); Donna Murch, *Living for the City: Migration, Education, and the Rise of the Black Panther Party in Oakland, California* (Chapel Hill: University of North Carolina Press, 2010); Richard P. McCormick, *Black Student Protest Movement at Rutgers* (New Brunswick: Rutgers University Press, 1990). There are exceptions, as some historians have paid more attention to administrators. Fabio Rojas offers the most sophisticated treatment of how institutions responded to the black campus activism. Still, Rojas focuses solely on the rise of black studies: Fabio Rojas, *From Black Power to Black Studies: How a Radical Social Movement Became an Academic Discipline* (Baltimore: Johns Hopkins University Press, 2007). Other exceptions include Jerome Karabel, *The Chosen: The Hidden History of Admission and Exclusion at Harvard, Yale, and Princeton* (New York: Mariner Books, 2005); John Aubrey Douglass, *The Conditions for Admission: Access, Equity, and the Social Contract of Public Universities* (Stanford, CA: Stanford University Press, 2007); Donald Alexander Downs, *Cornell '69: Crisis of the American University* (Ithaca, NY: Cornell University Press, 1999). Still, Karabel's and Downs's work don't explain how administrators limited the outcomes of the black campus movement after the 1970s. Douglass's work largely ignores campus activism.

4. Glasker's *Black Students in the Ivory Tower* is an exception, but he quickly moves through activism in the 1980s in a closing chapter. Rojas and Biondi also look at the evolution of black studies past the mid-1970s.

5. Derrick A. Bell, Jr., *"Brown v. Board of Education* and the Interest-Convergence Dilemma," *Harvard Law Review* 93, no. 3 (January 1980): 518–33; Kimberlé Crenshaw, "From Racial Liberalism to Racial Literacy: *Brown v. Board of Education* and the Interest-Divergence Dilemma," *Journal of American History* 91, no. 1 (June 2004): 92–118; Kimberlé Crenshaw, "Twenty Years of Critical Race Theory: Looking Back to Move Forward," *Connecticut Law Review* 43, no. 5 (July 2011): 1253–1352.

6. Scholars who have examined the more recent history of racial inclusion in universities include Ellen Berrey, *The Enigma of Diversity: The Language of Race and the Limits of Racial Justice* (Chicago: University of Chicago Press, 2015); Daniel Lipson, "Embracing Diversity: The Institutionalization of Affirmative as Diversity Management at UC-Berkeley, UT-Austin, and UW-Madison," *Law and Social Inquiry* 32, no. 4 (2007): 985–1026; Daniel N. Lipson, "The Resilience of Affirmative Action in the 1980s: Innovation, Isomorphism, and Institutionalization in University Admissions," *Political Research Quarterly* 64, no. 1 (2011): 132–44; William G. Bowen and Derek Bok, *The Shape of the River: Long-Term Consequences of Considering Race in College and University Admissions* (Princeton, NJ: Princeton University Press, 1999). Jerome Karabel spends the closing chapters of *The Chosen* on recent inclusion policies.

7. Some researchers have taken advantage of the University of Michigan's archives and written about the university's inclusion initiatives. Unfortunately, their use of the archives was limited. Consequently, the conclusions I come to in this book differ from many of their findings: Berrey, *Enigma of Diversity*; Lisa M. Stulberg and Anthony S. Chen, "The Origins of Race-Conscious Affirmative Action in Undergraduate Admissions: A Comparative Analysis of Institutional Change in Higher Education," *Sociology of Education* 87, no. 1 (2014): 36–52; Daniel Hirschman, Ellen Berrey, and Fiona Rose-Greenland, "Dequantifying Diversity: Affirmative Action and Admissions at the University of Michigan," *Theory and Society* 45, no. 3 (2016): 265–301.

8. For anyone interested in examining the law school's affirmative action history, the locator for the school's records can be accessed online at the Bentley Historical Library's website: http://bentley.umich.edu.

9. Gratz v. Bollinger, 539 U.S. 306 (2003).

## 1. Bones and Sinews

1. The University as a Racist Institution, 1970, Provost and Executive Vice President for Academic Affairs, Supplemental Files, box 2, folder: BAM [Demands], 1969–70, Bentley Historical Library, University of Michigan, hereafter BHL.

2. Howard H. Peckham, *The Making of the University of Michigan, 1817–1992* (Ann Arbor: University of Michigan Press, 1994), 3–7, 63.

3. Laura Calkins, "Samuel Codes Watson," *Michigan History* 86, no. 1 (January/February 2002): 8–52; Peckham, *Making of the University of Michigan*, 64; Ruth Bordin, *Women at Michigan: The "Dangerous Experiment," 1870s to the Present* (Ann Arbor: University of Michigan Press, 1999), 6; "Third November Meeting, 1839," *Regents' Proceedings with Appendixes and Index, 1837–1864* (Ann Arbor: University of Michigan, 1915), 22.

4. John R. Thelin, *A History of American Higher Education* (Baltimore: Johns Hopkins University Press, 2004), 41.

5. Roger L. Geiger, *The History of American Higher Education: Learning and Culture from the Founding to World War II* (Princeton, NJ: Princeton University Press, 2015), 187–93.

6. "November Meeting, 1841," *Regents' Proceedings*, 190, http://babel.hathitrust.org /cgi/pt?id=uiug.30112111896996;view=1up;seq=200.

7. "December Meeting, 1841," *Regents' Proceedings*, 212.

8. Jana Nidiffer and Jeffrey P. Bouman, "The Chasm between Rhetoric and Reality: The Fate of the 'Democratic Ideal' When a Public University Becomes Elite," *Educational Policy* 15, no. 3 (July 2001): 441; "December Meeting, 1841," 222; National Center for Education Statistics, *120 Years of American Education: A Statistical Portrait* (Washington, DC: U.S. Department of Education, 1993), 30, 7.

9. Peckham, *Making of the University of Michigan*, 36–42.

10. "October Meeting, 1854," *Regents' Proceedings*, 598; Henry Tappan, "Review by Rev. Dr. H. P. Tappan: Historic Statement of my Connection with the University," *Regents' Proceedings*, 1132–33; Geiger, *History of American Higher Education*, 252–56.

11. Peckham, *Making of the University of Michigan*, 8, 12, 23, 66–7; Thelin, *History of American Higher Education*, 75.

12. Geiger, *History of American Higher Education*, 254; Harold Wechsler, *The Qualified Student: A History of Selective Admission in America* (New York: John Wiley & Sons, 1977), 17–20.

13. Wechsler, *Qualified Student*, 17–20.

14. Nidiffer and Bouman, "The Chasm Between Rhetoric and Reality," 442–46.

15. Thelin, *History of American Higher Education*, 110–11; Edwin E. Slosson, *Great American Universities* (New York: Macmillan, 1910), vii–x, 474–525.

16. Ira M. Smith, "University of Michigan: Trend of Admission Requirements in the College of Literature, Science, and the Arts," *Michigan History* 14 (Spring 1930): 207–20, Ira M. Smith Papers, box 2; Peckham, *Making of the University of Michigan*, 127, 156.

17. David O. Levine, *The American College and the Culture of Aspiration, 1915–1940* (Ithaca, NY: Cornell University Press, 1986), 39; Thelin, *History of American Higher Education*, 261.

18. Benjamin Fine, *Admission to American Colleges: A Study of Current Policy and Practice* (New York: Harper & Brothers, 1946), 25, 148.

19. Smith, "University of Michigan," 207–20; Peckham, *Making of the University of Michigan*, 156.

20. Peckham, *Making of the University of Michigan*, 173, 177; C. C. Little, "The Second International Congress of Eugenics," *Eugenics Review* 13, no. 4 (1922): 511–24; Daniel J. Kevles, *In the Name of Eugenics: Genetics and the Uses of Human Heredity* (Cambridge: Harvard University Press, 2004), 69; Adam Cohen, *Imbeciles: The Supreme Court, American Eugenics, and the Sterilization of Carrie Buck* (New York: Penguin Books, 2016), 4. The army's use of intelligence tests during World War I proved the turning point: John Carson, *The Measure of Merit: Talents, Intelligence, and Inequality in the French and American Republics, 1750–1940* (Princeton, NJ: Princeton University Press, 2007), 197–228.

21. Ira M. Smith, "Freshman Admissions of the University of Michigan: A Review and a Glance Ahead," Ira M. Smith Papers, box 1, folder: Reminiscences, BHL; Nicholas Lemann, *The Big Test: The Secret History of the American Meritocracy* (New York: Farrar, Straus and Giroux, 1999), 29–30; Carl C. Brigham, *A Study of American Intelligence* (Princeton: Princeton University Press, 1923), 210.

22. Ira M. Smith resume, Ira M. Smith Papers, box 1, folder: Biographical Materials, BHL; Ira M. Smith, "Reminiscences of a Registrar," August 28, 1961, Ira M. Smith Papers, box 1, folder: Reminiscences, BHL.

23. Smith, "Freshman Admissions of the University of Michigan."

24. Smith, "Reminiscences of a Registrar."

25. Smith, "Freshman Admissions of the University of Michigan."

26. P. S. Dwyer, Charlotte Horner, and C. S. Yoakam, *A Statistical Summary of the Records of Students Entering the University of Michigan as Freshmen in the Decade 1927–1936*, University of Michigan Administrative Studies, vol. 1, no. 4 (Ann Arbor: University of Michigan Press, 1940), Evaluation and Examinations Division Records, box 2, BHL.

27. Jerome Karabel, *The Chosen: The Hidden History of Admission and Exclusion at Harvard, Yale, and Princeton* (Boston: Houghton Mifflin, 2005), 77–138; "President Little Resigns," University of Michigan Faculty History Project, http://faculty-history .dc.umich.edu/faculty/clarence-cook-little/president-little-resigns. There is evidence that there were unwritten quotas in hiring Jewish employees in at least one UM department: Jenner Hodges to Samuel Lipsky, October 2, 1939, President's Records, box 265, folder: Topical Files, 1991–1992, Minority Affairs, Jewish Community, BHL; Jenner Hodges to Samuel Lipsky, February 1, 1940, President's Records, box 265, folder: Topical Files, 1991–1992, Minority Affairs, Jewish Community, BHL.

28. Ibram H. Rogers, *The Black Campus Movement: Black Students and the Racial Reconstitution of Higher Education, 1965–1972* (New York: Palgrave Macmillan, 2012), 18; Henry Vance Davis, "From Coloreds to African-Americans: A History of the Struggle for Educational Equity at the University of Michigan and an Agenda for the Pluralistic Multicultural University of the Twenty-First Century," in *Sankofa: The University since BAM: Twenty Years of Progress? Conference Report*, ed. Henry Vance Davis (Ann Arbor: Office of Minority Affairs, 1991), 33. Population data comes from Campbell Gibson and Kay Jung, "Table 37: Michigan-Race and Hispanic Origin: 1880 to 1990," *Historical Census Statistics on Population Totals by Race, 1790 to 1990, and by Hispanic Origins, 1970 to 1990, for the United States, Regions, Divisions, and States* (Washington, DC: U.S. Census Bureau, 2002), 55, https://www.census.gov//content/dam/Census/library /working-papers/2002/demo/POP-twps0056.pdf.

29. These insights come from Lani Guinier, *The Tyranny of the Meritocracy: Democratizing Higher Education in America* (Boston: Beacon Press, 2015), 23, 40.

30. Jeffrey Mirel, *The Rise and Fall of an Urban School System: Detroit, 1907–81* (Ann Arbor: University of Michigan Press, 1993), 191, 255.

31. Historical certification reports for Detroit schools can be found in Bureau of School Services Records, 1871–1992, boxes 36–48, BHL.

32. Smith, "Freshman Admissions of the University of Michigan"; Smith, "Reminiscences of a Registrar"; Thelin, *History of American Higher Education*, 261.

33. *The President's Report for 1945–1946* (Ann Arbor: University of Michigan, 1946), 195–96, http://babel.hathitrust.org/cgi/pt?id=mdp.39015005494730;view=1up;seq =199; Laura M. Calkins, "The Origins of the Modern Multiversity at Michigan: Politics and Discourse on Race, Religion, and Gender, 1940–52," Laura Calkins Papers, box 1, folder: Reports and Articles, BHL. For Lawrie's position at the university, see "Alumnae Leaders Discuss Fellowship Programs," *Michigan Alumnus* 42, no. 2 (October 12, 1935): 272.

34. Harlan H. Hatcher, transcript of taped interview, December 1992, March 1992, Harlan Hatcher Papers, box 60, folder: Autobiographical-Interview, 1990–1992-Transcript, Tapes 1–3, BHL.

35. Hatcher, transcript of taped interview.

36. Informational Memorandum on Literary College Activities Bearing on Admissions Policy, June 12, 1956, College of Literature, Science, and the Arts Records, box 319, folder: Committee on Admissions, BHL.

37. Informational Memorandum on Literary College Activities Bearing on Admissions Policy; Report of the Committee on Admissions, L.S.&A; Faculty Minutes, 1955–56, College of Literature, Science, and the Arts Records, box 206; Roger W. Heyns, Memorandum to Vice-President Marvin L. Niehuss, "Experimental Use of Pre-Admissions Examinations for Freshmen Enrolling in This College in 1961–63," December 16, 1959, College of Literature, Science, and the Arts Records, box 319, folder: Admissions Examinations (Report to Niehuss), BHL; "Student Quality, Freshman Grades, and the Admissions Problem at the University of Michigan, 1958," Evaluation and Examinations Division Records, box 4, folder: Correspondence and Revisions to Report "Academic Quality of Entering Freshmen and the Admissions Problem," BHL.

38. College of Literature, Science, and the Arts Executive Committee Minutes and Statistical Studies, 1960–61, College of Literature, Science and the Arts Records, box 298, BHL.

39. Hatcher, transcript of taped interview.

40. Press release, June 29, 1981, News and Information Services Faculty and Staff Files, box 133, BHL.

41. David Marcus, "Change Affects New Freshmen," *Michigan Daily*, February 20, 1963.

42. Biographical Information: Benno G. Fricke, September 1964, News and Information Services, Faculty and Staff Files, box 45, folder: Fricke, Benno G., BHL; E. Lowell Kelly, "The Bureau of Psychological Services," *The University of Michigan: An Encyclopedic Survey* (Ann Arbor: Bentley Historical Library, 1977), 163–67; "For Release after 1:30 P.M. Tuesday, March 24, 1959," News and Information Services, Faculty and Staff Files, box 45, folder: Fricke, Benno G., BHL; "For Release after 9:30 A.M. Tuesday, September 2, 1958," News and Information Services, Faculty and Staff Files, box 45, folder: Fricke, Benno G., BHL; "Academic and Test Performance of Certain University of Michigan Freshmen," 1956, Evaluation and Examinations Division Records, box 4, folder: Fricke, Benno: Reports, Data, Tables and Correspondence Related to Freshmen Testing, BHL.

43. "Academic and Test Performance of Certain University of Michigan Freshmen, 1956," Evaluation and Examinations Division Records, box 4, folder: Fricke, Benno: Reports, Data, Tables and Correspondence Related to Freshmen Testing, BHL.

44. "Student Quality, Freshman Grades, and the Admissions Problem at the University of Michigan, 1958," Evaluation and Examinations Division Records, box 4, folder: Correspondence and Revisions to Report "Academic Quality of Entering Freshmen and the Admissions Problem," BHL.

45. "Student Quality, Freshman Grades, and the Admissions Problem at the University of Michigan."

46. Hatcher, transcript of taped interview.

47. "For Release after 9:30 A.M. Tuesday, September 2, 1958," News and Information Services, Faculty and Staff Files, box 45, folder: Fricke, Benno G., BHL; "For Release

after 1:30 P.M. Tuesday, March 24, 1959," News and Information Services, Faculty and Staff Files, box 45, folder: Fricke, Benno G., BHL.

48. Census of Negro Students, Fall Semester 1963–1964, Opportunity Award Program Records, box 1, folder: Student Census, BHL; "Some Characteristics of Negro Freshmen at the University of Michigan," Opportunity Award Program Records, box 1, folder: Student Census 1963, BHL.

49. All the faculty meeting minutes and reports available suggest that eugenics or race didn't infuse discussions about admissions in the 1920s.

50. Lemann, *Big Test*, 155–65; Mirel, *Rise and Fall of an Urban School System*, 255–60.

51. "Medic Admission Policy Defended," *Ann Arbor News*, March 9, 1950, Laura Calkins Papers, box 1, folder: Provost Documents, BHL; Lisa M. Stulberg and Anthony S. Chen, "The Origins of Race-Conscious Affirmative Action in Undergraduate Admissions: A Comparative Analysis of Institutional Change in Higher Education," *Sociology of Education* 87, no. 1 (2014): 36–52.

52. Calkins, "Origins of the Modern Multiversity at Michigan."

53. Calkins, "Origins of the Modern Multiversity at Michigan"; *To Secure These Rights: The Report of the President's Committee on Civil Rights* (Washington, DC: Government Printing Office, 1947). For an explanation of the rise of racial liberalism, see Leah N. Gordon, *From Power to Prejudice: The Rise of Racial Individualism in Midcentury America* (Chicago: University of Chicago Press, 2015); Walter Jackson, *Gunnar Myrdal and America's Conscience: Social Engineering and Racial Liberalism, 1938–1987* (Chapel Hill: University of North Carolina Press, 1990).

54. "Medic Admission Policy Defended."

55. Calkins, "Origins of the Modern Multiversity at Michigan."

56. Calkins, "Origins of the Modern Multiversity at Michigan"; Jackson, *Gunnar Myrdal and America's Conscience*, 33, 286, 292.

57. Census of Negro Students, Fall Semester 1963–1964, Opportunity Award Program Records, box 1, folder: Student Census, BHL; "Some Characteristics of Negro Freshmen at the University of Michigan," Opportunity Award Program Records, box 1, folder: Student Census 1963, BHL; Thomas Sugrue, *The Origins of the Urban Crisis: Race and Inequality in Postwar Detroit* (Princeton, NJ: Princeton University Press, 1996), 23.

58. Report of the Committee on Intercultural Relations, International Center Records, box 2, folder: Committee on Intercultural Relations, BHL; Center for International Student Affairs . . . A Prospectus to The Ford Foundation, International Center Records, box 11, folder: Student Relations: International House 1945–1955, BHL; *The President's Report for 1953–1954* (Ann Arbor: University of Michigan, 1954), 6.

59. Committee on Admissions Policy, June 27, 1945, International Center Records, box 2, folder: Admission (2-1), BHL; Committee on Admissions Policy, July 18, 1945, International Center Records, box 2, folder: Admission (2-1), BHL; Committee on Admissions Policy, July 25, 1945, International Center Records, box 2, folder: Minutes Committee on Intercultural Relations, 1943–1945, BHL; Committee on Intercultural Relations Meeting, April 30, 1946, International Center Records, box 2, folder: Minutes Committee on Intercultural Relations, 1943–1945, BHL; Committee on Intercultural Relations Meeting, May 28, 1940, International Center Records, box 2, folder: Minutes Committee on Intercultural Relations, 1943–1945, BHL; Earnest Boyco, Robert S. Ford, and Albert H. Marckwardt to Esson M. Gale, May 3, 1951, International Center Records, box 2, folder: Comm. on Intercultural 1946–1963, BHL.

60. *The President's Report for 1951–1952* (Ann Arbor: University of Michigan, 1952), 88; "A General Plan for Meeting the Needs of Postwar International Education," International Center Records, box 2, folder: Minutes Committee on Intercultural Relations, 1943–1945, BHL; "Fostering Intercultural Relations through the Interchange of Students and Teachers," International Center Records, box 2, folder: Minutes Committee on Intercultural Relations, 1943–1945, BHL; "International Center Spring Manual, 1949," International Center Records, box 19, folder: International Center Printed Manuals: International Center Manual 1949–1950, BHL.

61. "The International Center," International Center Records, box 19, folder: International Center Printed Pamphlets, The International Center 1942–1945, BHL; Center for International Student Affairs, A Prospectus to The Ford Foundation, International Center Records, box 11, folder: Student Relations: International House 1945–1955, BHL; Friends International Center, International Center Records, box 11, folder: Student Relations: Housing: Friend's Center, BHL; International House as an All University International Center, January 17, 1958, International Center Records, box 11, folder: Student Relations: International House 1958, BHL.

62. Proposed Minutes of the February 13, 1961, Faculty Meeting of the College of Literature, Science, and the Arts, L.S.&A. Faculty Minutes, 1960–1961, College of Literature, Science and the Arts Records, box 207, BHL; Proposed Minutes of the March 2, 1964, Faculty Meeting of the College of Literature, Science, and the Arts, L.S.&A Faculty Minutes, 1963–64, College of Literature, Science and the Arts Records, box 207, BHL.

63. Report of the Executive Committee of the College of Literature, Science, and the Arts to be Presented at the Meeting of the Faculty on Monday, March 7, 1960, L.S.&A. Faculty Minutes, 1959–60, College of Literature, Science, and the Arts Records, box 207, BHL; Proposed Minutes of the November 2, 1959, Faculty Meeting of the College of Literature, Science & the Arts, L.S.&A. Faculty Minutes, 1959–60, College of Literature, Science, and the Arts Records, box 207, BHL; Proposed Minutes of the February 13, 1961, Faculty Meeting of the College of Literature, Science, and the Arts, L.S.&A. Faculty Minutes, 1960–1961, College of Literature, Science and the Arts Records, box 207, BHL.

64. *The President's Report for 1945–1946* (Ann Arbor: University of Michigan, 1946), 5, 195–96; *The President's Report for 1946–1947* (Ann Arbor: University of Michigan, 1947), 9, 214, 225; Committee on Admissions Policy, August 8, 1945, International Center Records, box 2, folder: Admission (2-1), BHL; Committee on Admissions Policy, July 25, 1945, International Center Records, box 2, folder: Minutes Committee on Intercultural Relations, 1943–1945, BHL; Information for Prospective Freshmen, 1946, Office of Undergraduate Admissions, box 1, folder Leaflet-Admissions of Freshmen, BHL.

65. Conference on Foreign Student Problems and Adjustment, Chicago, April 29, 30, and May 1, 1946, International Center Records, box 2, folder: Comm. on Intercultural 1946–1963, BHL; Report of the Committee to Study the Academic Performance of Athletes in the Literary College, L.S.&A. Faculty Minutes, 1959–60, College of Literature, Science, and the Arts Records, box 207, BHL; "January Meeting, 1946," *Proceedings of the Board of Regents (1945–1948)*, 191–93.

66. *The President's Report for 1920–1921*, 122; *The President's Report for 1932–1933*, 223; *The President's Report for 1921–1922*, 142; *Michigan: Her Athletic Record, Facilities for*

*Physical Education, the Men Who Supervise the Program, and the Progress They Have Made* (Ann Arbor: University of Michigan, 1929).

67. Peckham, *Making of the University of Michigan*, 190; Davis, "From Colored to African-Americans"; Calkins, "Origins of the Modern Multiversity at Michigan." For a national context of discrimination in this period, see Rogers, *Black Campus Movement*, 9–28.

68. "Assignment of Negroes in South, East, and West Quadrangles," 1958, Housing Division Records, box 1, folder: Residence Halls-Discrimination Issue, 1958; BHL University of Michigan Survey Research Center, *Campus Attitudes toward Minority Groups* (Ann Arbor: University of Michigan, 1949).

69. "Plan to Open SL Office for Bias Hearing," *Michigan Daily*, April 15, 1949; Bob Keith, "SL Asks for Time Limit on Fraternity Bias Clause," *Michigan Daily*, November 16, 1950; Rich Thomas, "SL Passes New Anti-Bias Motion," *Michigan Daily*, December 14, 1950; "Fraternities Attempt Removal of Bias Clauses," *Michigan Daily*, October 9, 1951; Herb Heindenreich to Harlan Hatcher, March 8, 1962, Vice President of Student Affairs Records, box 6, folder: James A. Lewis, Topical, Human Relations Board (Race Discrimination), 1958–1963, BHL; "Hatcher Restates Bias Stand," *Michigan Daily*, February 23, 1963; Report on Interview with Mr. Frank Staffan, 1963, Vice President of Student Affairs Records, box 6, folder: James A. Lewis, Topical, Human Relations Board (Race Discrimination), 1958–1963, BHL; Report on Telephoning of Landlords, May 1961 Project, Vice President of Student Affairs Records, box 6, folder: James A. Lewis, Topical, Human Relations Board (Race Discrimination), 1958–1963, BHL; Suzanne M. Meyer, Report of Human Relations Counselor, May 23, 1962, Vice President of Student Affairs Records, box 6, folder: James A. Lewis, Topical, Human Relations Board (Race Discrimination), 1958–1963, BHL.

70. Dave Chudwin, "HRC Asks Rent Bias Hearing," *Michigan Daily*, April 17, 1969.

71. Kenneth F. Herrold, "Evaluation and Research in Group Dynamics," *Educational and Psychological Measurement* 10 (1950): 493; Bert Raven, "Workshop Planning and Evaluation—a Problem-Solving Approach," *Journal of Education Sociology* 26, no. 7 (March 1953): 318–19.

72. Heindenreich to Hatcher, March 8, 1962; "Hatcher Restates Bias Stand," 1; "Human Relations Board to Study Discrimination," *Michigan Daily*, November 1, 1955.

73. "November Meeting, 1959," *Proceedings of the Board of Regents (1957–1960)*, 1099.

74. George Palmer to James E. Lewis, May 22, 1958, Housing Division Records, box 1, BHL; "November Meeting, 1959," 1099.

75. Edd Miller to Roger Heyns, November 19, 1963, Provost and Executive Vice President for Academic Affairs, Central Files, box 1, folder: Negro, re 1963–1964, BHL; E. G. Williamson to Vice President Roger W. Heyns, October 22, 1963, Provost and Executive Vice President for Academic Affairs, Central Files, box 1, folder: Negro, re 1963–1964, BHL; "For Release at 12 Noon, Thursday, March 5, 1964," Provost and Executive Vice President for Academic Affairs, Central Files, box 1, folder: Negro, re 1963–1964, BHL; Harlan Hatcher, "The State of the University," *Michigan Quarterly Review* 3, no. 1 (Winter 1964): 1–7; Nancy Sundheim, "Tutorial Project Is Helping Culturally Deprived Children," *Michigan Daily*, September 2, 1965.

76. "Related Data on Negroes," *Michigan Daily*, February 23, 1963. Henry Johnson became the first black executive administrators in 1972: "VP's Top Priority Is Minori-

ties," *Michigan Daily*, August 22, 1972, News and Information Services, Faculty and Staff Files, box 65, BHL.

77. William H. Boone, "Problems of Adjustment of Negro Students at a White School," *Journal of Negro Education* 11, no. 4 (October 1942): 481.

78. Marshall B. Clinard and Donald L. Noel, "Role Behavior of Students from Negro Colleges in a Non-segregated University Situation," *Journal of Negro Education* 27, no. 2 (Spring 1958): 183–84.

## 2. The Origins of Affirmative Action

1. Compliance Report of Institutions of Higher Education under Title VI of the Civil Rights Act of 1964, Fall 1967, Assistant to the President Records, box 39, folder: Compliance Reports, 67–69, BHL; Census of Negro Students, Fall Semester 1963–1964, Opportunity Award Program Records, box 1, folder: Student Census, BHL; "Some Characteristics of Negro Freshmen at the University of Michigan," Opportunity Award Program Records, box 1, folder: Student Census 1963, BHL.

2. Thomas J. Sugrue, "Affirmative Action from Below: Civil Rights, the Building Trades, and the Politics of Racial Equality in the Urban North, 1945–1969," *Journal of American History* 91, no. 1 (2004): 148–52.

3. Terry H. Anderson, *The Pursuit of Fairness: A History of Affirmative Action* (Oxford: Oxford University Press, 2004), 19–27, 35–42, 50–51; Timothy M. Thurber, "Racial Liberalism, Affirmative Action, and the Troubled History of the President's Committee on Government Contracts," *Journal of Policy History* 18, no. 4 (2006): 446–76.

4. Anderson, *Pursuit of Fairness*, 24–48, 56; Thurber, "Racial Liberalism, Affirmative Action," 446–76.

5. Matthew J. Countryman, *Up South: Civil Rights and Black Power in Philadelphia* (Philadelphia: University of Pennsylvania Press, 2006), 83, 104–10. Examples of similar protests outside Philadelphia in the early 1960s can be found in Anderson, *Pursuit of Fairness*, 58; Quintard Taylor, "The Civil Rights Movement in the American West: Black Protest in Seattle, 1960–1970," *Journal of Negro History* 80 (Winter 1995): 4; Patrick D. Jones, "'Get Up Off Your Knees!': Competing Visions of Black Empowerment in Milwaukee during the Civil Rights Era," in *Neighborhood Rebels: Black Power at the Local Level*, ed. Peniel Joseph, 56–58 (New York: Palgrave Macmillan, 2010); Thomas Sugrue, "The Tangled Roots of Affirmative Action," *American Behavioral Scientist* 41, no. 7 (1998): 891.

6. Sugrue, *Sweet Land of Liberty: The Forgotten Struggle for Civil Rights in the North* (New York: Random House, 2008), 265–66; "1960 Democratic Party Platform," American Presidency Project, July 11, 1960, https://www.presidency.ucsb.edu/documents/1960-democratic-party-platform.

7. Hobart Taylor, interview by Stephen Goodell; Hobart Taylor, interview by Ed Edwin, April 2, 1977, transcript, Hobart Taylor Papers, box 1, folder: Personal, Oral History Interview, Middleburg, Virginia, 1977, BHL.

8. Richard L. Zweigenhaft and G. William Domhoff, *Diversity in the Power Elite: How It Happened, Why It Matters* (New York: Rowman & Littlefield, 2006), 95; Hobart Taylor Jr., interview by John F. Steward, January 11, 1967, transcript, Hobart Taylor Papers, box 1, folder: Personal, Oral History Interview, John F. Kennedy Library, 1967 (1), BHL.

9. Hobart Taylor, interview by Ed Edwin.

10. Hobart Taylor, interview by Stephen Goodell; John F. Kennedy, "Executive Order 10925," March 6, 1961, http://www.eeoc.gov/eeoc/history/35th/thelaw/eo -10925.html.

11. Jennifer Delton, *Racial Integration in Corporate America, 1940–1990* (New York: Cambridge University Press, 2009), 178–79; David Hamilton Golland, *Constructing Affirmative Action: The Struggle for Equal Employment Opportunity* (Lexington: University Press of Kentucky, 2011), 48–49; Anderson, *Pursuit of Fairness*, 64–65.

12. Nicholas Lemann, *The Big Test: The Secret History of Meritocracy* (New York: Farrar, Straus and Giroux, 1999), 162; Golland, *Constructing Affirmative Action*, 48; Sugrue, *Sweet Land of Liberty*, 277–78; Thomas Sugrue, *The Origins of the Urban Crisis: Race and Inequality in Postwar Detroit* (Princeton, NJ: Princeton University Press, 1996), 143–44.

13. Much of the scholarship on activism for jobs in the 1950s and early 1960s has focused on access to blue-collar jobs. One exception is Steven Gelber, *Black Men and Businessmen: The Growing Awareness of a Social Responsibility* (Port Washington, NY: National University Publication, 1974), 123–38. For Taylor's speeches, see Hobart Taylor, "Commencement Address at Prairie View Agricultural and Mechanical College," May 21, 1961, Hobart Taylor Papers, box 1, folder: Addresses, Speeches, and Remarks, 1961–1962, BHL; Hobart Taylor Jr., "Equal Employment Opportunity," in *Proceedings of New York University Fifteenth Annual Conference on Labor*, ed. Emanuel Stein, 35–36 (New York: New York University, 1962); Hobart Taylor Papers, box 1, folder: Addresses, Speeches, and Remarks, 1961–1962, BHL.

14. Taylor, "Commencement Address at Prairie View Agricultural and Mechanical College," May 21, 1961, Hobart Taylor Papers, box 1, folder: Addresses, Speeches, and Remarks, 1961–1962, BHL; Taylor, "Equal Employment Opportunity," 35–36, Hobart Taylor Papers, box 1, folder: Addresses, Speeches, and Remarks, 1961–1962, BHL; Sugrue, *Sweet Land of Liberty*, 277.

15. Kenneth E. Redd, "Historically Black Colleges and Universities: Making a Comeback," *New Directions for Higher Education* 102 (Summer 1998): 35; Enrest M. Collins, "Integration in the State-Supported Colleges and Universities of the South: The Extent of Progress," *Journal of Higher Education* 32, no. 5 (May 1961): 241; U.S. Census Bureau, "Table A-1: School Enrollment of the Population 3 Years Old and Over, by Level and Control of School, Race, and Hispanic Origin: October 1955 to 2017," https://www2.census.gov/programs-surveys/demo/tables/school-enrollment /time-series/cps-historical-time-series/tablea-1.xlsx.

16. A 1963 PCEEO report suggests that Taylor's first interventions on university campuses were at the University of Michigan and Wayne State University (President's Committee on Equal Employment Opportunity, *Report to the President* [Washington, 1963], 109); Hugh Davis Graham and Nancy Diamond, *The Rise of American Research Universities: Elites and Challengers in the Postwar Era* (Baltimore: Johns Hopkins University Press, 1997), 38; Paul D. Moreno, *From Direct Action to Affirmative Action: Fair Employment Law and Policy in America, 1933–1972* (Baton Rouge: Louisiana State University Press, 1997), 188–89; Golland, *Constructing Affirmative Action*, 41–42; University of Michigan Board of Regents, "March Meeting 1962," *Proceedings of the Board of Regents (1960–1963)*, 646; "Race Records Not Available," *Michigan Daily*, March 17, 1962, 1.

17. "Students, the University of Michigan and Discrimination," 1960, Vice President of Student Affairs Records, box 6, folder: James A. Lewis, Topical, Human Relations Board (Race Discrimination) 1958–1963, BHL; "Race Records Not Available"; University of Michigan Board of Regents, "March Meeting 1962," 646.

18. Gloria Bowles, "Labor Records: 'U' to Study Minorities," *Michigan Daily*, January 4, 1963, 1; Minutes of the Academic Affairs Advisory Council, January 9, 1963, Provost and Executive Vice President for Academic Affairs, Central Files, box 1, folder: Academic Affairs Advisory Council Minutes, 1962–1963, BHL; Bowles, "'U' to Study Minorities."

19. "Related Data on Negroes," *Michigan Daily*, February 23, 1963, 1; Ralph Gibson, Report Submitted to President Fleming and Members of the Senate, Spring 1968, Assistant to the President Records, box 38, folder: Academic Advisory Committee-Black Students, BHL. PCEEO was not the first agency to do this. While the PCEEO enjoyed more power to collect employment data, Eisenhower's PCGC understood the limitations of the individual complaint model as early as 1954 and began using workforce data to challenge companies claims that they weren't discriminating and to push companies beyond token hiring. Thurber, "Racial Liberalism, Affirmative Action," 454–55; Moreno, *From Direct Action to Affirmative Action*, 181–89; Sugrue, *Sweet Land of Liberty*, 269.

20. James A. Lewis to the President's Staff, RE: Report—Equal Employment Opportunity Program, May 4, 1966, Vice President Winfred A. Harbison Papers, Walter Reuther Library, Wayne State University, hereafter WRL. The topics of these meetings were later recounted in Inter-University Conference on the Negro in Higher Education, October 21, 1963, Provost and Executive Vice President for Academic Affairs, Central Files, box 1, folder: Negro, re 1963–1964, BHL.

21. Golland, *Constructing Affirmative Action*, 41; Hobart Taylor, interview by Stephen Goodell, January 6, 1969, transcript, Hobart Taylor Papers, box 1, folder: Personal, Oral History Interview, The University of Texas, 1969, BHL. Emphasis in original.

22. Compliance Report of Institutions of Higher Education under Title VI of the Civil Rights Act of 1964, Fall 1967, Assistant to the President Records, box 39, folder: Compliance Reports, 67–69, BHL. Scholars who emphasize PfP's failures include Nancy MacLean, *Freedom Is Not Enough: The Opening of the American Workplace* (New York: Russell Sage Foundation, 2006), 44; Moreno, *From Direct Action to Affirmative Action*, 197; Golland, *Constructing Affirmative Action*, 44–50. Jennifer Delton brings to light some of the successes of PfP in *Racial Integration in Corporate America*, 189–91.

23. Stephen Spurr, who also attended, recounted the meeting eight years later in S. H. Spurr, Draft, April 22, 1970, President's Records, box 12, folder: Black (Faculty/Students, re), BHL; A. H. Wheeler, NAACP Position Paper on University Student Black Action Movement, March 21, 1970, Center for AfroAmerican and African Studies Records, box 1, folder: BAM, Selected Documents, 1970–1987, BHL. Wheeler describes the same meeting at a recorded conference in 1980: "Prof. Wheeler Foster, Mood, Stone, 'U of M a Decade After BAM,'" Center for AfroAmerican and African Studies Records, box 28, BHL; Roger W. Heyns, interview by Harriet Nathan, Berkeley, 1987, in *Berkeley Chancellor, 1965–1971: The University in a Turbulent Society*, 54–56, https://archive.org/details/berkeleychancellor00heynrich; Vice-President to Francis A. Kornegay, February 28, 1963, Provost and Executive Vice President for Academic Affairs, Central Files, box 1, folder: Tuskegee Institute, 1962–63, BHL.

24. Timothy J. Minchin, *Hiring the Black Worker: The Racial Integration of the Southern Textile Industry, 1960–1980* (Chapel Hill: University of North Carolina Press, 1999), 50–51.

25. "Cites Result of Program," *Michigan Daily*, June 25, 1963, 1. For concerns about unemployed and underemployed African American youth in cities, see a brief description of the meeting in University of Michigan Board of Regents, "June Meeting, 1963," *Proceedings of the Board of Regents (1960–1963)*, 1218–19.

26. Glenn T. Eskew, *But for Birmingham: The Local and National Movements in the Civil Rights Struggle* (Chapel Hill: University of North Carolina Press, 1997), 222; Sugrue, "Affirmative Action from Below," 161–62; Sugrue, "Tangled Roots of Affirmative Action," *American Behavioral Scientist*, 892. For examinations of protests outside Philadelphia, see Brian Purnell, "'The Revolution Has Come to Brooklyn': Construction Trades Protests and the Negro Revolt of 1963," in *Black Power at Work: Community Control, Affirmative Action, and the Construction Industry*, ed. David Goldberg and Trevor Griffey, 1–47 (Ithaca, NY: Cornell University Press, 2010); Julie Rabig, "'The Laboratory of Democracy': Construction Industry Racism in Newark and the Limits of Liberalism," in Goldberg and Griffey, *Black Power at Work*, 48–67.

27. Golland, *Constructing Affirmative Action*, 50–58; Sugrue, *Sweet Land of Liberty*, 269–70; Sugrue, "Affirmative Action from Below," 164; "Supplemental Message on Civil Rights," June 14, 1963, Papers of John F. Kennedy, Presidential Papers, President's Office Files, series: Subjects, folder: Civil Rights: General, June 1963: 14–30, John F. Kennedy Presidential Library, http://www.jfklibrary.org/Asset-Viewer/Archives/JFKPOF-097-003.aspx. Just days before Kennedy brought education leaders to the White House, Theodore Sorensen, Kenney's special counsel, was crafting one of Kennedy's many 1963 speeches on civil rights. The speech reiterated what Hobart Taylor had been suggesting for the past year: that the United States needed to expand educational opportunities for African Americans because "too many . . . are equipped to work in those occupations where technology and other changes have reduced the need for manpower." John F. Kennedy, "Special Message to the Congress on Civil Rights and Job Opportunities," June 19, 1963, The American Presidency Project, http://www.presidency.ucsb.edu/ws/index.php?pid=9283.

28. Harlan Hatcher's September 30, 1963, speech was reprinted months later as "The State of the University," *Michigan Quarterly Review* 3 (Winter 1964): 1–7. Hatcher also admitted in a 1992 interview that his meeting with Kennedy played an important role in what he called the university's "first efforts . . . to incorporate . . . the Black group." See Harlan H. Hatcher, interview by Enid H. Galler, December 1991, March 1992, transcript, Harlan Hatcher Papers, box 60, folder: Autobiographical-Interview, 1990–1992-Transcript, Tapes 4–8, BHL.

29. Harlan Hatcher, "The State of the University," *Michigan Quarterly Review* 3, no. 1 (Winter 1964): 1–7.

30. "Sain Gets Entrance Job at 'U,'" *Michigan Daily*, September 13, 1963, 1; Leonard Sain, Résumé, News and Information Services, Faculty and Staff Files, box 112, folder: Sain, Leonard, BHL; H. Neil Berkson, "'Small Number': Surveys Negroes at 'U,'" *Michigan Daily*, February 16, 1964, 1.

31. Berkson, "'Small Number.'"

32. Harlan Hatcher, 1963 date book, Harlan Hatcher Papers, box 60, folder: Autobiographical-Yearly Datebooks-1962–1969, BHL; Heyns is quoted in "Inter-

University Conference on the Negro in Higher Education"; Harlan Hatcher, "Michigan and Tuskegee," Michigan Quarterly Review, Summer 1964, Robert Nederlander Papers, box 1, folder: Black Student Demands, 1970, BHL. For a few examples of other universities that embarked on similar exchange programs in the early 1960s, see Stanley S. Scott, "Spelman Students Return," *Atlantic Daily World*, March 3, 1961, 1; "Plan Exchange Program with Negro College," *Chicago Daily Defender*, February 20, 1962, 3; "Oberlin and Negro College Plan a Student Exchange," *New York Times*, November 7, 1963, 42; "Barnard Students in 2nd Exchange Program," *Chicago Defender*, March 3, 1962, 19; "Four Study at Negro Schools," *Los Angeles Times*, March 31, 1963, SG10.

33. Census of Negro Students, Fall Semester 1963–1964, Opportunity Award Program Records, box 1, folder: Student Census, BHL; Warner Rice to Leonard Sain, April 6, 1964, Provost and Executive Vice President for Academic Affairs, Central Files, box 1, folder: Negro, re 1963–1964, BHL; School of Education Faculty Meeting Minutes, January 1964, Opportunity Award Program Records, box 1, folder: Student Census Correspondence; Notecard, December 17, 1963, Opportunity Award Program Records, box 1, folder: Student Census Correspondence, BHL.

34. Census of Negro Students, Fall Semester 1963–1964, Opportunity Award Program Records, box 1, folder: Student Census, BHL; Some Characteristics of Negro Freshmen at the University of Michigan, Opportunity Award Program Records, box 1, folder: Student Census 1963, BHL. For the percentage of black athletes in the first-year student class, see John Chavis, "Words on the Tenth Anniversary of the Opportunity Program: The University of Michigan," November 14, 1974, 2, John Chavis Papers, box 1, BHL; Berkson, "'Small Number'"; "The President's Report for 1963–1964," 316, 327.

35. Suzanne M. Meyer to Dr. James Lewis, November 13, 1963, Vice President of Student Affairs Records, box 6, folder: James A. Lewis, Topical, Human Relations Board (Race Discrimination) 1958–1963, BHL; University of Michigan Board of Regents, "October Meeting 1964," *Proceedings of the Board of Regents, (1963–1966)*, 563, http://quod.lib.umich.edu/u/umregproc/ACW7513.1963.001/577?rgn=full+text; view=pdf.

36. Anderson, *Pursuit of Fairness*, 76–80. For the best analysis of attacks on early fair employment legislation, see Anthony Chen, *The Fifth Freedom: Jobs, Politics, and Civil Rights in the United States, 1941–1972* (Princeton, NJ: Princeton University Press, 2009), 88–114; Lisa M. Stulberg and Anthony S. Chen, "The Origins of Race-Conscious Affirmative Action in Undergraduate Admissions: A Comparative Analysis of Institutional Change in Higher Education," *Sociology of Education* 87, no. 1 (January 2014): 39; Howard Ball, *The* Bakke *Case: Race, Education, and Affirmative Action* (Lawrence: University Press of Kansas, 2000); Dennis Deslippe, *Protesting Affirmative Action: The Struggle over Equality After the Civil Rights Revolution* (Baltimore: Johns Hopkins University Press, 2012), 111–49.

37. Stulberg and Chen, "Origins of Race-Conscious Affirmative Action in Undergraduate Admissions," 39–43.

38. "ACE Plans Aid Programs for Negroes," *Michigan Daily*, October 19, 1963, 1; "Education Unit Aims to Widen Negro Scope," *Washington Post*, October 4, 1963, A13; "Inter-University Conference on the Negro in Higher Education."

39. Berkson, "'Small Number'"; "For Release at 12 Noon, Thursday March 5, 1964," Provost and Executive Vice President for Academic Affairs Records, Central

Files, box 1, folder: Negro, re 1963–1964, BHL; Leonard Sain to Anne H. Gray, June 30, 1964, Provost and Executive Vice President for Academic Affairs, Central Files, box 1, folder: Negro, re 1963–1964, BHL.

40. Roger W. Heyns to Hobart Taylor, February 8, 1964, Provost and Executive Vice President for Academic Affairs, Central Files, box 1, folder: Negro, re 1963–1964, BHL; W. K. McInally to Roger Heyns, January 24, 1964, Provost and Executive Vice President for Academic Affairs, Central Files, box 1, folder: Negro, re 1963–1964, BHL.

41. The University of Michigan Opportunity Award Program, 1964–1968, Provost and Executive Vice President for Academic Affairs, Central Files, box 8, folder: Chavis, John, BHL; John Chavis to VP Allan Smith, November 25, 1968, Provost and Executive Vice President for Academic Affairs, Central Files, box 14, folder: Chavis, John, BHL; John Chavis Biographical Data, John Chavis Papers, box 1, folder: Biographical Info, BHL.

42. University Steering Committee on the Development of Academic Opportunities, Racial Origin Survey, January 1967, Housing Division Records, box 1, folder: Academic Opportunities (Minorities), BHL; John M. Allen to Professor Norman R. Scott, November 7, 1966, Housing Division Records, box 1, folder: Academic Opportunities (Minorities), BHL.

43. John Brubacher, *Higher Education in Transition: A History of American Colleges and Universities* (New Brunswick: Transaction, 1997), 369.

44. Draft, December 9, 1968, John Chavis Papers, box 1, folder: Opportunity Award Programs, 1965–1968, BHL; Z. A. Johnson to Dr. Vroman, Provost and Executive Vice President for Academic Affairs, box 7, folder: Admissions, BHL; Goodman recounted these practices in a public talk in 1980: George Goodman, "Black Students at U of M in the 1970's," February 13, 1980, Tape 1, Center for Afroamerican and African Studies, box 28, BHL.

45. Draft, December 9, 1968, John Chavis Papers, box 1, folder: Opportunity Award Programs, 1965–1968, BHL; Z. A. Johnson to Dr. Vroman, Provost and Executive Vice President for Academic Affairs, box 7, folder: Admissions, BHL; Goodman recounted these practices in a public talk in 1980: George Goodman, "Black Students at U of M in the 1970's," February 13, 1980, Tape 1, Center for Afroamerican and African Studies, box 28, BHL.

46. Ruth Eckstein, "Black Opportunity Undergraduates at the University of Michigan, 1964–1970: A Retrospective View," August 15, 1971, Provost and Executive Vice President for Academic Affairs, Staff Files, box 50, folder: Black Opportunity Undergraduates at the University of Michigan, 1964–1970, BHL; "The University of Michigan Opportunity Award Program, 1964–1968," Provost and Executive Vice President for Academic Affairs, Central Files, box 8, folder: Chavis, John, BHL.

47. For an explanation of the difference between "soft" and "hard" programs, see Stulberg and Chen, "Origins of Race-Conscious Affirmative Action in Undergraduate Admissions," 38.

48. Judith Barnett, "Program Seeks to Help Negro Students," *Michigan Daily*, April 26, 1964, 1; Philip Sutin, "Heyns Reveals New Plan to Assist 'Disadvantaged,'" *Michigan Daily*, March 6, 1964, 1; "The Opportunity Award Program," 1968, Provost and Executive Vice President for Academic Affairs, Supplemental Files, box 1, folder: Opportunity Awards Program: W. L. Cash, 1968–71, BHL; "The Need to Recruit Poor Cited at U-M," *Ann Arbor News*, January 11, 1967, 2.

49. UM administrators didn't begin tracking the race of all university students until 1967, when HEW began requiring annual compliance reports: Compliance Report of Institutions of Higher Education under Title VI of the Civil rights Act of 1964, Fall 1967, Assistant to the President Records, box 39, folder: Compliance Reports, 67–69, BHL.

50. "Need to Recruit Poor Cited at U-M," *Michigan Daily*, January 11, 1967, 2; John Chavis to Vice President Allan Smith, Subject: Opportunity Award Program, June 7, 1968, President's Records, box 4, folder: Opportunity Award Program, BHL.

51. Nellie Varner and George Goodman to Coordinating Committee for Human Relations, February 18, 1969, Provost and Executive Vice President for Academic Affairs, Staff Files, box 60, folder: Robert B. Holmes, Topical Files: Admissions Office: Opportunity Program Office Changes, Sept. 1975–July 1979 and undated, BHL.

52. "Black Opportunity Undergraduates at the University of Michigan, 1964–1970"; "Draft," December 9, 1968, John Chavis Papers, box 1, BHL.

53. This 1965 study was summarized in "Patricia O'Connor and Doris Miller to Members of the University Steering Committee on the Development of Academic Opportunities," December 9, 1966, Provost and Executive Vice President for Academic Affairs, Central Files, box 8, folder: Committees-University Steering Committee on development of Academic Opportunities II, BHL.

54. "Patricia O'Connor and Doris M. Miller to Members of the University Steering Committee on the Development of Academic Opportunities," December 9, 1966, Provost and Executive Vice President for Academic Affairs, Central Files, box 8, folder: Committees-University Steering Committee on Development of Academic Opportunities II, BHL; Doris Miller, "The Relationship between Achiever Personality Scores and Grade Point Average for Opportunity Award Students," 1966, Provost and Executive Vice President for Academic Affairs, Central Files, box 8, folder: Committees-University Steering Committee on Development of Academic Opportunities II, BHL.

55. Ruth Eckstein, "The State of the Opportunity Undergraduate Enrollment, Fall 1972," November 17, 1972, Provost and Executive Vice President for Academic Affairs, Staff Files, box 50, folder: Opportunity Program: Enrollment of Minority Students, 1969–73, BHL; LSA Minority Student Attrition Study, April 8, 1973, Thomas A. Butts Papers, box 1, folder: OFA, Student Loan Programs, Minority Projections since BAM (Black Action Movement, 1972–1973), BHL; Outline of Discussion with Regents on Attrition of Minority Undergraduate Students, Provost and Executive Vice President for Academic Affairs, Staff Files, box 65, folder: Robert B. Holmes, Topical Files: Minority Reports: Miscellaneous U. of M. Reports and Memos (includes notes), June 1975–March 1980, BHL.

56. Compliance Report of Institutions of Higher Education under Title VI of the Civil rights Act of 1964, Fall 1967, Assistant to the President Records, box 39, folder: Compliance Reports, 67–69, BHL.

57. Walter Greene to Harlan Hatcher, June 28, 1966, Marvin L. Niehuss Paperes, box 28, folder: Compliance Review, BHL; "The Civil Rights Act of 1964," *National Archives*, https://www.docsteach.org/documents/document/civil-rights-act-of-1964; Christopher Loss, *Between Citizens and the State: The Politics of American Higher Education in the 20th Century* (Princeton, NJ: Princeton University Press, 2012), 171–76.

58. "For Immediate Release," March 19, 1967, John Chavis Papers, box 1, folder: Correspondence, BHL.

59. Recommendations for Broadening Equal Opportunities under Provisions of Title VI, Civil Rights Bill, Provost and Executive Vice President for Academic Affairs, Supplemental Files, box 1, folder: Equal Employment Opportunity Report, 1967–68, BHL.

60. Anderson, *Pursuit of Fairness*, 92; Walter Greene to Harlan Hatcher, September 13, 1966, Marvin L. Niehuss Papers, box 28, folder: Niehuss: Compliance Review, 1966–1968, BHL; Jack H. Hamilton to Executive Vice President Marvin Niehuss, Re: Title VII, Civil Rights Act, 1964, Compliance Review Report, March 7, 1967, Provost and Executive Vice President for Academic Affairs, Supplemental Files, box 1, folder: Equal Employment Opportunity Report, 1967–68, BHL.

61. Bryce Nelson, Michigan: Ruckus over Race Has Relevance to Other Universities, *Science*, June 2, 1967, Provost and Executive Vice President for Academic Affairs, Supplemental Files, box 1, folder: Equal Employment Opportunity Report, 1967–68, BHL.

62. Nelson, Michigan, BHL.

63. Jack H. Hamilton to Executive Vice President Marvin Niehuss, Re: Title VII, Civil Rights Act, 1964, Compliance Review Report, March 7, 1967, Provost and Executive Vice President for Academic Affairs, Supplemental Files, box 1, folder: Equal Employment Opportunity Report, 1967–68, BHL.

64. Hamilton to Niehuss, Re: Title VII, Civil Rights Act, 1964, BHL; "Patricia O'Connor and Doris Miller to Members of the University Steering Committee on the Development of Academic Opportunities," December 9, 1966, BHL; Doris Miller, "The Relationship between Achiever Personality Scores and Grade Point Average for Opportunity Award Students," December 9, 1966, Provost and Executive Vice President for Academic Affairs, Central Files, box 8, folder: Committees-University Steering Committee on Development of Academic Opportunities II, BHL; Hamilton to Niehuss, March 7, 1967, Provost and Executive Vice President for Academic Affairs, Supplemental Files, box 1, folder: Equal Employment Opportunity Report, 1967–68, BHL.

## 3. Rise of the Black Campus Movement

1. Terry Anderson, *The Movement and the Sixties: Protest in America from Greensboro to Wounded Knee* (New York: Oxford University Press, 1995), 39. Robert Cohen's *Freedom's Orato: Mario Salvo and the Radical Legacy of the 1960s* (New York: Oxford University Press, 2009), 2.

2. Anderson, *Movement and the Sixties*, 160–61.

3. Cohen, *Freedom's Orator*, 2; David Farber, *The Age of Great Dreams: America in the 1960s* (New York: Hill and Wang, 1994), 78, 156; Bill Ayers, *Fugitive Days: Memoirs of an Antiwar Activist* (Boston: Beacon Press, 2009), 39–58; Howard H. Peckham, *The Making of the University of Michigan, 1817–1992* (Ann Arbor: University of Michigan Press, 1994), 290–93.

4. "Remembering BAM," *Ann Arbor News*, March 25, 1990, Vice Provost for Multicultural Affairs, box 4, folder: BAM, BHL; Joy Ann Williamson, *Black Power on Campus: The University of Illinois, 1965–75* (Urbana: University of Illinois Press, 2003), 1. For more background on Black Power's fundamental principles and their influence on college campuses, see Peniel E. Joseph, "The Black Power Movement: A State of the

Field," *Journal of American History* (December 2009): 752–53; Peniel Joseph, "Dashikis and Democracy: Black Studies, Student Activism, and the Black Power Movement," *Journal of African American History* 88, no. 2 (Spring 2003): 182–203; Ibram H. Rogers, "The Black Campus Movement: The Case for a New Historiography," *The Sixties: A Journal of History, Politics and Culture* 4, no. 2 (December 2011): 171–86. For the best treatment of Black Power's adaptation of colonial critiques, see Robert O. Self, *American Babylon: Race and the Struggle for Postwar Oakland* (Princeton, NJ: Princeton University Press, 2003), 215–327.

5. Donna Jean Murch, *Living for the City: Migration, Education, and the Rise of the Black Panther Party in Oakland, California* (Chapel Hill: University of North Carolina Press, 2010), 103–11; Ibram H. Rogers, "The Black Campus Movement and the Institutionalization of Black Studies, 1965–1970," *Journal of African American Studies* 16, no. 1 (March 2012): 23–24; Martha Biondi, *The Black Revolution on Campus* (Berkeley: University of California Press, 2012), 31.

6. Sidney Fine, *Violence in the Model City: The Cavanagh Administration, Race Relations, and the Detroit Riot of 1967* (East Lansing: Michigan State University Press, 2007), 1–125, 155–63, 291, 294, 299; Robben W. Fleming, interview by Enid H. Galler, Fall 1992, transcript, History and Traditions of the University Committee, box 1, folder: Robben Fleming, BHL.

7. Robben Fleming, *Tempest into Rainbows: Managing Turbulence* (Ann Arbor: University of Michigan Press, 1996), 158.

8. Matthew Levin, *Cold War University: Madison and the New Left in the Sixties* (Madison: University of Wisconsin Press, 2013), 3–7; Fleming, *Tempest into Rainbows*, 150–51.

9. Fleming, *Tempest into Rainbows*, 113–21, 147–56; Bruce Weber, "Robben W. Fleming, University President in Turbulent Times, Dies at 93," *New York Times*, January 21, 2010, http://www.nytimes.com/2010/01/22/education/22fleming.html; Fleming, interview by Enid H. Galler, Fall 1992, transcript, History and Traditions of the University Committee, box 1, folder: Robben Fleming, BHL.

10. Fleming, *Tempest into Rainbows*, 158.

11. Levin, *Cold War University*, 149–59.

12. Fleming, interview by Enid H. Galler, Fall 1992, transcript, History and Traditions of the University Committee, box 1, folder: Robben Fleming, BHL.

13. Fleming, *Tempest into Rainbows*, 165.

14. "The History of the Negro American Petition," March 29, 1968, CAAS, box 2, folder: BAM Conferences and Scholarship; Richard H. Ross, "Brief Chronological 'The History of the Negro American' Course (Black History Course) and the Early Stages of the Michigan Students Movement on Campus from 1966 to 1970," Items #1–27, BHL; W. B. Wilcox, "To the Editor," *Michigan Daily*, January 17, 1968, 4.

15. Henry Johnson became the first black vice president in 1972; UM didn't host a black regent in the 1960s until 1967: Otis Smith, "G.M. Executive and Ex-Justice," *New York Times*, June 30, 1974, 72, http://www.nytimes.com/1994/06/30/obituaries/otis-smith-72-gm-executive-and-ex-justice.html.

16. "Norman R. Scott," University of Michigan Faculty History Project, https://www.lib.umich.edu/faculty-history/faculty/norman-r-scott/memoir; Norman R. Scott to President-Designate Robben W. Fleming, December 19, 1967, Provost and Executive Vice President for Academic Affairs, Central Files, box 8, folder: Committees-University Steering Committee on Development of Academic Opportunities I, BHL;

"Ralph M. Gibson," University of Michigan Faculty History Project, http://www
.lib.umich.edu/faculty-history/faculty/ralph-m-gibson/memoir; Norman Scott to
Robben Fleming, July 24, 1967, John Chavis Papers, box 1, folder: Steering Committee for the Development of Academic Opportunities, 1965–1967, BHL; The University Steering Committee on the Development of Academic Opportunities, October 3,
1967, Provost and Executive Vice President for Academic Affairs, Central Files, box 8,
folder: Committees-University Steering Committee on Development of Academic
Opportunities I, BHL; "Albert Wheeler," in *Sankofa: The University since BAM: Twenty
Year of Progress? Conference Report*, ed. Henry Vance Davis, 64 (Ann Arbor: Office of
Minority Affairs, 1991).

17. A. H. Wheeler to Vice Presidents Smith and Pierpont and Steering Committee
for Academic Opportunities, Subject: Equal Opportunities Program at the University
of Michigan, May 9, 1967, Albert H. and Emma M. Wheeler Papers, box 6, folder:
Steering Committee on Academic Opportunities, 1965–67, BHL.

18. The following article comments on Smith's response to the committee's policy
recommendations: Marcia Abramson, "5 Hours for Grievances: King Shootings Sparks
Building Seizure," *Michigan Daily*, August 27, 1968, 3; Affirmative Action Plan, 1968,
Provost and Executive Vice President for Academic Affairs, Central Files, box 8,
folder: Committees-University Steering Committee on Development of Academic Opportunities I, BHL; Allan F. Smith to Deans, Directors and Department Chairman,
August 10, 1967, John Chavis Papers, box 1, folder: Steering Committee for the Development of Academic Opportunities, 1965–1967, BHL.

19. Marcia Abramson, "5 Hours for Grievances: King Shooting Sparks Building
Seizure," *Michigan Daily*, August 27, 1968, 3.

20. "For Release P.M. July 13, 1967," July 10, 1967, Provost and Executive Vice
President for Academic Affairs, Supplemental Files, box 1, folder: Equal Employment
Opportunity Report, 1967–68, BHL; "Programs of the University of Michigan Related to Minority Groups," April 16, 1968, Assistant to the President Records, box 38,
folder: Black Students, 68–83, BHL; "An Administrative Internship Program for Ju-
niors in Selected Negro Colleges," President's Records, box 1, folder: Affirmative
Action Programs, BHL; Dr. Martin Luther King Jr. Memorial Fund, Draft, July 19,
1968, Otis M. Smith Papers, box 2, folder: Regent Papers, Martin Luther King Memorial Scholarship Fund, 1968–1970, BHL.

21. Ibram H. Rogers, *The Black Campus Movement: Black Students and the Racial Reconstitution of Higher Education, 1965–1972* (New York: Palgrave Macmillan, 2012), 96;
Anderson, *The Movement and the Sixties*, 192; William Haber to Richard Ross, April 8,
1968, President's Records, box 1, folder: Affirmative Action Programs, BHL.

22. Fleming started his job in January 1968. Robben Fleming, *Tempest into Rainbows*, 165; Abramson, "5 Hours for Grievances"; "Black Students: Action, Assurance
after Lock-in," *Michigan Daily*, August 27, 1968, 3.

23. Abramson, "5 Hours for Grievances," 3.

24. Abramson, "5 Hours for Grievances."

25. Marcia Abramson, "Black Student Demands: Finding the Answers," *Michigan
Daily*, May 16, 1968, 1; Henry Grix, "'U' May Formalize Black Studies," *Michigan Daily*,
August 14, 1968, 1.

26. Alvin M. Bentley to Robben Fleming, April 19, 1968, President's Records, box
1, folder: Bentley, Alvin (Regent), BHL.

27. Otis Smith to President R. W. Fleming and Regents, April 11, 1968, Provost and Executive Vice President for Academic Affairs, Central Files, box 11, folder: Negro, re 1967–1968, BHL.

28. "Michigan University Office Seized by Students," *New York Times*, April 10, 1968, 66; Abramson, "Black Student Demands," 1; Robben Fleming, "Statement on Student Unrest," May 8, 1969, Otis M. Smith Papers, box 1, folder: Regent Papers, Administration, 1967–1971, BHL.

29. David Cunningham, "State versus Social Movement: FBI Counterintelligence Against the New Left," *States, Parties, and Social Movements* (New York: Cambridge University Press, 2003), 48; Anonymous to Director, FBI, Counterintelligence Program: Internal Security: Disruption of the New Left, June 1, 1968, Bret Enyon Papers, box 1, folder: Government Intelligence Activities COINTELPRO (Michigan) 1968, BHL; Friend of the University to Dear X, 1968, Bret Enyon Papers, box 1, folder: Government Intelligence Activities COINTELPRO (Michigan) 1968, BHL. The critical letters Fleming received can be found in: President's Records, box 1, folder: Complaints (re President Fleming), BHL.

30. Questions & Answers: Information for the Use of Solicitors for the Dr. Martin Luther King Jr. Memorial Fund, Provost and Executive Vice President for Academic Affairs, Central Files, box 16, folder: Martin Luther King Fund, 1968–69, BHL.

31. R. W. Fleming to Mr. Anthony G. De Lorenzo, December 20, 1968, Provost and Executive Vice President for Academic Affairs, Staff Files, box 51, folder: Martin Luther King Committee, 1968–69, BHL; James M. Roche to R. W. Fleming, May 9, 1969, Otis M. Smith Papers, box 2, folder: Regent Papers, Martin Luther King Memorial Scholarship Fund, 1968–1970, BHL; Robben W. Fleming to Mr. Henry Ford II, Draft, 1968, Provost and Executive Vice President for Academic Affairs, Staff Files, box 51, folder: Martin Luther King Committee, 1968–69, BHL; R. W. Fleming to James W. Roche, April 11, 1969, Otis M. Smith Papers, box 2, folder: Regent Papers, Martin Luther King Memorial Scholarship Fund, 1968–1970, BHL; Contribution to the University of Michigan Graduate School of Business, April 25, 1969, Otis M. Smith Papers, box 2, folder: Regent Papers, Martin Luther King Memorial Scholarship Fund, 1968–1970, BHL.

32. "William L. Cash," University of Michigan Faculty History Project, https://www.lib.umich.edu/faculty-history/faculty/william-l-cash/memoir; "For Release Tuesday A.M. July 16, 1968," July 15, 1968, News and Information Services, Faculty and Staff Files, box 20, folder: Cash, William L. Jr., BHL.

33. Minutes, April 10, 1968, College of Literature, Science, and the Arts Executive Committee Minutes and Statistical Studies, 1967–68, College of Literature, Science, and the Arts Records, box 300, BHL; J. Frank Yates, Curriculum Vitae, November 12, 2015, http://www.bus.umich.edu/FacultyBios/CV/jfyates.pdf.

34. George Goodman, "Black Students at U of M in the 1970's," February, 13, 1980, Tape 1, Center for Afroamerican and African Studies Records, box 28, BHL.

35. "For Immediate Release," December 16, 1968, News and Information Services, Faculty and Staff Files, box 20, folder: Cash, William L. Jr., BHL.

36. Henry Grix, Honors Course: Black History Is Beautiful, *Michigan Daily*, July 17, 1968, 1; Henry Grix, "Efforts to Expand Black Studies Increase," *Michigan Daily*, September 12, 1968, 1; "Harold Wright Cruse," University of Michigan Faculty History Project, https://www.lib.umich.edu/faculty-history/faculty/harold-wright-cruse

/memoir; Christopher Lehmann-Haupt, "Harold Cruse, Social Critic and Fervent Black Nationalist, Dies at 89," *New York Times*, March 30, 2005, http://www.nytimes.com/2005/03/30/us/harold-cruse-social-critic-and-fervent-Black-nationalist-dies-at-89.html.

37. Sharon Weiner, 'U' Committee Plans Black Major, *Michigan Daily*, February 6, 1969, 1; Henry Grix, "'U' May Formalize Black Studies," *Michigan Daily*, August 14, 1968, 1; Create Black Major, *Michigan Daily*, April 8, 1969, 1.

38. Henry Vance Davis, "From Coloreds to African-Americans: A History of the Struggle for Educational Equity at the University of Michigan and an Agenda for the Pluralistic Multicultural University of the Twenty-First Century," in *Sankofa: The University since BAM: Twenty Years of Progress? Conference Report*, ed. Henry Vance Davis (Ann Arbor: Office of Minority Affairs, 1991); College of Literature, Science, and the Arts Black Students' Union, "A Center for Afro-American Studies: A Proposal, Center for Afroamerican and African Studies Records," box 16, folder: CAAS: Archives, History of the Center and Program, 1970–2000, BHL.

39. J. F. Yates, "Proposal for a Center for Afro-American Studies," Madison Foster Papers, box 1, folder: BAM Strike, BHL; Rick Perloff, "Afro-American Center Considered," *Michigan Daily*, February 9, 1969, 1.

40. Robben Fleming to Barbara W. Newell, November 7, 1968, University of Michigan Housing Division Records, box 7, BHL.

41. Robben Fleming, Statement on Student Unrest, May 8, 1969, Otis M. Smith Papers, box 1, folder: Regent Papers, Administration, 1967–1971; Thomas J. Sugrue, *Sweet Land of Liberty: The Forgotten Struggle for Civil Rights in the North* (New York: Random House, 2008), 348.

42. Fleming to Newell, November 7, 1968; Barbara Newell to John Feldkamp, November 12, 1968, Vice President for Student Affairs, box 9, BHL.

43. John Feldkamp to Barbara Newell, "Housing Issues Concerning Black Students," January 2, 1969, Housing Division Records, box 7, BHL.

44. Williamson, *Black Power on Campus*, 30; "Black Students Win Many Demands After 38-Hour Bursar's Office Sit-in," *Daily Northwestern*, May 6, 1968, 2; Biondi, *Black Revolution on Campus*, 91–92; John Feldkamp to Barbara Newell, "Housing Issues concerning Black Students," January 2, 1969, Housing Division Records, box 7, BHL. Martha Biondi also found that universities created similar living spaces that focused on cultural identity, rather than race, to get around legal problems.

45. John Feldkamp to Barbara Newell, Re: Housing Issues concerning Black Students, January 2, 1969, Vice President of Student Affairs Records, box 9, folder: B. W. Newell Administrative Student Organization Black Student Union, 1969–1970, BHL.

46. R. W. Fleming, Martin Luther King Jr. Commemoration Service, April 4, 1969, Robben W. Fleming Papers, box 19, folder: R. W. Fleming (Speeches) (Lists II), BHL.

47. Neil Paterson, "Blues Festival: Breathtaking Tour of a Very Rich Sound," *Michigan Daily*, August 2, 1969, 2; Lindsay Chaney, "Black Arts Festival Intriguing," *Michigan Daily*, November 16, 1969, 2. For work on African Americans' place in popular culture, see William L. Van Deburg, *Black Camelot: African-American Culture Heroes in Their Times, 1960–1980* (Chicago: University of Chicago Press, 1997).

48. Fleming, Martin Luther King Jr. Commemoration Service.

49. Goodman recounts these problems in George Goodman, "Black Students at U of M in the 1970's," February 13, 1980, Tape 1, Center for Afroamerican and African Studies Records, box 28, BHL.

50. Notes on a Special Two-Year Curriculum for "High Academic Risk" Students, March 25, 1968, President's Records, box 1, folder: Affirmative Action Programs, BHL; William L. Hays to Professor John Milholland, September 19, 1969, Provost and Executive Vice President for Academic Affairs, Supplemental Files, box 2, folder: BAM: Black Student Program, 69–70, BHL.

51. Notes on a Special Two-Year Curriculum for "High Academic Risk" Students; William L. Hays to Professor John Milholland, September 19, 1969, Provost and Executive Vice President for Academic Affairs, Supplemental Files, box 2, folder: BAM: Black Student Program, 69–70, BHL; Black Opportunity Undergraduates at the University of Michigan, 1964–1970: A Retrospective View, College of Literature, Science and the Arts Records, box 211, folder: Opportunity Program, 1971–72, BHL; Ruth Eckstein, "A Study of Black Opportunity Award Freshmen at the University of Michigan, 1964–1967," January 30, 1969, John Chavis Papers, box 1, BHL; Patricia O'Connor and Doris Miller to Members of the University Steering Committee on the Development of Academic Opportunities, December 9, 1966, Housing Division Records, box 1, BHL.

52. "A Proposal for a Freshman Year of Studies Program," July 9, 1969, Provost and Executive Vice President for Academic Affairs Records, box 2, folder: BAM: Black Student Program, 69–70, BHL.

53. "Proposal for a Freshman Year of Studies Program."

54. "Proposal for a Freshman Year of Studies Program."

55. William L. Hays to R.W. Fleming, July 29, 1969, Provost and Executive Vice President for Academic Affairs, Supplemental Files, box 2, folder: BAM: Black Student Program, 69–70, BHL; William L. Hays to Professor John Milholland, September 19, 1969, Provost and Executive Vice President for Academic Affairs, Supplemental Files, box 2, folder: BAM: Black Student Program, 69–70, BHL.

56. William L. Hays to Robben Fleming, July 29, 1969; R. W. Fleming to Dean William L. Hays, August 4, 1969, Provost and Executive Vice President for Academic Affairs Records, box 2, folder: BAM: Black Student Program, 69–70, BHL; LSA faculty meeting minutes confirmed that Yates never received funding for the program: "Proposed Meeting Minutes of the November 1, 1971 Faculty Meeting," L.S.&A. Faculty Minutes, 1970–71, College of Literature, Science and the Arts Records, box 208, BHL.

57. Supplementary Information, March 1969, Otis M. Smith Papers, box 2, folder: Regent Papers, Martin Luther King Memorial Scholarship Fund, 1968–1970, BHL.

58. Affirmative Action Plan, 1968, Provost and Executive Vice President for Academic Affairs, Central Files, box 8, folder: Committees-University Steering Committee on Development of Academic Opportunities I, BHL; For Immediate Release After Regents Meeting Friday, April 19, 1968, Provost and Executive Vice President for Academic Affairs, Supplemental Files, box 1, folder: Equal Employment Opportunity Report, 1967–68, BHL.

59. "For Immediate Release," April 7, 1969, News and Information Services, Faculty and Staff Files, box 20, folder: Cash, William L. Jr., BHL.

60. Equal Employment Opportunity Affirmative Action Program, June 4, 1969, Provost and Executive Vice President for Academic Affairs, Central Files, box 13, folder: Affirmative Action Program, BHL.

61. "For Immediate Release," June 27, 1969, Assistant to the President Records, box 39, folder: Compliance Reports, 67–69, BHL.

62. William L. Hays and Allan Smith, Request for the Establishment of a Center, Name: Center for Afro-American and African Studies, July 1970, Center for Afroamerican and African Studies Records, box 16, folder: CAAS: Archives, History of the Center and Program, BHL. This document explains the administrative process involved in approving the center, stretching back to 1969.

63. Survey of Progress in Broadening Educational Opportunity for American Negroes at State Universities and Land-Grant Colleges, Fall 1969, Assistant to the President Records, box 39, folder: Compliance Reports, 67–69, BHL.

64. Ibram X. Kendi, "The Black Campus Movement: The Case for a New Historiography," *The Sixties: A Journal of History, Politics and Culture* 4 (December 2011): 175; Biondi, *Black Revolution on Campus*, 43–78; Donald Alexander Downs, *Cornell '69: Crisis of the American University* (Ithaca, NY: Cornell University Press, 1999), 198–99; "Cornell Officials Yield to Armed Students," *Chicago Tribune*, April 21, 1969, 1; "Cornell Students Urged to Turn in Firearms," *Washington Post*, April 26, 1969, A8; "36-Hour Seizure: Negro Students End Cornell Armed Sit-In," *Los Angeles Times*, April 21, 1969, A5; Stephan Bradley, *Harlem vs. Columbia University: Black Student Power in the Late 1960s* (Urbana-Champaign: University of Illinois Press, 2009), 94–99.

65. Biondi, *Black Revolution on Campus*, 158–59.

66. Fleming, *Tempest into Rainbows*, 187, 193, 196, 202.

67. Peter W. Forsythe to Wilber K. Pierpont, Preliminary Memorandum-Confidential, Office of the General Counsel, William P. Lemmer Records, box 1, folder: Student Unrest, Memos from P. W. Forsythe, attorney, to W. K. Pierpont, labeled confidential, 1969, BHL. The memorandum notes that this is in response to questions sent by Fleming on May 18, 1969.

68. Peter W. Forsythe to Wilber K. Pierpont, Preliminary Memorandum-Confidential, Office of the General Counsel, William P. Lemmer Records, box 1, folder: Student Unrest, Memos from P. W. Forsythe, attorney, to W. K. Pierpont, labeled confidential, 1969, BHL.

69. Alan Glenn, "The Battle of Ann Arbor: June 16–20, 1969," *Ann Arbor Chronicle*, June 16, 2009, http://annarborchronicle.com/2009/06/16/the-battle-of-ann-arbor-june-16-20-1969/; Bill Schmidt and Gene Goltz, "Tear Gas Scatters Students," *Detroit Free Press*, June 18, 1969, 1A, 9A.

70. Fleming, interview by Enid H. Galler, Fall 1992, transcript, History and Traditions of the University Committee, box 1, folder: Robben Fleming, BHL; Richard L. Kennedy, interview by Enid H. Galler, Winter 1995, transcript, History and Traditions of the University Committee, box 1, folder: Richard Kennedy, BHL; Alan Glenn, "The Battle of Ann Arbor: June 16–20, 1969," *Ann Arbor Chronicle*, June 16, 2009, http://annarborchronicle.com/2009/06/16/the-battle-of-ann-arbor-june-16-20-1969/.

71. Glenn, "Battle of Ann Arbor."

72. Students Seize LSA Building as over 1000 Mass in Support; "'U' Obtains Injunction: Demand 'U' Regents Meet on Bookstore," September 26, 1969, 1; Fleming, *Tempest into Rainbows*, 189–92. Fleming mistakenly writes that this unfolded in 1968 in his book.

73. Sharon Weiner, "Discuss Demands: Blacks Call Mass Meeting," *Michigan Daily*, February 3, 1970, 1; Sharon Weiner, "Closed Session: Black Students Confer over Admissions Issue," *Michigan Daily*, February 5, 1970, 1.

74. United Black Population of the University of Michigan, Black Student Demands, 1970, Vice President of Student Affairs Records, box 9, folder: B. W. Newell Administrative Student Organization Black Student Union, 1969–1970, BHL; Sharon Weiner and W. E. Schrock, "Blacks Present Demands to Fleming," *Michigan Daily*, February 6, 1970, 1; Lynn Weiner, "Increased Minority Admissions asked," *Michigan Daily*, January 18, 1970, 1.

75. United Black Population of the University of Michigan, Black Student Demands, 1970, Vice President of Student Affairs Records, box 9, folder: B. W. Newell Administrative Student Organization Black Student Union, 1969–1970, BHL.

76. "The University as a Racist Institution," 1970, Provost and Executive Vice President for Academic Affairs, Supplemental Files, box 2, folder: BAM Demands, 1969–70, BHL.

77. "The University as a Racist Institution."

78. "The University as a Racist Institution."

79. Rob Bier, "Regents Seek 5-Year Minority Admissions Plan," *Michigan Daily*, February 20, 1970, 1.

80. Bier, "Regents Seeks 5-Year Minority Admissions Plan"; Susan Brune, "Conflict and Conciliation: A Review of the Black Action Movement Strike at the University of Michigan," *Michigan Journal of Political Science* 5, 46–47; W. Ellison Chalmers, "The University of Michigan and the Black Action Movement," April 17, 1971, President Records, box 106, BHL.

81. Brune, "Conflict and Conciliation," 48.

82. William Haber to A. F. Smith et al., March 3, 1970, Vice President of Student Affairs Records, box 9, folder: B. W. Newell, Topical File Black Action Movement, 1970, BHL.

83. William Haber to A. F. Smith et al., March 3, 1970.

84. William Haber to A. F. Smith et al., March 3, 1970.

85. William Haber to A. F. Smith et al., March 3, 1970; Statement on Increased Enrollment of Black Students, March 4, 1970, Robert Nederlander Papers, box 1, folder: Black Student Demands, 1970, BHL; R. W. Fleming to Members of the Black Action Movement, March 5, 1970, L.S.&A. Faculty Minutes, 1969–70, College of Literature, Science and the Arts Records, box 208, BHL. The proposal is untitled and attached to Fleming's letter.

86. Jack H. Hamilton to President Fleming et al., Subject: Response to BAM Demands, March 4, 1970, Provost and Executive Vice President for Academic Affairs, Supplemental Files, box 2, folder: BAM General, 1969–70, BHL; R. W. Fleming to Members of the Black Action Movement, March 5, 1970, L.S.&A. Faculty Minutes, 1969–70, College of Literature, Science and the Arts Records, box 208, BHL.

87. W. Ellison Chalmers, "The University of Michigan and the Black Action Movement," April 17, 1971, President Records, box 106, BHL; Bob Bier, "BAM Leaders Reject Regental Resolution," *Michigan Daily*, March 20, 1970, 1.

88. Gertrude E. Huebner, interview by Enid H. Galler, April 2004, transcript, History and Traditions of the University Committee, box 1, folder: Huebner, Gertrude E., BHL.

89. Data: Fleming Questions, March 18, 1970, Provost and Executive Vice President for Academic Affairs, Supplemental Files, box 2, folder: BAM General, 1969–70, BHL.

90. W. Ellison Chalmers, "The University of Michigan and the Black Action Movement," April 17, 1971, President Records, box 106, BHL; Bob Bier, "BAM Leaders Reject Regental Resolution," *Michigan Daily*, March 20, 1970, 1.

91. Bier, "BAM Leaders Reject Regental Resolution."

92. Robert Kraftowitz, "BAM Asks U Strike, Rally on Admissions," *Michigan Daily*, March 19, 1970, 1, 8; Robert Kraftowitz, "Blacks, Supporters March around Campus," *Michigan Daily*, March 20, 1970, 1, 6.

93. Kraftowitz, "Blacks, Supporters March around Campus."

94. Kraftowitz, "Blacks, Supporters March around Campus."

95. "Day-by-Day, Here Is a Summary of What Was Reported by the News Media as Happening during the Black Action Movement's Strike on the Ann Arbor Campus in Late March and Early April," Michigan Alumnus, May 1970, Robert Nederlander Papers, box 1, folder: Black Action Movement, 1970, BHL.

96. Kim Clarke, "Remembering BAM," Ann Arbor News, March 27, 1990, Vice Provost for Multicultural Affairs, box 4, folder: BAM, BHL; "Day-by-Day, Here Is a Summary," BHL.

97. Fleming, interview by Enid H. Galler.

98. Fleming, interview by Enid H. Galler.

99. W. E. Schrock, Eric Schenk, and Chris Uhl, "Estimate Effect at Up to 50%," *Michigan Daily*, March 24, 1970, 1.

100. Special Meeting of the Senate Assembly Meeting Minutes, March 25, 1970, Vice President of Student Affairs Records, box 9, folder: B. W. Newell, Topical File Black Action Movement, 1970, BHL; Niara Sudarkasa (formerly Gloria Marshall) Curriculum Vitae, Fall 1974, Provost and Executive Vice President for Academic Affairs, Staff Files, box 65, folder: Niara Sudarkasa, Personal: Resumes, 1974–1985.

101. "Special Meeting of the Senate Assembly Meeting Minutes," March 25, 1970, Vice President of Student Affairs Records, box 9, folder: B. W. Newell, Topical File Black Action Movement, 1970, BHL.

102. "Special Meeting of the Senate Assembly Meeting Minutes"; Executive Committee of the Political Science Department to Regents, Administration, and Colleagues, March 25, 1970, Provost and Executive Vice President for Academic Affairs, Supplemental Files, box 2, folder: BAM: Faculty Reactions, 1969–70, BHL; School of Dentistry, Faculty Meeting Minutes of March 27, 1970, Provost and Executive Vice President for Academic Affairs, Supplemental Files, box 2, folder: BAM: Black Enrollment (Quotas) 1969–70, BHL; School of Public Heath Agenda for Faculty Meeting, March 30, 1970, Eugene Feingold Papers, box 3, folder: UM Minority Concerns: Black Action Movement, 1970, BHL; Minutes of Special Faculty Meeting, March 26, 1970, Provost and Executive Vice President for Academic Affairs, Supplemental Files, box 2, folder: BAM: Black Enrollment (Quotas) 1969–70, BHL; Graduate School of Business Administration, Special Faculty Meeting, March 30, 1970, Thomas A. Butts Papers, box 1, folder: OFA, Student Loan Programs, Minority Projections Since BAM (Black Action Movement, 1972–1973), BHL; Minutes of the March 27, 1970 Special Faculty Meeting of the College of Literature, Science, and the Arts, Provost and Executive Vice President for Academic Affairs, Supplemental Files, box 2, folder: BAM: Black Enrollment (Quotas) 1969–70, BHL.

103. "Day-by-Day, Here Is a Summary," BHL; Fleming, interview by Enid H. Galler.

104. Fleming, interview by Enid H. Galler.

105. Office of the President, Untitled, April 3, 1970, Provost and Executive Vice President for Academic Affairs, Supplemental Files, box 2, folder: BAM General, 1969–70, BHL; Statement of the Board of Regents, the University of Michigan, April 1, 1970, Provost and Executive Vice President for Academic Affairs, Supplemental Files, box 2, folder: BAM General, 1969–70, BHL.

106. Office of the President, Untitled, April 3, 1970; Robert Kraftowitz, "Regents Act on Demands," *Michigan Daily*, April 2, 1970, 1.

## 4. Controlling Inclusion

1. Dave Chudwin, "BAM Ends Class Strike: Accepts Regental Statement," *Michigan Daily*, April 2, 1970, 1; Manifesto of Intent of the Black Action Movement, Madison Foster Papers, box 1, folder: BAM Strike (aftermath) June 1971-Feb-1980, BHL.

2. "The University as a Racist Institution," 1970, Provost and Executive Vice President for Academic Affairs, Supplemental Files, box 2, folder: BAM Demands, 1969–70, BHL.

3. "'U' Commencement: Grads Hear Wharton, Fleming," *Michigan Daily*, May 6, 1970, 3; University Relations Office, "Answers to Some Frequently-Asked Questions about the Expanded Opportunity Award Program at the University of Michigan."

4. Robert J. Donovan, "Michigan U's Plan for 10% Black Quota Assailed by Agnew," *Los Angeles Times*, April 14, 1970, 1; Cheryl Arvidson, "Agnew Hits Colleges' Open Door Policy," *Chicago Daily Defender*, April 15, 1970, 4; "Agnew's Commons Sense," *Chicago Tribune*, April 15, 1970, 20. Only two months earlier, Agnew had scored political points by criticizing what he saw as racial quotas in university admissions. Seth S. King, "Agnew Denounces University Quotas to Help Minorities," *New York Times*, February 13, 1970, 1; Arvidson, "Agnew Hits Colleges' Open Door Policy," 4; William Godfrey, "At the University of Michigan," *Chicago Tribune*, April 28, 1970, 16; Rollin L. McNitt, "Michigan U.'s Cave-In to Blacks' Demands Will Drag Down Standards," *Los Angeles Times*, April 19, 1970, D6.

5. "Answers to Some Frequently-Asked Questions about the Expanded Opportunity Program at the University of Michigan"; Robben Fleming, "'We Must Put Our House in Order': Fleming Looks at His University," *Detroit Free Press*, May 16, 1970, 8A; R. W. Fleming to Douglas G. Wilson, March 24, 1970, Center for Afroamerican and African Studies Records, box 1, folder: Correspondence Alumni Opposition to the Strike, BHL.

6. Dave Chudwin, "Black Admissions: Seeking Funds to the Pay the Bill," *Michigan Daily*, February 3, 1971, 1.

7. On Fleming's concerns about declining state support and other financial problems, see R. W. Fleming, "The BAM Dispute," March 23, 1970, Robert Nederlander Papers, box 1, folder: Black Student Demands, 1970, BHL. For information on the College of Engineering's Minority Projects Office, see Keith Cooley, "Annual Report Minority Projects Office, 1970–71," Thomas A. Butts Papers, box 1, folder: OFA, Student Loan Programs, Minority Projections since BAM (Black Action Movement, 1972–1973), BHL; Robben Fleming to William Milliken, October 29, 1976, President Records, box 97, BHL; University of Michigan, Ann Arbor, Budget vs. Expense Report, 1975–76, President Records, box 97, BHL; Rebecca Warner, "Fleming Says Black

Enrollment Not 'Eroding' Academic Standards," *Michigan Daily*, November 6, 1973, 1; Robben W. Fleming, interview by Enid H. Galler, Fall 1992, History and Traditions of the University Committee Interviews, box 1, BHL.

8. James F. Brinkerhoff, Campus Disorder-Planning, May 10, 1971, Office of the General Counsel, William P. Lemmer Records, box 1, folder: Student Unrest, Planning for Containment, 1970–1971, BHL.

9. Executive Officers to the Regents, March 18, 1970, Provost and Executive Vice President for Academic Affairs, Supplemental Files, box 2, folder: BAM (University Statements), BHL.

10. Status of Campus Disruption Proceedings as of November 9, 1971, Office of the General Counsel, William P. Lemmer Records, box 1, folder: Student Unrest, Reports on Status of Campus Disruption Proceedings, 1970–1971, BHL.

11. The rules created on April 17, 1970 were reprinted in "The University of Michigan Interim Rules and Disciplinary Procedures," *Michigan Daily*, July 1, 1970, 10.

12. John Zeh, "Closing Coffers to College Protesters," *Michigan Daily*, March 28, 1969, 4; Judy Sarasohn, "LSA Sit-In Participants May Lose U.S., State Aid," *Michigan Daily*, January 28, 1970, 1; "States Pass Campus Disorder Laws," June 24, 1970, 10.

13. "Michigan's Disruption Statute," *Michigan Daily*, June 24, 1970, 10.

14. James F. Brinkerhoff, Campus Disorder-Planning, May 10, 1971, Office of the General Counsel, William P. Lemmer Records, box 1, folder: Student Unrest, Planning for Containment, 1970–1971, BHL.

15. Brinkerhoff, Campus Disorder-Planning, May 10, 1971, BHL.

16. Fleming, interview by Enid H. Galler; Niara Sudarkasa Curriculum Vitae, Fall 1974, Provost and Executive Vice President for Academic Affairs, Staff Files, box 65, folder: Niara Sudarkasa, Personal: Résumés, 1974–1985, BHL.

17. Rebecca Warner, "'U' Academic Image Concerns Smith," *Michigan Daily*, January 25, 1974, 1.

18. "English 123-A Racially Homogenous Courses for Black Freshmen," 1973, Vice President for Academic Affairs, Central Files, box 50; Gilbert Maddox, "A Plan for the Creation of a Supportive Environment for Black Students at the University of Michigan," December 1970, Vice President for Academic Affairs, Staff Files, box 51; "Coalition for the Use of Learning Skills: Schedule of Options: Study Groups, Classes, Writers' Clinic," Winter 1971, Housing Division Records, box 2, BHL.

19. "Statement of Increased Enrollment of Black Students," March 4, 1970, Robert Nederlander Papers, box 1, BHL.

20. Professor P. Roe to Stephen Spurr, April 3, 1970, Vice President for Academic Affairs, Staff Files, box 51, BHL.

21. Martha Biondi, *Black Revolution on Campus* (Berkeley: University of California Press, 2012), 114–41.

22. George Goodman, "Black Students at U of M in the 1970's," February 13, 1980, Tape 1, Center for Afroamerican and African Studies Records, box 28, BHL.

23. Dave Chudwin, "Black Admissions: Seeking Funds to Pay the Bill," *Michigan Daily*, February 3, 1971, 1; Questions & Answers: Information for the Use of Solicitors for the Dr. Martin Luther King Jr. Memorial Fund, Provost and Executive Vice President for Academic Affairs, Central Files, box 16, folder: Martin Luther King Fund, 1968–69, BHL. Minority Student Survey, April 19, 1973, Provost and Executive

Vice President for Academic Affairs, Staff Files, box 50, folder: Opportunity Program-General, 1969–70, BHL.

24. "Special Report on Opportunity Program," October 1970, Vice President of Academic Affairs, Staff Files, box 51, BHL; George D. Goodman, Minority Enrollment Report, Ann Arbor Campus, 1974, Vice President for Government Relations Records, box 16, folder: Minorities 1974, BHL.

25. Analysis and Evaluation of the University of Michigan Opportunity Award Program, January 30, 1969, Provost and Executive Vice President for Academic Affairs, Supplemental Files, box 1, folder: Opportunity Awards Program: W. L. Cash, 1968–71, BHL; George D. Goodman, Minority Enrollment Report, Ann Arbor Campus, 1974, Vice President for Government Relations Records, box 16, folder: Minorities 1974, BHL.

26. "The State of Opportunity Undergraduate Enrollment, Fall 1972," College of Literature, Science and the Arts Records, box 221, BHL.

27. Education and Housing Program to Wilma Bledsoe, Subject: University of Michigan Fact-Finding, March 7, 1972, Robert E. Nederlander Papers, box 1, folder: Afro-American Living Quarters, 1972, BHL.

28. Lee Gill, Phone interview with author, January 19, 2011; Education and Housing Program to Wilma Bledsoe, Subject: University of Michigan Fact-finding, March 7, 1972, Robert E. Nederlander Papers, box 1, folder: Afro-American Living Quarters, 1972, BHL.

29. William L. Hays and Allan F. Smith, Request for the Establishment of a Center: Center for Afro-American and African Studies, July 1, 1970, Center for Afroamerican and African Studies Records, box 16, folder: CAAS: Archives, History of the Center and Program, BHL; Godfrey Uzoigwe, the Center for Afroamerican and African Studies, 1970–1975, December 6, 1979, Center for Afroamerican and African Studies Records, box 16, folder: CAAS: Archives, History of the Center and Program, BHL; Rojas, *From Black Power to Black Studies*, 210.

30. "Press Release," September 17, 1970, News and Information Services Faculty and Staff Files, box 81, BHL.

31. Maddox, "A Plan for the Creation of a Supportive Environment for Black Students at the University of Michigan"; Dennis Lampron, "Throwing the White Masks Away," *Huron Valley Advisor*, October 27, 1971, News and Information Services Faculty and Staff Files, box 81, BHL; "Release on Receipt," September 17, 1970, News and Information Services Faculty and Staff Files, box 81, BHL.

32. Stephen H. Spurr to Gilbert Maddox, October 24, 1970, Vice President for Academic Affairs, Staff Files, box 51, BHL; "Education: Bushwaked in Texas," *Time*, October 28, 1974, http://www.time.com/time/magazine/article/0,9171,908939,00 .html. Spurr also refused to support the admission of friends of regent members to the Law School and refused to discipline the student newspaper, which was especially critical of the regents.

33. Carla Rapoport, "Blacks at 'U': Support Lags Behind," *Michigan Daily*, December 3, 1971, 6; Carla Rapoport, "'U': Enrolling Blacks with Both Eyes Closed," *Michigan Daily*, December 8, 1971, 4.

34. The first of these studies that questioned prevailing assumptions about attrition was circulated in November 1972: Ruth Eckstein, "The State of the Opportunity

Undergraduate Enrollment, Fall 1972," November 17, 1972, Provost and Executive Vice President for Academic Affairs, Staff Files, box 50, folder: Opportunity Program: Enrollment of Minority Students, 1969–73, BHL.

35. Rapoport, "Blacks at 'U'"; Support Lags Behind"; Carla Rapoport, "'U.'"

36. Rapoport, "'U.'"

37. Charles Kidd, Gilbert Maddox, Dave Wesley, and Frank Yates, "Black Administrators: Responsibility without Power," *Michigan Daily*, April 10, 1971, 4.

38. Charles Kidd, Curriculum Vitae, News and Information Services Faculty and Staff Files, box 71, BHL; Press Release, April 16, 1971, News and Information Services Faculty and Staff Files, box 71, BHL.

39. "Charles Kidd: Univ. of Michigan: A Decade After B.A.M.," tape recording, Center for Afroamerican Studies Records, box 25, BHL.

40. P. E. Bauer, "Trotter House to Provide New Services for Blacks," *Michigan Daily*, July 20, 1971, 3.

41. Shawn Leigh Alexander, *An Army of Lions: The Civil Rights Struggle Before the NAACP* (Philadelphia: University of Pennsylvania Press, 2012), 187, 244–45; P. E. Bauer, "Trotter House to Provide New Services for Blacks," *Michigan Daily*, July 20, 1971, 3. Kidd recalls the conversation with an executive officer in "Charles Kidd: Univ. of Michigan: A Decade After B.A.M," 1980, CAAS Records, box 28, BHL.

42. Bauer, "Trotter House to Provide New Services for Blacks"; "Press Release," September 16, 1971, News and Information Services Faculty and Staff Files, box 71, BHL.

43. Georgia Williams to John Feldkamp, Re: Racial Climate in South Quad, February 14, 1972, Detroit Urban League Records, box 79, folder: Kornegay, Exec. Director, 1971 Annual File University of Michigan Black Living Unit, 1971–1972.

44. Education and Housing Program to Wilma Bledsoe; "Proposal for an All-Black Corridor by the Black Women of Stockwell," December 10, 1971, Vice President of Student Affairs Records, box 24, BHL.

45. Lee Gill, phone interview with author, January 19, 2011; Wayne C. Glasker, *Black Students in the Ivory Tower: African American Student Activism at the University of Pennsylvania, 1967–1990* (Amherst: University of Massachusetts Press, 2002), 89.

46. Lee Gill, phone interview with author; "Proposal for an Afro-American and African Cultural Residence Hall," January 26, 1972, Vice President of Student Affairs Records, box 24, BHL.

47. Biondi, *Black Revolution on Campus*, 91; John Feldkamp to Barbara Newell, Re: Housing Issues concerning Black Students, January 2, 1969, Vice President of Student Affairs Records, box 9, folder: B.W. Newell Administrative Student Organization Black Student Union, 1969–1970, BHL.

48. Linda Dreeben, "Regents to Consider Afro Housing Units," *Michigan Daily*, March 29, 1972, Robert Nederlander Papers, box 1, BHL.

49. R. K. Daane to Robben Fleming, March 17, 1972, Robert Nederlander, box 1, BHL; Dreeben, "Regents to Consider Afro Housing Units."

50. Civil Rights Commission to William Bledsoe, March 7, 1972, Robert Nederlander Papers, box 1, BHL; "The Michigan Civil Rights Commission & Department of Civil Rights," Michigan.gov, December 1, 2010, http://www.michigan.gov/mdcr/0,1607,7-138-4951-9283—,00.html.

51. Francis Kornegay to Robben Fleming, March 15, 1972, Robert Nederlander, box 1, BHL; "Resolution Adopted by the Executive Board of the Ann Arbor-Wastenaw

County Branch of the American Civil Liberties Union," March 13, 1972, Robert Nederlander Papers, box 1, BHL; David Holmes to Robben Fleming, March 29, 1972, Robert Nederlander Papers, box 1, BHL.

52. Lee Gill, "Building a Black Power Base in the Dormitories," *Michigan Daily*, February 17, 1972, Robert Nederlander Papers, box 1, BHL.

53. "Organizing Structure and Proposed Educational Programs," March 10, 1972, Campus Broadcasting Network Records, box 3, BHL.

54. Student Government Council, "Position Statement on the Proposed Afro-American/American Cultural Living Unit," March 16, 1972, Robert Nederlander, box 1, BHL.

55. "Organizing Structure and Proposed Educational Programs."

56. Barbara Meyer, And the Case Against the Afro-American Units," *Michigan Daily*, February 17, 1972, Robert E. Nederlander Papers, box 1, folder: Afro-American Living Quarters, 1972; Barbara Ann Meyer to Robben Fleming, March 25, 1972, Robert Nederlander Papers, box 1, BHL. Natasha R. Warikoo finds that self interest still frames white students understanding of the benefits of diversity in *The Diversity Bargain: And Other Dilemmas of Race, Admissions, and Meritocracy at Elite Universities* (Chicago: University of Chicago Press, 2016).

57. Charles Kidd to University of Michigan Regents, March 8, 1972, Robert Nederlander Papers, box 1, BHL; The first of these studies that supported Kidd was circulated in November 1972: Eckstein, "The State of the Opportunity Undergraduate Enrollment."

58. Tony Schwartz, "Regents Reject Afro Unit, New Committee Probe," March 30, 1972, Robert Nederlander, box 1, folder: Afro-American Living Quarters, 1972, BHL.

59. Linda Dreeben, "Regents to Consider Afro Housing Units," March 29, 1972, Robert Nederlander Papers, box 1, folder: Afro-American Living Quarters, 1972, BHL.

60. Schwartz, "Regents Reject Afro Unit, New Committee Probe"; Roy Reynolds, "'Afro' Housing Vetoed," *Ann Arbor News*, March 30, 1972, Robert Nederlander Papers, box 1, BHL; "Special March Meeting, 1972," *Proceedings of the Board of Regents* (1969–1972), 1437.

61. Johnson explains his role in this in the following memo: Henry Johnson to Gerald Dunn, 1982, Vice President of Student Affairs Records, box 17, folder: H. Johnson 1983–1984 Annual File, Trotter House, 1972–1983, BHL; Janet Cooper to Robben Fleming, September 13, 1972, Robert Nederlander Papers, box 1, folder: Afro-American Living Quarters, 1972, BHL; Lee Gill, phone interview by author, January 19, 2011.

62. Melvia Miller, "Proposal for the Establishment of 'Project Awareness,'" June 22, 1972, Vice President of Student Affairs, box 24, BHL; *Black History—Lost, Stolen or Strayed?* Columbia Broadcasting Company, 1968; G. F. Burkhouse to Leonard Spillane, October 12, 1972, University of Michigan Housing Division Records, box 7, BHL.

63. Georgia Williams to John Feldkamp, August 28, 1972, Vice President for Academic Affairs, Central Files, box 47, folder: Georgia Williams, 1972–73, BHL; John Feldkamp to Georgia Williams, Re: Appointment Status, September 1, 1972, Vice President for Academic Affairs, Central Files, box 47, folder: Georgia Williams, 1972–73 BHL; John Feldkamp to Georgia Williams, Re: Resignation, September 21, 1972, Vice President for Academic Affairs, Central Files, box 47, folder: Georgia Williams, 1972–73, BHL.

64. Marilyn Riley, "VP's Top Priority Is Minorities," *Michigan Daily*, August 22, 1972, 3.

65. Henry Johnson, "Black Students at White Institutions: Coping with Conflicts," March 26, 1974, Assistant to the President Records, box 38, BHL.

66. Sue Sommer, "'U' Short of 10% Black Enrollment Goal," *Michigan Daily*, April 7, 1973, 1.

67. Sommer, "'U' Short of 10% Black Enrollment Goal"; Cindy Hill, "'U' Projects Failure to Meet 10 Per cent Black Enrollment," *Michigan Daily*, April 20, 1973, 1.

68. Hill, "'U' Projects Failure to Meet 10 Per cent Black Enrollment," 1.

69. Sommer, "'U' Short of 10% Black Enrollment Goal," 1; Hill, "'U' Projects Failure to Meet 10 Per cent Black Enrollment," 1.

70. Rebecca Warner, "Fleming Says Black Enrollment Not Eroding Academic Standards," *Michigan Daily*, November 6, 1973, 1.

71. Ruth Eckstein, "The State of the Opportunity Undergraduate Enrollment, Fall 1972," November 17, 1972, Provost and Executive Vice President for Academic Affairs, Staff Files, box 50, folder: Opportunity Program: Enrollment of Minority Students, 1969–73, BHL.

72. President Fleming to W. L. Cash and Jack Hamilton, Subject: Black Student Enrollment, December 13, 1972, Provost and Executive Vice President for Academic Affairs, Staff Files, box 50, folder: Opportunity Program: Enrollment of Minority Students, 1969–73, BHL; "Attrition Rate: Some Underlying Causes Affecting Michigan Opportunity Students," Vice President for Government Relations Records, box 16, folder: Minorities 1973, BHL.

73. LSA Minority Student Attrition Study, April 8, 1973, Thomas A. Butts Papers, box 1, folder: OFA, Student Loan Programs, Minority Projections since BAM (Black Action Movement, 1972–1973), BHL.

74. Della Dipietro, "Black Enrollment at 7.3%," *Michigan Daily*, December 11, 1973, 1.

75. Office of the President, Untitled, April 3, 1970, Provost and Executive Vice President for Academic Affairs, Supplemental Files, box 2, folder: BAM General, 1969–70, BHL; The University as a Racist Institution, 1970, Provost and Executive Vice President for Academic Affairs, Supplemental Files, box 2, folder: BAM [Demands], 1969–70, BHL.

76. Interview with Bernice Sandler, July 1, 2001, Women's Activism Against Sex Discrimination: The 1970 HEW Investigation of the University of Michigan Records, box 1, folder: Women's Activism Against Sex Discrimination: The 1970 HEW Investigation of the University of Michigan-Administrative Files, 2001, Interview Transcripts-Bernice Sandler, BHL.

77. Interview with Bernice Sadler; R. W. Fleming to Don F. Scott, November 3, 1970, in Eric A. Stein, "Women's Activism Against Sex Discrimination: The 1970 HEW Investigation of the University of Michigan," Institute for Research on Women and Gender Working Paper Series, Working Paper #63, January 24, 2002, Women's Activism Against Sex Discrimination: The 1970 HEW Investigation of the University of Michigan Records, box 1; R. W. Fleming to Don F. Scott, November 3, 1970, in Eric A. Stein, "Women's Activism Against Sex Discrimination: The 1970 HEW Investigation of the University of Michigan," Institute for Research on Women and Gender Working Paper Series, Working Paper #63, January 24, 2002, Women's Activism

Against Sex Discrimination: The 1970 HEW Investigation of the University of Michigan Records, box 1; Lynn Weiner, "HEW Accepts 'U' Proposals to End Sex Bias in Employment," *Michigan Daily*, January 6, 1971, 1.

78. News and Information Services, for Release After Regents Meeting Friday, September 15, 1972, News and Information Services, Faculty and Staff Files, box 132, folder: Varner, Nellie Mae (folder 1), BHL.

79. Affirmative Action Progress Report, April 1, 1974–March 31, 1975, Affirmative Action Office, Publications 1973–1995, box 1, folder: Affirmative Action Program Printed Reports, Affirmative Action Program, 1974–1975, BHL.

80. Sara Rimer, "'U' Keeps Mum on LSA Deanship," *Michigan Daily*, January 21, 1975, 1; "Billy E. Frye," *University of Michigan Faculty History Project*, https://www.lib.umich.edu/faculty-history/faculty/billy-e-frye/accepts-post-emory-university.

81. "Report on the Cobb Affair: LSA Deanship Probed," *Michigan Daily*, May 15, 1975, 6.

82. Sara Rimer, "Search for LSA Dean Set," *Michigan Daily*, May 7, 1975, 1; University Steering Committee on the Development of Academic Opportunities, Racial Origin Survey, January 1967, Housing Division Records, box 1, folder: Academic Opportunities (Minorities), BHL; John M. Allen to Professor Norman R. Scott, November 7, 1966, Housing Division Records, box 1, folder: Academic Opportunities (Minorities), BHL; "Billy E. Frye," *University of Michigan Faculty History Project*, https://www.lib.umich.edu/faculty-history/faculty/billy-e-frye/accepts-post-emory-university.

83. Robben W. Fleming, interview by Enid H. Galler, Fall 1992, transcript, History and Traditions of the University Committee, box 1, folder: Robben Fleming, BHL; Judy Ruskin, Dan Biddle, and Sara Rimer, "Fleming Hedges on Tenure Issue," *Michigan Daily*, February 4, 1975, 1.

84. "Cobb Chronology: Candor Lost," *Michigan Daily*, February 18, 1975, 4; Wini Warren, "Jewel Plummer Cobb," *Black Women Scientists in the United States* (Bloomington: Indiana University Press, 1999), http://www.csun.edu/~ghe59995/MSE302/2-2%20Jewel%20Cobb.pdf.

85. Sara Rimer, Dan Biddle, and Judy Ruskin, "Initial Cobb Offer Sparks Uproar," *Michigan Daily*, January 29, 1975, 1.

86. Sara Rimer, "200 Protest Offer to Cobb," *Michigan Daily*, January 31, 1975, 1.

87. Sara Rimer and Dan Biddle, "Cobb Rejects Initial 2-Year, No-Tenure Deanship Offer; Regents Meet Again," *Michigan Daily*, January 28, 1975, 1; Rimer, "200 Protest Offer to Cobb."

88. "Cobb Chronology: Candor Lost," *Michigan Daily*, February 18, 1975, 4; "Report on the Cobb Affair: LSA Deanship Probed," *Michigan Daily*, May 15, 1975, 6; Ann Marie Lipinksi and Ken Parsigian, "Cobb Not among 10 Dean Finalists," *Michigan Daily*, February 4, 1976, 1.

89. "Report on the Cobb Affair: LSA Deanship Probed," *Michigan Daily*, May 15, 1975, 6; Dan Biddle and Sara Rimer, "'U' Blasts Cobb Report," *Michigan Daily*, May 17, 1975, 1.

90. News and Information Services, Release On Receipt, February 24, 1976, News and Information Services, Faculty and Staff Files, box 132, folder: Varner, Nellie Mae (folder 2), BHL; R. W. Fleming to Executive Officers, Subject: Reorganization of

Affirmative Action Programs, March 16, 1976, Provost and Executive Vice President for Academic Affairs, Staff Files, box 60, folder: Robert B. Holmes, Topical Files: Affirmative Action Office: General Correspondence, March 1976–April 1977, BHL.

91. Ruth Eckstein, Black Opportunity Undergraduates at the University of Michigan, 1964–1970: A Retrospective View, August 15, 1971, Provost and Executive Vice President for Academic Affairs, Staff Files, box 50, folder: Black Opportunity Undergraduates at the University of Michigan, 1964–1970, BHL; "A Proposal for Presentation to the Regents of the University of Michigan concerning the University's Obligation to the American Indian," May 5, 1971, Vice President for Government Relations Records, box 16, folder: Minorities, 1971, BHL; Compliance Report of Institutions of Higher Education, Fall 1968, Assistant to the President Records, box 39, folder: Compliance Reports, 67–69, BHL; Ruth Eckstein, Black Opportunity Undergraduates at the University of Michigan, 1964–1970: A Retrospective View, August 15, 1971, Provost and Executive Vice President for Academic Affairs, Staff Files, box 50, folder: Black Opportunity Undergraduates at the University of Michigan, 1964–1970, BHL; "A Proposal for Presentation to the Regents of the University of Michigan concerning the University's Obligation to the American Indian."

92. Raymond Padilla, interview with author, 2012; Robert Kraftowitz, "Regents Act on Demands," *Michigan Daily*, April 2, 1970, 1.

93. Raymond Padilla, LA RAZA and the University of Michigan Opportunity Program: An Evaluation, August 14, 1970, Provost and Executive Vice President for Academic Affairs, Staff Files, box 50, folder: Opportunity Program Committee, 1969–72, BHL; The State of Opportunity Undergraduate Enrollment, Fall 1972, Provost and Executive Vice President of Academic Affairs, Staff Files, box 50, folder: Opportunity Program: Enrollment of University Students, 1969–1973, BHL; Thomas A. Butts to FADs (Financial Aid Officers, Analysts and Directors), Re: United Migrants for Opportunity Incorporated (UMOI), June 13, 1974, Office of Financial Aid Records, box 4, folder: Policies-Opportunity Students-General, 1971–82, BHL; Compliance Report of Institutions of Higher Education under Title VI of the Civil Rights Act of 1964, Fall 1970, Assistant to the President Records, box 39, folder: Compliance Reports 70–71, BHL; Compliance Report of Institutions of Higher Education under Title VI of the Civil Rights Act of 1964 and Title IX of the Education Amendments of 1972 Student Enrollment Survey, Fall 1974, Assistant to the President Records, box 39, folder: Compliance Reports 72–80, BHL.

94. Compliance Report of Institutions of Higher Education under Title VI of the Civil Rights Act of 1964, Fall 1970, Assistant to the President Records, box 39, folder: Compliance Reports 70–71, BHL; Jim Irwin, "Indians Threaten U with Suit," *Michigan Daily*, July 30, 1971, 1.

95. "A Proposal for Presentation to the Regents of the University of Michigan concerning the University's Obligation to the American Indian."

96. Irwin, "Indians Threaten U with Suit"; P. E. Bauer and Chris Parks, "Indians File Suit Against U on Treaty," *Michigan Daily*, August 7, 1971, 1; Foot of the Rapids (Fort Meigs), 1817, Clarke County Historical Library, https://www.cmich.edu/library/clarke/ResearchResources/Native_American_Material/Treaty_Rights/Text_of_Michigan_Related_Treaties/Pages/Foot-of-the-Rapids-(Fort-Meigs),-1817.aspx.

97. Thomas Butts recounts Daane's strategy in the following: Thomas A. Butts to Roderick K. Daane, Re: Free Tuition for North American Indian Students, September

17, 1976, Provost and Executive Vice President for Academic Affairs, Staff Files, box 62, folder: Robert B. Holmes, Topical Files: Financial Aid, Native Americans, July 1976–July 1979, BHL; Thomas A. Butts to Richard A. English, Re: HB4130, Free Tuition for American Indians, August 19, 1976, Provost and Executive Vice President for Academic Affairs, Staff Files, box 62, folder: Robert B. Holmes, Topical Files: Financial Aid, Native Americans, July 1976–July 1979, BHL; Rene Becker, 'U' Challenges Indians in Court, Michigan Daily Sep, 1978, 1; *Children of the Chippewa, Ottawa, and Potawatomy Tribes v. Regents of the University of Michigan*, 305 N.W. 2d 522 (Mich. App. 1981); Allan F. Smith to Dr. Ernest R. Zimmerman, August 18, 1971, Assistant to the President Records, box 38, folder: American Indian, BHL.

98. Compliance Report of Institutions of Higher Education, Fall 1968, Assistant to the President Records, box 39, folder: Compliance Reports, 67–69, BHL; Compliance Report of Institutions of Higher Education under Title VI of the Civil Rights Act of 1964, Fall 1970, Assistant to the President Records, box 39, folder: Compliance Reports 70–71, BHL; Compliance Report of Institutions of Higher Education under Title VI of the Civil Rights Act of 1964 and Title IX of the Education Amendments of 1972 Student Enrollment Survey, Fall 1974, Assistant to the President Records, box 39, folder: Compliance Reports 72–80, BHL.

99. Peter S. Xenos, Robert W. Gardner, Herbert R. Barringer, and Michael J. Levin, "Asian Americans: Growth and Change in the 1970s," special issue, *Center for Migration Studies* 5, no. 3 (May 1987): 253; Minutes of Opportunity Program Committee, January 30, 1974, Office of Financial Aid Records, box 4, folder: Policies-Opportunity Students-General, 1971–82, BHL.

100. Proposal for an Asian American Advocate, Vice President for Student Affairs Records, box 14, folder: H Johnson, 1977–1978 Annual File, Asian Americans, 1974–1976, BHL.

101. Ellen D. Wu, *The Color of Success: Asian Americans and the Origins of the Model Minority* (Princeton, NJ: Princeton University Press, 2014), 2; Proposal for an Asian American Advocate, Vice President for Student Affairs Records, box 14, folder: H Johnson, 1977–1978 Annual File, Asian Americans, 1974–1976, BHL; Confidential Memorandum for the President (Amended), 1944, International Center Records, box 2, folder: Minutes Committee on Intercultural Relations, 1943–1945, BHL; Laura M. Calkins, "The Origins of the Modern Multiversity at Michigan: Politics and Discourses on Race, Religion, and Gender, 1940–52," Laura Calkins Papers, box 1, folder: Reports and Articles, BHL; Applications from Japanese American students in internment camps can be found in Ira M. Smith Papers, box 3, folder: Papers 1941–42 concerning Admission of Japanese American Students, BHL.

102. Enrollment of Non-Citizen Students Fall Term 1970–71 as Compared with 1969–70, International Center Records, box 19, folder: International Center-printed Statistics, Enrollment of Non-citizen Students, 1965–1970, BHL; Proposal for an Asian American Advocate, Vice President for Student Affairs Records, box 14, folder: H Johnson, 1977–1978 Annual File, Asian Americans, 1974–1976, BHL.

103. Cheryl Pilate, "Asian Discrimination: Activist Battles for Rights," *Michigan Daily*, February 24, 1974, 1; Proposal for an Asian American Advocate, Vice President for Student Affairs Records, box 14, folder: H Johnson, 1977–1978 Annual File, Asian Americans, 1974–1976, BHL.

104. "'75 BAM' Demands," *Michigan Daily*, February 19, 1975, 8.

105. "'75 BAM' Demands."

106. "'75 BAM' Demands."

107. Bob Meachum, "Students End Ad. Bldg. Sit-In," *Michigan Daily*, February 21, 1975, 1.

108. Gordon Atcheson, "Tranquil Mood Pervades Takeover," *Michigan Daily*, February 19, 1975, 1.

109. David Weinberg, "Sit-in '75: Ain't the Old Days," *Michigan Daily*, February 27, 1975, 7.

110. Weinberg, "Sit-in '75."

## 5. Affirmative Action for Whom?

1. The University of Michigan Fall 1976 Minority Enrollment Report, December 1976, Provost and Executive Vice President for Academic Affairs, Supplemental Files, box 1, folder: 1976, Minority Enrollment Report, BHL; The University of Michigan Ann Arbor, Enrollments in Degree Credit Programs by Racial/Ethnic Category, Fall 1985–1975, Provost and Executive Vice President for Academic Affairs, Staff Files, box 187, folder: VPAA-OMA-Enrollment, Comparative 1985–1986, BHL.

2. Cliff Sjogren Résumé, Spring 1974, News and Information Services University of Michigan Faculty and Staff Files, box 119, folder: Sjogren, Clifford F., BHL; Clyde Vroman took the position in 1949: James P. Adams to Ira M. Smith and Clyde Vroman, September 1, 1949, Ira M. Smith Papers, box 4, folder: Correspondence of Clyde Vroman, 1949–1950, BHL; News and Information Services, Release on Receipt, March 26, 1973, News and Information Services, Faculty and Staff Files, box 50, folder: Goodman, George D., BHL.

3. George Goodman, phone interview by author, February 15, 2011. I use "resistance" rather than "backlash" because the term "backlash" is often tied to a specific genre of scholarship in the 1980s and 1990s that sometimes focused too closely on violent resistance and usually avoided investigating how whites' views of race intertwined with other issues. Still, as this scholarship has evolved, it still focuses on whites who undermined the activism and victories of the civil rights movement. Most often, it focuses on whites who resisted by protesting, moving outside cities, filing lawsuits, and sometimes using violence. That's why I refer to this scholarship together as work on resistance. Some examples of scholarship on resistance include Dan T. Carter, *The Politics of Rage: George Wallace, the Origins of the New Conservatism, and the Transformation of American Politics* (Baton Rouge: Louisiana State University Press, 1995); Kevin Kruse, *White Flight: Atlanta and the Making of Modern Conservatism* (Princeton, NJ: Princeton University Press, 2007); Arnold R. Hirsch, *Making the Second Ghetto: Race and Housing in Chicago, 1940–1960* (Cambridge: Cambridge University Press, 1983); Thomas Sugrue, *The Origins of the Urban Crisis: Race and Inequality in Postwar Detroit* (Princeton, NJ: Princeton University Press, 1996); Jonathan Rieder, *Canarsie: The Jews and Italians of Brooklyn against Liberalism* (Cambridge, MA: Harvard University Press, 1985); Ronald P. Formisano, *Boston against Busing: Race, Class, and Ethnicity in the 1960s and 1970s* (Chapel Hill: University of North Carolina Press, 1991); Dennis Deslippe, *Protesting Affirmative Action: The Struggle over Equality after the Civil Rights Revolution* (Baltimore: Johns Hopkins University Press, 2012).

4. George Goodman, phone interview by author, February 15, 2011; Cliff Sjogren, phone interview by author, August 15, 2010.

5. Committee on Admissions Report, December 4, 1967, L.S.&A. Faculty Minutes, 1967–68, College of Literature, Science and the Arts Records, box 208, BHL; Lance Erickson, "A Discussion of the Current LSA Admissions Situation," January 21, 1975, LSA, box 237, folder: Admissions, Office of 1974–75, BHL; Proposed Minutes of the November 7, 1977, Faculty Meeting, L.S.A. Fac. Min., 1977–78, College of Literature, Science and the Arts Records, box 208, BHL; Freshman Admissions Count for Fall Term 1969, January 16, 1969, Provost and Executive Vice President for Academic Affairs, Central Files, box 13, folder Admissions Office, Statistics, BHL.

6. Cliff Sjogren to Richard English, "Item: Comments on Dave Robinson's 'Summary Report on Current Admissions Office Effort for Minority Student Recruitment,'" January 5, 1978, Provost and Executive VP for Academic Affairs, Staff Files, box 64, folder: Robert B. Holmes: Topical Files: Minority Enrollment: Reports (correspondence) (includes notes and tables), Jan.–Dec. 1978; Andrew Wiese, *Places of Their Own: African American Suburbanization in the Twentieth Century* (Chicago: University of Chicago Press, 2004), 5, 255, 232–33.

7. Cliff Sjogren to Richard English, January 5, 1978.

8. G. D. Goodman and P. Wilson-Crawford, Proposal for Change in the University of Michigan's Opportunity Program, March 16, 1976, Office of Financial Aid Records, box 4, folder: Policies-Opportunity Students-General, 1971–83, BHL; Goodman and Wilson-Crawford, Proposal for Change in the University of Michigan's Opportunity Program; Goodman, phone interview by author.

9. Richard A. English to Frank H.T. Rhodes, December 9, 1976, Provost and Executive Vice President for Academic Affairs, Staff Files, box 65, folder: Robert B. Holmes, Topical Files: Registrar's Office: Racial Ethnic Information, Aug. 1976–June 1978, BHL.

10. Nili Tannenbaum, "Building Diversity in Leadership: The Joint Doctoral Program in Social Work and Social Science," UM School of Social Work website, August 5, 2002, https://ssw.umich.edu/stories/48880-building-diversity-in-leadership -the-joint-doctoral-program-in-social-work-and-social-science.

11. Richard A. English, "Trends in Undergraduate Enrollment Quality Indicators, and Financial Support," October 18, 1976, Provost and Executive Vice President for Academic Affairs, Staff Files, box 44, folder: Scholarships-Merit vs. Need issue, 1976–77, BHL.

12. Harris D. Olson to William L. Cash and Richard A. English, Re: Degrees by Racial/Ethnic Group and Level, September 10, 1976, Vice President of Student Affairs, box 29, folder: VPSA Topical Files, Minority Affairs, Office of-General, BHL.

13. Richard A. English to Frank H. T. Rhodes.

14. George Goodman, "Proposed New Directions for the Opportunity Program," November 1975, Vice President of Academic Affairs, Staff Files, box 60, BHL.

15. Cliff Sjogren to Richard English, January 5, 1978.

16. "U Short of 10% Black Enrollment," *Michigan Daily*, April 7, 1973, 1; Ruth Eckstein, "The State of the Opportunity Undergraduate Enrollment, Fall 1972," November 17, 1972, Provost and Executive Vice President for Academic Affairs, Staff Files, box 50, folder: Opportunity Program: Enrollment of Minority Students, 1969–73,

BHL; LSA Minority Student Attrition Study, April 8, 1973, Thomas A. Butts Papers, box 1, folder: OFA, Student Loan Programs, Minority Projections since BAM (Black Action Movement, 1972–1973), BHL; Outline of Discussion with Regents on Attrition of Minority Undergraduate Students, Provost and Executive Vice President for Academic Affairs, Staff Files, box 65, folder: Robert B. Holmes, Topical Files: Minority Reports: Miscellaneous U. of M. Reports and Memos (includes notes), June 1975–March 1980, BHL.

17. Cliff Sjogren to Richard English, Re: Grand Rapids Adjunct Office, June 9, 1976, Provost and Executive Vice President for Academic Affairs, Staff Files, box 60, folder: Robert B. Holmes, Topical Files: Admissions Office: General Correspondence, Jan. 1976–July 1977, BHL.

18. Sjogren, phone interview with author. I searched through all the LSA meeting minutes, correspondence between the admissions office and other officials available in the archives, and the student newspaper to make this conclusion.

19. Proposed Minutes of the January 7, 1974, Faculty Meeting, L.S.A. Fac. Min., 1973–74, College of Literature, Science and the Arts Records, box 208, BHL; Proposed Minutes of the April 14, 1975, Faculty Meeting, L.S.A. Fac. Min., 1975–76, College of Literature, Science and the Arts Records, box 208, BHL; Proposed Minutes of the September 13, 1976, Faculty Meeting, L.S.A. Fac. Min., 1976–77, College of Literature, Science and the Arts Records, box 208, BHL.

20. Thomas A. Butts to David Aminoff, Re: Scholarships, March 15, 1977, Provost and Executive Vice President for Academic Affairs, Staff Files, box 44, folder: Scholarships-Merit vs. Need issue, 1976–77, BHL.

21. Pat Wilson, "Changes in Admissions Guidelines for Opportunity Program Applicants," September 22, 1975, Provost and Executive Vice President of Academic Affairs, Staff Files, box 60, folder: Robert B. Holmes, Topical Files: Admissions Office: Opportunity Program Office Changes, Sept. 1975–July 1979 and undated, BHL.

22. Proposed Minutes of the January 7, 1974, Faculty Meeting; Minutes of the April 14, 1975, Faculty Meeting; Proposed Minutes of the September 13, 1976, Faculty Meeting.

23. Adon Gordus, "Some Projections and Problems for the Future," L.S.A. Fac. Min., 1975–76, College of Literature, Science and the Arts Records, box 208, BHL.

24. For an excellent overview of the austerity politics of the 1970s, see Kim Phillips-Fein, *Fear City: New York's Fiscal Crisis and the Rise of Austerity Politics* (New York: Metropolitan Books, 2017); *The President's Report to the Board of Regents for 1974/1975*, vol. 2 (Ann Arbor: University of Michigan, 1975), 3; "September Meeting, 1975," *Proceedings of the Board of Regents*, 58; University of Michigan Ann Arbor General Fund Budget vs. Expense Report, 1975–76, President Records, box 97, folder: Budgets, 1975–76, BHL; Ellen Berrey, *The Enigma of Diversity: The Language of Race and the Limits of Racial Justice* (Chicago: University of Chicago Press, 2015), 63.

25. Proposed Minutes of the January 7, 1974, Faculty Meeting; Jim Danzinger, "Freshperson SAT Marks Drop," *Michigan Daily*, August 7, 1976, 5; "Release on Receipt," November 20, 1975, Provost and Vice President for Academic Affairs, Supplemental Files, box 1, folder: 1975 Enrollment Report, BHL; Lance Erickson, "A Discussion of the Current LSA Admissions Situation," January 21, 1975, LSA, box 237, folder: Admissions, Office of 1974–75, BHL.

26. Sjogren, phone interview with author.

27. William M. Bulkeley, "Learning Frugality," *Wall Street Journal*, May 31, 1977, 1.

28. Joyce A. Baugh, *The Detroit School Busing Case:* Miliken v. Bradley *and the Controversy over Desegregation* (Lawrence: University of Kansas Press, 2011); Paul A. Sracic, San Antonio v. Rodriguez *and the Pursuit of Equal Education: The Debate over Discrimination and School Funding* (Lawrence: University of Kansas Press, 2006).

29. Baugh, *Detroit School Busing Case.*

30. Paul A. Sracic, San Antonio v. Rodriguez *and the Pursuit of Equal Education.*

31. Jeffrey Mirel, *The Rise and Fall of an Urban School System: Detroit, 1907–81* (Ann Arbor: University of Michigan Press, 1993), 353; Bulkeley, "Learning Frugality." By 1978, Sjogren was placing more emphasis on advanced placement courses: Proposed Minutes of the November 6, 1978 Faculty Meeting, L.S.A. Fac. Min., 1978–79, College of Literature, Science and the Arts Records, box 208, BHL.

32. Julilly Kohler-Hausmann, *Getting Tough: Welfare and Imprisonment in 1970s America* (Princeton, NJ: Princeton University Press, 2017), 6.

33. "'Small Scale Riot' in Detroit Brings Curfew on Youth," *Washington Post*, August 18, 1976, A20; Charles A. Krause, "Motor City Fighting for Its Life Again," *Washington Post*, August 23, 1976, A1; William Grant and Billy Bowles, "Schools Learn to Live with Violence," *Detroit Free Press*, September 30, 1976, 1A, 12A.

34. William Serrin, "Detroit: A Midsummer's Nightmare," *New York Times*, August 25, 1976, 29.

35. Heather Ann Thompson, *Whose Detroit? Politics, Labor, and Race in a Modern American City* (Ithaca, NY: Cornell University Press, 2001).

36. Recall the backlash to William Haber's statement about changing the character of the institution during the BAM strike in chapter 3.

37. Sjogren, phone interview by author.

38. Proposed Meeting Minutes of the April 14, 1975, Faculty Meeting of the College of Literature, Science, and the Arts, Carl Cohen, Remarks before the University of Michigan Senate Assembly, November 15, 1976, *L.S.A. Fac. Min., 1975–76*, College of Literature, Science and the Arts Records, box 208; Provost and Executive Vice President for Academic Affairs, Staff Files, box 62, folder: Robert B. Holmes, Topical Files: Financial Aid, Merit Scholarships, February 1976–June 1978, BHL.

39. Examples of Cohen's comments on improving the quality of the student body include Proposed Minutes of the December 3, 1973, Faculty Meeting of the College of Literature, Science, and the Arts, *L.S.A. Fac. Min., 1973–74*, College of Literature, Science and the Arts Records, box 208, BHL; Proposed Meeting Minutes of the April 14, 1975, Faculty Meeting of the College of Literature, Science, and the Arts, Carl Cohen, Remarks before the University of Michigan Senate Assembly, November 15, 1976, *L.S.A. Fac. Min., 1975–76*, College of Literature, Science and the Arts Records, box 208; Proposed Minutes of the October 6, 1975, Faculty Meeting, *L.S.A. Fac. Min., 1975–76*, College of Literature, Science and the Arts Records, box 208, BHL; Proposed Minutes of the September 13, 1976, Faculty Meeting of Literature, Science, and the Arts, *L.S.A. Fac. Min., 1976–77*, College of Literature, Science and the Arts Records, box 208, BHL.

40. Reynold H. Colvin to Carl Cohen, May 10, 1977, Carl Cohen Papers, box 46, folder: Bakke Correspondence, Miscellaneous, BHL; Carl Cohen to Reynold H. Colvin, June 1, 1977, Carl Cohen Papers, box 46, folder: Bakke Correspondence, Miscellaneous, BHL; Carl Cohen to Terry, June 30, 1977, Carl Cohen Papers, box 46, folder:

Bakke Correspondence, Miscellaneous, BHL; John Bennett to Carl Cohen, November 15, 1977, Carl Cohen Papers, box 46, folder: Bakke Correspondence, Miscellaneous, BHL; Terry H. Anderson, *The Pursuit of Fairness: A History of Affirmative action* (New York: Oxford University Press, 2004), 151.

41. Regents of the University of California v. Bakke, 438 U.S. 265 (1978).

42. Rene Becker, "'U' Says Programs Safe," *Michigan Daily*, June 29, 1978, 1. The analyses of the case that administrators collected made no suggestion that universities needed to emphasize the educational benefits of diversity in order to comply with *Bakke*: "Responding to the *Bakke* Decision," June 29, 1978, VP for Academic Affairs, Central Files, box 100, folder: Bakke (re: alleged discrimination at UC-Davis in admissions) (2011, doc. 56, p. 23); *Professional Education after Bakke: A Report on Eleven Post-Bakke Policy Conferences of High-Demand Academic Programs* (American Council of Education, 1979).

43. Lance Erickson to Counselors, Supervisors, and Secretaries, Re: Guidelines for Minority and Opportunity Recruitment Policies and Procedures, September 6, 1979, Provost and Executive Vice President for Academic Affairs, Staff Files, box 60, folder: Robert B. Holmes, Topical Files: Admissions Office: General Correspondence, July 1979–July 1980, BHL.

44. "Who Won?" *New York Times*, June 29, 1978, A24.

45. Thomas J. Kane, "College Entry by Blacks since 1970: The Role of College Costs, Family Background, and the Returns of Education," *Journal of Political Economy* 102, no. 5 (1994): 878–82.

46. The University of Michigan Ann Arbor Undergraduate Enrollment in Degree Credit Programs by Racial/Ethnic Category and Unit, Fall 1983–Fall 1975, Provost and Executive Vice President for Academic Affairs, Staff Files, box 187, folder: VPAA-OMA-Enrollment, comparative (for years 1971–1984), BHL.

47. George D. Goodman, Minority Enrollment Report, Ann Arbor Campus, 1974, Vice President for Government Relations Records, box 16, folder: Minorities 1974, BHL; Applications, Admissions Offers and New Enrollment for the Ann Arbor Campus, Fall 1978 through 1982, Provost and Executive Vice President for Academic Affairs, Staff Files, box 108, folder: Minority Enrollment, 1983–84, BHL; The University of Michigan Ann Arbor Undergraduate Enrollment in Degree Credit Programs by Racial/Ethnic Category and Unit, Fall 1983–Fall 1975, Provost and Executive Vice President for Academic Affairs, Staff Files, box 187, folder: VPAA-OMA-Enrollment, comparative (for years 1971–1984), BHL.

48. Evaluative Reports of Special Recruiting Activities, 1979–1980. Office of Undergraduate Admissions, box 3, folder: Evaluative Reports of Special Recruiting Activities, 1979–80, BHL.

49. David Robinson to Richard English, Re: Minority Students Selected for Academic Recognition Scholarship Program, April 14, 1977, Provost and Executive Vice President for Academic Affairs, Staff Files, box 60, folder: Robert B. Holmes, Topical Files: Admissions Office: General Correspondence, Jan. 1976–July 1977, BHL; William L. Grothe to Richard English, Re: Interim Report on Selections for the Academic Recognition Scholarship (ARS) Program, the Regents-Alumni Scholarship Program (RAS), and the Michigan Annual Giving (MAG) Program, March 13, 1979, Provost and Executive VP for Academic Affairs, Staff Files, box 62, Robert Holmes: Topical Files:

Financial Aid: Native Americans (includes notes, tables, and graphs), July 1976–July 1979 and undated, BHL.

50. David Robinson, Cancellation Survey of Midwest Black Students Admitted to the University of Michigan for Fall Term, 1984, September, 19, 1984, Vice President for Academic Affairs, Staff Files, box 102, BHL.

51. Carla Rapoport, "Black Enrollment Swells," *Michigan Daily*, December 2, 1971, 1; Ruth Eckstein, "Entry Characteristics of New Freshmen, Fall 1976–1978," July 1978, Vice President for Academic Affairs, Staff Files, box 63, folder: Robert B. Holmes, Topical Files: Minority Enrollment: Ruth Eckstein (includes notes and reports), Dec. 1975–Sept. 1980 and undated, BHL.

52. Edward P. St. John and Eric H. Asker, *Refinancing the College Dream: Access, Equal Opportunity, and Justice for Taxpayers* (Baltimore: Johns Hopkins University Press, 2003), 18–22, 80.

53. Office of Financial Aid, "Report on Minority Student Recruitment and Retention," January 1982, Provost and Executive Vice President of Academic Affairs, Staff Files, box 108, BHL; Niara Sudarkasa, Undergraduate Minority Enrollment: Policy Issues and Recommendations Related to Recruitment and Financial aid, October 1984, Office of Financial Aid Records, box 3, folder: Policies-Minority Student Programs-Recruitment and Retention, 1982–86. I used the inflation calculator on the Bureau of Labor Statistics website to determine inflation: http://www.bls.gov/data/inflation_calculator.htm.

54. Office of Financial Aid, "Report on Minority Student Recruitment and Retention"; United States Department of Labor, Bureau of Labor Statistics, http://www.bls .gov/data/inflation_calculator.htm.

55. Cliff Sjogren to Robert B. Holmes, September 22, 1983, Provost and Executive Vice President for Academic Affairs, Staff Files, box 102, folder: VPAA Staff-Holmes-Admissions-General-1983/84 (2), BHL.

## 6. Sustaining Racial Retrenchment

1. Pam Gordon, "University Budget Speech," Vice President for Government Relations Records, 1979, box 16, folder: Minorities-1979, BHL; Susan R. Pollack, "Colleges Grapple with Lag in Minority Enrollment," *Detroit News*, February 18, 1979, Provost and Executive Vice President for Academic Affairs, Supplemental Files, box 1, folder: Minority Enrollment, Fall 1978, BHL.

2. Gordon, "University Budget Speech,"

3. Gordon, "University Budget Speech."

4. Black Student Union Presentation, April 19, 1979, Eugene Feingold Papers, box 3, folder: UM Minority Concerns: Minority Student Concerns Task Force-Correspondence, 1979–1981, BHL.

5. Harold T. Shapiro to President Allan F. Smith, May 29, 1979, Subject: Regent Waters Resolution of April 19, 1979, Vice President for Government Relations Records, box 16, folder: Minorities-1979; Report of the Task Force on Minority Student Concerns, March 1981 (revised), Provost and Executive Vice President for Academic Affairs, Staff Files, box 108, folder: VPAA Staff-Holmes-Topical-Minority Enrollment, 1981/2 (1), BHL.

6. George D. Goodman to President Harold T. Shapiro, Re: Thoughts on Minority Enrollment, March 12, 1980, Provost and Executive Vice President for Academic

Affairs, Staff Files, box 65, folder: Robert B. Holmes, Topical Files: Minority Enrollment: Reports (correspondence) Jan.–May 1980, BHL.

7. Carl Cohen, "Racial Preference Is Dynamite," *Chronicle of Higher Education*,
May 2, 1977, 10, 40; Carl Cohen, "The DeFunis Case: Race & the Constitution," *Nation*,
February 8, 1975, 145.

8. George Goodman, "Black Students at U of M in the 1970's," February 13, 1980,
Tape 1, Center for Afroamerican and African Studies Records, box 28, BHL.

9. Steve Raphael, "Opportunity Knocks," *Detroit News Magazine*, June 22, 1980,
Provost and Executive Vice President for Academic Affairs, Staff Files, box 65, folder:
Robert B. Holmes, Topical Files: Minority Enrollment: Reports (correspondence)
Jan.–Sep. 1981, BHL.

10. Task Force on Minority Concerns Statement, Eugene Feingold Papers, box 3,
folder: UM Minority Concerns: Minority Student Concerns Task Force-Correspondence,
1979–1981, BHL.

11. Task Force on Minority Student Concerns Minutes, February 28, 1980, Eugene
Feingold Papers, box 3, folder: UM Minority Concerns: Minority Student Concerns
Task Force-Minutes, 1979–1980, BHL.

12. Cliff Sjogren and Lance Erickson to Vice President B. E. Frye, Subject: Minority
Student Enrollment, February 11, 1981, Provost and Executive Vice President for Aca-
demic Affairs, Staff Files, box 65, folder: Robert B. Holmes, Topical Files: Minority
Enrollment: Reports (correspondence) Jan.–Sep. 1981, BHL.

13. Task Force on Minority Student Concerns Minutes, February 28, 1980.

14. "Q. Harold Shapiro: What's Next for U-M?" *Detroit Free Press*, July 29, 1979, 1A.

15. "U-M Conference Will Explore Impact of BAM," *Ann Arbor News*, March 17,
1980, A4, CAAS box 2, folder: BAM Conferences and Scholarship, Decade after BAM
(1980), BHL.

16. Harold Shapiro, "Harold Shapiro's Address, U of M: A Decade after BAM,
Panel: The organization and significance of BAM," March 20, 1980, CAAS Records,
box 29, BHL.

17. Shapiro, "Harold Shapiro's Address, U of M."

18. Rene Becker, "'U' Says Programs Safe," *Michigan Daily*, June 29, 1978, 1; "Responding to the *Bakke* Decision," June 29, 1978, VP for Academic Affairs, Central
Files, box 100, folder: Bakke (re: alleged discrimination at UC-Davis in admissions),
BHL; *Professional Education after Bakke: A Report on Eleven Post-Bakke Policy Conferences
of High-Demand Academic Programs* (American Council of Education, 1979).

19. Shapiro, "Harold Shapiro's Address, U of M."

20. Shapiro, "Harold Shapiro's Address, U of M."

21. Shapiro, "Harold Shapiro's Address, U of M."

22. Shapiro, "Harold Shapiro's Address, U of M."

23. Cliff Sjogren to Richard English, "Item: Comments on Dave Robinson's 'Summary Report on Current Admissions Office Effort for Minority Student Recruitment,'" January 5, 1978, Provost and Executive VP for Academic Affairs, Staff Files,
box 64, folder: Robert B. Holmes: Topical Files: Minority Enrollment: Reports (correspondence) (includes notes and tables), Jan.–Dec. 1978, BHL; Minority Data,
1990, Minority Data, 1990, James J. Duderstadt Papers, box 4, folder: Speeches-Michigan
Mandate, Two Year Status Report, 1990, BHL.

24. Sean Jackson, "Panel Says 'U' Support for Minorities Must Increase," *Michigan Daily*, September 8, 1984, 1.

25. Shapiro, "Harold Shapiro's Address, U of M"; Harold Shapiro, "Inauguration Address: Critic and Servant; The Role of the University," April 14, 1980, http://um2017 .org/2017_Website/Shapiros_Inauguration_Address.html.

26. Shapiro, "Harold Shapiro's Address, U of M."

27. Shapiro, "Harold Shapiro's Address, U of M"; "Partners in Growth," *Michigan Alumnus*, May 1981, 9.

28. Shapiro, "Harold Shapiro's Address, U of M."

29. Report of the Task Force on Minority Concerns, March 1981 (revised), Provost and Executive Vice President for Academic Affairs, Staff Files, box 108, folder: VPAA Staff-Holmes-Topical-Minority Enrollment, 1981/2 (1), BHL.

30. Report of the Task Force on Minority Concerns, March 1981.

31. Report of the Task Force on Minority Concerns, March 1981.

32. Wiliam L. Grothe to Richard English, Re: Interim Report on Selections for the Academic Recognition Scholarship (ARS) Program, the Regents-Alumni Scholarship Program (RAS), and the Michigan Annual Giving (MAG) Program, March 13, 1979, Provost and Executive VP for Academic Affairs, Staff Files, box 62, Robert Holmes: Topical Files: Financial Aid: Native Americans, BHL; Robert Seltzer to Robert Holmes, Re: Recruiting and Enrolling Outstanding Minority Students, November 2, 1982, Provost and Executive Vice President for Academic Affairs, Staff Files, box 103, folder: Admissions: Adm Issues, 1983–1983 (2), BHL.

33. Elizabeth M. Hawthorne to Associate Dean Jack Walker, February 6, 1985, Provost and Executive Vice President for Academic Affairs, Staff Files, box 102, folder: VPAA-Staff-Holmes-Admissions-General-1984/85 (1), BHL.

34. Report of the Task Force on Undergraduate Student Aid, June 1984, President's Records, box 207, folder: Undergraduate Student Aid, Report of the Task Force on, 1984, BHL.

35. George Kovanis, "Sudarkasa Set to Challenge 'U,'" *Michigan Daily*, February 12, 1984, 2; "Dr. Niara Sudarkasa," Provost and Executive Vice President for Academic Affairs, Staff Files, box 65, folder: Sudarkasa, Niara, Personal: Background Materials, 1984–1986 and undated, BHL; Lincoln University Appoints First Woman President, September 29, 1986, Provost and Executive Vice President for Academic Affairs, Staff Files, box 65, folder: Sudarkasa, Niara, Personal: Background Materials, 1984–1986 and undated, BHL.

36. Lawes, "Black Student Union Making a Comeback," 1; Sharon Silbar, "Black Student Groups Tries to Revive Spirit of BAM," *Michigan Daily*, November 21, 1982, 1.

37. Niara Sudarkasa to Provost James J. Duderstadt, Re: Minority Student Recruitment and Retention: What Have We Accomplished? Where Do We Go from Here?, July 23, 1986, Provost and Executive Vice President for Academic Affairs, Staff Files, box 67, folder: Staff Files: Sudarkasa, N: Minority Issues Briefing Book 1987, BHL.

38. Niara Sudarkasa, U-M Steps Up Minority Recruitment, September 1984, Provost and Executive Vice President for Academic Affairs, Staff Files, box 65, folder: Sudarkasa, Niara, Personal: Appearance, Speeches, Articles, March 1985–April 1986 and undated, BHL.

39. Niara Sudarkasa, Admissions and Recruitment Activities, Discussion Paper on Undergraduate Minority Enrollment, the University of Michigan, October 1984, VP for Academic Affairs, Central Files, box 202, Minorities: Minority Student Recruitment and Retention Unit Task Force, BHL; Niara Sudarkasa to Mr. Carl Tidd, November 14, 1984, Provost and Executive Vice President of Academic Affairs, Staff Files, box 103, folder: VPAA-Staff-Holmes-Admissions-General-1984/85 (3), BHL; Niara Sudarkasa to Ron Aramaki, April 22, 1985, Provost and Executive Vice President for Academic Affairs, Staff Files, box 66, folder: Topical Files: Niara Sudarkasa: Council for Minority Concerns, April 1985, BHL.

40. Niara Sudarkasa, Admissions and Recruitment Activities, Discussion Paper on Undergraduate Minority Enrollment, the University of Michigan, October 1984, VP for Academic Affairs, Central Files, box 202, Minorities: Minority Student Recruitment and Retention Unit Task Force, BHL.

41. Niara Sudarkasa, Undergraduate Minority Enrollment: Issues and Recommendations Related to Recruitment and Financial Aid: Summary, March 1985, Provost and Executive Vice President for Academic Affairs, Staff Files, box 108, folder: VPAA-Staff-Holmes-Minority Enrollment-1984/85 (3), BHL; Niara Sudarkasa, Admissions and Recruitment Activities, Discussion Paper on Undergraduate Minority Enrollment, the University of Michigan, October 1984, VP for Academic Affairs, Central Files, box 202, Minorities: Minority Student Recruitment and Retention Unit Task Force, BHL; Warner V. Slack and Douglas Porter, "The Scholastic Aptitude Test: A Critical Appraisal," *Harvard Education Review* 50, no. 2 (1980): 170–72; Cliff Sjogren to Vice President B. E. Frye, Subject: Minority Student Enrollment, February 11, 1981, Provost and Executive VP for Academic Affairs, Staff Files, box 64, folder: Robert B. Holmes: Topical Files: Minority Enrollment: Reports Jan.–Sept. 1981, BHL.

42. Niara Sudarkasa, Admissions and Recruitment Activities, October 1984.

43. Notes for HTS Interview with *Detroit Free Press* from N. Sudarkasa, May 7, 1985, Provost and Executive Vice President for Academic Affairs, Staff Files, box 67, folder: Staff Files: Sudarkasa, N: Minority Issues Briefing Book 1987.

44. Blue Ribbon Commission Meeting Minutes, December 5, 1983, Provost and Executive Vice President for Academic Affairs, Staff Files, box 66, folder: Topical Files: Niara Sudarkasa: Admissions, Office of, March 1983–October 1986, BHL; Sean Jackson, "LSA's Inside Review," *Michigan Daily*, November 16, 1984, 3.

45. Bill Frye to Clifford F. Sjogren, July 15, 1982, Provost and Executive Vice President for Academic Affairs, Staff Files, box 102, folder: Admissions: General, 1982–1984 (2), BHL; Cliff Sjogren to Vice President B. E. Frye, Subject: Minority Student Enrollment, February 11, 1981, Provost and Executive VP for Academic Affairs, Staff Files, box 64, folder: Robert B. Holmes: Topical Files: Minority Enrollment: Reports Jan.–Sept. 1981, BHL; B. E. Frye to Clifford Sjogren and Lance Erickson, February 19, 1981, Provost and Executive VP for Academic Affairs, Staff Files, box 64, folder: Robert B. Holmes: Topical Files: Minority Enrollment: Reports Jan.–Sept. 1981, BHL; Bill Frye to Clifford F. Sjogren, July 15, 1982, Provost and Executive Vice President for Academic Affairs, Staff Files, box 102, folder: Admissions: General, 1982–1984 (2), BHL; Cliff Sjogren to Robert Holmes, May 31, 1983, Provost and Executive Vice Present for Academic Affairs, Staff Files, box 66, folder: Niara Sudarkasa Topical Files: Admissions, Office of, March 1983–Oct. 1986, BHL; Cliff Sjogren to Robert Holmes, June 7, 1983, Provost and Executive Vice Present for Academic Affairs, Staff Files, box

66, folder: Niara Sudarkasa Topical Files: Admissions, Office of, March 1983–Oct. 1986, BHL; Robert B. Holmes to Lance Erickson and Clifford Sjogren, March 24, 1983, Provost and Executive Vice President of Academic Affairs, Staff Files, box 103, folder: Admissions Issues, July 1982–June 83 (1), BHL.

46. Sjogren references Sudarkasa's criticism in Cliff Sjogren to Niara Sudarkasa, November 8, 1985, Provost and Executive Vice President of Academic Affairs, Staff Files, box 103, folder: VPAA-Staff-Holmes-Admissions-General-1985-1986 (1), BHL.

47. Cliff Sjogren to Niara Sudarkasa, November 8, 1985.

48. Niara Sudarkasa to Cliff Sjogren, November 12, 1985, Provost and Executive Vice President of Academic Affairs, Staff Files, box 103, folder: VPAA-Staff-Holmes-Admissions-General-1985-1986 (1), BHL.

49. Robert B. Holmes to Clifford Sjogren, December 17 1985, Provost and Executive Vice President of Academic Affairs, Staff Files, box 103, folder: VPAA-Staff-Holmes-Admissions-General-1985-1986 (3), BHL; Clifford Sjogren to Niara Sudarkasa, Draft, December 13, 1985, Provost and Executive Vice President of Academic Affairs, Staff Files, box 103, folder: VPAA-Staff-Holmes-Admissions-General-1985-1986 (3), BHL.

50. Billy E. Frye to Niara Sudarkasa, November 18, 1985, Provost and Executive Vice President for Academic Affairs, Staff Files, box 66, folder: Topical Files: Niara Sudarkasa: Admissions, Office of, March 1983–October 1986, BHL.

51. Notes for HTS Interview with Detroit Free Press from N. Sudarkasa, May 7, 1985; "At Michigan . . . Shapiro Talks about Effort to Reach Elusive 10% Black Enrollment Goal," 1B, 4B.

52. Niara Sudarkasa to B. E. Frye, November 26, 1985, Vice President for Academic Affairs, Central Files, box 202, folder: Minorities, BHL; Charles Kidd, Gilbert Maddox, Dave Wesley, and Frank Yates, "Black Administrators: Responsibility without Power," *Michigan Daily*, April 10, 1971, 4.

53. Walter R. Allen, Résumé, Summer 2004, http://www.unc.edu/edp/people/cv/pdf/allen.pdf.

54. Barry Beckham, ed., *The Black Student's Guide to Colleges* (New York: E.P. Dutton, 1982); Barry Beckham, ed., *The Black Student's Guide to Colleges*, 2nd ed. (Providence, RI: Beckham House 1984), 281–82; Veronica Woolridge, "University of Michigan," *New York Times*, April 5, 1985, Vice Provost for Multicultural Affairs, box 1, folder: Articles and Clippings, BHL; Eric Young, "Stanford University," *New York Times*, April 5, 1985, Vice Provost for Multicultural Affairs, box 1, folder: Articles and Clippings, BHL; Jeff Turner, "University of Georgia," *New York Times*, April 5, 1985, Vice Provost for Multicultural Affairs, box 1, folder: Articles and Clippings, BHL.

55. Bill Spindle, "Are Blacks on Campus Losing Out?" *Michigan Daily*, October 22, 1982, 1, 4, 5; "New Black Student Union," *Michigan Daily*, September 30, 1982, 4.

56. Niara Sudarkasa, Undergraduate Minority Enrollment: Issues and Recommendations Related to Recruitment and Financial Aid: Summary, March 1985, Provost and Executive Vice President of Academic Affairs, Staff Files, box 186, folder: VPAA-OMA-Admissions Task Force, 1986 (4), BHL.

57. Joel Thurtell, "Being Black at UM," *Detroit Free Press*, March 31, 1985, B1.

58. News and Information Services, 2nd Draft, April 3, 1985, Provost and Executive Vice President for Academic Affairs, Staff Files, box 66, folder: Topical Files: Niara Sudarkasa: *Detroit Free Press*, April–May 1985 and undated, BHL; Harold T. Shapiro to David Lawrence Jr., April 8, 1985, Provost and Executive Vice President for Academic

Affairs, Staff Files, box 66, folder: Topical Files: Niara Sudarkasa: *Detroit Free Press*, April–May 1985 and undated, BHL; Joel Thurtell, "Report of Bias Unfair, U-M Officials Charge," *Detroit Free Press*, April 7, 1985, 14A, Provost and Executive Vice President for Academic Affairs, Staff Files, box 66, folder: Topical Files: Niara Sudarkasa: *Detroit Free Press*, April–May 1985 and undated, BHL.

59. "U-M 'Insensitive' to Blacks, Lawyer Says," *Enquirer and News*, June 27, 1985, Provost and Executive Vice President for Academic Affairs, Staff Files, box 65, folder: Sudarkasa, Niara, Personal: Appearance, Speeches, Articles, March 1985–April 1986 and undated, BHL.

60. Ellen Berrey, *The Enigma of Diversity: The Language of Race and the Limits of Racial Justice* (Chicago: University of Chicago Press, 2015), 61, 71.

61. Sudarkasa describes these meetings in "Proposal for a Year on Understanding the Value of Diversity at the University and in Society," November 20, 1985, Vice President for Academic Affairs, Central Files, box 202, folder: Minorities, BHL.

62. "Proposal for a Year on Understanding the Value of Diversity at the University and in Society," November 20, 1985, Vice President for Academic Affairs, Central Files, box 202, folder: Minorities, BHL.

63. "Proposal for a Year on Understanding the Value of Diversity at the University and in Society."

64. Committee on Diversity, Report to the President, "A Year on Understanding the Value of Diversity at the University and in Society," July 11, 1986, VP for Student Affairs, box 22, folder: Diversity-Task Force.

65. Harold Shapiro to Colleagues, July 22, 1986, Vice President for Student Affairs Records, box 22, folder: Diversity-Task Force, 1986, BHL.

66. Niara Sudarkasa to Provost James J. Duderstadt, Re: Minority Student Recruitment and Retention: What Have We Accomplished? Where Do We Go from Here? July 23, 1986, Provost and Executive Vice President for Academic Affairs, Staff Files, box 67, folder: Staff Files: Sudarkasa, N: Minority Issues Briefing Book 1987, BHL.

67. Lincoln University Appoints First Woman President, September 29, 1986, Provost and Executive Vice President for Academic Affairs, Staff Files, box 65, folder: Sudarkasa, Niara, Personal: Background Materials, 1984–1986 and undated, BHL.

## 7. The Michigan Mandate

1. James Tobin, "Big Man on Campus," *Michigan: The Magazine of the Detroit News*, May 21, 1989, News and Information Services, Faculty and Staff Files, box 4, folder: Atkins, Daniel, BHL.

2. Dinesh D'Souza, *Illiberal Education: The Politics of Race and Sex on Campus* (New York: Free Press, 1991), 15–21.

3. Rebecca Blumenstein, "Dudserstadt Assumes Interim Presidency," *Michigan Daily*, January 7, 1987, 1.

4. Paul McNaughton, Open Letter to the Residents of Couzens, January 29, 1987, CAAS, box 55, BAM III, UCAR Racist Flyers at Couzens Hall, 1987, BHL; Eugene Pak, "Racist Flier Sparks Forum at Couzens," *Michigan Daily*, February 2, 1987, 1.

5. Pak, "Racist Flier"; Jerry Markon, "Student Admits He Sent Flier," *Michigan Daily*, March 10, 1987, 1.

6. George Curry, "Racial Climate Turns Cool on College Campuses," *Chicago Tribune*, February 17, 1987, 1, 8; Lee Altken, "Racism on Campus: Beyond the Citadel," *People Weekly*, December 15, 1986, 58; Raoul Dennis, "Racism on the Rise," *Black Enterprise*, April 1987, 17; Dudley Clendines, "Citadel's Cadets Feeling Effects of a Klan-Like Act," *New York Times*, November 23, 1986, 26; Carolyn Lumsden, "Race Tensions Smolder in College Community," *Washington Post*, November 11, 1986; "Racism Rising at Colleges," *New Pittsburgh Courier*, January 10, 1987, 3; "Racism: From Closet to Quad," *New York Times*, April 1, 1987, A30.

7. Lisa Pollak, "Ransby Speaks Out on Campus," *Michigan Daily*, September 10, 1987, Section: "Activism," 3; Dov Cohen, "Apartheid Protesters Fight Racism with Shanty," *Michigan Daily*, March 24, 1986, 3.

8. David Webster, "Diag Rally Fights 'U' Racism," February 9, 1987, 3; Eugene Pak, "Coalition Organizes against Racism," *Michigan Daily*, February 18, 1987, 1.

9. Rebecca Blumenstein, "Affirmative Action Initiative Disclosed," *Michigan Daily*, February 12, 1987, 1.

10. Ted Sevransky Show, "Racial Jokes," Tape recording, February 4, 1987, CAAS, box 34, BHL.

11. Barbara Ransby, "UCAR Continues Fight," *Michigan Daily*, April 9, 1987, 4; Barbara Ransby, "UCAR Keeps Up Pressure," *Michigan Daily*, April 10, 1987, 4.

12. Wendy Lews, "Confrontation: Coalition Demands Action on Racism," *Michigan Daily*, March 5, 1987, 1; "Duderstadt: Country Boy with a New Image," *Ann Arbor News*, June 10, 1988, News and Information Services, Faculty and Staff Files, box 31, News and Information Services, Faculty and Staff Files, box 31, folder: Daane, Roderick K, BHL.

13. "Harold T. Shapiro" University of Michigan Faculty History Project, https://www.lib.umich.edu/faculty-history/faculty/harold-t-shapiro/memoir; "Duderstadt: Country Boy with a New Image."

14. Morris Hood Hearings, 1987, Tape 1, CAAS, box 34; Morris Hood Hearings, Tape 2, CAAS, box 34; Morris Hood Hearings, Tape 3, CAAS, box 34; Morris Hood Hearings, Tape 4, CAAS, box 34; Morris Hood Hearings, Tape 5, CAAS, box 34; Hood Hearing: Higher Education Subcommittee of the Appropriations Committee, Office of Human Resources and Affirmative Action box 8, folder: State of Michigan, Morris Hood Inquiry, Re: Racism 3/87, BHL; David Webster, "'U' Draws National Attention," *Michigan Daily*, March 6, 1987, 5; Stephen Gregory, "Hearing on Racism Sparks Emotion," *Michigan Daily*, March 6, 1987, 1.

15. Martha Sevetson, "Students Unite Against Racism," *Michigan Daily*, February 17, 1987, 3; Stephen Gregory, "Hearing on Racism Sparks Emotion," *Michigan Daily*, March 6, 1987, 1.

16. "Black Action Movement III Demands," *University Record*, March 23, 1987, CAAS, box 1, folder: BAM III: Newspaper Clippings, Ann Arbor News, *Detroit Free Press*, *Michigan Daily*, BAM/UCAR Demands, BHL.

17. Wendy Lewis, "UCAR Stages Sit-In at Fleming Building," *Michigan Daily*, March 20, 1987, 1; Ruth Seymour, "New Breed of Protesters Focuses on U-M Racism," *Detroit Free Press*, March 22, 1987, 1B.

18. Eugene Pak, "Rev. Jesse Jackson Speaks at Hill Today," *Michigan Daily*, March 23, 1987, 1; Bill McGraw, "Jackson Managed to Defuse Racial Tension," *Detroit Free Press*, March 29, 1987, 5B; James Duderstadt, "The History of the Michigan Mandate: A Personal Narrative," June 15, 1991, 7, in author's possession.

19. James Duderstadt, "The History of the Michigan Mandate: A Personal Narrative," June 15, 1991, 9.

20. Brodie and Banner, *The Research Presidency*, 172–73; Duderstadt, "The History of the Michigan Mandate: A Personal Narrative," 9; Keith Brodie and Leslie Banner, *The Research University Presidency in the late Twentieth Century: A Life Cycle/Case History Approach* (Westport, CT: Praeger, 2005), 81–82; Barbara Ransby, "UCAR Continues Fight," *Michigan Daily*, April 9, 1987, 4.

21. Brodie and Banner, *Research University Presidency in the Late Twentieth Century*, 81–82; James Duderstadt, "The History of the Michigan Mandate: A Personal Narrative," June 15, 1991, 6, in author's possession.

22. The Diversity Agenda, November 6, 1987, James J. Duderstadt Papers, box 23, folder: Strategic Planning, Increasing Diversity, University of California Study (September 1987), BHL.

23. Interview with James Duderstadt, March 15, 2017.

24. Diversity Strategic Plan, February 16, 1988, Vice President for Academic and Multicultural Affairs Records, box 5, folder: Diversity Agenda, 1987–1990, BHL.

25. Diversity Strategic Plan, February 16, 1988; Mary Jo Frank, "'Raiding' for Faculty is Encouraged by Moody," *University Record*, May 15, 1988, News and Information Services, Faculty and Staff Files, box 91, folder: Moody Charles (folder 2), BHL.

26. Diversity Strategic Plan, February 16, 1988.

27. "Fleming Considers Changing Racial Harassment Proposal," *Ann Arbor News*, January 16, 1988, News and Information Services, Faculty and Staff Files, box 132, folder: Varner, Nellie Mae (folder 2), BHL; Steve Knopper, "Fleming's New Policy Debated," *Michigan Daily*, March 1, 1988, 1; "Offensive Speech," *Michigan Daily*, January 11, 1988, 1; Steven Knopper, "Officials Discuss Code Draft," *Michigan Daily*, January 18, 1988, 1; January Meeting, January 15, 1988, Proceedings of the Board of Regents, 1987–1988, http://quod.lib.umich.edu/u/umregproc/acw7513.1987.001/163?page=root; size=100;view=imag.

28. "The University of Michigan Policy on Discrimination and Discriminatory Harassment by the Students in the University Environment," Fall 1988 Eugene Feingold Papers, box 3, folder: UM Minority Concerns: Harassment Policies 1988–1989, BHL; Jim Poniewozik, "Code Vote Prompted Mixed Reaction," *Michigan Daily*, March 21, 1988, 1; Jim Poniewozik and Ryan Tutak, "Anti-Code Group Storms Fleming Building Lobby," *Michigan Daily*, April 15, 1988, 1; David Schwartz, "Code Approval Prompts Protests," *Michigan Daily*, April 18, 1988, 1; Noah Finkel, "President Invokes New Policy," *Michigan Daily*, September 18, 1989, 1.

29. "What Students Should Know about Discrimination and Discriminatory Harassment by Students in the University Environment," Fall 1988 Eugene Feingold Papers, box 3, folder: UM Minority Concerns: Harassment Policies 1988–1989, BHL.

30. Ryan Tutak, "It's President Duderstadt," *Michigan Daily*, June 10, 1988, extra ed., 1.

31. The Michigan Mandate: A Strategic Linking of Academic Excellence and Social Diversity, Draft 5.1, March 1989, James J. Duderstadt Papers, box 4, folder: Speeches-Michigan Mandate, 1989 (1), BHL.

32. The Michigan Plan: A Strategy for the Enhancement of Excellence through Diversity, Version 1.2 May 1, 1988, James J. Duderstadt Papers, box 22, folder: Michigan

Plan, Comments on Draft (1989), BHL; James Duderstadt, "Appendix A: The Early History of the Michigan Mandate," *The 50 Year History of Social Diversity at the University of Michigan* (Ann Arbor: Millennium Project, 2015), 36; Draft 3.0: The Michigan Mandate: A Strategic Linking of Academic Excellence and Social Diversity, James J. Duderstadt Papers, box 4, folder: Speeches-Michigan Mandate, 1989 (2), BHL.

33. The Michigan Mandate, September 11, 1988, James J. Duderstadt Papers, box 23, folder: Michigan Mandate, Reflected Materials (scattered dates), BHL; James Duderstadt, "The History of the University of Michigan: A Personal Narrative," June 15, 1991, 11, unpublished in author's possession.

34. Duderstadt talked about the apathetic environment in James Duderstadt, interview with author, March 15, 2017.

35. Charles David Moody Sr., Biography, News and Information Services, Faculty and Staff Files, box 91, folder: Moody Charles (folder 1), BHL; Mark Chesler to Shirley Jackson, James J. Duderstadt Papers, box 22, folder: Michigan Plan, Comments on Draft (1989); Duderstadt, "Appendix A: The Early History of the Michigan Mandate," 34.

36. "U Goals Examined: EOs, Faculty Begin Racism Awareness Retreats," *University Record*, June 22, 1987, Lana Pollack Papers, box 4, folder: MI Senate, Org., UM, Racism Hearing, 1987–1990, BHL.

37. "U Goals Examined." On backlash against affirmative action, see Dennis Deslippe, *Protesting Affirmative Action: The Struggle over Equality After the Civil Rights Revolution* (Baltimore: Johns Hopkins University Press, 2012); Lee Cokorinos, *The Assault on Diversity: An Organized Challenge to Racial and Gender Justice* (New York: Rowman & Littlefield, 2003).

38. The Diversity Agenda, November 6, 1987, James J. Duderstadt Papers, box 23, folder: Strategic Planning, Increasing Diversity, University of California Study (September 1987), BHL; ABPA Michigan Plan Committee to James J. Duderstadt, Subject: The Michigan Plan, July 5, 1988, James J. Duderstadt Papers, box 23, folder: Diversity Reading Materials, BHL.

39. The Michigan Mandate: A Strategic Linking of Academic Excellence and Social Diversity, Draft 6.0, March 1990, 3–4, https://books.google.com/books?id=AufhAAAAMAAJ&pg=PP7&lpg=PP7&dq=michigan+mandate+march+1990&source=bl&ots=khUrAxDZWg&sig=toVBvt0pnBYzqdDLn40PrCDEhe4&hl=en&sa=X&ved=0ahUKEwip9YvmsuPTAhULjVQKHU_kDyQQ6AEIODAD#v=onepage&q=michigan%20mandate%20march%201990&f=false.

40. The Michigan Mandate, September 11, 1988, James J. Duderstadt Papers, box 23, folder: Michigan Mandate, Reflected Materials (scattered dates), BHL; Barbara Misle, "Black Students Express Concern over Pact," *Ann Arbor News*, April 29, 1987, A4, CAAS box 1, folder: BAM III, Newspaper Clippings, President Harold Shapiro Resignation, BHL; Barbara Ransby, "UCAR Continues Fight," *Michigan Daily*, April 9, 1987, 4, CAAS box 1, folder: BAM III: Newspaper Clippings, *Ann Arbor News*, *Detroit Free Press*, *Michigan Daily*, BAM/UCAR Demands, BHL.

41. The Michigan Plan: A Strategy for the Enhancement of Excellence through Diversity, Version 1.2 May 1, 1988, James J. Duderstadt Papers, box 22, folder: Michigan Plan, Comments on Draft (1989), BHL.

42. Ryan Tutak, "It's President Duderstadt," *Michigan Daily*, June 10, 1988, extra ed., 1

43. Jack W. Meiland to James J. Duderstadt, January 20, 1989, James J. Duderstadt Papers, box 4, folder: Speeches-Michigan Mandate, 1989 (1), BHL; James S. Jackson to Shirley Clarkson, Subject: Michigan Mandate, January 29, 1989, email, James J. Duderstadt Papers, box 22, folder: Michigan Plan, Comments on Draft (1989), BHL; Mark Chesler, Dealing with Racism at the University of Michigan, March 18, 1987, CAAS, box 55, BAM III, UCAR Recommendations on Negotiated Agreements, 1987, BHL; James Duderstadt, interview with author, March 15, 2017.

44. "Introducing Our New Director," *Points of Entry* 2, no. 1 (Winter 1989), Office of Undergraduate Admissions, Publications, box 1, folder: Office of Undergraduate Admissions, Newsletter, Points of Entry (for Faculty and Staff), BHL.

45. "Admissions Office's Shaw Heads for Yale: Ted Spencer Appointed Interim Chief," University Record, June 22, 1992, News and Information Services University of Michigan Faculty and Staff Files, box 121, folder: Spencer, Ted (doc. 1, p. 21); Theodore L. Spencer, Résumé, News and Information Services, Faculty and Staff Files, box 121, folder: Spencer, Ted, BHL.

46. Cliff Sjogren, Monique Washington, and Don Swain to Counseling Staff, Supervisors, Secretaries, Re: Guidelines for the admission to the College of Literature, Science, and the Arts for All Terms, 1987, August 1986, College of Literature, Science and the Arts Records, box 342, folder: Dean's Files-Topical-Admissions and Admissions Committees, 1987–1988, BHL.

47. Preliminary Expert Witness Report of William T. Trent, Gratz et al. v. Bollinger et al., June 17, 2000, Admissions Lawsuit Collection, box 15, BHL; Sjogren, Washington, and Swain to Counseling Staff, Supervisors, Secretaries, August 1986.

48. Richard Shaw, interview with author, April 5, 2017; Theodore Spencer, interview with author, May 19, 2017; Sjogren, Washington, and Swain to Counseling Staff, Supervisors, Secretaries, August 1986; Office of Undergraduate Admissions, College of Literature, Science and the Arts Guidelines for All Terms of 1996, Vice Provost for Academic and Multicultural Affairs Records, box 38, folder: Student Academic Services, Admissions-Carl Cohen, 1996, BHL.

49. Theodore Spencer, interview with author, May 19, 2017.

50. Richard Shaw, interview with author, April 5, 2017; Theodore Spencer, interview with author, May 19, 2017.

51. Richard Shaw, interview with author, April 5, 2017.

52. Lydia Smigielski, State Offers Free Tuition to Minorities, *Detroit Free Press*, June 17, 1988, 1A; James Duderstadt to Bob Rorke, September 15, 1989, Vice Provost for Academic and Multicultural Affairs Records, box 3, folder: Topical, DPS, Wade McCree Incentive Scholarship Program, General, 1987–92, BHL.

53. "Table 2. Michigan Public High Schools (Sorted by % Black)," in Preliminary Expert Report of William T. Trent, *Gratz v. Bollinger* No. 97-75231 (E.D.) Mich.), Admissions Lawsuit Collection, box 15, BHL.

54. Ted Spencer and Rob Seltzer, Undergraduate Admissions Data, Fall 1995, Office of Undergraduate Admissions, Publications, box 1, folder: Repots: Undergraduate Admissions Data, Fall 1995, BHL.

55. Office of the Registrar, University of Michigan–Ann Arbor, Enrollment in Degree Credit Programs by Ethnicity, Fall 1996–Fall 2006, http://www.ro.umich.edu/report/06fa837.xls. The university almost reached 9 percent in fall 1995: Josh White, "'U' Minority Enrollment Rises to 25%," *Michigan Daily*, October 20, 1995, 1.

56. Recall black students' efforts to create intraracial spaces in chapters 3 and 4. They emphasized the importance of addressing social alienation over UM officials' vision for improving race relations.

57. Henry Goldblatt, "Mandate Promises Racial Equality," *Michigan Daily*, September 5, 1991, 6.

58. Proposed Minutes of the October 4, 1990, Meeting of the Faculty of the College of Literature, Science, and the Arts, LSA Records, box 373, folder: ROE/UC Adoption, 89–90, BHL.

59. Living-Learning Intervention to Improve Student Retention, April 24, 1990, Provost and Executive Vice President for Academic Affairs, Staff Files, box 287, folder: VPAA, Staff, Swain, Topical: Steele, Claude (retention project), BHL; Supplement to Proposal: "Protective Dis-Identification and Its Mediation of Academic Outcomes among Black College Students," Provost and Executive Vice President for Academic Affairs, Staff Files, box 287, folder: VPAA, Staff, Swain, Topical: Steele, Claude (retention project), BHL.

60. Living-Learning Intervention to Improve Student Retention; Supplement to Proposal: "Protective Dis-Identification and Its Mediation of Academic Outcomes among Black College Students."

61. Living-Learning Intervention to Improve Student Retention; Supplement to Proposal: "Protective Dis-Identification and Its Mediation of Academic Outcomes Among Black College Students."

62. Karen Emerson, "New Living Arrangement Stresses Academic Success," September 3, 1991, News and Information Services University of Michigan Faculty and Staff Files, box 123, folder: Steele, Claude Mason, BHL.

63. Monita C. Thompson, Teresa Graham Brett, and Charles Behling, "Educating for Social Justice: The Program on Intergroup Relations, Conflict, and Community at the University of Michigan," in *Intergroup Dialogue: Deliberative Democracy in School, College, Community, and Workplace*, ed. David Schoem and Sylvia Hurtado, 99–114 (Ann Arbor: University of Michigan Press, 2001).

64. Thompson, Brett, and Behling, "Educating for Social Justice," 99–114; "'U' Should Invest in Group Relations," *Michigan Daily*, March 9, 1992, 4.

65. Thompson, Brett, and Behling, "Educating for Social Justice," 99–114.

66. Charles D. Moody Sr. to James J. Duderstadt, Re: Update on Research Study on Racial and Gender Perspective of UM Fall Term 1990, Freshpersons and First Time Teaching Assistants in LSA and Engineering, June 26, 1990, Vice Provost for Academic and Multicultural Affairs Records, box 11, folder: Administrative, Committees, Advisory Committee to Study of Racial, Ethnic and Diversity Attitudes of Freshpersons, 1990, BHL.

67. John Matlock, Gerald Gurin, and Katrina Wade-Golden, *The Michigan Student Study: Students' Expectations of and Experiences with Racial/Ethnic Diversity* (Ann Arbor: University of Michigan Office of Academic Multicultural Initiatives, 2002).

68. Ted Spencer and Rob Seltzer, Undergraduate Admissions Data, Fall 1995, Office of Undergraduate Admissions, Publications, box 1, folder: Repots: Undergraduate Admissions Data, Fall 1995, BHL; Office of the Registrar, University of Michigan-Ann Arbor, Enrollment in Degree Credit Programs by Ethnicity, Fall 1996–Fall 2006, http://www.ro.umich.edu/report/06fa837.xls. The university almost reached 9 percent in fall 1995: Josh White, "'U' Minority Enrollment Rises to 25%," *Michigan Daily*, October 20, 1995, 1.

### 8. *Gratz v. Bollinger*

1. Greg Stohr, *A Black and White Case: How Affirmative Action Survived Its Greatest Legal Challenge* (Princeton, NJ: Bloomberg Press, 2004), 2–3.

2. Michel Marriot, "Black Enrollment in College Up after Long Decline, U.S. Says," *New York Times*, March 30, 1990, A1; Jennifer Toth, "College Affirmative Action: How Serious Is the Backlash?," *Los Angeles Times*, May 16, 1991, SBA5; Carol Jouzaitis, "Affirmative Action under Campus Attack," *Chicago Tribune*, May 28, 1991, N1; Carol Jouzaitis, "Affirmative Action Feels Student Heat," *Chicago Tribune*, May 28, 1991, C1.

3. Andrew Hartman, *A War for the Soul of America: A History of the Culture Wars* (Chicago: University of Chicago Press, 2015), 227–33; Charles Krauthammer, "A Battle Lost at Stanford," *Washington Post*, April 22, 1988, A23; George F. Will, "Stanford's Regression," *Washington Post*, May 1, 1988, 53; Dinesh D'Souza, "The Politics of Force-Fed Multiculturalism," *Christian Science Monitor*, April 22, 1991, 19. For the most comprehensive scholarly coverage of the Stanford curriculum debate, see Lora Dawn Burnett, "Canon Wars: The Stanford 'Western Culture' Debates and the Neoliberal Assault on American Higher Education" (PhD diss., University of Texas-Dallas, 2015).

4. Brian Pusser, *Burning Down the House: Politics, Governance, and Affirmative Action at the University of California* (Albany, NY: State University of New York Press, 2004), 36–39; Amy Wallace and Dave Lesher, "UC Regents, in Historic Vote, Wipe Out Affirmative Action," *Los Angeles Times*, July 21, 1995, http://articles.latimes.com/1995-07-21/news/mn-26379_1_regents-vote-affirmative-action-university-of-california-regents; James Carney, "Affirmative Action: Mend It, Don't End It," *Time*, Monday July 31, 1995, http://www.time.com/time/magazine/article/0,9171,983257,00.html; Ethan Bronner, "U. of Washington Will End Race-Conscious Admissions," *New York Times*, November 7, 1998, A12; Charles Krauthammer, "Taking Affirmative Action Out of the Judges' Hands," *Seattle Times*, June 19, 1995, http://community.seattletimes.nwsource.com/archive/?date=19950619&slug=2127126; "How Affirmative Action Will Meet Its Demise," *Chicago Tribune*, June 16, 1995, http://articles.chicagotribune.com/1995-06-16/news/9506160090_1_adarand-constructors-affirmative-action-abortion-law; "Legislative Death Awaits Affirmative Action," *Desert News*, June 18, 1995, http://www.deseretnews.com/article/423228/LEGISLATIVE-DEATH-AWAITS-AFFIRMATIVE-ACTION.html.

5. Sean Wilentz, *The Age of Reagan: A History, 1974–2008* (New York: Harper, 2008), 187–88, 311–12.

6. Girardeau A. Spann, *The Law of Affirmative Action: Twenty-Five Years of Supreme Court Decisions on Race and Remedies* (New York: New York University Press, 2000), 164–65; Ashutosh Bhagwat, "Affirmative Action and Compelling Interests: Equal Protection Jurisprudence at the Crossroads," *University of Pennsylvania Journal of Constitutional Law* 4 (January 2002): 270.

7. Goodwin Liu, "Affirmative Action in Higher Education: The Diversity Rationale and the Compelling Interest Test," *Harvard Civil Rights-Civil Liberties Law Review* 33 (Summer 1998): 385; City of Richmond v. J.A. Croson Co., 488 U.S. 493 (1989) (plurality opinion).

8. "White Woman Denied to Law School Challenges Texas Affirmative Action," *Baltimore Sun*, July 13, 1994, 10A.

9. Stohr, *Black and White Case*, 27; Lee Cokorinos, *The Assault on Diversity: An Organized Challenge to Racial and Gender Justice* (Lanham, MD: Roman & Littlefield, 2003), 60, 66–67.

10. Carl Cohen to Lewis A. Morrissey, December 19, 1995, Vice Provost for Academic and Multicultural Affairs Records, box 38, folder: Student Academic Services, Admissions-Carl Cohen, 1996, BHL.

11. Lewis A. Morrissey to Carl Cohen, March 12, 1996, Vice Provost for Academic and Multicultural Affairs Records, box 38, folder: Student Academic Services, Admissions-Carl Cohen, 1996, BHL; Stohr, *Black and White Case*, 17–19.

12. Stohr, *Black and White Case*; Brent E. Simmons, "Affirmative Action: The Legislative Debate in the Michigan House of Representatives," *Thomas M. Cooley Law Review* 14 (1997): 267–316.

13. Stohr, *Black and White Case*, ix, 36–37, 46–49; Dawson Bell, "Legislators Aim to Sue U-M over Race Policy," *Detroit Free Press*, May 2, 1997, 1B.

14. Regents of the Univ. of Cal. v. Bakke, 438 U.S. 265 (1978); Hopwood v. Texas, 78 F.3d 932 (5th Cir. 1996).

15. He explained this in a public event: "Affirmative Action: Where Do We Stand?" Tape recording, September 29, 1999, Affirmative Action Lawsuits Collection, box 27, BHL.

16. The Michigan Mandate: A Strategic Linking of Academic Excellence and Social Diversity, Draft 6.0, March 1990, 3–4, https://books.google.com/books?id =AufhAAAAMAAJ&pg=PP7&lpg=PP7&dq=michigan+mandate+march+1990&sou rce=bl&ots=khUrAxDZWg&sig=toVBvt0pnBYzqdDLn40PrCDEhe4&hl=en&sa =X&ved=0ahUKEwip9YvmsuPTAhULjVQKHU_kDyQQ6AEIODAD#v =onepage&q=michigan%20mandate%20march%201990&f=false.

17. Maryanne George, Hugh McDiarmid, and Matthew G. Davis, "Duderstadt Steps Down, Denies Ouster," *Detroit Free Press*, September 29, 1995, 1A; Maryanne George, "Deal Sealed for Bollinger, U-M," *Detroit Free Press*, November 13, 1996, 1B; Stohr, *Black and White Case*, 34; Lee Bollinger, "Inauguration Address," September 19, 1997, http://um2017.org/2017_Website/Bollingers_Inaugural_Address.html. Quotes from admissions office documents, which were submitted as exhibits in the case, come from Duggan's decision against the intervenors; Payton used the other documents as exhibits in the case; see Defendants' Opposition to Plaintiffs' Motion for Partial Summary Judgment.

18. Laura Calkins, interview with author, May 8, 2017.

19. Calkins, interview with author.

20. James B. Angell, *The Higher Education: A Plea for Making It Accessible to All* (Ann Arbor: Board of Regents, 1879), http://umich.edu/~bhlumrec/c/commence/1879 -Angell.pdf.

21. See footnote 34 in Brief for Respondents, Grutter v. Bollinger, 539 U.S. 306 (2003).

22. Deposition of James Duderstadt, January 8, 1999, Admissions Lawsuit Collection, box 14, BHL; The Michigan Mandate: A Strategic Linking of Academic Excellence and Social Diversity, Draft 6.0, March 1990, 3–4, https://books.google.com /books?id=AufhAAAAMAAJ&pg=PP7&lpg=PP7&dq=michigan+mandate+march+ 1990&source=bl&ots=khUrAxDZWg&sig=toVBvt0pnBYzqdDLn40PrCDEhe4&hl

=en&sa=X&ved=0ahUKEwip9YvmsuPTAhULjVQKHU_kDyQQ6AEIODAD#v=onepage&q=michigan%20mandate%20march%201990&f=false.

23. Neil H. Berkson, "'Small Number': Surveys Negroes at 'U,'" *Michigan Daily*, February 16, 1964, 1; O. Jackson Cole and J. Frank Yaes, "BAM Demands: Meeting the Needs of the People," *Michigan Daily*, April 2, 1970, 4; Niara Sudarkasa, Undergraduate Minority Enrollment: Issues and Recommendations Related to Recruitment and Financial Aid: Summary, March 1985, Provost and Executive Vice President for Academic Affairs, Staff Files, box 65, folder: Sudarkasa, Niara, Personal: Appearance, Speeches, Articles, March 1985–April 1986 and undated, BHL; Kim Clarke, "Minorities at U-M: Progress, but 'a Long Way to Go,'" *Ann Arbor News*, March 25, 1990, News and Information Services, Faculty and Staff Files, box 91, folder: Moody Charles (folder 1), BHL.

24. First Amended Motion to Intervene, *Gratz v. Bollinger*, E.D. Mich. 97-CV-75231-DT.

25. Stohr, *Black and White Case*, 127–31; Plaintiff's Memorandum in Opposition for Intervention, *Gratz v. Bollinger*, 97-75231.

26. Expert Report of James Anderson, Admissions Lawsuit Collection, box 15, BHL.

27. Preliminary Expert Witness Report of William T. Trent, Gratz et al. v. Bollinger et al., June 17, 2000, Admissions Lawsuit Collection, box 15, BHL; Stohr, *Black and White Case*, 49.

28. Preliminary Expert Witness Report of William T. Trent, Gratz et al. v. Bollinger et al., June 17, 2000, Admissions Lawsuit Collection box 15, BHL.

29. Brief for Patterson Respondents, Gratz v. Bollinger, 539 U.S. 244 (2003).

30. Defendants' Opposition to Plaintiffs' Motion for Partial Summary Judgment, 9–10.

31. Expert Report of Patricia Gurin, *Gratz et al. v. Bollinger et al.*, No. 97-75321 (E.D. Mich.).

32. Expert Report of Patricia Gurin.

33. Expert Report of Patricia Gurin.

34. Expert Report of Patricia Gurin.

35. Expert Report of Patricia Gurin; Brief for Respondents, Gratz v. Bollinger, 539 U.S. 244 (2003).

36. Expert Report of Joe Feagin, Admissions Lawsuit Collection, box 15, BHL; Expert Report of Walter Allen, Admissions Lawsuit Collection box 15, BHL.

37. Expert Report of Joe Feagin.

38. Walter Allen, "Campus Racial Climate at the University of Michigan: A Case Study," October 11, 2000, in Expert Report of Walter Allen, Admissions Lawsuit Collection, box 15, BHL.

39. Brief for Respondents, Gratz v. Bollinger; Defendants' Opposition to Plaintiff's Motion for Partial Summary Judgment, Gratz et al. v. Bollinger et al.

40. "Transcript of Oral Arguments," December 6, 2001, Gratz v. Bollinger, https://diversity.umich.edu/admissions/legal/gratz/gra-oatrans2.html; "Transcript of Oral Arguments," Grutter v. Bollinger, https://www.supremecourt.gov/oral_arguments/argument_transcripts/2002/02-516.pdf.

41. Expert Report of Joe Feagin; Expert Report of Walter Allen.

42. Brief of the Authors of the Texas Tech Percent Plan as *Amicus Curiae* in Support of Respondents, Gratz v. Bollinger.

43. Brief for Respondents, Gratz v. Bollinger.

44. Brief for Respondents, Gratz v. Bollinger; William Haber to A. F. Smith et al., March 3, 1970, Vice President of Student Affairs Records, box 9, folder: B. W. Newell, Topical File Black Action Movement, 1970.

45. Expert Report of William G. Bowen, Gratz et al. v. Bollinger et al.; William G. Bowen and Derek Bok, *The Shape of the River: Long-Term Consequences of Considering Race in College and University Admissions* (Princeton, NJ: Princeton University Press, 1998).

46. Expert Report of William G. Bowen, Gratz et al. v. Bollinger et al.; Bowen and Bok, *Shape of the River*, 46–52.

47. Expert Report of William G. Bowen, Gratz et al. v. Bollinger et al.; Bowen and Bok, *Shape of the River*.

48. Brief for the University of Pittsburgh, Temple University, Wayne State University, and the University of Arizona, Gratz v. Bollinger.

49. Brief for Amherst College, et al., Gratz v. Bollinger.

50. Brief of the Authors of the Texas Tech Percent Plan.

51. Brief for Respondents, Gratz v. Bollinger; Brief of Amici Curiae Columbia University, Cornell University, Georgetown University, Rice University, and Vanderbilt University in Support of Respondents, Gratz v. Bollinger.

52. Brief for the Patterson Respondents, Gratz v. Bollinger.

53. Frank Dobbin, *Inventing Equal Opportunity* (Princeton, NJ: Princeton University Press, 2009), 133–60.

54. Brief for 65 Leading American Businesses as Amicus Curiae Supporting Respondents, Gratz v. Bollinger; Brief of MTV Networks as Amicus Curiae Supporting Respondents, Gratz v. Bollinger; Brief of General Motors Corporation as Amicus Curiae Supporting Respondents, Gratz v. Bollinger.

55. Brief for 65 Leading American Businesses as Amicus Curiae Supporting Respondents; Brief of MTV Networks as Amicus Curiae Supporting Respondents; Brief of General Motors Corporation as Amicus Curiae Supporting Respondents.

56. Brief of General Motors Corporation as Amicus Curiae Supporting Respondents.

57. Gratz v. Bollinger; Grutter v. Bollinger.

58. Gratz v. Bollinger; Grutter v. Bollinger.

59. Grutter v. Bollinger.

60. Grutter v. Bollinger.

61. Grutter v. Bollinger.

62. Grutter v. Bollinger.

63. Gratz v. Bollinger; Grutter v. Bollinger.

64. Grutter v. Bollinger.

65. Grutter v. Bollinger.

66. Grutter v. Bollinger.

67. Grutter v. Bollinger.

68. James Kolvunen and Samantha Woll, "Students Divided over Methods Used to Achieve Diverse Campus," *Michigan Daily*, June 24, 2003, 1; Linda Greenhouse,

"Justices Back Affirmative Action by 5 to 4 Vote, but Wider Vote Bans a Racial Point System," *New York Times*, June 24, 2003, A1; Jeffrey Brainard and Julianne Basinger, "Bollinger Accepts 'Once-in-a-Lifetime' Chance to Lead Columbia University," *Chronicle of Higher Education*, October 8, 2001, https://www.chronicle.com/article/Bollinger-Accepts/109232.

### Epilogue

1. Suzette Hackney, "Affirmative Action Ban Ok'd," *Detroit Free Press*, November 8, 2006, 9A.

2. "Summary of Workshop on the Judicial Impact of Ballot Initiatives and Judicial Decisions," January 23–24, 2007, in author's possession.

3. "University of Michigan 2010–2011 Undergraduate Application," in author's possession.

4. Kristen Jordan Shamus, "U-M Targets a Mix of Traits," *Detroit Free Press*, March 29, 2007, http://www.freep.com/apps/pbcs.dll/article?AID=2007112130044.

5. Chris Herring, "Minority Enrollment Dips for 2008 Class," *Michigan Daily*, October 22, 2008, 1A.

6. Rather than archiving annual tables with data on race and ethnicity online, the University of Michigan's Office of the Registrar now allows researchers to search for data and create their own data tables. See the "Ethnicity Reports," https://ro.umich.edu/reports/ethnicity.

7. Chris Herring, "Minority Enrollment Dips for 2008 Class," *Michigan Daily*, October 22, 2008, 1A; Stephanie Steinberg, "In typically Low-Key Setting, Students Press Coleman on Diversity Issues," *Michigan Daily*, October 28, 2009, https://www.michigandaily.com/content/fireside-chat-students-press-coleman-diversity-issues.

8. Christopher E. D'Alessio, "A Bridge Too Far: The Limits of the Political Process Doctrine in *Schuette v. Coalition to Defend Affirmative Action*," *Duke Journal of Constitutional Law and Public Policy Sidebar* 9 (2013): 104–24; David Bernstein, "*Schuette v. Coalition to Defend Affirmative Action* and the Failed Attempt to Square a Circle," *Journal of Law and Liberty* 8, no. 1 (2013): 210–27.

9. Motion of the Regents of the University of Michigan, the Board of Trustees of Michigan State University, and the Board of Governors of Wayne State University for Preliminary Injunction Relief, December 11, 2006, *Schuette v. Coalition to Defend Affirmative Action*, E.D. Mich. 2-06-CV-15024, http://diversity.umich.edu/wp-content/uploads/2015/10/1442_001.pdf. On Spencer's testimony, see Brief for Respondents the Regents of the University of Michigan, the Board of Trustees of Michigan State University, Mary Sue Coleman, and Lou Anna K. Simon, *Schuette v. Coalition to Defend Affirmative Action*, 572 U.S. (2014), http://diversity.umich.edu/wp-content/uploads/2015/10/12-682_bs_um.pdf.

10. Kellie Woodhouse, "What's It Like to Be Black at the University of Michigan? Just Check #BBUM on Twitter," *Michigan Live*, November 19, 2013, http://www.mlive.com/news/ann-arbor/index.ssf/2013/11/whats_it_like_to_be_brown_at_t.html.

11. Woodhouse, "What's It Like?"

12. Ben Freed, "Being Black at University of Michigan Organizers Threaten 'Physical Action' If Demands Aren't Met," *Michigan Live*, January 20, 2014, http://www

.mlive.com/news/ann-arbor/index.ssf/2014/01/being_Black_at_university_of_m.html.

13. Coleman Addresses Diversity and Campus Climate in Feb. 20 Remarks, *University Record*, February 20, 2014, https://record.umich.edu/articles/coleman-addresses-diversity-and-campus-climate-feb-20-remarks.

14. Steve Friess, "Diversity at U-M: What's Next," *Michigan Alumnus* 121, no. 1 (Fall 2014): 39; Kellie Woodhouse, "University of Michigan Renews Decades-Long Struggle to Increase Black Enrollment," *Michigan Live*, February 2, 2014, http://www.mlive.com/news/ann-arbor/index.ssf/2014/02/university_of_michigan_renews.html.

15. *Schuette v. Coalition to Defend Affirmative Action*, 572 U.S. (2014); Kellie Woodhouse, "University of Michigan President Mary Sue Coleman to Retire in 2014," *Ann Arbor News*, April 18, 2003, http://www.annarbor.com/news/university-of-michigan-president-mary-sue-coleman-to-retire-in-july-2014/.

16. Jeremy Allen, "Read U-M President Mark Schlissel's Full Inauguration Speech," *Michigan Live*, September 5, 2014, http://www.mlive.com/news/ann-arbor/index.ssf/2014/09/read_u-m_president_mark_schlis.html.

17. Provost's Committee on Diversity, Equity and Inclusion, "Report: Achieving Equity & Inclusion at Michigan," May 2014, *University of Michigan, Office of the Provost*, http://www.provost.umich.edu/reports/div-equity-inclusion.html#rec.

18. *Fisher v. University of Texas at Austin*, 133 U.S. 2411 (2013); *Fisher v. University of Texas at Austin*, 579 U.S. (2016).

19. Brief of the University of Michigan as *Amicus Curiae* in Support of Respondents (2016) (No. 14-981).

20. Brief of the University of Michigan.

21. Emma Kinery, "One Year In, Schlissel Says Diversity Plan Moving Ahead," *Michigan Daily*, September 29, 2015, https://www.michigandaily.com/section/news/campus-context-series-diversity.

22. David Jesse, "Tuition at U-M to Be Free for Some," *Detroit Free Press*, June 16, 2017, 1A, 9A.

23. David Jesse, "University of Michigan to Invest $85M in Efforts to Boost Diversity, Inclusiveness," *Detroit Free Press*, October 7, 2016, 4A, 7A; David Jesse, "U-M College Prep Program to Offer Full Scholarships," *Lansing State Journal*, October 24, 2015, 2A; "Wolverine Pathways," University of Michigan, https://wolverinepathways.umich.edu/.

24. Blake Alsup, "UM Efforts to Aid Lower-Income Students Begin to Bear Fruit," *Detroit News*, June 28, 2018, https://www.detroitnews.com/story/news/local/michigan/2018/06/29/um-efforts-aid-lower-income-students-begin-bear-fruit/721229002/.

25. "Ethnicity," University of Michigan Office of the Registrar, November 10, 2018, https://ro.umich.edu/reports/ethnicity; Shaun R. Harper and Isaiah Simmons, *Black Students at Public Colleges and Universities: A 50-State Report Card* (Los Angeles: USC Race and Equity Center, 2018).

26. Harper and Simmons, *Black Students at Public Colleges and Universities*.

27. Office of Planning, Evaluation and Policy Development, Office of the Under Secretary, U.S. Department of Education, *Advancing Diversity and Inclusion in Higher Education: Key Data Highlights Focusing on Race and Ethnicity and Promising Practices* (Washington, D.C.: U.S. Department of Education, 2016), https://www2.ed.gov/rschstat/research/pubs/advancing-diversity-inclusion.pdf.

28. Emily Jane Fox, "Stanford Offers Free Tuition for Families Making Less Than $125,000," *CNN*, April 3, 2015, https://money.cnn.com/2015/04/01/pf/college/stanford-financial-aid/; "Financial Aid Initiatives Unique to Brown University," https://www.brown.edu/about/administration/financial-aid/financial-aid-initiatives-unique-brown-university; Chris Morris, "Rice University Announces Free Tution for Low and Middle-Income Students," *Fortune*, September 18, 2018; "Financial Aid Initiatives," Cornell University, Financial Aid, November 10, 2018, https://finaid.cornell.edu/cost-attend/financial-aid-initiatives; "How Aid Works," Columbia University Financial Aid & Educational Financing, November 10, 2018, https://cc-seas.financialaid.columbia.edu/how/aid/works; "How Does It Work," Duke University Office of Undergraduate Financial Support, November 10, 2018, https://financialaid.duke.edu/undergraduate-applicants/how-does-it-work; "How Aid Works," Dartmouth Financial Aid Office, November 10, 2018, https://financialaid.dartmouth.edu/how-aid-works/how-much-help-will-i-get; "Making MIT Affordable," MIT Student Financial Services, November 10, 2018, https://sfs.mit.edu/undergraduate-students/the-cost-of-attendance/making-mit-affordable/.

29. Natasha Bach, "Why the University of Chicago Is Dropping Its SAT/ACT Test Requirement," *Fortune*, June 15, 2018, http://fortune.com/2018/06/15/university-of-chicago-drops-act-sat-test-requirement-for-admissions/; "320+ 'Top Tier' Schools That Deemphasize the ACT/SAT in Admissions Decisions per U.S. News & World Report *Best Colleges Guide* (2019 Edition)," FairTest: The National Center for Fair and Open Testing, November 10, 2018, http://www.fairtest.org/sites/default/files/Optional-Schools-in-U.S.News-Top-Tiers.pdf; "Standardized Testing Requirements," Hamilton College, November 10, 2018, https://www.hamilton.edu/admission/apply/requirements.

30. Steven T. Syverson, Valerie W. Franks, and William C. Hiss, "Defining Access: How Test-Optional Works," National Association for College Admission Counseling, Spring 2018, https://www.nacacnet.org/globalassets/documents/publications/research/defining-access-report-2018.pdf.

31. The National Center for Fair and Open Testing keeps the most up-to-date records on institutions that have eliminated or currently offer test-optional policies: https://www.fairtest.org/university.

32. Scott Jaschik, "Chicago Drops SAT/ACT Requirement. Will Others Follow?" *Inside Higher Education*, June 19, 2018, https://www.insidehighered.com/admissions/article/2018/06/19/university-chicago-drops-satact-requirement.

33. Anya Kamenetz, *DIY U: Edupunks, Edupreneurs, and the Coming Transformation of Higher Education* (White River Junction, VT: Chelsea Green, 2010); Kevin Carey, *The End of College: Creating the Future of Learning and the University of Everywhere* (New York: Riverhead Books, 2015); Jeffrey J. Selingo, *College (Un)Bound: The Future of Higher Education and What It Means for Students* (Las Vegas: Amazon, 2013).

34. Carey, *End of College*, 255.

35. Kamenetz is unique in that she offers a short chapter on race in *DIY U*, but she fails to anticipate the problems that students of color will face in the system she proposes. For a good history of for-profit colleges, see A. J. Angulo, *Diploma Mills: How for-Profit Colleges Stiffed Students, Taxpayers, and the American Dream* (Baltimore: Johns Hopkins University, 2016).

36. Lani Guinier, *The Tyranny of the Meritocracy: Democratizing Higher Education in America* (Boston: Beacon Press, 2015), xii–xiii, 4, 23, 25, 29.

37. I'm not the first to use the hospital metaphor. See Guinier, *Tyranny of Meritocracy*, 7–8.

38. Scott Jaschik, "The 'U.S. News' Rankings' (Faux?) Embrace of Social Mobility," *Inside Higher Ed*, September 10, 2018, https://www.insidehighered.com/admissions/article/2018/09/10/us-news-says-it-has-shifted-rankings-focus-social-mobility-has-it; "2018 College Guide and Rankings," *Washington Monthly*, https://washingtonmonthly.com/2018college-guide?ranking=2018-rankings-national-universities.

39. Suzanne Mettler, *Degrees of Inequality: How the Politics of Higher Education Sabotaged the American Dream* (New York: Basic Books, 2014), 12, 189–200; Geraldine Fabrikant, "Yale's Endowment Grew 12%, While Harvard's Grew 10%," *New York Times*, October 2, 2018, B3; Martin Slagter, "University of Michigan Endowment Grew $1 Billion in 2018," *Ann Arbor News*, October 19, 2018, https://www.mlive.com/news/ann-arbor/index.ssf/2018/10/university_of_michigan_endowme_4.html.

# Index